ORDNANCE SURVEY MEMOIRS OF IRELAND

Volume Thirty-Nine

PARISHES OF COUNTY DONEGAL II
1835–6

Published 1997.
The Institute of Irish Studies,
The Queen's University of Belfast,
Belfast.
In association with
The Royal Irish Academy,
Dawson Street,
Dublin.

Reprinted 2013 by Ulster Historical Foundation

Grateful acknowledgement is made to the Economic and Social Research Council and the Department of Education for Northern Ireland for their financial assistance at different stages of this publication programme.

We would also like to thank the office of the Taoiseach and the Department of Education in Ireland for contributing towards the costs of this volume.

Copyright 1997.

All rights reserved. No part of this publication may be reproduced, stored in a retrieval system or transmitted, in any form or by any means, electronic, mechanical, photocopying, recording or otherwise, without the prior permission of the publisher.

British Library Cataloguing-in-Publication Data.
A catalogue record for this book is available from the British Library.

ISBN: 978-0-85389-659-3

Printed in Ireland by SPRINT-print Ltd

Ordnance Survey Memoirs of Ireland
VOLUME THIRTY-NINE

Parishes of County Donegal II
1835–6

Mid, West and South Donegal

Edited by Angélique Day and Patrick McWilliams

The Institute of Irish Studies
in association with
The Royal Irish Academy

EDITORIAL BOARD

Angélique Day (General Editor)
Patrick S. McWilliams (Executive Editor)
Dr B.M. Walker (Publishing Director)
Professor R.H. Buchanan

CONTENTS

	Page
Introduction	ix
Brief history of the Irish Ordnance Survey and Memoirs	ix
Definition of terms used	x
Note on Memoirs of County Donegal	x

Parishes in County Donegal

Clonleigh	1
Convoy	18
Conwal	24
Donaghmore	28
Donegal	42
Drumhome	58
Glencolumbkille	64
Inishkeel	67
Kilbarron	74
Killea and Taughboyne	79
Killymard	94
Kilteevoge	111
Leck	115
Raphoe	121
Raymoghy	132
Taughboyne	148
Templecarn	156
Tullaghobegley	172
Urney	174
Miscellaneous Papers	183

List of selected maps and drawings

County Donegal, with parish boundaries	vi
County Donegal, 1837, by Samuel Lewis	viii
Letterkenny, OS map, 1830s	25
Donegal town, OS map, 1830s	43
Killybegs, OS map, 1830s	66
Ballyshannon, OS map, 1830s	75
Ballybofey and Stranorlar, OS map, 1830s	110
Raphoe, OS map, 1830s	122
Belleaghan Abbey and Raymoghy old church	134
Station Island, Lough Derg	159

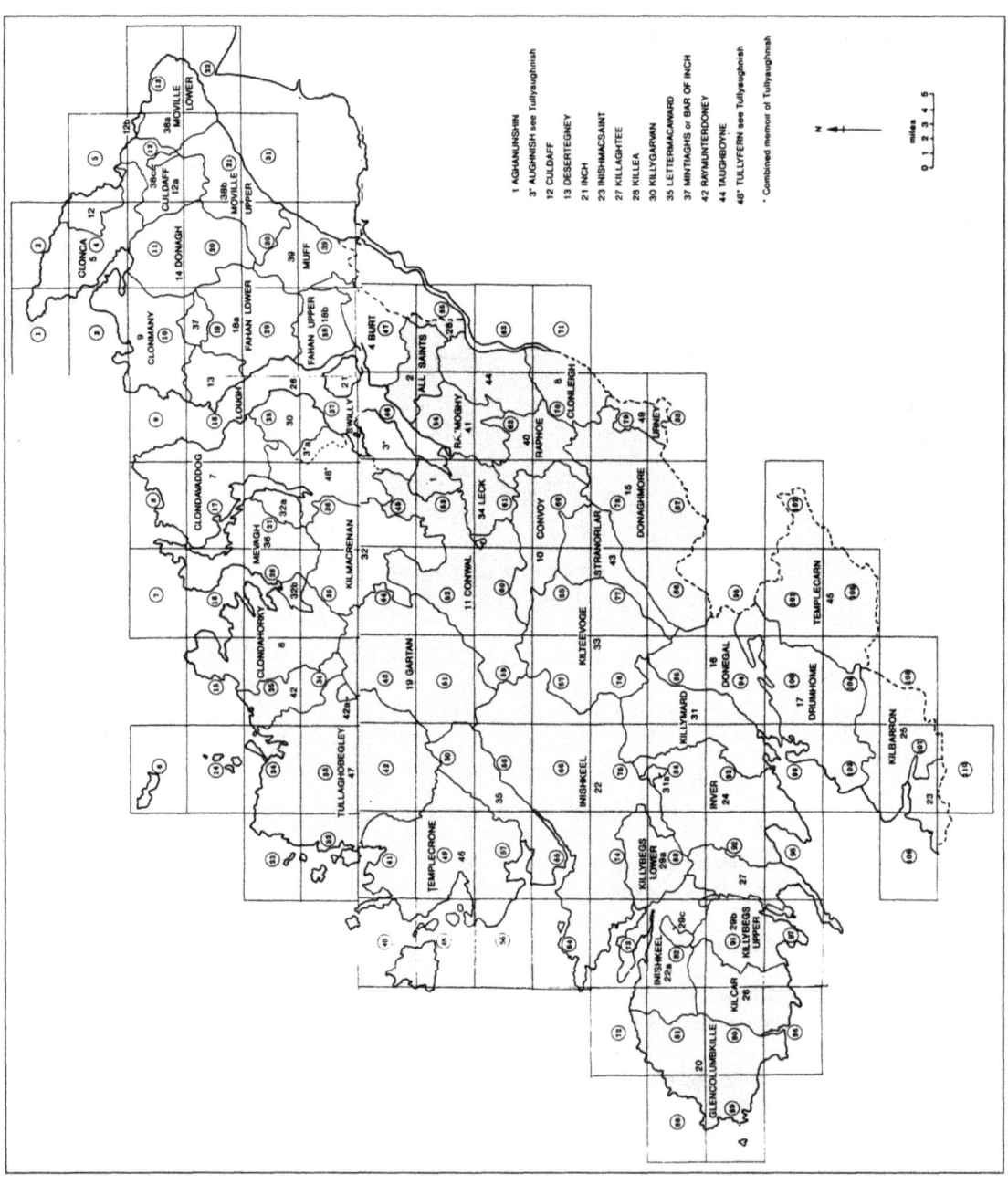

ACKNOWLEDGEMENTS

During the course of the transcription and publication project many have advised and encouraged us in this gigantic task. Thanks must first be given to the Royal Irish Academy which has made available to us the original manuscripts. We are also greatly indebted to Librarian Siobhán O'Rafferty and her staff for their continuing help in deciphering indistinct passages of manuscript.

We should like to acknowledge the following individuals for their special contributions. Dr Brian Trainor led the way with his edition of the Antrim Memoir and provided vital help on the steering committee. Dr Ann Hamlin and her staff in the Environment and Heritage Service have also provided valuable support, especially for database work. Professor R.H. Buchanan's unfailing encouragement has been an inspiration to us. Without Dr Kieran Devine the initial stages of the transcription and the computerising work would never have been completed successfully: the project owes a great deal to his constant help and advice. Dr Kay Muhr's contribution to the work of the project is appreciated, as is that of former editor Nóirín Dobson. Mr W.C. Kerr's interest and expertise have been invaluable. Professor Anne Crookshank and Dr Edward McParland were most generous with practical help and advice concerning the drawings amongst the Memoir manuscripts.

We would like to thank the Director of the Ordnance Survey, Dublin and the keepers of the fire-proof store, among them Leonard Hines. Finally, all students of the nineteenth-century Ordnance Survey of Ireland owe a great deal to the pioneering work of Professor J.H. Andrews, and his kind help in the first days of the project is gratefully recorded.

Special mention must be made of Colán MacArthur's kind help with the Memoirs. We would also like to thank Liam Ronayne, the Donegal County Librarian, for his support and interest.

The essential task of inputting the texts from audio tapes was done by Miss Eileen Kingan, Mrs Christine Robertson, Miss Eilis Smyth, Miss Lynn Murray and, most importantly, Miss Maureen Carr.

We are grateful to the Linen Hall Library for lending us their copies of the first edition 6" Ordnance Survey maps: also to Ms Maura Pringle of QUB Cartography Department for the index maps showing the parish boundaries. For providing financial assistance at crucial times for the maintenance of the project, we would like to take this opportunity of thanking the trustees of the Esme Mitchell trust and The Public Record Office of Northern Ireland.

Left:
Map of parishes of County Donegal. The area described in this volume, the parishes of Mid, West and South Donegal, has been shaded to highlight its location. The square grids represent the 1830s 6" Ordnance Survey maps. The encircled numbers relate to the map numbers as presented in the bound volumes of maps for the county. The parishes have been numbered in all cases and named in full where possible, but if this has not been possible a key is provided.

The following parishes are not recorded in the Memoirs: Aghanunshin, Clonca, Clondahorky, Fahan Lower, Fahan Upper, Gartan, Inishmacsaint, Inver, Kilcar, Killaghtee, Killybegs Lower, Killybegs Upper, Lettermacaward, Raymunterdoney, Stranorlar, Templecrone.

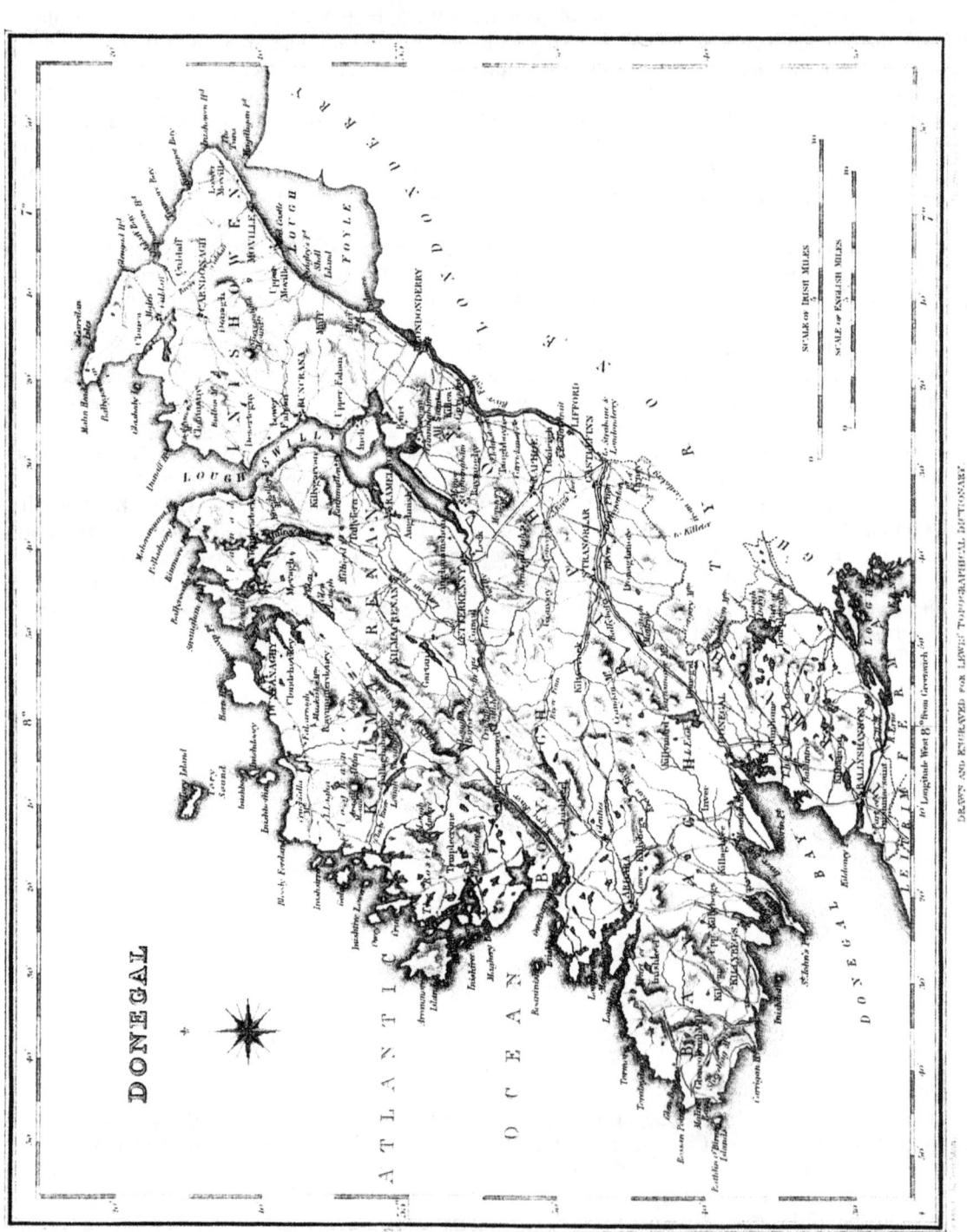

Map of County Donegal, from Samuel Lewis' *Atlas of the counties of Ireland* (London, 1837)

INTRODUCTION AND GUIDE TO THE PUBLICATION OF THE ORDNANCE SURVEY MEMOIRS

The following text of the Ordnance Survey Memoirs was first transcribed by a team working in the Institute of Irish Studies at The Queen's University of Belfast, on a computerised index of the material. For this publication programme the text has been further edited: spellings have been modernised in most cases, although where the original spelling was thought to be of any interest it has been retained and is indicated by angle brackets in the text. Variant spellings for townland and lesser place-names have been preserved, although parish and major place-names have been standardised and the original spelling given in angle brackets. Names of prominent people, for instance landlords, have been standardised where possible, but original spellings of names in lists of informants, emigration tables and on tombstones have been retained. We have not altered the Memoir writers' anglicisation of names and words in Irish.

Punctuation has been modernised and is the responsibility of the editors. Editorial additions are indicated by square brackets: a question mark before and after a word indicates a queried reading and tentatively inserted information respectively. Original drawings are referred to in the text, and some have been reproduced. Manuscript page references have been omitted from this series. Because of the huge variation in size of Memoirs for different counties, the following editorial policy has been adopted: where there are numerous duplicating and overlapping accounts, the most complete and finished account, normally the Memoir proper, has been presented, with additional unique information from other accounts like the Fair Sheets entered into a separate section, clearly titled and identified; where the Memoir material is less, nothing has been omitted. To achieve standard volume size, parishes have been associated on the basis of propinquity.

There are considerable differences in the volume of information recorded for different areas: counties Antrim and Londonderry are exceptionally well covered, while the other counties do not have quite the same detail. This series is the first systematic publication of the parish Memoirs, although individual parishes have been published by pioneering local history societies. The entire transcriptions of the Memoirs made in the course of the indexing project can be consulted in the Public Record Office of Northern Ireland and the library at the Queen's University of Belfast. The manuscripts of the Ordnance Survey Memoirs are in the Royal Irish Academy, Dublin.

Brief history of the Irish Ordnance Survey in the nineteenth century and the writing of the Ordnance Survey Memoirs

In 1824 a House of Commons committee recommended a townland survey of Ireland with maps at the scale of 6", to facilitate a uniform valuation for local taxation. The Duke of Wellington, then prime minister, authorised this, the first Ordnance Survey of Ireland. The survey was directed by Colonel Thomas Colby, who had under his command officers of the Royal Engineers and three companies of sappers and miners. In addition to this, civil assistants were recruited to help with sketching, drawing and engraving of maps, and eventually, in the 1830s, the writing of the Memoirs.

The Memoirs were written descriptions intended to accompany the maps, containing information which could not be fitted on to them. Colonel Colby always considered additional information to be necessary to clarify place-names and other distinctive features of each parish; this was to be written up in reports by the officers. Much information about parishes resulted from research into place-names and was used in the writing of the Memoirs. The term "Memoir" comes from the abbreviation of the word "Aide-Memoire". It was also used in the 18th century to describe topographical descriptions accompanying maps.

In 1833 Colby's assistant, Lieutenant Thomas Larcom, developed the scope of the officers' reports by stipulating the headings or "Heads of Inquiry" under which information was to be reported, and including topics of social as well as economic interest. By this time civil assistants were writing some of the Memoirs under the supervision of the officers, as well as collecting information in the Fair Sheets.

The first "Memoirs" are officers' reports covering Antrim in 1830, and work continued on the Antrim parishes right through the decade, with special activity in 1838 and 1839. Counties Down and Tyrone were written up from 1833 to 1837, with both officers and civil assistants working on Memoirs. In Londonderry and Fermanagh research and writing started in 1834. Armagh was worked on in 1835, 1837 and 1838. Much labour was expended in the Londonderry parishes. The plans to publish the Memoirs commenced with the parish of Templemore, containing the city and liberties of Derry, which came out in 1837 after a great deal of expense and effort.

Between 1839 and 1840 the Memoir scheme collapsed. Sir Robert Peel's government could not countenance the expenditure of money and time on such an exercise; despite a parliamentary commission favouring the continuation of the writing of the Memoirs, the scheme was halted before the southern half of the country was covered. The manuscripts remained unpublished and most were removed to the Royal Irish Academy, Dublin from the Ordnance Survey, Phoenix Park. Other records of the Ordnance Survey, including some residual material from the Memoir scheme, have been transferred to the National Archives, Bishop Street, Dublin.

The Memoirs are a uniquely detailed source for the history of the northern half of Ireland immediately before the Great Famine. They document the landscape and situation, buildings and antiquities, land-holdings and population, employment and livelihood of the parishes. They act as a nineteenth-century Domesday book and are essential to the understanding of the cultural heritage of our communities. It is planned to produce a volume of evaluative essays to put the material in its full context, with information on other sources and on the writers of the Memoirs.

Definition of descriptive terms

Memoir (sometimes Statistical Memoir): an account of a parish written according to the prescribed form outlined in the instructions known as "Heads of Inquiry", and normally divided into three sections: Natural Features and History; Modern and Ancient Topography; Social and Productive Economy.

Fair Sheets: "information gathered for the Memoirs", an original title describing paragraphs of information following no particular order, often with marginal headings, signed and dated by the civil assistant responsible.

Statistical Remarks/Accounts: both titles are employed by the Engineer officers in their descriptions of the parish with marginal headings, often similar in layout to the Memoir.

Office Copies: these are copies of early drafts, generally officers' accounts and must have been made for office purposes.

Ordnance Survey Memoirs for County Donegal

This volume, the thirty-ninth in the series and the second of two for the county, contains the Memoirs for 20 parishes in the west, south, middle and Lagan districts of Donegal. These accounts follow the types of description seen in the first

Donegal volume and consist of statistical reports written by young engineer officers, Lieutenants Delves Broughton, Lancey and Wilkinson, between 1835 and 1836, and replies written by local correspondents, mostly clergy and farmers, to queries from the 1820s by the North West of Ireland Farming Society, an organisation that sought to improve agricultural practices.

For parish and other major place-name spellings we have looked to *Donegal History and society* eds William Nolan, Liam Ronayne and Mairead Dunlevy (Geographical Publications, 1995) as a standard. There are many variant spellings for townland and other places and, as this reflects the linguistic heritage of the area, the editors have tried to preserve as many of them as possible.

Many of the comments we have made about the Memoirs of volume 38 would be applicable here: the portrayal of a predominantly agricultural economy in which the domestic linen industry played an important, if declining, role; fishing, both in the Atlantic and Loughs Swilly and Foyle, that provided a valuable source of nutrition and income; and the importance of the fertilizing products of Lough Swilly, especially shells, sand and sea-mud, to the Lagan parishes.

As might be expected, the imposing Jacobean and earlier structure of Donegal Castle is described competently by Lancey, while other more ancient and problematic objects such as the sheila-na-gig found on an island in Lough Eske are recorded in drawings only. The famous site of St Patrick's Purgatory on Lough Derg provokes a detailed, if unsympathetic, description from Lancey, while the ancient religious station of Glencolumbkille is very briefly sketched in by a local farmer.

We would like to acknowledge as useful a transcription of the Inishkeel Memoir prepared by Thomas Gildea Cannon of Wisconsin, USA.

Drawings in the Memoir papers are listed below and are cross-referenced in the text; some are illustrated. The manuscript material is to be found in Boxes 21 and 22 of the Royal Irish Academy's collection of Ordnance Survey Memoirs, and section references are given beside each parish below in their printed order.

Clonleigh	Box 21 III 2, 1
Convoy	Box 21 V 1
Conwal	Box 21 VI 1
Donaghmore	Box 21 X 1
Donegal	Box 21 IX 2, 1
Drumhome	Box 21 XI 1, 2
Glencolumbkille	Box 21 XII 1
Inishkeel	Box 21 XIII 1
Kilbarron	Box 21 XIV 1
Killea and Taughboyne	Box 21 XV 1
Killymard	Box 21 XVIII 2, 1
Kilteevoge	Box 21 XXI 1
Leck	Box 21 XXII 1, Box 22 XII 6
Raphoe	Box 22 VI, 2
Raymoghy	Box 22 VI 1, 2
Taughboyne	Box 22 VIII 1
Templecarn	Box 22 IX 1, 2
Tullaghobegley	Box 22 IV 1
Urney	Box 22 XI 1
Miscellaneous Papers (All Saints, Clonleigh, Killea, Raymoghy, Taughboyne)	Box 22 XII 8

Drawings

[by W. Lancey except where specified]

Donegal (section 2):

Donegal Castle, detailed view of front elevations, with dimensions.

Decorated fireplace in Donegal Castle with arms of Brooke family and scale.

Donegal Abbey, south and east windows, with dimensions.

Donegal church, side elevation with dimensions.

Gravestone with arms of Bishop O'Gallagher of Raphoe, with dimensions.

Franciscan friary in Magherabeg, with dimensions.

Tomb of Dean Marshall in graveyard, with funerary devices.

2 sculpted stones preserved in St Ernan's garden.

Drumhome (section 1):

East view of Temple McMillighan showing gable wall and window, with dimensions.

Killymard (section 2):

Pigeon house in Lough Eske Demesne, with dimensions.

Ruins in Lough Eske Demesne showing arches and inset window, with dimensions.

Sheila-na-gig in Lough Eske Demesne.

Tombstone in Lough Eske Demesne.

Raymoghy (section 1):

Balleaghan Abbey showing east window and side elevation [illustrated].

Old church of Raymoghy showing east window and side elevation [illustrated] [by Lieutenant I.I. Wilkinson].

Templecarn (section 1):

Magrath's Castle near Pettigo, with dimensions.

Sculpted stone at chapel door, Station Island, Lough Derg, showing arms of Prior Dogherty, with dimensions.

Cross from beds of St Patrick's Purgatory, Station Island, with annotations and dimensions.

St Patrick's Cross, Lough Derg, with dimensions.

Station Island, Lough Derg, tracing showing St Patrick's chapel, prior's house, penitential beds and other features.

View of Station Island, Lough Derg, from the shore [illustrated].

St Deavog's Chair, with dimensions.

Miscellaneous (section 5):

Copy of early map of St Patrick's Purgatory, Lough Derg, with buildings and penitential beds.

Parish of Clonleigh, County Donegal

Statistical Report by Lieutenant I.I. Wilkinson, December 1835

Natural State

Situation and Boundaries

The parish of Clonleigh is situated in the eastern part of the county of Donegal, in the barony of Raphoe and diocese of Derry.

It is bounded on the north by the parish of Taughboyne, on the west by the parishes of Raphoe and Donaghmore, on the south by the parish of Urney and on the east by the River Finn and the River Foyle, which is formed by junction of the Finn and the Mourne immediately above Lifford bridge, a structure of 12 arches.

Extent and Divisions

The outline of the parish is irregular, but its greatest length from north east to south west is 7 miles and a half and its greatest breadth from north west to south east 4 miles, including an area of 12,600 statute acres nearly.

The parish is divided into 89 denominations, of which 26 are churchlands held of the Bishop of Derry, 39 the property of the Earl of Erne, 5 of Colonel Creighton, 2 of Mr Crawford of Letterkenny, 10 of Mr Sinclair, 2 of the Revd Mr Alexander, 1 of Mr Montgomery of Convoy and 4 of Peter Maxwell Esquire of Birdstown, which are tithe free.

Natural Features and Productive Economy

Rivers

The Finn separates the parish of Clonleigh from the adjoining one of Urney in the county of Tyrone for 3 miles, flowing through an alluvial soil in a deep narrow channel. It is subject to large floods and barely fordable in 2 places at a depth of 6 feet, one opposite Urney House, the residence of the rector of that parish, the other nearer to Lifford.

Above the bridge it meets the River Mourne flowing from the eastward and both unite to form the Foyle, which separates Clonleigh from the adjoining parishes of Camus and Leckpatrick in the county Tyrone for about 4 miles. It forms several islands and, running over sand and gravel, is fordable immediately below Lifford, and in several places the tide from the sea rises about 18 inches at the Lifford bridge and reaches as far as Claudy bridge.

The Burndale river, a small stream rising among the mountains in the parishes of Convoy and Conwal near Loughdale, the source of which is upwards of 860 feet above the sea, flows from west to east and, dividing the parish of Clonleigh into 2 nearly equal parts, joins the Foyle 1 mile below Lifford; it is subject to floods.

The Swilly burn rises near Raphoe and falls into the Foyle about 4 miles below Lifford.

There are a number of smaller streams and springs. No mineral springs have been discovered. Lifford is well supplied with water from the hill above it.

Fisheries

There is an excellent salmon fishery belonging to the Irish Society in the Foyle and Finn; the Burndale river also affords trout.

Hills

There are no mountains in the parish but a number of small hills, most of them cultivated to the summit. The principal one, named Crohan, rises to the height of 722 feet, on which is a trigonometrical station, a pile formed of earth and stones. The summit of Crohan is barren and its sides so steep that the manure necessary for cultivation is carried up on horses' backs.

Manures and Bogs

The manures are chiefly lime, bog and animal manure.

The bog extends in detached portions along the Swilly burn, principally in Mossmore, Mullinaveigh, Drimlene, Boyagh and Porthall. The general height above the sea is 23 feet.

Modern Topography

Towns: Lifford

Lifford, situated on the left bank of the Foyle, in north latitude 54 degrees 49 minutes nearly and west longitude 7 degrees 23 minutes nearly, is the only town in the parish. Here is the parochial church and, as Lifford is also the county town of Donegal, where assizes are held twice in the year, there is a court house, county house and gaol which is kept remarkably clean.

The average number of prisoners in 6 months was 140, principally confined for illicit distillation. They are employed at stone-breaking. Here prisoners awaiting their trial who are not able to provide themselves with subsistence are obliged to work.

There is: a barrack for a company of infantry; it is not government property but hired from an individual; an infirmary, where the average number of patients is 65, of whom, accidents excepted, three-fourths are afflicted with scrofulous ulcers and chronic rheumatism; cases of fever are not admitted; a distillery; a lunatic asylum for 16 patients, which number it contains at present; a post office; 192 houses, 12 of which are public; and 725 inhabitants, 324 males, 401 females (census May 1830).

Ballindrait

On the road from Lifford to Raphoe is the largest village in the parish. Here a Presbyterian meeting house, the Roman Catholic chapel and the residence of the Roman Catholic priest adjoining it are situated on the road between Ballindrait and Lifford. Ballindrait contains 134 houses, of which 4 are public, 1 corn mill, 1 flax mill, 3 forges and 348 inhabitants, 166 males, 182 females.

Schools

There are 3 schools in the parish, 1 at Lifford, founded by Sir R. Hanson [Hansard], 40 scholars; 1 at Blackrock, founded by the Revd W. Knox, 50 boys and 50 girls; and 1 in Ballindrait, 15 boys and 11 girls, by the Kildare Place Society; and others now founding under the care of the Revd W. Knox, rector.

Gentlemen's Seats

The Revd William Knox, rector of the parish, by whom this information respecting it was chiefly afforded, has a mansion at Gortgranagh, not Glebe, and Benjamin Humfrey Esquire a residence at Cavanacor. These are the only magistrates in the parish.

PRODUCTIVE ECONOMY

Farms

The size of the farms vary from 15 to 30 acres and produce oats, potatoes, which in large farms generally occupy a tenth and in small ones a fourth of the ground, flax and latterly wheat. The best land is let from 25s to 30s per acre, the second rate from 10s to 15s and portions from 5s to 10s, except in Kirkminister (Mr Maxwell's) where the land, being tithe-free, about 4s on the acre may be added.

Crops

The value of the crops on the ground per acre of oats are from 6 pounds to 4 pounds, of wheat from 12 pounds to 9 pounds, potatoes from 20 pounds to 12 pounds or 8 pounds, flax from 12 pounds to 8 pounds or 6 pounds and barley from 10 pounds to 6 pounds (Cunningham acre).

General Economy

The wages of a day labourer vary from 8d to 10d per diem, with a horse and cart from 2s 6d to 3s 6d. There are no manufactories. Meal and potatoes constitute the principal subsistence of labourers.

There is a cattle fair held annually at Ballindrait on the 20th November, but no market in the parish. This is to be attributed to the neighbourhood of Strabane, which possesses good ones and is within a mile of Lifford.

SOCIAL ECONOMY

Population

The parish contains 830 houses, 900 families, of whom 440 persons belong to the Church of England, 2,035 are Presbyterians, 1,562 Roman Catholics and 237 Covenanters (census 1821). No registry of births, marriages and deaths being kept by the Presbyterians and Roman Catholics, the increase or decrease of population is not known.

Advowson

The living of Clonleigh is distinct and in the gift of the Lord Bishop of Derry. The tithes are valued under the Tithe Composition Act at 840 pounds per annum. There are also 40 and a half statute acres of glebe in the parish, and the townlands of Carrickadawson (378 and a half acres) and Carnshannagh (293 acres), situated in the parish of Taughboyne, are glebe lands attached to the rectory of Clonleigh. These glebes are valued at 320 pounds; the total value of the living is therefore 1,160 pounds per annum. There is no glebe house in the parish.

Natural History

Geology

The geological features of the parish are entirely confined to the primitive class, mica slate being the prevailing rock. Limestone is very abundant, appearing in strata alternating with the mica slate. The limestone itself is parted by thin layers of mica in the direction of the beds, so that on the cross fracture nothing but lime appears, while on the leading fracture mica or mica slate is alone visible. This circumstance, however, makes the limestone the more valuable for economical purposes, as it can be raised of any thickness and several feet long, splitting afterwards with great facility in the direction of the layers of mica.

That species of serpentine by some called potstone makes its appearance in the townland of Camus. It is so soft in some places as to admit of being dressed with the knife. It is not much sought after though, from its well-known property as a firestone, it might be very useful. It is not of great extent nor can its connection with the including strata be traced.

A few hundred yards to the north a rock makes its appearance, composed of a paste of a reddish-brown colour (compact felspar?) containing numerous interspersed crystals of greenish-black hornblende which are sometimes confusedly aggregated. The bed is only a few feet thick and is conformable to the including strata. It may be traced to a considerable distance. It is cut off by the opening between Kirkminister and Crohan but reappears on one of the points of the former hill with precisely the same characters.

There is not the least appearance of stratification in the bed. It is rent by numerous vertical fissures. Its connection with the rock below it, which is an impure limestone, cannot be traced, while above it may be seen a rock highly micaceous which appears to have filled up the hollows, neither rock appearing to be altered at the point of contact. The adhesion is slight, but with care a hand specimen might be obtained, part of which would have a porphyritic aspect, while the remainder of a different colour would have a schistose structure. No metallic veins have been discovered.

Coal

A report prevails in the country that coal has been and may be found by sinking in Crohan. If any coal does exist it, of course, can only be anthracite. It appears that many years ago a soldier belonging to a regiment quartered in Lifford, who had been a miner, visited the spot and told the inhabitants that coal existed and would be found by sinking in the spot he pointed out. He knew it, he said, by the colour and taste of the water. Now the spot is close to a limestone quarry behind Mr Clarke's house in the townland of Carraghlane. The dip of the strata is to the north 5 degrees west at an angle of 21 degrees and the direction of course east 5 degrees north. The inferior strata may be traced to the south for hundreds of feet. They continue of the same character. No one has any of the coal.

General Remarks

There are considerable tracts of alluvial land on the banks of the Foyle and Burndale rivers, but that on the Finn alone presents anything remarkable. Here are small isolated hills of gravel rising to the height of 43 feet in the middle of the flat alluvial land. The gravel is of all sizes, quite rounded by attrition and is entirely composed of the primitive rocks, principally mica slate with some few larger boulders of granite. I am indebted for this geological notice to Captain T. Jones, Royal Navy, Member of Parliament for the county of Londonderry.

Modern and Ancient Topography

Roads

The principal roads in the parish lead from Lifford to Stranorlar, distance 13 and a quarter miles, to Raphoe 6 miles, Letterkenny 16 miles and Londonderry 15 miles. Of these, none are well laid out or kept in good order.

Antiquities

The remains of an old church or friary at Edenmore; another at Ballybogan still used as a burial ground; a remarkable stone in the townland of Lower Kirkminister called the Gallows Stone, close to a cottage on the roadside leading from Raphoe to Castlefinn; some large stones called a giant's grave in the townland of Drimnaha; a similar object in that of Gortnagole; and also a circular enclosure of upright stones in the townland of Middle Kirkminister; and several circular enclosures called Danish forts. No tradition respecting them could be learnt.

Social Economy

Table of Schools

[Table contains the following headings: situation, number of scholars subdivided by religion and sex, remarks as to how supported].

Murlogh: Protestants 6 males, 5 females; Roman Catholics 29 males, 44 females; this national school is taught by Mr Sherdin and his son, both Roman Catholics, who receive separate salaries of 8 pounds and 4 pounds per annum from the government; he also charges each scholar from 1s 1d to 1s 6d per quarter. There is also a female teacher who receives no salary.

Ballybogan: Protestants 1 male, 4 females; Roman Catholics 37 males, 22 females; this school is taught by Mr Diver, a Roman Catholic, who receives a salary of 8 pounds per annum; he also charges each scholar 1s 1d per quarter.

Cloghfin: Protestants 15 males, 14 females; Roman Catholics 38 males, 34 females; this school is taught by Patrick Braceland, a Roman Catholic, who receives a salary of 8 pounds per annum from government; he also charges each scholar from 1s 1d to 1s 4d per quarter.

Tamnawood, female school: Protestants 19, Roman Catholics 3; this is a female school taught by Ann Sprowles, a Protestant, who receives a salary of 12 pounds from the Erne fund, also from the scholars about 14 pounds 8s per annum. She teaches reading, writing and sewing.

Tamnawood, male school: Protestants 28 males, Roman Catholics 2 males; there is also attached a male school taught by Mathew Buchannan, a Presbyterian; he receives from the Erne fund (left by Lord Erne) 12 pounds and from the scholars 24 pounds 8s per annum.

Trades or Callings in Lifford

Shoemakers 14, tailors 12, painters 2, blacksmiths 2, wheelwrights 1, weavers 2, carpenters 8, bakers 2, grocers 5, publicans 10, land surveyors 2, Protestant clergymen 1, stonemasons 11, land agent 1.

Population of the parish of Clonleigh in the year 1834: 806 members of the Established Church, 3,540 Roman Catholics, 1,674 Presbyterians, total 6,020.

From published abstract of report by W.J. Hamilton Esquire, barrister-at-law, signed I.I. Wilkinson, Lieutenant Royal Engineers, 12th December 1835.

Replies by Reverend John Graham to Queries of North West Farming Society, October 1821.

Natural State

Locality and Proprietors

This parish is situated in the county of Donegal, in the barony of Raphoe and diocese of Derry. The ancient and modern name of it is Clonleigh but it is generally called Lifford; Revd William Knox, incumbent.

The landed proprietors are the Bishop of Derry, Colonel Maxwell, Charles Crawford, resident in the county; James Sinclair Esquire resident in Tyrone; the Earl of Erne, the Revd John Barker, not residents.

Productive Economy

Holdings and Farms

On looking over the annexed table of landholders, it will be seen that the size of farms varies from 10 to 80 acres; but Mr James Ball occupies 155 acres in the townland of Shannon, where he sets an example of an improved mode of agriculture and care of improving the breed of cattle which cannot fail to be useful to the landholders in his vicinity. Mr Thomas Keys occupies an 100 acres in Glenfad which appear to be in a productive state. Mr Maxwell holds 75 acres, a very handsome demesne in Gortnagranagh, highly improved and judiciously planted.

Pasture-lands are to no great extent here; a few acres in each farm are appropriated to this purpose in proportion to the arable land. Milch cows are the general stock, with a horse to each of the smaller-sized farms. The aftergrass of the meadows generally fatten a cow or more for the owner, and the soil round the ditches of the cornfields serve oftentimes in good stead, when Lammas or Michaelmas floods have tinged the meadows and pasture with mud.

Agricultural Methods

The mode of cultivating land here is by the plough chiefly, but in winter and the earlier part of spring the furrows of ground intended for potatoes or oats are frequently dug up and spread on the top of the ridge; the succession of crops usually in this way: potatoes, barley, a little wheat, oats, flax and oats again.

The most likely means of improvement would be the general introduction of lime as a manure

Parish of Clonleigh

and, from the existence of limestone in the parish and the facilities of water carriage for fuel, great facilities for obtaining this advantage may be found here. The pasture-lands are generally capable of improvement and this might be effected by a judicious application of them to tillage and letting them out in full heart.

A more general use of clover and green fodder would enable the farmer to turn most of their pasture into tillage; and from the accumulation of manure from stall-feeding, as well as the protection of the cattle from heat, flies and running in hot weather, it is probable that the system of pasturage will eventually be given up for stall-feeding. Pasture appears to the writer of this report to be a waste of land in feeding cattle.

NATURAL FEATURES

Mountains and Water

The only mountain in this parish is one of considerable height and extent, Croaghan. A great proportion of it has been reclaimed and is now in a productive state, particularly on the southern side, where it runs parallel or nearly so to the River Finn. The summit and some parts on the side of this mountain appear to be irreclaimable.

It affords an abundant supply of excellent water, and from a well in it the gaol and town of Lifford might be supplied with water in a part of the country often inundated; yet when good water is so often hard to be got that the permission to go for it, to a small well in one of the gardens near the hospital, is paid for quarterly.

Bogs

The principal bog is at Porthall. It contains 149 acres and belongs to the Bishop of Derry. On Drumleen are 100 acres of bog belonging to the Earl of Erne. There is a very considerable tract of bog at Ardgre belonging to James Sinclair Esquire and another of some extent, and containing bog fir, at Glenfad on the see lands of Derry.

The quantity of timber in the bogs here is not great. It consists chiefly of fir with some black oak, seldom found at any great distance from the surface but always on or very near the substratum of the bog.

Woods

There is an old oakwood on the south side of Croaghan but the trees are of small size and little value. There are thriving plantations at Gortgranagh belonging to R. Maxwell Esquire, at Ardgre belonging to Mr Sinclair and at Porthall belonging to Mr James Clark. That at Ardgre is a long skirting planted in moory soil and the trees appear to be of slower growth and less promising than the others, which are in better soil.

There are many orchards in this parish, particularly about Ballindrait, and the apples are of an excellent quality. An orchard has been observed as one of the characteristics of an English settler's farm. There is a very fine quince tree in the garden adjoining the schoolhouse at Lifford.

With respect to forest trees, we observe that alder and ash thrive best in a moist low soil and the larch in mountainous ground. There are no nurseries of trees here, but the want is supplied by those at Strabane in the immediate neighbourhood.

PRODUCTIVE ECONOMY

Rents

The rent of land in this parish varies from 5s to 2 pounds 2s per acre, according to its quality, situation and the time it was taken. Town Parks near Lifford set at 3 pounds and some at 3s per acre. 2 pounds 2s may be a fair average as the acreable rent of arable land here, or perhaps 2 pounds, green pasture at 10s and moory at 5s an acre; so the best land may be rated at 3 pounds or guineas, the second at 2 pounds or guineas and the third from 10s to 30s.

The value of turf bog depends on its quality and distance from Lifford and Strabane. In general the tenants pay no rent for it and some do.

Implements and Fences

The Scotch plough and harrow and carts have been introduced here with great advantage, as also some few threshing and winnowing machines and other improved implements.

No very general change in the mode of fences has been made, but in many places stone walls have been advantageously substituted for quickset ditches which afford harbours for birds and vermin, to the injury of the crops, and moreover occupies too great a proportion of the ground. The fences in general use yet are the quick and ditch, and what is called "the stone ditch and [?] line fence." These are thought best adapted to the situation of the lands and are valued for the shelter they afford from the prevailing winds.

Employment and Wages

Employment is not abundant here; if it were, we would have little or no distress amongst us, for the labour of the head of the family in agriculture and that of his wife and family in linen manufacture would keep them all well fed, clothed and housed. In spring and harvest, of course, there is most employment, but one of our wants most severely felt is that of work for old and young, of which the people seem always desirous, few instances of voluntary idleness occurring here.

The wages of servants here now is from 2 to 4 guineas for the half-year, the hire of a labourer without food is from 10d to 1s (British) per day. Some farmers are said to have unfortunate men to labour for them at 8d a day, upon which, low as provisions are, no man could support a family.

Green Crops

Some clover but scarcely any other green crops are cultivated here; rye grass and clover are sown here.

Drainage

Surface draining is most generally used here. Few of the small farmers could, in times like the present, afford the expense of underdraining. At Shannon and a few other places the underdraining has been practised, particularly at Gortnagranagh and Curraghalane.

Manures

The principal manure here is stable and cowhouse dung, with the ashes and soot and some other such materials as accumulates about houses and farmyards. Composts of lime and bog are not made as frequently as they ought to be and are in other parts of the country, but bog is not conveniently interspersed through the parish; neither is the manuring by shells carried to such an extent as it might be in a parish possessing such great facilities of water carriage. Lime or dung is said to be superior as a manure to burned clay, which has been but little used here.

Irrigation

The farmers here are in the habit of watering the meadows and the practice is found to be very generally beneficial. The situation of the meadow is favourable to irrigation; on the higher grounds is abundance of water. The occasional overflow of the river, though severely injurious in too many occasions, enriches our lowlands by a deposit of rich earth on them.

Dairies

Many dairies have been established in this parish with success, particularly at Ardgre, the milk and butter of which are almost always superior to any other brought into Strabane or Lifford. Whether this is to be ascribed to superiority in the soil or in the management of these dairies is not known, but such is the fact. Some few choices are made here for domestic use.

Oxen and Spade Tillage

We have oxen used here in husbandry.

Spade tillage is not practised here, but if it were it is thought it would prove much more useful than plough tillage.

Grain Crops

Barley, wheat and oats are the only descriptions of grain raised here. Barley sells generally for 1s, oats from 9d to 10d and wheat from 1s 4d to 1s 6d a stone. Provisions of all kinds, flesh, fowl and fish, are cheap here, particularly the latter, of which our indented coast supplies us with a great abundance of the finest kind.

The measurement of land is by the Cunningham or Scotch acre.

Cattle

The black cattle are of a mixed breed and capable of great improvement. Mr James Ball of Shannon has got a bull of a superior English breed, and some opportunity of improving our stock by an intermixture of the Ayrshire and other British kinds exist in the neighbouring county Tyrone.

The description of stock kept on our pasturelands is milch cows, bullocks and a small proportion of sheep. In the summer and autumn considerable numbers of young cattle are fed in the mountainous pastures.

Sheep

Sheep thrive here; they are generally of a small kind. The mutton from 9 to 14 lbs a quarter, and as much excelling the new lights in flavour as they are inferior in appearance and tallow. They appear to be peculiarly adapted to the climate and soil but perhaps they might be improved by crossing the strain, which is generally thought to be good for man and beast. New combinations may be as surprisingly made in flesh and blood as well as in the kaleidoscopes or alphabet. An exchange in the longitude of the legs of our sheep might be made with some advantage for the breadth in the posterior of some of the English breeds.

Mineral Spring

The pump in the debtors' end of Lifford gaol affords water slightly impregnated with iron, but no other mineral water is known in this parish.

Horses

The horses used here for agricultural purposes, with the exception of a few large and strong enough to draw heavy loads on Scotch carts, are of a light hardy kind, as fit for the saddle as the drafts. Perhaps the breed is capable of improvement, but the writer of this report, considering the soil and the climate, does not think it is.

Swine

The description of swine bred here is generally of the old Irish long-legged breed with a slight and advantageous mixture of the Dutch flat rumps; considering the number of potatoes and other excellent vegetables raised here, the feeding of pork is a most ample resource to us. Great is the advantage of feeding 3 or 4 pigs and, though pork no longer pays the rent of small holdings, a dish of bacon and cabbage with a barn-door fowl, also the produce of the potato field, form as agreeable a kind of food as ever it did and render the possessor of it independent of the market.

Memoir Writing

The probable quantity of each description of stock the writer of this article has been hitherto unable to ascertain; but, if agreeable to the North Western Society, he will endeavour, and he hopes with success, to make out an accurate account of it this winter as an appendix to this return.

It is much to be regretted that this was not required of the enumerator under the new population act, in place of the useless and indelicate task of ascertaining the ages of old maids and ancient bachelors whose returns in the reports are as inaccurate as they are unimportant.

Improvements in Stock

A comparison of the quantity and value of our stock of cattle now, of that of the unhappy time when they were enumerated, in prospect of their being driven or destroyed before an invading enemy, would be a most important document for the political economist.

The improvement in the breed of horses here and in the neighbouring county of Fermanagh is not thought to be great within the last 20 years. Many people think there has been no improvement in it but that it has rather declined. Sheep are said to be rather stationary, black cattle improved, swine somewhat. If any kind of horse breed has been ameliorated, it is said to be that of the draft. The old mountain garran breed seems to be on the decline or nearly extinct. Some good small ponies remarkable for soundness of mind and safety of foot have been imported from Scotland, and the breed improved with mixture of others in this country.

The breeding of blooded horses was formerly much encouraged in this part of Ulster by racing, but the idleness and deprivation of the lower orders, and perhaps of the upper too, which this amusement may be said to occasion, formed too strong a counterbalance to the advantage of improving the breed of horses to render it desirable that this mode of entertainment and gambling should ever [sic] become general in Ireland.

NATURAL FEATURES AND NATURAL HISTORY

Rivers and Pearls

The River Finn divides the parish from the county of Tyrone and parish of Camus or Mourne <Morne>, and also from the parish of Leckpatrick. The River Sooly or Swilly separates it from the parishes of Raphoe and Taughboyne, and the River Burndale divides it into nearly 2 equal parts, runs through it from west to north east, passing through Ballindrait and falling into the Foyle nearly opposite to Islandmore.

The Finn and Mourne unite near the county hospital and not far from Lifford bridge, and in the union of these rivers is called Foyle, though in the original grant to Sir Richard Hansard, and in his will, the river so united is called the Finn.

It is said that the rivers about Omagh and others in the county of Donegal which run into the Foyle produce a kind of mussel-shells in which pearls are found, and some have been very lately picked up in the Tyrone rivers. On the 13th October 1688, Sir Robert Redding wrote a curious letter on the subject to Dr Lyster which was published by the ingenious Dr Thomas Molyneux of Dublin; now out of print.

The pearl of most value found here are our salmon, which form a very agreeable variety of delicious food to us in its season and is salted for spring use by many of our housekeepers, who use it pounded up with potatoes.

Mines and Quarries

No mines have been discovered here within the memory of man, but indications of iron and coal have been noticed. There is no scarcity of stone quarries in this parish. Those in Croaghan consist both of grit building stone and of blue limestone. The quantity of the limestone is very good. It is burned with turf in small kilns. The stone of Croaghan has the appearance of being strongly impregnated with iron and it gives a sombre appearance to the Gothic front of Lifford gaol which is built of it.

Lime being sold here for 10d a barrel by retail, and at a lower price when any quantity of it is bought, the expense of burning it must be little and would be less if we availed ourselves fully of water carriage which this parish possesses. The quarries here are most conveniently situated for the exportation of their produce and if there were any inducement to build houses in Lifford, few places could they be erected on more easy terms: lime and cars and stone on the spot, slate quarries in the neighbouring parishes and the sea open to foreign timber and iron.

No coal has been found here.

Springs and Marl

The pump in the debtors' yard at Lifford gaol is the only mineral water known here. Very few of the Irish mineral waters are strong enough to be efficacious as medicines and on that account are the more useful for domestic purposes.

No marl has been discovered in this parish, the subsoil of which appears in general to be either rocky or sandy.

Social Economy

Habits of the People

The situation of inhabitants in general as to domestic comforts and conveniences, though much similar to that of the inhabitants of many other parts of Ulster, is not yet such as to warrant an opinion of its being incapable of improvement. The windows do not open as generally as they ought to do. They are in many places lead lights nailed upon frames so as never to admit fresh air except when broken. The houses are not white-washed inside and outside, as they ought to be several times in the year when lime can be so easily procured. The dung-pits, except those of the richer farmers, are still kept too near the front doors and the beds are more calculated for warmth than for neatness.

The late calamity of the times has left dark traces upon the abodes and attire of our peasantry, and it is to be hoped that an amelioration of them will make our distressed but industrious and kindhearted people to renew their clothing and render their decayed habitations more comfortable than they are at present.

Their disposition to industry is very observable and can only be equalled by their heroic patience under privations, which would render Englishmen desperately mischievous to others or to themselves. The habits of the greater part of them are those of cleanliness and their internal comforts greater than their circumstances would lead a stranger to expect.

Their means of earning money is either by labour or the sale of the produce of their farms; some live by weaving, a few by fishing and a due proportion by manufacturing shoes, by carpenter or smith's work, dressing flax etc. The money earned is seldom more than what is necessary for the discharge of rent and other demands, and for the relief of present wants. The days of money hoarding have passed away with the noise of war.

The farm and cottage houses, as already observed, are not generally in that thorough state of repair in which they were when the parish was perhaps one of the best appointed in that way known in the province of Ulster.

Fuel

In some parts of the parish, as appears from the statements of the quantity and situation of bog in it, fuel is abundant, but in other parts, as at Shannon and Lifford, it is not so easily to be had. Mr Ball finds it cheaper to burn coal even in his kitchen than to buy turf for that purpose, as the expense of drawing it would be enormous. A bog which once supplied Lifford with turf has been entirely cut away and is now rushy pasture of an indifferent quality. Turf costs from 5 pounds to 8 pounds a hundred of 240 barrels, being sometimes higher and seldom much lower, but it is of an excellent kind, brought from the mountains of Tyrone over Strabane, hard and black, and nearly equalling coal in the heat it gives.

Parish of Clonleigh

Food

The general food of the farming class consists of oaten and wheaten bread with milk or tea, with butter and eggs for breakfast; beef, bacon, vegetables, poultry, fish (fresh or salted) for dinner; potatoes or stirabout or flummery with milk for supper. The food of the manufacturing class is nearly the same but not quite so varied or expensive as that of the farming class.

The poor or labouring class live but scantily, their food being chiefly potatoes with a short allowance of buttermilk and too often with salt only. An occasional influx of very fine herrings often relieves them. But he who feedeth the young ravens one way or other maintains the poorest of the people, so that few feel actual hunger without the means of allaying it.

Education

The general desire for education which at present characterises the Irish population exists nowhere in a greater degree than here, but it has been somewhat repressed by the late distresses of the farming part of our community and the peasantry to whom they had been in the habit of affording employment.

At Lifford is a classical school maintained by a small endowment. The charge in it is 1 guinea and 1 guinea per quarter. That in the other schools (of which a list is subjoined) is usually for arithmetic, writing and reading 7s 6d, for writing and reading 5s, and for spelling from 1s 8d to 3s 4d a quarter. The general wish for education is pretty equal in all classes but the poorest are unable to gratify it.

The schools are kept at Porthall by John Doogan; Glencock, Michael Quinn; Slievdool, Matthew Buchanan; Ballindrait, Hugh Gallagher; Church Minister, Alexander Eglinton; Keelogue, Robert McKinnen; Curraghalane, John Burn; Lifford, J. Starrat, J. Arbuckle, the Revd J. Graham.

It has been observed that the peasantry have been generally improved in their manners and conduct by the little education they have got, which has combined, with some other causes, to render inebriety, writing and idleness much less observable than it was in other times not very remote from the present.

Health

The general state of health here is good, the situation being very favourable except about Porthall, which is low and marshy, but even there no disease prevails occasioned by damp or moisture. Typhus fever has prevailed here when it was general in Ireland, but with comparatively few fatal results: alternate doses of Glauber salts and fresh buttermilk proved an almost infallible cure for it.

If the gaol, through which a large proportion of this large and populous county unfortunately pass from the operation of the revenue laws, may be taken as a fair test of the healthiness of the people, it may be reckoned proofs of the soundness of our constitution and salubrity of our air, that from the autumn of 1817 to the present day there has been no fever of any kind in Lifford gaol nor any other sickness of a serious nature, with the exception of one or two aged men who come there with broken constitutions.

The diseases incident to children prevail here occasionally as in other places but are usually of a mild nature, except on a late occasion when the smallpox was most mischievously propagated in Lifford by inoculation; but as this was done in error by a very young person otherwise of excellent conduct, there is no danger of an recurrence of the evil.

Friendly Societies

There are no friendly societies here for the improvement of the condition of the poor, but it is to be hoped that this will not be the case much longer and that Lifford or the more central town of Ballindrait may be considered as a proper place for establishing a branch of the North West Farming Society.

There is intelligence and spirit enough in the parish to render the inhabitants of it very competent to such an effort for the good of the country, and the most unaffected harmony and goodwill to each other prevails among us.

MODERN TOPOGRAPHY AND SOCIAL ECONOMY

Towns

The only towns in this parish are those of Lifford and Ballindrait, both of them in a state of decline. Lifford, although the shire town of the county of Donegal, has neither fair, market or post office, though there is a patent as early as the grant of the lands by King James I for a weekly market on Mondays and for 2 fairs in the year, one on Ascension Thursday and the other on the feast of St Matthew; date of the patent, 31st January 1612.

The want of a post office is well supplied by a very regular mail coach kept by Mr Oliver Jenkins in Strabane, one and the same town with Lifford, which in that case would form the west end of a provincial metropolis. There is but one fair held in Ballindrait and that on the 21st November, although it is said there is a patent for several others.

Progress of Improvement

The spirit of improvement appears to be repressed by the low state of the county with respect to money matters, but there seems to be ground for hoping that, as the circumstances of the people improve, their observable inclination to seek and adopt the means of bettering their condition will be brought into action again. The quantity of coarse ground recovered from a state of nature during the late war, together with the great improvement in the roads, as well as the intelligence and habits of our people, afford that they have no natural disinclination to making improvements.

Memoir Writing

Informants

The proprietors or farmers who are most skilful improvers and most likely to be useful correspondents to the North West Society: James Sinclair, James Ball, Robert Maxwell, Andrew Ball Esquire, Mr Andrew McCrea of Ardgee, Captain Humphries of Murlogh, Revd Mr Huston of Gortin, John Chambers Esquire, Lifford, Mr William Clark, Lifford, Mr George Knox, Lifford, William Spence Esquire, Coneyberry, Dr Clarke of Curraghlane, Mr Thomas Keys, Clonfad, Mr Tasker Keys, Mr Crocket of Edenmore, the Revd Andrew Kernaghan of Rossgier, Mr Sproule of Coneyberry, Mr James Clark of Porthall, Surgeon Prior of Ballindrait, Mr Gabriel Montgomery, Lifford, Mr Irwin Aiken, Lifford, Mr Patrick Scanlan, Mr John Morton, Dr Gillespie, all of Lifford, Mr James Galbraith of Edenmore, Mr William Burns of Church Minister.

Productive Economy

Linen Manufacture

The linen manufacture is increasing. There are no mill works connected with it here.

The ground is prepared for flax by being twice ploughed. It usually exceeds oats as a crop. It is both exported and used for home manufacture. Very little seed is saved. The moisture of the climate and the hurry of brittle harvests are not favourable to this branch of agricultural economy.

Preparation of Yarn

Flax is prepared for the manufacturer both by mills and by manual labour, and fire is used in the preparation. The grist of yarn is in general from 2 to 4 hanks in the lb. The spinner earns 4d or 5d a day. The price of a spangle is from 2s to 2s 8d. It is used both in home manufacture and sold in Strabane market for exportation. Some spinners grow their flax but many more purchase it.

The double wheel has not yet been introduced here, but those who have and examined the thread spun by it say it is much superior, being more even than that spun on the single wheel; and this seems to be a great advantage in it which was probably not foreseen by the inventor. The idle hand in the old spinning wheel was, like idle hands on all other occasions, worse than useless. It tempted the spinner frequently to try to aid the hand employed and so occasioned a doubling or lump in the thread so spun. The manufacturer usually prepared the yarn for the loom himself.

There are no yarn greens in this parish. What is called the Coleraine linen is generally manufactured here and sold in Derry and Strabane from 1s to 1s 4d a yard.

There is no woollen manufactory here. There is no cotton manufactured here.

Fisheries

This not being on the sea-coast, kelp is not made here.

There is a salmon fishery at Lifford in which 2 small boats with 5 men to each are employed. It has been very unproductive this year. No fish is cured here for a foreign market.

The fishing does not appear to be capable of much improvement in any but one, which would be giving it a jubilee now and then for a year to suffer the fish to multiply. See Archbishop King's account of our salmon and eel fisheries.

Answers by Reverend John Graham to Queries of Shaw Mason

Memoir Writing

Memoir Writing

Appendix consisting of replies to some of Shaw Mason's queries, retrospective statistics and suggestions for improvement.

Parish of Clonleigh

SOCIAL ECONOMY

Disposition of the People

The genius and disposition of the people of this parish seems to be of a superior kind, as appears at once to those who converse with them. They are much better acquainted with civil and ecclesiastical history than persons of the same rank in almost any other place and such is the variety of religious opinions amongst them, and so disposed are they to acquire a knowledge of the different systems of faith held in the world, that many of them, from whose appearance little intelligence could be expected, exhibit information on religious and other subjects which it would puzzle a stranger to account for.

It is customary at the wakes of Presbyterians and other professors of the Reformed faith to have a chapter of the New or Old Testament read at certain intervals of the 2 nights during which the wake is held, and this practice has frequently given rise to warm but amicable debates among the persons present concerning the different modes of faith held by them.

The disposition of the people is remarkable, fair, open and generous: individual exceptions must of course exist, but it is only just to say that the inhabitants of this parish are a well-disposed and good-natured kind of people.

Customs and Traditions

The customs here are those of an English colony intermingled for a considerable time with Scotch and Irish neighbours. Those in agriculture are giving way to others of a more improved description; some few in rural economy and in the management of diseased cattle mark a slight degree of superstition which is also wearing away.

The Scottish mode of "running for the broze," as it is termed, and firing shots after those who are galloping for it is also getting into disuse, and altogether such has been the effort of the difficulties of the times that many idle customs have been brushed away by the keen blast of adversity and we are likely to benefit in this way very considerably by the trials we have passed through.

Christenings

The baptism of the children belonging to the Established Church are usually, except in cases of delicacy or illness, performed in the church. It was formerly a custom to have entertainment at christenings here but that practice, which was often as inconvenient to the finances as injurious to the health of families, is growing obsolete, being discouraged by the clergy.

Marriage

The marriages are celebrated here usually in the church when the parties are of the Established religion. The Roman Catholics and Dissenters are married in private houses.

Wakes and Funerals

akes and funerals are conducted here with a great deal of decency and propriety, much retrenchment as unnecessary expense having been made in this way; but still it is a practice to expend more on them than prudence would require.

It is an annoyance of no small magnitude to have the house of affliction filled with guests for whom an entertainment must at least be laid on the table, though few taste of it. Scarves are frequently given, which should be received to make shirts for the orphans, and a mahogany coffin sometimes makes its appearance.

Medicines

The knowledge and practice of medicine is improving in the neighbourhood, but perhaps it may be one cause of the superior healthiness of the parish that we have not an apothecary's shop in it; but this want is amply remedied by 3 vendors of medicines in Strabane.

The county surgeon is the only medical practitioner but, except as an accoucheur and in his capacity of hospital surgeon, there is little practice for him or any other medical man in this parish, which is not infested, like many other parts of Ireland, with ignorant peasants assuming to be physicians and creating work for themselves and others as they proceed in their adopted profession.

Appearance of the People

The people are generally of the middle stature and of a prepossessing appearance. The practice of inoculating for the smallpox in the first instance, and the introduction of the cowpock latterly, have tended to preserve the symmetry of our people's features and diminish the number of scarred blind faces.

Diseases

A low typhus sometimes, but seldom, prevails here. Rheumatism, from the damp of the climate and the situation of some of the houses, seems to prevail here more than in the south of Ireland. The poorer class are sometimes troubled with indigestion, and an oppression on the breast which they call a weight on their hearts. In some, perhaps too many, cases these latter diseases arrive from bad and scanty [food?] [and] from despondency.

Longevity

In this and most of the parishes in Ireland which have been surveyed there are many instances of persons attaining the age of 80 years and upwards. The following is a list of those here [insert note: list of names not copied]. Abstract: from 80 to 85 years 57 persons, from 86 to 90 years 7 persons, above 90 years 4 persons; of these 29 are women, 19 men.

Proprietors

The Earl of Erne: [?] Moreen, Cavanacor in part, Tamnawood, Mullen, Shiercloon, Guystown, Ballindrait, Melsesshaugh, Drumnahan, Chapel Green, Murlogh, Ballinabrine, Birdstown, Springhill, Hermitage, Tubberoneill, Slensmoyle, Anciany Upper, Legoneill, Spring Grove, Gortinriagh, Backhill, Shannon, Calhame, Dhoorish Croagh, Cunninghams Town, Tobernabrock, Gortin, Gortmagole, Keelogue, Croghanwood, Portanare, Anciany Lower, the Haw, Legandoragh, Curraghalane, Coneyberry, Roughan, Wood Island, Lifford or Ballyduff, Newtown Croaghan, Clamperlane and New Bridge.

The Bishop of Derry: Rossgier, Edenmore, Braid, Coolatee, Blackrock, Gortgrana, Sixty Acres, Drumina, Mosshill, Clonfad, Porthall, Boyagh, New Row, Glencosh, Cavan, Dromore, Drumleen, Mullinageeny, Holland, Mullinawye, Gortinmore, Cavanacor (a part), Milltown Ballylogan, Churchtown Ballylogan, Islandmore and Corkin Island.

James Sinclair Esquire: Mossbeg, Mossmore, Mullaghaney, Lurganshaney, Cloghfin, Tobery, Lishy and Simonstown.

The Revd John Baskin [Barker], resident in England: Ardnaglass, Aghavee, Camus, Gortnavilly.

Charles Crawford Esquire: Crawford's Croaghan or Card's Croaghan, and Tirkery. [Insert note: List of landowners not complete].

MODERN TOPOGRAPHY

Modern Buildings: Gaol

The gaol was finished and first occupied in the month of September 1793. It cost the county 11,032 pounds and was very badly built, the arches throughout cracked and the walls quite insufficient for want of a sufficiency of lime in the mortar and from the bad laying of the stones. The walls of the yards are split in many places and can be easily climbed. The "T" form of this gaol, though favourable to the prisoners hearing divine service, in all parts of it is very inconvenient in one respect; by means of it, the prisoners in the debtors' and women's end may converse from their windows with those in the Crown end.

These and other impediments to classification and improvements of the prisoners, it is hoped, will be avoided in the structure of the additions about to be made to this prison.

Sessions House

The sessions house is a commodious one, considering that 73 years have elapsed since it was built. The underground storey is used as a receptacle for 33 lunatics and a miserable cold damp place it is. It was formerly the county gaol.

On the front of this building, and under the king's arms, is the following inscription: "This building was raised by the county of Donegal under the direction of Andrew Knox, Oliver McCausland, George Vaughan, Nathaniel Nesbitt, Francis Mansfield, trustees; designed and executed by Michael Priestley A.D. 1746, Gilmore fecit."

County Hospital

This was originally and for many years a barrack for cavalry. It is built exactly on the same plan with the present horse-barrack of Granard in the county of Longford. In the *Londonderry Journal* for October 19th 1782 appeared the following advertisement relative to this building.

"Donegal infirmary: the governors of the Donegal infirmary having resolved to expend the sum of 600 pounds in repairing the old barrack of Lifford and converting it into an infirmary and apartments for the surgeon, such persons as chuse to propose the said work are desired to send their plans and estimates before the 5th of November next to the Revd Dr Knox, the Revd N. Spence, Richard Cowan Esquire, Charles Nesbitt Esquire or the treasurer, signed J. Lammay, treasurer."

Towns: Lifford

The town of Lifford was built by Sir Richard Hansard, who settled 30 inhabitants in it with a field of 3 acres 3 roods to each of them, with commonage for grazing. It was not any time large, but since the peace it has declined from the removal of a considerable body of troops which had been quartered in it during the war. Neither fair or market is held in it, nor is it a post town, but these inconveniences are in some degree remedied by its vicinity to Strabane, to which it would probably have been long since united but for the violence of the floods which annually inundate the lowlands between them.

Ballindrait

Ballindrait is a small old town about 1 and a half miles from Lifford, on the road to Raphoe. Near it was the residence of Sir Robert Hansard, the proprietor of Lifford estate in 1619, but almost all the traces of that mansion are obliterated. It stood on a rising over the river opposite the mill. Lifford and Ballindrait are both celebrated in a very curious old poem found in a library at Armagh and republished in the *Derriana* in 1794:

> The Mourne from south, the Finn from west commence,
> At Lifford they can join their confluence;
> From thence to Derry in full streams they flow,
> And guard the south of Derry from the foe.
> Horror and death our flying troops pursue,
> The Irish horse our scattered forces slew;
> They intercept our troops from Castlefinn,
> With death and slaughter and their country win;
> Brave Wigton of Raphoe at the long causey
> Oppos'd their horse till the foot got away;
> And in few hours at Ballindrait they were.

Gentlemen's Seats

Porthall, the residence of Mr James Clark, formerly the family seat of the Vaughans: this is a considerable building in the style of the earliest part of the large century. It stands in a low swampy situation very near the northern bank of the River Foyle and enjoys the facilities of a ready communication by water with Derry and Strabane. This building has the appearance of a very strong castle when viewed at some distance and, not being commanded by hills and being surrounded by bog and water, it might easily be made very difficult of access.

Clonlee, the seat of Robert Maxwell Esquire, pleasantly situated and laid out, both as to building and plantation, with much taste: this house and offices have been lately built and add much to the improved appearance of that part of the parish in which they stand. 2 springs of very fine water accommodate the house and rise within the area of it.

Clonfad, the residence of Thomas Keys, a small comfortable house with a good garden and some old planting about it: this place and Clonlee have the advantage of being in the immediate vicinity of a bog in which there is a great deal of bog timber. There is a small but fruitful garden and orchard in it.

Shannon, the residence of James and Andrew Ball Esquires, whose farm, very beautifully situated, is always kept in the very highest state of cultivation: the ancient name of this townland was Shandon, as appears by a patent of James I.

Bellmount or Curraghalane, the seat of Dr Clarke, a handsome house lately erected within about a mile of Lifford on the Castlefinn road: it is situated on an eminence upon the south side of Croaghan hill, a few hundred yards from the River Finn. The land attached is about 30 acres held in perpetuity.

Coneyberry: there has been a comfortably slated house lately erected here by Mr Shuse on a small scale. The ground about it is in full heart and good cultivation, and it is well sheltered.

At Murlogh a comfortable slated house 2-storeys high, the residence of the Revd Arthur McHugh, parish priest of Clonleigh and the adjoining parish of Camus and Strabane: the Roman Catholic chapel stands near the house but the quantity of the land around it is much too small for the convenience of the occupier, of whom it is but just to observe that his steady and committed efforts to discountenance sedition and preserve the peace of the country would obviously point him out as a person meriting a more suitable accommodation of land in it.

There is also at Murlogh one of the completest cottages in the province of Ulster, considering the small size of it. It is at present occupied by Captain Humphreys.

The situation of both these residences at the foot and on the east side of Croaghan hill is very interesting and some aged trees add very considerably to its beauty. Some inconveniences, however, arise from the vicinity of so steep a mountain.

Inns

There are several houses of entertainment in Lifford, on different scales of convenience, though no more than two or three of them can be called inns. These are kept by Mr John Gwynn, Mrs Risk and Mr Patrick Scanlon. Mr John

Sharkey keeps a small but much frequented house for the accommodation of those who resort to the assizes, sessions and gaol of Lifford from all parts of the country. Such are the happy days in which we live that when a shoal of herrings visited our shores in the spring of 1821, Sharkey was able to give plentiful dinners to his guests at 2d ha'penny a head.

At Ballindrait there are several houses of entertainment as far as drink goes but no inn. The vicinity of Raphoe and Strabane renders one unnecessary in it.

Bridges

The chief bridges are those over the Foyle at Lifford and those over Burndale in Ballindrait and at Mulrine's on the Derry road. The last of these, after sometime being in a dilapidated state, has been effectually repaired; but the bridges at Lifford and Ballindrait are in a most shameful state of ruin, partly occasioned by time and the action of floods but more so by the practice of some evil-disposed persons who pull stones from them and throw them into the water clandestinely.

Roads

The principal roads are that leading from Strabane to Raphoe which passes through Lifford and Ballindrait, and that from Lifford to Letterkenny also passes through Ballindrait. There is, however, a new road nearly finished from Lifford to Letterkenny, of considerable width and on level ground, avoiding the inconvenience of passing over Mongorry mountain or going round by Convoy to Letterkenny.

The road from Lifford to Londonderry through this parish has lately been in part repaired, but one of the most remarkable and inconvenient operations of a late amendment of the road act has been the suffering of many of roads and bridges to fall into a state of decay, which will render their future repair difficult and expensive.

Scenery

The scenery in many parts of this parish and neighbourhood is remarkably beautiful, notwithstanding a perceptible want of trees. From the bridge at Lifford the view of the great valley between the surrounding mountains of Tyrone and Donegal is particularly beautiful. The same may be said of the view of the hospital at Lifford, just at the meeting of the Mourne and the Finn.

The scenery at the old church and from Mr Maxwell's handsome residence at Glenlee is of the same description, and from these points the river and islands in it are seen to great advantage. Mr Ball's residence at Shannon is in itself a handsome object, though the house is an old one; but a surrounding farm in a high state of cultivation and stocked with cattle of a superior kind forms the most agreeable scenery in any country.

ANCIENT TOPOGRAPHY

Ancient Buildings

At Lifford, on the bank of the river behind the house now occupied by Mrs Stevenson, stood the old castle of Lifford but all traces of its foundation have for many years been obliterated. It is probably not older than the foundation about the year 1610, though there is a vague tradition here that it was once the asylum of Perkin Warbeck.

At Ballindrait, on an eminence rising over the River Swilly and opposed to the mill, the ruins of a castle and garden walls may yet be traced, though not without some difficulty. This was the residence of Sir Richard Hansard, to whom the town of Lifford and the lands adjoining to it were granted by King James I, in consideration of his eminent services against Shane O'Neill and Sir Cahir O'Dogherty.

Old Church

At Clonleigh the ruins of the ancient parish church are very considerable and there seems to have been 2 or 3 distinct houses adjoining to each other after the manner of monasteries, one of then probably a refectory and another a dormitory. There is, however, no record to warrant our concluding that it ever was an abbey. The walls are exceedingly thick and the mortar as used in all such buildings much harder than the stones which it cements.

The arch of a window which remains is such as would indicate that it was built before the pointed Gothic style of architecture was known in these parts, and traces in the almost impenetrable mortar which lines the inside of this arch prove that in the erection of it matted twigs or a bent hurdle was used as a temporary support instead of boards.

MODERN TOPOGRAPHY

Religious Establishments

Churches and other houses of worship: the parish of Clonleigh is an entire rectory in the gift of the

Parish of Clonleigh

Bishop of Derry and, beside the tithes of wheat, oats, barley, flax, meadow and potatoes, has annexed to it 420 acres of glebe land. According to the Ecclesiastical Register lately published by Mr [?] Erck of the Record Tower, Dublin Castle, a gift of 100 pounds and a loan of 1,500 pounds has been granted by the Board of First Fruits for the purpose of building a glebe house in this parish.

The larger of the 2 glebes is in the adjoining parish of Raphoe and therefore unsuited for the residence of the incumbent. The smaller one is in the townland of Rosgier, and being also inconvenient an attempt was made during the incumbency of the late rector to exchange some part of the larger glebe for grounds near the town of Lifford, but without success.

Church

The church of Lifford was originally built by the executors of Sir Richard Hansard, the original patentee, according to the following item in his will dated in the 17th year of the reign of King James I, September 9th.

"My will is that the church be built where usually the dead be buried in Lifford, the breadth of it to be 22 feet, the length 60 feet with a chancel at the east end of it 20 feet long and in breadth equal to the said church, the wall to be in height both of the church and chancel 16 feet."

In the body of the church is a monument of Sir Richard and Lady Hansard, upon which is the following inscription which, to within a year or two, was covered over so as to be rendered illegible by several coats of whitewash: "Of Berkenthorpe in the county of Lincoln, [blank] his wife, daughter of Sir Edward Marbury of Geisly in the said county, knight, who died the 3rd day of October 1619. Sir Richard Hansard, after he had [blank] of Arlin, Cambridge, took on him the profession of a soldier in the prime of life; he had divers and sundry honourable places of command in the wars, made governor of Lifford and the parts adjoining, where he did many good services in Tyrone's rebellion, and last of all in Sir Cahir O'Dogherty's rebellion.

King James I gave him this town of Lifford and 4 quarters of Croaghan hill to found a corporation there, which he effected. At his death he disposed of these lands and others to divers of his name not near of kindred to him; but for want of a feofment to enable him to dispose of his lands by will, by law it fell to his younger brother William Hansard of Berkenthorpe in Lincolnshire, Esquire.

He ordained by his will Sir John Vaughan Knight, Sir George Marbury Knight and Thomas Perkins Esquire, then lieutenant of his company, his executors and directed them to build the church, the school and schoolhouse in this town, as they now are done, and likewise gave 86 pounds per annum in perpetuity out of his lands videlicet: the warden of Lifford [blank] pounds, to the recorder thereof [blank] pounds, to the 2 sergeants [blank] pounds, to the schoolmaster [blank] pounds, to the usher [blank] pounds per annum; and for that, by law, this land fell to his younger brother, whereby these pious intentions were like to be frustrated; therefore the 3 forementioned executors did purchase off his said brother these whole lands for 1,500 pounds and so have finished the said work and perpetual donation according to the will and intent of the said Sir Richard."

Improvements to Church

A gallery was erected in the church in the year 1777 by subscription of 26 pounds 3s 2d.

During the incumbency of the late rector a very handsome steeple was erected to this church, and Mr Daniel bought a small organ and had the communion window and the upper parts of all other windows glazed with stained glass. The organ has been long out of repair and is quite useless.

The church requires a stronger roof than that at present on it which, from the rafters being too far asunder, is liable to be stripped by almost every gale of wind that blows. The whole of the woodwork requires a coat of paint.

MODERN TOPOGRAPHY AND SOCIAL ECONOMY

Catholic Chapel

At Murlogh is the Roman Catholic chapel built about 30 years ago by subscription, and near it a manse house has been erected by the present priest, the Revd Arthur McHugh, who expended upwards of an 100 guineas on it.

Mr McHugh's residence in the parish has been productive of much of that tranquillity and goodwill which characterises it, and both in his capacity of a parochial clergyman and as a chaplain of the county gaol has uniformly co-operated with the gentlemen of the county in pursuing the peace and preventing every effort to disturb the country.

Presbyterian Minister

Mr Houston, the Presbyterian minister, whose meeting house is in Ballindrait, co-operates in the same laudable and efficient manner on every occasion which requires his aid.

Suggestions for Improvement: Bridges

The bridge at Lifford, which connects the counties of Tyrone and Donegal, is in a state of decay requiring immediate repair, particularly on the Tyrone side of it where it is likely to be undermined by a current of water directed against it by some very injudicious enclosures lately made on this road to Strabane, in place of a railing which formerly was used there or an arched footpath which perhaps ought to be made there. At present the passage from Lifford to Strabane has been converted into something like a canal and is in a dangerous and most inconvenient state.

Canal

The rendering of the River Swilly and Burndale navigable, and by embankments and natural cuts for irrigation, this parish might be much improved; but one of the most important improvements of this and many surrounding parishes would be the union of Lough Swilly and Lough Foyle by means of a canal from Castleforward to Carrigans, by which means the finest shells in the world for manure could be brought here in lighters and furnish us with a manure so valuable that the burning of land for that purpose would become unnecessary.

The shells of Lough Swilly are different from those of Lough Foyle and of a much superior kind. They are of a soft decayed kind of oyster-shell easily decomposed and amalgamating with clay, whereas those of Lough Foyle are of harder kind like periwinkle, cockle, limpet.

Communications

The communication between the counties of Donegal and Tyrone is frequently impeded by floods, and this inconvenience might in a great degree be remedied by the erection of a bridge a little higher up over the Finn and nearly opposite to the house lately built by Mr Spence in Coneyberry. By this bridge an entire passage would be had at all times to the Urney side of Strabane, and the road from Raphoe, Letterkenny and Lifford to Dublin would be shortened nearly a mile.

It may also be observed here that a very fine line of road to Derry might be made through the townlands of Lifford, Drumboy, Coolatee, Gortnagranagh, Glenfad and Porthall, which would probably be the most eligible line for a mail coach road as it was considered by the engineers who planned a canal from Lough Erne to Lough Foyle as the proper side of the river for that purpose.

Asylum

If our lunatics, now 36 in number, viz. 33 in the asylum and 3 in the gaol, are not to be removed to the provincial hospital now erecting at Armagh, it would be necessary to have a place prepared for them in which they could exercise or work or read. Their present abode is miserably dark and damp.

SOCIAL AND PRODUCTIVE ECONOMY

Education

It would be desirable to have schoolhouses built on a cheap plan in at least 4 different parts of the parish and that Ball's simple but efficacious and speedy mode should be adopted in them. The schoolhouse at Lifford is, in many parts of it, in a state of dangerous decay, particularly the loft and roof over the schoolhouse and dormitory. The present master wants a schoolroom and an usher, and it would be much for the advantage of the neighbourhood if the school were on an efficient plan.

The advantages of a classical education need not be proved. They are very obvious and the present master of the school is very willing to contribute his part to the extension of the benefit of it to the neighbourhood for whose accommodation it was founded.

Local Government

The abolition of seneschal courts throughout this island would be a blessing to our people. As the quarter sessions are constituted here and elsewhere, men have opportunities of recovering small debts sufficiently often, perhaps too much so.

Seneschals give decrees every 6 weeks and have concurrent jurisdiction with the assistant barrister. They harass the poor most unmercifully in 9 cases out of 10. Many of them are drunken, ill-principled men and the practitioners in these courts are often disgraceful rogues, swindling the unhappy tenants brought into them and contributing to spread over the country a disregard for the sanction of an oath truly shocking.

Parish of Clonleigh

Agriculture

The introduction of hemp, rape and green crops of various kinds would be useful here, as also a better kind of black cattle and swine and a more general burning of lime, which latter would be much facilitated by the proposed union of Lough Swilly with Lough Foyle, as an additional ingress would thereby be opened for coal, culm etc.

Fisheries

The eel fishery which was tried here a short time ago without success ought to be attempted again, and perhaps it would be the interest of the proprietors of the salmon fishery whether the cessation from fishing for a year or two would bring that department into a more productive state than it has been for many years.

"I can see", said Archbishop King in his *Observations on salmon fishing*, "that it is with these fisheries as with land: if the farmer plough it every year, he will have little return; but by giving it intermission, it will again get heart. So, if a fishery be plied every year, the produce of fish will certainly diminish; and this I take to be one reason why fisheries formerly great and profitable are now come to little or nothing.

The constant fishing not only destroyed the breed but frightened away those that are left, whereas if the fishings were interrupted for a year or two by certain intervals, they would return to their first fruitfulness. This appeared by the intermission given to the fisheries in the county of Londonderry during the wars, which made them very valuable for some years afterwards, and the fish would not only multiply but increase greatly in their bulk.

After the long cessation of fishing in 1641 and the troubles which succeeded that year, salmon were taken in brooks some 6 feet long and in great quantities, where there have been none at all for many years past."

North West Society

It would be desirable that a branch of the North West Society should be established here and also a benefit society for the relief of its members when afflicted by sickness or any other misfortune; turbulent or dishonest conduct or a disregard for the sanctity of an oath to be deemed sufficient cause for exclusion or expulsion.

Sources of Information

The parochial registry should not be confined to the Established Church, but one should be composed of authentic returns from the other denominations of ministers and, with it, should be combined many other particulars not at present deemed necessary to be recorded, such as the general state of the weather and crops each year; the prevailing diseases; rare medical cases; popular discoveries in medicines, such as that of liverwort, found to be efficacious of late in relieving bilious affections and removing indications of jaundice and dropsy; the amount of the stock of cattle each year etc. Thus in some years might be collected a fund of detailed knowledge which might prove extremely useful to the philosopher and legislator.

Manufactures

The manufacture of wool for domestic use, at least, should be encouraged here and the double wheel for spinning flax introduced.

Periodical Paper

It would conduce much to the information and improvement of our people if a low-priced periodical paper were provided for them. It might be denominated the *Farmer's magazine* and, beside the publication of the transactions of the North West Farming Society, could contain extracts from the agricultural magazines and newspapers.

A weekly publication paged so as to form a volume at the end of the year might be productive of much good if conducted judiciously, and the suggestion is particularly recommended to the notice of the North West Society. Signed John Graham, Lifford, 8th October 1821.

Parish of Convoy, County Donegal

Memoir by Lieutenant I.I. Wilkinson, January 1836

NATURAL STATE

Situation and Extent

The parish of Convoy is situated in the county of Donegal, in the barony and diocese of Raphoe.

The outline is very irregular: the greatest length is 12 miles from east to west, the greatest breadth 5 and a half miles from north to south, comprising an area of 20,090 acres nearly.

Divisions and Boundaries

The parish of Convoy is divided into 57 denominations or townlands. The principal proprietors are Sir Edmund Hayes Bart, M.P. for Donegal, Robert Montgomery Esquire of Convoy.

The parish of Convoy is bounded by the parishes of Kilteevoge <Kilteevogh>, Conwal, Leck, Raphoe, Donaghmore and Stranorlar.

NATURAL FEATURES

Surface

The surface is much diversified, from highly cultivated ground to barren and wild mountains. The highest in the parish (Kirk) rises to 1,198 feet above the sea. There are a number of smaller hills very similar to each other in appearance.

Lakes and Rivers

Lough Dale, situated between the parishes of Convoy and Conwal, near the north western extremity of the former and at a height of [blank] feet nearly above the sea, is the only lake.

The Burndale river, which rises near it, is the principal stream traversing the parish and, after a course of 20 miles nearly, joins the Foyle about 1 mile below Lifford. The parish is well supplied with water; no mineral springs.

MODERN TOPOGRAPHY

Towns: Convoy

Convoy, situated on the principal road from Raphoe to Stranorlar, and about 3 miles from the former and 6 from the latter place, is the largest village in the parish. Here is placed the parochial church, built 12 years since at an expense of about 1,200 pounds. It will contain about 200 people.

A Roman Catholic chapel built about 50 years at an expense of nearly 600 pounds, for about 700 persons. A Presbyterian meeting house, built about 80 years at an expense of 700 pounds, will hold about 600 persons.

There are 5 public houses, 3 grocer's shops, a post office, 2 blacksmith's forges and 2 public bakeries. No market is held but there are 2 fairs in the year, on the 17th May and 26th October.

Houses and Roads

The houses are in general low, some are built 2-storeys high and slated but not many.

The road through Convoy is the most direct between Londonderry and Ballyshannon.

Meeting House

There is in the townland of Ballyboe a place of worship called a "mountain house" or Covenanters' meeting house. It was built in the year 1805 by subscription from all sects of persuasion in religion and will hold about 300 persons, but not more than 100 usually attend. People resort hither from the parishes of All Saints, Taughboyne, Raymoghy and Kilteevoge. They have no placed clergyman, nor is divine service performed every Sunday. The minister who performs is paid from 10s to 15s per Sunday. A graveyard is attached to this meeting house.

SOCIAL ECONOMY AND MODERN TOPOGRAPHY

Protestant Colony

In the townland of Aughkelly, belonging to Sir Edmund Hayes and which was formerly only mountain pasture, a Protestant colony has been established, dwelling houses and a schoolhouse built. A road from Letterkenny to Stranorlar passes through Aughkelly, which is situated about half-way. The colonists have therefore 2 weekly markets within 6 miles. The first colonists failed chiefly through ignorance of agriculture and a subscription was raised to send them to their homes near Dublin.

Mills

There is in the mill town of Convoy a corn mill with a flax mill attached to it, the joint property of Robert Montgomery Esquire of Convoy and Mr Norman of Dublin. It grinds about 7 tons per diem. It is undershot, of about 20 horsepower, with hanging troughs 16 inches in width. The waterfall is about 5 feet. The tenants are bound to the mill under penalty of 10s every time they pass it.

The 20th was formerly paid and the mills sometimes passed, but now that the 30th grain only is paid the mill is never passed. The flax mill dresses about 6 cwt of flax per diem. The same wheel serves both.

In the townland of Starritstown is a corn mill belonging to William McGowan of Pluck. It grinds about 3 tons a day, is undershot, of about 10 horsepower, with hanging troughs about 16 inches in breadth. The fall of water is about 22 feet and the wheel about 11 and a half feet in diameter.

Gentlemen's Seats

The only gentleman's seat in the parish is that of Robert Montgomery Esquire near Convoy. It is called Greenfield, in which townland the mansion is situated. About one-third of this townland is arable and pasture. The remainder is occupied by plantation, chiefly firs, ash and oak.

Advowson

Convoy is a ecclesiastical division of Raphoe, which parish was divided in 1821 into the parishes of Raphoe and Convoy. The Roman Catholic parish remains as before. The benefice is a perpetual curacy attached to the deanery of Raphoe.

ANCIENT TOPOGRAPHY

Antiquities

An old church or friary is supposed to have existed in the townland of Drimkeen, of which there are no remains at present except a wall shown as part of it from 4 to 9 feet high. The graveyard adjoining is still used by the inhabitants of the neighbourhood, and in it a shed is built to shelter the priest who says mass, which is celebrated there to this day.

There are several of the circular enclosures called Danish forts in the parish; they present nothing remarkable.

SOCIAL ECONOMY

Census and Enquiry in 1831

Statistical table of the parish of Convoy from the census and enquiry made in 1831. [Table contains the following headings: name of townland, population subdivided by religion and sex, analysis of occupations and houses].

Augheygault: Church of England 10 males, 13 females; Presbyterians 21 males, 29 females; Roman Catholics 30 males, 21 females; population 124; 14 inhabited houses, 7 outhouses, 21 buildings; 10 looms, 10 weavers; size of farms 4 to 24 acres, rent 15s to 1 pound 2s; landlord Robert Montgomery.

Augheygault Big: Church of England 10 males, 16 females; Presbyterians 30 males, 30 females; Roman Catholics 15 males, 20 females; population 121; 18 inhabited houses, 10 outhouses, 28 buildings; 10 looms, 10 weavers; size of farms 6 to 20 acres, rent 1 pound; landlord Robert Montgomery.

Artykellys: Church of England 2 males, 1 female; Presbyterians 2 males, 5 females; Roman Catholics 32 males, 29 females; population 71; 7 inhabited houses, 2 uninhabited houses, 2 outhouses, 11 buildings; 1 loom, 1 weaver; size of farms 6 to 15 acres, rent 15s to 1 pound 4s; landlord Sir Edmund Hayes Bart, M.P.

Aughkelly: Church of England 16 males, 13 females; Roman Catholics 4 males, 2 females; population 35; 7 inhabited houses, 2 outhouses, 9 buildings; 1 loom, 1 weaver; size of farms 5 acres; landlord Sir E. Hayes Bart, M.P.

Breen: Roman Catholics 16 males, 15 females; population 31; 5 inhabited houses, 3 outhouses, 8 buildings; size of farms 28 to 40 acres, rent 5s; landlord Sir E. Hayes Bart, M.P.

Ballyboe: Presbyterians 3 males, 4 females; Roman Catholics 6 males, 3 females; population 16; 3 inhabited houses, 5 outhouses, 8 buildings; size of farms 40 acres, rent 1 pound 1s; landlord Mr Gardner.

Broadpath: Presbyterians 9 males, 6 females; Roman Catholics 29 males, 21 females; population 65; 10 inhabited houses, 8 outhouses, 18 buildings; 2 looms, 2 weavers; size of farms 5 to 36 acres, rent 17s to 1 pound 2s; landlord Counsellor Johnston.

Cloughgore: Presbyterians 2 males, 2 females; Roman Catholics 4 males, 1 female; population 9; 2 inhabited houses, 1 outhouse, 3 buildings; size of farms 25 acres, rent 1 pound 2s; landlord Sir E. Hayes Bart, M.P.

Clougheroe: Church of England 19 males, 23 females; Presbyterians 23 males, 17 females; Roman Catholics 29 males, 26 females; population 137; 29 inhabited houses, 6 outhouses, 35 buildings; size of farms 7 to 50 acres, rent 7s 6d to 12s 6d; landlord Sir E. Hayes Bart, M.P.

Callen: Church of England 13 males, 13 females; Presbyterians 36 males, 30 females; Roman Catholics 7 males, 15 females; population 114; 20 inhabited houses, 1 uninhabited house, 11 outhouses, 32 buildings; 7 looms, 7 weavers; size of farms 7 to 30 acres, rent 12s 6d to 1 pound; landlord Sir E. Hayes Bart, M.P.

Callencor: Church of England 17 males, 22 females; Presbyterians 8 males, 4 females; Roman Catholics 33 males, 28 females; population 112; 10 inhabited houses, 11 outhouses, 21 buildings; 7 looms, 11 weavers; size of farms 6 to 12 acres, rent 9s 6d to 1 pound; landlord Sir E. Hayes Bart, M.P.

Castletorrison: Church of England 7 males, 10 females; Presbyterians 30 males, 37 females; Roman Catholics 6 males, 9 females; population 99; 20 inhabited houses, 19 outhouses, 39 buildings; 7 looms, 7 weavers; size of farms 15 to 60 acres, rent 5s to 1 pound; landlord Sir E. Hayes Bart, M.P.

Cornagillagh: Church of England 6 males, 8 females; Presbyterians 28 males, 30 females; Roman Catholics 33 males, 34 females; population 139; 31 inhabited houses, 33 outhouses, 64 buildings; 1 loom, 1 weaver; size of farms 5 to 30 acres, rent 15s to 1 pound 5s; landlord Sir E. Hayes Bart, M.P.

Corradooey: Church of England 9 males, 7 females; Presbyterians 42 males, 29 females; Roman Catholics 46 males, 44 females; population 177; 30 inhabited houses, 12 outhouses, 42 buildings; 3 looms, 3 weavers; size of farms 4 to 42 acres, rent 10s to 1 pound; landlord Mr Verscoyle.

Calhame: Presbyterians 9 males, 8 females; Roman Catholics 7 males, 8 females; population 32; 5 inhabited houses, 3 outhouses, 8 buildings; size of farms 7 to 30 acres, rent 4s to 15s; landlord Mr Montgomery.

Craigdhu: Roman Catholics 25 males, 27 females; population 52; 11 inhabited houses, 7 outhouses, 18 buildings; size of farms 4 to 24 acres, rent 8s 3d; landlord Mr Mehaffey.

Convoy Townparks: Church of England 49 males, 38 females, Presbyterians 44 males, 71 females; Roman Catholics 92 males, 111 females; population 405; 41 inhabited houses, 37 outhouses, 78 buildings; size of farms 2 to 23 acres, rent 1 pound 10s to 2 pounds; landlord Mr Montgomery.

Convoy Demesne: Church of England 29 males, 18 females; Presbyterians 23 males, 19 females; Roman Catholics 36 males, 28 females; population 153; 25 inhabited houses, 14 outhouses, 39 buildings; 2 looms, 2 weavers; size of farms 3 to 22 acres, rent 15s to 1 pound 10s; landlord Mr Montgomery.

Carrickbrack: Church of England 3 males, 1 female: Presbyterians 42 males, 41 females; Roman Catholics 31 males, 32 females; population 150; 25 inhabited houses, 36 outhouses, 61 buildings; 2 looms, 2 weavers; size of farms 16 to 60 acres, rent 10s to 1 pound; landlord Mr Gardner.

Corcashey: Presbyterians 12 males, 2 females; population 14; 2 inhabited houses, 4 outhouses, 6 buildings; size of farms 26 to 56 acres, rent 7s 2d; landlord Mr Tinton.

Drimkeen: Church of England 2 males, 5 females; Presbyterians 31 males, 29 females; Roman Catholics 76 males, 92 females; population 235; 36 inhabited houses, 1 uninhabited house, 14 outhouses, 51 buildings; 7 looms, 7 weavers; size of farms 5 to 26 acres, rent 7s 6d to 1 pound; landlord Mr Young.

Drimnacrow: Church of England 1 male, 1 female: Presbyterians 9 males, 9 females; Roman Catholics 6 males, 4 females; population 30; 5 inhabited houses, 4 outhouses, 9 buildings; 1 weaver, 1 loom; size of farms 28 to 35 acres, rent 12s; landlord Mr Young.

Drumgumberland: Church of England 1 female: Presbyterians 29 males, 31 females; Roman Catholics 9 males, 12 females; population 82; 13 inhabited houses, 14 outhouses, 27 buildings; size of farms 12 to 50 acres, rent 6s to 18s; landlord Mr Gardner.

Fargans: Roman Catholics 15 males, 12 females; population 27; 4 inhabited houses, 1 uninhabited house, 3 outhouses, 8 buildings; size of farms 10 to 16 acres, rent 2s 4d to 4s; landlord Sir E. Hayes Bart.

Finneydurk Glebe: Presbyterians 20 males, 29 females; Roman Catholics 19 males, 12 females; population 80; 2 inhabited houses, 2 outhouses, 4 buildings; 2 looms, 2 weavers; size of farms 11 to 27 acres, rent 1s to 1 pound 2s; landlord see of Raphoe.

Findrum: Church of England 7 males, 5 females; Presbyterians 24 males, 36 females; Roman Catholics 36 males, 34 females; population 142; 16 inhabited houses, 1 uninhabited house, 10 outhouses, 27 buildings; 2 looms, 2 weavers; size of farms 3 to 46 acres, rent 10s to 1 pound 3s; landlord Messrs McClenahan and Montgomery.

Greenfield: Church of England 5 males, 1 female: Roman Catholics 3 males, 5 females; population 14; 2 inhabited houses, 9 outhouses, 11 buildings; landlord Mr Montgomery.

Glassley: Church of England 3 males, 3 females; Roman Catholics 8 males, 21 females; population 35; 8 inhabited houses, 4 outhouses, 12 buildings; size of farms 2 to 12 acres, rent 1 pound 3s; landlord Mr Montgomery.

Gobnascale: Church of England 10 males, 10 females; Presbyterians 11 males, 14 females; Roman Catholics 3 males, 2 females; population 50; 8 inhabited houses, 5 outhouses, 13 buildings; size of farms 14 to 40 acres, rent 10s 6d to 1 pound; landlord Mr Gardner.

Gurtadragon: Church of England 2 females; Presbyterians 14 males, 21 females; Roman Catholics 24 males, 23 females; population 84; 11 inhabited houses, 3 outhouses, 14 buildings; 5 looms, 5 weavers; size of farms 17 to 24 acres, rent 11s 2d to 1 pound 4s; landlord Sir Edmund Hayes Bart, M.P.

Kark: Roman Catholics 52 males, 64 females; population 116; 22 inhabited houses, 10 outhouses, 32 buildings; 2 looms, 2 weavers; size of farms 4 to 436 acres, rent 1s to 8s 6d; landlord Sir E. Hayes Bart, M.P.

Killynure: Church of England 7 males, 11 females; Presbyterians 15 males, 12 females; Roman Catholics 27 males, 15 females; population 87; 18 inhabited houses, 15 outhouses, 33 buildings; 1 loom, 1 weaver, size of farms 7 to 33 acres, rent 11s to 1 pound; landlord Mr Kane.

Knockygarron: Church of England 7 males, 9 females; Presbyterians 13 males, 9 females; Roman Catholics 14 males, 13 females; population 65; 15 inhabited houses, 13 outhouses, 28 buildings; 2 looms, 3 weavers; size of farms 5 to 15 acres, rent 8s 5d to 1 pound 5s; landlord Mr Kane.

Labadoo: Presbyterians 12 males, 12 females; Roman Catholics 10 males, 4 females; population 38; 5 inhabited houses, 6 outhouses, 11 buildings; size of farms 23 to 128 acres, rent 5s to 9s; landlord Mr Hutton.

Lisnaree; size of farms 700 acres, rent 2s 6d; landlord Mr Stewart.

Lissenisk: Presbyterians 11 males, 8 females; Roman Catholics 3 males, 5 females; population 27; 5 inhabited houses, 7 outhouses, 12 buildings; 1 loom, 1 weaver; size of farms 6 to 13 acres, rent 6s to 15s; landlord Sir E. Hayes Bart, M.P.

Lissenore: Church of England 9 males, 17 females; Presbyterians 4 males, 7 females; Roman Catholics 3 males, 3 females; population 43; 6 inhabited houses, 10 outhouses, 16 buildings; size of farms 13 to 15 acres, rent 1 pound 1s; landlord Sir E. Hayes Bart, M.P.

Lettermore: Church of England 6 males, 11 females; Presbyterians 4 males, 7 females; Roman Catholics 116 males, 133 females; population 277; 37 inhabited houses, 1 uninhabited house, 11 outhouses, 49 buildings; 18 looms, 18 weavers; size of farms 5 to 20 acres, rent 2s 4d to 12s 2d; landlord Sir E. Hayes Bart, M.P.

Leagueland: Roman Catholics 43 males, 44 females; population 87; 14 inhabited houses, 5 outhouses, 19 buildings; size of farms 6 to 43 acres, rent 5s to 1 pound; landlord Sir E. Hayes Bart, M.P.

Lettershamboe: Roman Catholics 16 males, 20 females; population 36; 8 inhabited houses, 2 outhouses, 10 buildings; size of farms 20 to 37 acres, rent 6s; landlord Sir E. Hayes Bart, M.P.

Mullaghfin: Presbyterians 5 males, 3 females; Roman Catholics 48 males, 38 females; population 94; 19 inhabited houses, 21 outhouses, 40 buildings; size of farms 12 to 36 acres, rent 5s to 7s; landlord Sir E. Hayes Bart, M.P.

McMeenstown: Church of England 10 males, 6 females; Presbyterians 16 males, 15 females; Roman Catholics 37 males, 38 females; population 122; 16 inhabited houses, 2 outhouses, 18 buildings; 1 loom, 1 weaver; size of farms 3 to 30 acres, rent 16s to 1 pound 8s; landlord Mr Montgomery.

Milltown: Church of England 5 males, 15 females; Presbyterians 9 males, 10 females; Roman Catholics 15 males, 23 females; population 77; 5 inhabited houses, 2 outhouses, 7 buildings; size of farms 5 to 28 acres, rent 15s; landlord Mr Montgomery.

Magheranappin: Church of England 7 males, 7 females; Presbyterians 30 males, 19 females; Roman Catholics 39 males, 40 females; population 142; 25 inhabited houses, 20 outhouses, 45 buildings; 3 looms, 3 weavers; size of farms 10 to 35 acres, rent 5s to 1 pound 6s; landlord Mr Montgomery.

Mullinard: Presbyterians 22 males, 14 females; Roman Catholics 20 males, 21 females; population 77; 16 inhabited houses, 9 outhouses, 25 buildings; 1 loom, 1 weaver; size of farms 8 to 40 acres, rent 10s 6d; landlord Mr Johnston.

Meenavally: Presbyterians 4 males, 5 females; Roman Catholics 2 males; population 11; 1 inhabited house, 4 outhouses, 5 buildings; size of farms 101 acres, 5d ha'penny per acre; landlord Mr Hone.

Magherycorrin: Church of England 7 males, 7 females; Presbyterians 32 males, 32 females; Roman Catholics 47 males, 57 females; population 182; 27 inhabited houses, 2 uninhabited houses, 15 outhouses, 44 buildings; 6 looms, 6 weavers; size of farms 8 to 55 acres, rent 8s 4d to 1 pound 3s; landlord Bishop of Raphoe.

Magheryvale: Church of England 6 males, 5 females; Presbyterians 3 males, 4 females; Roman Catholics 43 males, 42 females; population 103; 13 inhabited houses, 8 outhouses, 21 buildings; 5 looms, 5 weavers; size of farms 10 to 17 acres, rent 8s; landlord Sir E. Hayes Bart, M.P.

Minticat: Roman Catholics 9 males, 6 females; population 15; 3 inhabited houses, 4 outhouses, 7 buildings; size of farms 12 to 400 acres, rent 2s 6d; landlord Sir E. Hayes Bart, M.P.

Meenalaban: Roman Catholics 11 males, 11 females; population 22; 4 inhabited houses, 1 uninhabited house, 2 outhouses, 7 buildings; size of farms 17 acres, rent 8s; landlord Sir E. Hayes Bart, M.P.

Prieststown: Church of England 8 males, 6 females; Presbyterians 15 males, 13 females; Roman Catholics 17 males, 12 females; population 71; 12 inhabited houses, 6 outhouses, 18 buildings; 2 looms, 2 weavers; size of farms 17 to 28 acres, rent 12s to 15s; landlord Sir E. Hayes Bart, M.P.

Starritstown: Church of England 6 males, 1 female: Presbyterians 2 males, 4 females; Roman Catholics 6 males, 2 females; population 21; 3 inhabited houses, 4 outhouses, 7 buildings; 1 loom, 1 weaver; size of farms 17 acres, rent 15s; landlord Sir E. Hayes Bart, M.P.

Strongibbagh: Roman Catholics 67 males, 49 females; population 116; 15 inhabited houses, 1 uninhabited house, 8 outhouses, 24 buildings; 2 looms, 2 weavers; size of farms 10 to 25 acres, rent 5s to 7s; landlord Sir E. Hayes Bart, M.P.

Stralamford: Roman Catholics 81 males, 67 females; population 148; inhabited houses 20, 5 outhouses, 25 buildings; size of farms 2 to 70 acres, rent 3d ha'penny to 1 pound; landlord Mr Montgomery.

Trentabwee: Church of England 7 males, 6 females; Presbyterians 16 males, 21 females; Roman Catholics 113 males, 202 males; population 365; 39 inhabited houses, 22 outhouses, 61 buildings; 11 looms, 11 weavers; size of farms 4 to 30 acres, rent 3s 6d to 1 pound 5s; landlord Mr Montgomery.

Trainbuoy: Church of England 1 male, 2 females; Presbyterians 10 males, 8 females; Roman Catholics 4 males, 10 females; population 35; 6 inhabited houses, 10 outhouses, 16 buildings; size of farms 11 to 47 acres, rent 6s 6d to 11s; landlord Sir E. Hayes Bart, M.P.

Tommyscroft: Church of England 4 males, 7 females; Presbyterians 3 males, 8 females; Roman Catholics 19 males, 15 females; population 56; 11 inhabited houses, 12 outhouses, 23 buildings; 1 loom, 1 weaver; size of farms 2 to 47 acres, rent 1s 5d to 1 pound 2s; landlord Sir E. Hayes Bart, M.P.

Total or average in the parish: Church of England 308 males, 321 females; Presbyterians 728 males, 744 females; Roman Catholics 1,542 males, 1,625 females; population 5,268; 785 inhabited houses, 11 uninhabited houses, 532 outhouses, 1,328 buildings; 127 looms, 131 weavers.

Summary of Population

Population of the parish of Convoy from government census taken in 1834: 522 Protestants, 3,353 [sic] Presbyterians, 1,759 [sic] Roman Catholics, total 5,634.

Table of Schools

[Table contains the following headings: situation, number of pupils subdivided by religion and sex, remarks as to how supported].

Lettershamboe: Roman Catholics 14 males, 9 females; this school is taught by John McDevit, a Roman Catholic; the charge is 1s 3d per quarter each scholar, value 5 pounds 15s per annum.

Aughkelly: Protestants 7 males, 3 females; this school is taught by a Protestant whose name is John Morrow; he receives 12 pounds per annum from the Protestant colony.

Trentabwee: Protestants 4 males, 6 females; Roman Catholics 16 males, 14 females; this school is taught by James Haughey, a Roman Catholic; he charges from 1s 6d to 2s per quarter, value 12 pounds 8s per annum.

Augheygault Big: Protestants 32 males, 18 females; Roman Catholics 44 males, 69 females; this school is taught by James Cowan, a Presbyterian; he receives a salary of 12 pounds per annum from the Hibernian Society, also 5 pounds per year from the scholars.

Augheygault Little: Protestants 29 females, Roman Catholics 12 females; this school is taught by Margret Ramsey, a Presbyterian; it is under the direction of the Hibernian Society; she receives from the scholars 4 pounds per annum.

Drimkeen: Roman Catholics 17 males, 7 females; this school is taught by Ferdinand Devit, a Roman Catholic; he charges each scholar 1s 3d per quarter, value 6 pounds per annum.

Drimkeen: Protestants 15 males, 9 females; Roman Catholics 6 males, 5 females. This school is taught by John Morrow, a Protestant, who receives 10 pounds per annum from a society called the Association for Discountenancing Vice and Promoting Knowledge of the Christian Religion. He has a house and 2 and a half acres of land rent free; he makes no charge on the scholars.

Convoy: Protestants 32 males, 24 females; Roman Catholics 10 males, 9 females; a parish school, proprietors Mr Montgomery, Revd Mr Beatty and Revd Mr Wray.

[Signed] I.I. Wilkinson, Lieutenant Royal Engineers, 22nd January 1836.

Parish of Conwal, County Donegal

Statistical Report by Lieutenant I.I. Wilkinson, February 1836

NATURAL STATE

Name and Locality

The name is generally pronounced as it is written; derivation unknown.

The parish of Conwal is situated in the county of Donegal and diocese of Raphoe, partly in the barony of Kilmacrenan and partly in that of Raphoe.

The portion of the parish situate in the barony of Raphoe is bounded by the barony of Kilmacrenan on the north and west, on the east by the parish of Leck and on the south by the parishes of Convoy and Kilteevoge. It is in the north western part of the barony.

Its greatest length from west to east is about 9 and a half miles and its greatest breadth from north to south about 3 and three-quarters miles. Mean length 7 and a half miles, mean breadth 2 and a half miles.

The area comprises about 12,523 acres of land and 31 acres of water, part of Lough Dale. This area is divided into 2 unequal parts by a tongue of land belonging to the barony of Kilmacrenan which extends from Lough Dale to the River Swilly. The Raphoe part of Conwal comprises 23 townlands.

NATURAL FEATURES

Hills

The western portion is all mountain and, as yet, uncultivated. The eastern portion is partly cultivated, particularly those parts of it adjoining the River Swilly. The hills are not usually distinguished by name from the townlands in which they are situated.

The principal points are Drimnaght, which rises to a height of 1,004 feet above the sea, Ballystrang, 966 feet, Cronamuck, in the townland of Killymasney, 1,132 feet, Cronaglacken, in the townlands of Carrickalaugan and Treankeel, 1,127 feet and Altineerin, in the townland of that name in Kilmacrenan, 941 feet above the sea.

Lakes

Lough Dale, on the boundary between the parishes of Convoy and Conwal, is the principal lake. Its site is about [blank] feet above the sea and its area about 62 acres. There is also a small lake in the townland of Rariagh called Lough Arroughdale.

Rivers

The Swilly, which flows between this portion of Conwal and that belonging to the barony of Kilmacrenan, is the only river. It is picturesque but wholly useless as to navigation. The bed is gravelly and rocky, fordable in many places but, in common with other mountain streams, is often much swollen by heavy rains and torrents from the hills.

The Burndale river, which rises at a height of nearly 860 feet above the sea near Lough Dale, forms for about 2 and a half miles the boundary between Conwal and Convoy. In this part of its course it is merely a mountain stream.

There is a good supply of water from springs and rivulets. No mineral springs have been discovered.

Bogs

This portion of the parish is very well supplied with turf, principally from the bogs in Tullyhonour, Carrickalaugan and Rariagh. Very little timber occurs imbedded in the bogs.

The price of turf at Letterkenny during the winter is usually 5d per barrel.

MODERN TOPOGRAPHY

Public Buildings

There are no churches, chapels etc. in the Raphoe portion of Conwal. The Protestant inhabitants attend divine service at Letterkenny, a distance of from 2 and a half to 8 miles. The Roman Catholics generally attend Glenswilly chapel.

Gentlemen's Seats

Colonel Pratt has a mansion house much out of repair in the townland of Currowaddy. It is merely occupied by his steward, he himself residing at Letterkenny during his visits to his estate. There are some plantations about the house. The steward Mr Dunn, a north Briton, has made great improvements in agriculture and gives instructions to the tenants.

Parish of Conwal

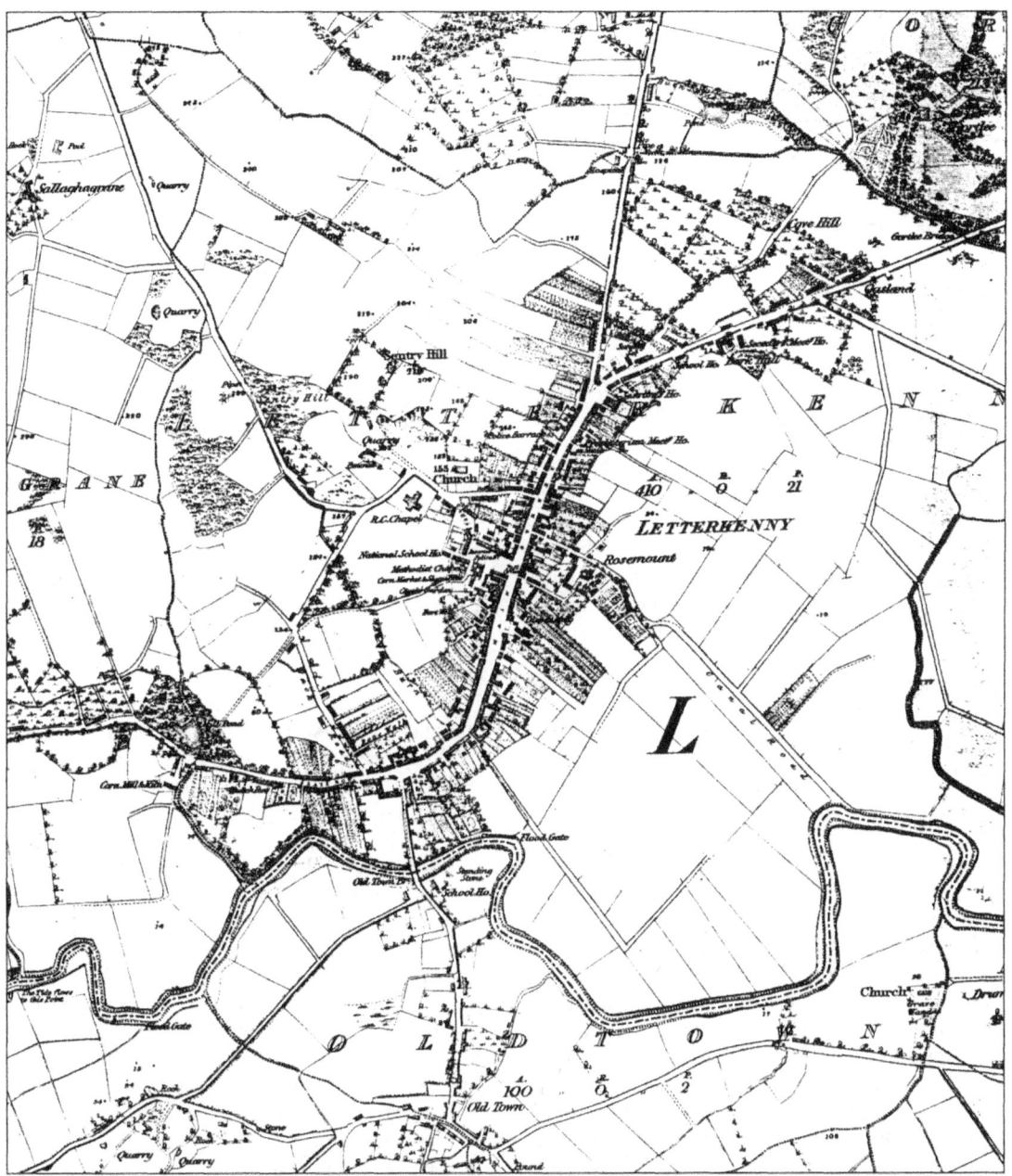

Map of Letterkenny from the first 6" O.S. maps, 1830s

Manufactories

The manufacture of linen yarn and worsted stockings is carried on to some extent in private houses. There is also a great deal of illicit distillation, principally from oats, occasionally from a mixture of oats and barley, and but rarely from barley alone. The spirit is readily disposed of among the licensed publicans in the neighbouring towns.

Communications

The roads are very bad, barely passable for carts (which are in general use) with the exception of the principal road leading from Letterkenny to Fintown and Dungloe <Dunlo>.

Religion

From the government census taken in 1834, the population of the whole parish, distinguishing each religious persuasion, was as follows: Established Church 1,519, Roman Catholics 8,498, Presbyterians 3,407, total 13,424. And from statistical enquiry made in 1835, vide table, it appears that in the Raphoe part of Conwal there were 401 families which, at an average of 6 to each, would give a population of 2,406.

Fairs and Markets

An annual fair is held on the 15th September at Rashedag. The market resorted to is Letterkenny, held weekly on Fridays.

The fairs at Rashedag are chiefly supplied with cattle of the small breed, usually kept in the mountains, and are bought up by dealers and taken to better pasture. There are few horses and those merely the mountain ponies, which are usually inferior to the Shetland ponies though they are larger. This inferiority arises from the want of pasturage.

Coarse socks manufactured from wool by the country people themselves are also brought thither and linen yarn in very small quantity, owing to the vicinity of Letterkenny market.

Habits of the People

There is a great want of cleanliness and exertion on the part of the people to improve themselves or their houses, which are wretched in the extreme. In Glenswilly the people are dressed on Sundays in blue frieze of the country manufacture, but on ordinary occasions are clothed in rags, not so much from poverty as from a system of hoarding up money to purchase cattle or lands, which seem to be their greatest objects.

This system prevails so far that even farm servants, whose wages are from 5 pounds to 7 pounds yearly for men and from 2 pounds to 2 pounds 10s for women (with board and lodging), find means to save sufficient to purchase by degrees from 15 pounds to 30 pounds' worth of cattle. This is considered a fortune upon which they marry.

The cattle, as they are purchased, are sent to the mountains to graze during the summer and are fed during the winter, for which the servants pay out of their wages. The person who lets the mountains is responsible for the cattle, which are sent from all parts, and keeps herds for the purpose of watching and taking care of them. The charge for grazing is from 4s to 8s a head for 3-year-old cattle; yearlings or 2-year old cattle pay in proportion. In winter the charge is from 8s to 10s.

Illicit Distillation

The inhabitants formerly supported themselves by illicit distillation and improvement is beginning to be manifested owing to its being repressed and their attention turned to agriculture.

ANCIENT TOPOGRAPHY

Antiquities

In the portion of Conwal belonging to the barony of Raphoe there are several of the circular enclosures commonly called Danish forts; they present nothing remarkable.

SOCIAL ECONOMY

Census and Enquiry in 1835

Statistical table of the parish of Conwal, as taken from census and enquiry made in the year 1835. [Table contains the following headings: name of townland, analysis of houses, name of landlord].

Ballystrang: 10 inhabited buildings, 15 dwelling houses and families, 6 outhouses, 2 ruined buildings, total 18 buildings; landlord Colonel Pratt.

Barrick or Ballymagic: 7 inhabited buildings, 8 dwelling houses and families, 5 ruined buildings, total 12 buildings; landlord Mr Hart.

Ballygawley: 5 inhabited buildings, 7 dwelling houses and families, 1 outhouse, 1 ruined building, total 7 buildings; landlord Mr Humphreys.

Brownhall: 2 inhabited buildings, 5 dwelling houses and families, 4 outhouses, total 6 buildings; landlord Mr William Boyd.

Bomany: 19 inhabited buildings, 31 dwelling houses and families, 9 outhouses, 2 uninhabited houses, 1 ruined building, total 31 buildings; landlord Mr William Boyd.

Ballygallon: 8 inhabited buildings, 10 dwelling houses and families, 3 outhouses, 1 uninhabited house, 1 ruined building, total 13 buildings; landlord Mr James Johnston.

Carrickalaugan: 16 inhabited buildings, 23 dwelling houses and families, 7 outhouses, 3 ruined buildings, total 26 buildings; landlord Mr James Johnston.

Currowaddy: 5 inhabited buildings, 5 dwelling houses and families, 3 outhouses, 1 ruined building, total 9 buildings; landlord Colonel Pratt.

Drimnaght, 35 inhabited buildings, 55 dwelling houses and families, 27 outhouses, 7 ruined buildings, total 69 buildings; landlord Mr James Watts.

Drimnahoagh, 2 inhabited buildings, 3 dwelling houses and families, 2 outhouses, total 4 buildings; landlord Mr James Johnston.

Kirkneedy, 37 inhabited buildings, 46 dwelling houses and families, 17 outhouses, 6 ruined buildings, total 60 buildings; landlord Mr James Watts.

Killymasney, 33 inhabited buildings, 47 dwelling houses and families, 12 outhouses, 7 ruined buildings, total 52 buildings; landlord Mr John Boyd.

Lenelea, 2 inhabited houses, 3 dwelling houses and families, 7 outhouses, 1 ruined building, total 10 buildings; landlord Mr James Watts.

Listack, 7 inhabited houses, 11 dwelling houses and families, 7 outhouses, total 14 buildings; landlord Colonel Pratt.

Letterleague, 24 inhabited houses, 30 dwelling houses and families, 6 outhouses, 2 uninhabited houses, 5 ruined buildings, total 37 buildings; landlord Colonel Pratt.

Milltown, 14 inhabited houses, 19 dwelling houses and families, 7 outhouses, 1 uninhabited house, 1 ruined building, total 23 buildings; landlord Mrs Boyde.

Meenadaura or Drimnahoagh Mountain, 1 inhabited building, 1 house and family, total 1 building; landlord Mr James Johnston.

Rashedag, 1 inhabited house, 1 dwelling house and family, 1 outhouse, total 2 buildings; landlord Mr Watt.

Roughan, 10 inhabited houses, 14 dwelling houses and families, 3 outhouses, 2 ruined buildings, total 15 buildings; landlord Mrs Boyde.

Rariagh, 18 inhabited houses, 28 dwelling houses and families, 11 outhouses, 2 ruined buildings, total 31 buildings; landlord Colonel Pratt.

Treankeel, 5 inhabited houses, 7 dwelling houses and families, 6 outhouses, 1 uninhabited house, 1 ruined building, total 13 buildings; landlord Mr James Johnston.

Tullyhonour, 15 inhabited houses, 32 dwelling houses and families, 11 outhouses, 1 uninhabited house, 4 ruined buildings, total 31 buildings; landlord Mr James Johnston.

Tueslenagh, 1 ruined building, total 1 building; landlord Mr James Johnston.

Total: 276 inhabited houses, 401 dwelling houses and families, 150 outhouses, 8 uninhabited houses, 51 ruined buildings, total 485 buildings.

Table of Schools

[Table contains the following headings: situation, number of pupils subdivided by religion and sex, remarks as to how supported].

Letterleague: Presbyterians 29 males, Roman Catholics 40 males, total 69; the teacher's name is William McClenaghan, a Protestant; he teaches reading, writing and arithmetic. He receives about 4 pounds per annum from the London Hibernian Society, as the children pass the inspector. He receives nothing from the parents of the children but he has a house and garden worth about 2 pounds per annum from Mr Scott, proprietor of the soil.

Letterleague: Protestants 5 females, Presbyterians 30 females, Roman Catholics 44 females, total 79; the teacher's name is Mrs Pearson, a Presbyterian; she teaches reading, writing and arithmetic. She receives about 8 pounds 10s per annum from the London Hibernian Society, as her scholars pass the inspector. She receives nothing from the parents of the children nor has she any other remuneration. These schools are in the same house but in separate apartments. It was built by the late Revd Joseph Pratt in the year 1822.

Drimnahoagh: Protestants 4 males, 2 females, Presbyterians 5 males, Roman Catholics 25 males, 5 females, total 41. The teacher's name is John Rankan. He is a Presbyterian and is supported by the scholars. The average value of his school is 10 pounds per annum. He teaches reading, writing and arithmetic. The charges are 1s 6d per quarter of a year for reading and 2s for writing and arithmetic.

Bomany: Protestants 2 males, 2 females, Presbyterians 5 males, 4 females, Roman Catholics 6 males, 5 females, total 24. The teacher's name is John Curran, a Roman Catholic. He is supported by the scholars and estimates his school to be worth 6 pounds per annum. He also boards with the scholars and goes to each scholar day about.

Signed I.I. Wilkinson, Lieutenant Royal Engineers, 2nd February 1836.

Parish of Donaghmore, County Donegal

Statistical Report by Lieutenant I.I. Wilkinson, April 1836

NATURAL STATE

Name and Locality

Donaghmore: this name is usually pronounced as it is written.

The parish of Donaghmore is situated in the county of Donegal, in the barony of Raphoe and diocese of Derry. It is the most southerly parish in the barony and is bounded by the parishes of Donegal, Stranorlar, Convoy, Raphoe, Clonleigh and Urney in the county of Donegal and by the parishes of Skirts of Urney and Ardstraw <Ardstra> and Termonamongan in the county of Tyrone.

Its greatest length from north east to south west is about 17 miles and its greatest breadth from south east to north west about 7 miles, comprising an area of about 46,055 acres 1 rood 26 perches of land and 335 acres 3 roods 6 perches of water. The outline is irregular.

NATURAL FEATURES

Hills

The parish of Donaghmore comprehends portions of 3 distinct ranges of hills which are not in general distinguished by name from the townland in which they are situated. Those in the western extremity of the parish are a part of the Barnesmore range and extend from the Gap of Barnesmore to the valley of the Mournebeg river.

The principal points are the mountain forming the south side of the gap called Barnesmore Owen and rising to the height of 1,489 feet above the sea; Crosshill in the townland of Meenbog, which rises to 1,260 feet; and Brandy hill in the parish of Termonamongan near its boundary with Donaghmore (1,024 feet).

From the Mournebeg river a lower range occupies the extent of the parish in an easterly direction from that of the Mournebeg. The principal points are Trush, in the townland of that name, 856 feet above the sea; Lissmullyduff, also called Droghert mountain, in the townland of Lissmullyduff, 867 feet; Croonalaghy, in the townland of that name, 767 feet; Mounthall, in the townland of the same name, 720 feet; and Rawshill, in the townland of Raws Upper.

The third and lowest range is in the north eastern part of the parish, to the north of the River Finn which it divides from the valley of the Burndale river. The principal points are Leaghthill, in the townland of that name, 398 feet above the sea, and Carnowen, in the townland of Carnowen, 400 feet.

Lakes

Lough Mourne, on the boundary of the parish of Donaghmore with the parish of Stranorlar (close to the south of the mail coach road from Londonderry to Sligo, at about 6 miles west of Ballybofey), is the largest lake. It contains about 174 acres, is nearly 556 feet above the level of the sea and about 48 feet deep. There is one very small island in the lough. The Mournebeg river rises in the lough and issues from its south west extremity.

Trusk lough, about 2 and a half miles to the south of Ballybofey, <Ballyboefay>, on the west of the road from Stranorlar by Aghyarran Lodge to Killeter, contains about 52 acres, is situated about 556 feet above the sea and is about 20 feet deep. The water from Trusk lough supplies the mills at Navenny.

Lough Carney is situate in the townland of Crohonagh about a quarter of a mile westward of Lough Mourne. It contains about 6 acres, is 554 feet above the sea and about 8 feet deep. It is surrounded by a marsh, from the drainings of which it appears formed. A stream flows from Lough Carney to join the Mournebeg river about 8 chains from its issue from Lough Mourne.

Lough Napaise is partly in the townland of Meenbog and situated on the boundary of the parishes of Donaghmore and Donegal. It is 1,050 feet above the sea, contains about 3 and a half acres and is about 10 feet deep. A mountain stream called the Swannagh river flows from Lough Napaise and, after an easterly course of about 3 and a half miles, joins the Mournebeg river.

Lough Namaskher is also partly in the townland of Meenbog and situated on the boundary of the parishes of Donegal and Donaghmore. It is 1,041 feet above the sea, contains about 8 and a half acres and is about 12 feet deep.

Lough Innaghachole is also partly in the townland of Meenbog and is situated at the junction of the 3 parishes of Donaghmore, Donegal and

Parish of Donaghmore

Termonamongan. It is 1,111 feet above the sea, contains about 3 and a half acres and is about 8 feet deep. A stream flows from this lough towards the south east, between the parishes of Donaghmore and Termonamongan.

Lough Swannagh is situated in the townland of Meenbog about half a mile north of Lough Innaghachole. It is 1,044 feet above the sea, contains about 2 acres and is about 10 feet deep. A stream flows from this lake to the north east and joins the Sawanah river. The lake receives a stream from a blind lough or swamp about an eighth of a mile westward of it.

Lough Carrickaduff, situated in the townland of Meenbog near its south extremity: it is 999 feet above the sea, contains about 1 and a half acres and is about 9 feet deep.

Lough Gunick is a small lake situated in the townland of Kinleater about a mile to the south south east of Trusk lough. It is 660 feet above the sea, contains about 1 acre and is about 6 feet deep. A small stream flows from it into Trusk lough.

Lough Yeelignihin is situated at the junction of the townlands of Gortachork, Meenreagh and Meenahenisk. It is about 733 feet above the sea, contains about 1 acre and is about 8 feet deep. A stream flows from this lake forming the boundary between Gortachork and Meenahenisk.

Lough Beg is situated in the townland of Tieveclogher. It is 683 feet above the sea, contains about 2 acres and is about 6 feet deep. A small stream flows from this lake to join the Mournebeg river.

Lough Shinnagh is situated in the townland of Trusk about half a mile west south west of Trusk lough. It is 638 feet above the sea, contains about 5 acres and is about 13 feet deep. A stream from Lough Shinnagh flows naturally towards the south south east and joins the Mournebeg river, but a channel has been made near the lough by which this stream is divided and a branch made to flow into Trusk lough.

These lakes in general contain black trout, eels and perch, and salmon come up the Mournebeg river into Lough Mourne.

Rivers

River Finn: this river is navigable to Castlefinn for vessels carrying from 40 to 60 tons and for about a mile above Castlefinn for pleasure boats drawing less than a foot of water. After this the shoals effectually impede the progress of even the smallest craft. Large floods rise in the Finn about 6 hours after falls of rain in the mountains.

The Mournebeg river rises in Lough Mourne and, after flowing for about 4 miles through the parish of Donaghmore, forms for about 5 miles its southern boundary with that of Termonamongan. It then traverses this latter parish for about 4 and a half miles and falls into the Derg river about 2 miles below Killeter bridge. The Mournebeg river is not navigable in any part of its course; the bed is rocky.

The Burndale river, which is for about [blank] miles the boundary between Raphoe and Donaghmore, is unnavigable, subject to floods and flows in a gravelly and rocky channel.

There is also the Sawanah river, a stream called Mary Breen's burn, which both join the Mournebeg river, and many other mountain streams and rivulets.

The parish is well supplied with springs, some of which are deeply tinged with bog iron.

The salmon fishery at Killygordon is the property of Ralph Mansfield Esquire, who holds his estate by a grant from the Crown given to his ancestors in the reign of James I. It is rented by Mr Connolly of Killygordon at the sum of 4 pounds 4s per annum.

Bogs

The parish of Donaghmore is well supplied with turf from extensive bogs, principally situated in Meenbog, Tieveclogher etc. Timber occurs, but not in great plenty, in Tieveclogher bog, principally fir. The logs are sold from 2s 6d to 1 pound and used for axle-trees and roofs for building. A good deal is raised for fuel and makes an excellent fire.

Turf is cheap in comparison with the neighbouring parishes. It is usually sold at from 3d to 4d per barrel in Ballybofey and Killygordon. The bogs are grazed at seasons. Charcoal made from turf is generally used in the smiths' forges.

Modern Topography

Communications: Roads

The mail coach road from Londonderry to Sligo passes through the parish for about 8 miles and the crossroads from Castlefinn and Killygordon to Castlederg and Killeter on the road to Enniskillen. These roads are all made and repaired at the expense of the county by grand jury presentments and are often very much out of repair. Great want of skill or of superintendence appears in their construction, though good materials are at hand and in abundance.

Bridges

Castlefinn bridge, at the entrance of that town from Castlederg, is a structure of 6 water arches and 6 land ones; the depth of the water near the bridge is generally about 5 feet and the fall not more than 2 feet.

It was built by a Mr Mason and cost about 900 pounds, raised by assessment from the county, and was built at so little cost on account of the stones being procured from the ruins of a castle which stood close to the place.

A large corn store and quay for loading and unloading boats have been built at the bridge by Dr Rogan of Londonderry, who is the principal proprietor of Castlefinn. 4 boats are usually employed.

Liscooley bridge crosses the Finn on the road from Raphoe to Killeter through the townland of Liscooley. It was built in the year 1801 at the expense of about 1,100 pounds, raised by grand jury assessment. It has 5 water arches and 2 land ones to increase the waterway in time of floods. The fall of water at this bridge is about 3 feet.

Killygordon bridge crosses the Finn on the road from Killygordon to Killeter. It was built in the year 1782 and cost about 1,120 pounds, raised by assessment from the county. The fall of water through the bridge is about 4 feet. There are 7 arches. The depth of the ford at this bridge is usually about 3 feet.

The general depth of the Finn river from Stranorlar to Castlefinn is about 6 feet, but it is navigable very little way above Castlefinn on account of the fords and also of weirs to convey water to the corn and flax mills on its banks.

SOCIAL ECONOMY

Local Government

Petty sessions are held at Stranorlar every fortnight on Wednesdays. The magistrates who usually attend are James Johnston Esquire of Woodlands, Captain Mansfield of Killygordon, Samuel Delap Esquire of Monellan, John Corcoran Esquire of Edenmore; and also Sir Edmund Hayes Bart, M.P. and Sir Charles Style Bart attend when resident.

Dispensary

The Donaghmore dispensary is established at Killygordon and supported by a grant from the grand jury of the county equal to the amount raised by private subscription. The medical attendant is Dr Babbington and his salary 70 pounds per annum. The days of attendance at the dispensary are Wednesdays and Saturdays from 10 o'clock a.m. till 2 o'clock p.m. About 1,400 persons are annually relieved.

Religion

According to the government census taken in 1834, the population of the parish of Donaghmore was, distinguishing each religious persuasion, as follows: 1,677 members of the Established Church, 8,234 Roman Catholics, 3,346 Presbyterians, total 13,257; and by enquiry made in 1835, vide statistical table, it would appear that there were in the parish 2,360 families which, on an average of 5 and a half to each, gives a population of 12,980 persons.

PRODUCTIVE ECONOMY

Fairs and Markets

A weekly market is held in Castlefinn on Saturdays and in Ballybofey on Thursdays, by which the farmers of the parish of Donaghmore obtain a ready sale for their produce such as butter, grain, flax, as the Londonderry merchants send agents to these places every market day to make purchases on commission.

Annual fairs are held at Castlefinn on the Monday before Christmas Day (old style), on the Monday before Candlemas Day (old style), 17th March, Easter Monday, Whit Monday, 28th June, Monday before Lammas (old style), Monday before Michaelmas (old style) and on the 22nd November.

Annual fairs are held at Ballybofey on the last Thursdays in January, February and March. A fair is also held on the last Thursday in April, should it arrive before Easter Sunday, on the 22nd May and the 22nd December.

Annual fairs are held at Stranorlar on the 29th March, 12th August, 12th October and 13th December.

These fairs are principally for the sale of cattle, pigs, sheep etc. They are not good horse fairs. Linen yarn etc. are also sold.

Farms and Rents

The size of farms in the lowlands vary from 12 to 40 acres. They are usually held by lease from the head landlord either in perpetuity or for 31 years and 3 lives. The best land in the lowlands is let at 2 pounds per acre, the middling 1 pound 5s and the worst quality at about 15s. The rents are paid wholly in money. The farmers in general farm for subsistence. The tenants are liable to tithe and county cess.

The farm buildings are not in general good and commodious. They are usually erected and kept in repair by the tenants.

In the mountains the farms vary from 50 to 500 acres and the arable part of them produces chiefly oats and potatoes. A farm in Tieveclogher of about 500 acres is let on lease of 31 years at 30 pounds per annum.

Crops and Grazing

The lowlands produce potatoes, oats, barley, flax and wheat in considerable quantity about Castlefinn.

The mountains are used for cattle grazing, which are sent to them from the lowlands. Very few sheep are fed on the hills as they are considered too cold for sheep-walks.

The rotation of crops is as follows: potatoes, flax or oats (in the former case the land is again set with potatoes), wheat or barley and potatoes again.

The lands in the valley of Finn are rich and productive. Cultivation is carried up the mountain to the height of [blank] above the sea.

Manures

The manures used are usually lime, which is abundant, compost and farmyard manure. Every cottage has a receptacle as close to it as possible (generally indeed so close that the wall of the house has the manure heaped up against it) which receives the drainage and refuse of the house. In this receptacle the manure is made, the foundation of it being a quantity of earth drawn from the fields, road scrapings etc. If the inhabitants of the cottage be rich enough to keep a cow, the manure benefits by the addition of some animal matter.

In very many instances, however, the person is so poor as not to be able to keep horse or cow. In these cases it is clear that the clay drawn in is not better when it is restored to the field, than insomuch as it may have improved by turning, exposure to sun, rain and frost, and the very small quantity of manure which may be contained in the drainage from the house (the people themselves call this souring).

It is not to be wondered at that with such a system as this the lands are deteriorated, the crops except in very favourable seasons scanty and the face of the country (cultivated lands) covered with weeds. Another serious evil attending this system is that such collections of filth at the door of every habitation must inevitably have the effect of creating disease and spreading infection.

MODERN TOPOGRAPHY

Gentlemen's Seats

On the river, about half a mile above Castlefinn, the Glebe House of Donaghmore is situated. The house is a remarkably good one and the grounds are very tastefully laid out, and by former rectors have been much improved by plantations and enclosures. Some of the finest old trees that I have seen in this district were growing on the mensal lands. The present rector Revd Charles Irving has, in the last 3 years, quite denuded the place by unsparingly cutting down every tree of any growth.

Following the mail coach road, and to the south of it about 3 miles farther towards Stranorlar, are the houses and demesnes of Mount Hall, [blank] Young Esquire; Monellan, Samuel Delap Esquire; adjoining Killygordon is Killygordon demesne, the residence of Captain Mansfield; and from hence, proceeding towards Stranorlar on the road to the south of the River Finn, are Woodlands, Edenmore, John Corcoran Esquire; and Summerhill, the residence of James Johnston Esquire, an extensive linen bleacher.

In all these places are young plantations of some extent and the residence of these gentlemen at their several country houses is of much benefit to their immediate tenants and neighbours.

Public Buildings: Church

The church is a plain but neat building of modern date, having no tower, and is calculated to hold about 300 persons. About it were many fine old trees which have not escaped the axe. The church has just been newly roofed and slated by the Ecclesiastical Commissioners.

There is a chapel of ease at the crossroads above Killygordon which has been lately erected by the Board of First Fruits. It is a neat plain building without a tower and will contain 400 persons. The churchyard has been very tastefully laid out and planted by the curate Revd Robert Delap.

Catholic Chapels

There are 3 Roman Catholic chapels and 3 meeting houses in the usual style, plain barn-roofed buildings.

The Roman Catholic chapel at Castlefinn was built in 1822 by the congregation at an expense of about 250 pounds and calculated to hold about 350 persons.

There was also a schoolhouse built on part of the ground belonging to the chapel, but no school is taught there at present owing to the death of the person appointed to teach in it and to his widow keeping possession of the premises, contrary to the wish of the congregation.

The chapel yard is used as a burial ground. It is held by lease granted by the late Mrs Fox at the yearly rent of 2 pounds 14s.

The Roman Catholic chapel in the townland of Ballinacor was built in 1790 at an expense of about 800 pounds, by subscription from the congregation. It will hold about 900 persons.

The Roman Catholic chapel in the townland of Sessaghoneill has been lately built by the congregation, assisted by public subscription. It cost about 500 pounds and is calculated to contain about 800 persons.

Meeting Houses

There is a small Presbyterian meeting house in the townland of Lower Raws. It was built at the expense of the congregation and cost about 300 pounds. The minister receives a regium donum of 75 pounds per annum and 25 pounds from his hearers.

The Seceders' meeting house in the townland of Carnone was built in the year 1768 by the congregation at an expense of about 250 pounds. It will hold about 400 persons. The Revd William Dicky is the minister. His salary is about 54 pounds per annum. People are said to attend this meeting house from the parishes of Clonleigh, Urney, Donaghmore, Convoy and Raphoe.

The Presbyterian meeting house in the townland of Carrickashane was built in the year 1771 at the expense of the congregation and cost about 500 pounds. It will hold about 700 persons. The minister is the Revd Richard Dill.

Towns: Castlefinn

Castlefinn, owing to its being situated at the commencement of the navigation of the river, and the energy and enterprise of the proprietor Dr Francis Rogan of Derry, is likely to rise into importance. Already a corn market has been established and the quantity of grain shipped during the season for the Derry merchants is very considerable.

When a contemplated new line of road by Derg to Enniskillen shall have been completed much, indeed all, of the produce of the interior of Fermanagh which now finds its way to Derry via Strabane will be shipped at Castlefinn, the freight being considerably under what the bargemen, who ply from Strabane to Derry, can carry for, in consequence of the tolls of their canal.

There is a market house here built about 230 years, and the number of inhabitants amount to about 700. As usual the proportion of houses licensed to retail whiskey is very great as compared to shops of all other descriptions in the town. There is a weekly market on Mondays, a post office, and the mail to and from Londonderry and Sligo passes daily through the town.

Houses in Castlefinn

The houses in Castlefinn adjoining the market house are 2-storeys high, slated and many of them newly built. Those in the outskirts are in general merely thatched cottages. There is a mansion house adjoining Castlefinn which was part of the estate and the residence of the late Mrs Fox. It is unoccupied at present. A man named Scott, employed as a spy by King William's army, was taken by King James and hanged over the southern arch of the market house (1688). It was roofed about 20 years since.

Killygordon

Killygordon consists principally of a street or row of houses on the mail coach road from Londonderry to Sligo. There is a post office and daily post, dispensary and tanyard. The houses in general are low thatched cottages. There are a few 2-storeys high and slated. Killygordon demesne, the residence of Captain Mansfield, a magistrate, adjoins the village.

No markets are held but there are 5 annual fairs, on the 31st May, 31st August, 28th September, 1st December and 3rd March, principally for the sale of cattle, sheep, pigs.

Manufactories

Weaving linen and spinning yarn forms the winter occupations of the peasantry. There are bleach greens of some extent at Navenny and Dreenan, the property of James Johnston Esquire, at which are annually bleached 20,000 to 14,000 pieces of linen and 60 men are constantly employed. Their wages are from 4s 7d ha' penny to 15s a week each and there are besides other men employed to raise and cut turf in the mountain.

Mr Johnston states that the fuel for the green cost 200 pounds per annum, notwithstanding the convenience of bog. The linen is generally seven-eighths yard width, of a strong and useful description.

Parish of Donaghmore

The water which supplies the mills is bound to them by the proprietor of the soil, Marquis Conyngham, and Mr Johnston can prevent any persons erecting mills on the water between its source at Trusk lough and the green.

Permission was granted to Mr Walker to build a corn mill on certain conditions, and he would also have built a tanyard but this was considered by Mr Johnston injurious to the water and its erection forbidden.

There is no peculiar arrangement at these greens. The wheels are all breast shot, from 12 to 14 feet in diameter and from 3 to 4 and a half in breadth. The cloth when bleached is sent to Dublin and Liverpool.

SOCIAL AND PRODUCTIVE ECONOMY

Advowson

The living of Donaghmore is of considerable value, about 2,000 pounds per annum. The former incumbent, the Revd Sir John Lighton Bart, sold the perpetual advowson of it to Captain John Irving of Dublin, who presented his son the Revd Charles Irving, the present rector, to the parish.

The board of Trinity College of Dublin were in treaty with Sir John Lighton for the purchase of this living but afterwards declined it. They have been since desirous of obtaining it from the present proprietor.

A family of the name of Spence were originally in possession of the advowson and still make some claim to it. Though not in the gift, it is under the episcopal jurisdiction of the Bishop of Derry. The rector of Donaghmore has the appointment of the curate to the chapel of ease, subject to the approval of his nominee by the Bishop of Derry.

The tithes were valued under the Tithe Composition Act at 1,440 pounds per annum, the glebes, which include the townlands of Upper Alt and Calhame in the parish of Urney, at 740 pounds, total 2,180 pounds, subject to the charges made by recent acts of parliament.

Obstacles to Improvement

The great and leading impediment in the way of improvement here, as elsewhere, strikes me to be the absence of the natural guardians and protectors of the people, viz. their landlords. There are some exceptions, highly creditable to the individuals, in which the contrary conduct on the part of proprietors of estates proves clearly that were the solitary examples of kind, considerate and resident landlords universally adopted, very rapid and lasting benefits would result to the people and country.

Improving Landlords

I can point out no better exemplification of this than is afforded by a property belonging to Sir Robert Ferguson Bart in this parish, on the left bank of the Finn proceeding upwards and about 1 mile from Castlefinn. The farmhouses here are of a thriving [nature] and in comfort, and altogether there is an absence of that squalid wretchedness that meets you but too generally in the dwellings of the lower orders.

This is entirely attributable to the personal investigation by the landlord into the circumstances of his tenantry and the entrusting the management of his property in his absence to the superintendence of a humane and intelligent agent, who sees the enlightened and benevolent views of his employer carried into effect.

The same history is to be told of improvement wherever Sir Robert's property is to be found and, while it confers comfort and happiness on his people, he finds his account in the augmented value of his estates and the punctual payment of his rents.

I have already alluded to the activity and enterprise of the proprietor of Castlefinn (Dr Francis Rogan), by whose exertions the navigation of the river has been opened and the trade of the town created.

Plantations

Sir Robert Ferguson has made some judicious plantations on his estate which are thriving and luxuriant. The ground occupied by them was formerly of little or no value. The trees are of about 12 or 15 years' growth. The thinnings of these plantations he makes use of, chiefly in roofing and repairing his tenants' houses.

ANCIENT TOPOGRAPHY

Antiquities: Castle

A castle, belonging to the O'Donnell family, is said to have stood at Castlefinn, commanding the ford at which the present bridge is built. No trace of the castle remains, the stones having been used in the construction of the bridge.

In the reign of James I the castle and estate of Castlefinn are said to have been confiscated and granted to a General Kingsmill, for his conduct in suppressing the rebel O'Donnell. General

Kingsmill having no male heir, the estate was divided among his 4 daughters and has descended by marriage to its present possessors.

The site of another castle belonging to the O'Donnells is still shown in the townland of Killygordon, near the left bank of the River Finn at a place called Lower farm. In the reign of James I, Manus O'Donnell (brother to Earl O'Donnell of Donegal), who then held this castle being in the rebellion, an English force was sent against him and in a few days he and his adherents dispersed. An English officer named Mansfield having greatly distinguished himself on this occasion, the king granted the castle and estate called the estate of Killygordon to him and his heirs, by whom it is still possessed.

Holy Wells

There is a well in the townland of Carrick, close to the roadside from Castlefinn to Killygordon, which is called a holy well. Roman Catholics still resort to it to perform ceremonies and receive benefit for sore eyes, pains.

The spring was discovered about 30 years since by a man digging a French drain and, finding the spring remarkably strong, the drain was sunk deeper than usual and a bell discovered with a Latin inscription on it. The parish priest, named McBride, hearing of the discovery, asked to see this bell and, having read the inscription, would not return it to the finder but sent it to Rome; and from the date of its arrival there the well has been believed and affirmed to be "a well of cures."

There is another holy well in the townland of Killtown to which the Roman Catholics still go to obtain relief for sore eyes etc. by making what is called a station.

Curious Stones

In the wall of the parish church of Donaghmore is a stone with the figure of a greyhound on it. The tradition: that it is the representation of a favourite greyhound bitch belonging to a giant named Ossian, whom St Patrick was anxious to convert to Christianity and at whose request it was engraved on a stone placed beside the altar. In the old church about 70 years since, during the incumbency of the Revd Mr Spence, the church was rebuilt on a larger scale and, in pulling down the former one, this stone was broken but replaced in the wall, where it still remains.

The Roman Catholics claim a portion of the burial ground attached to the church and bury there.

On the mearing between Garvagh in the county of Tyrone and Coradooey in the county of Donegal there are a number of stones standing upright and called the County Cairn. It is said to be the grave of a favourite greyhound belonging to a giant named Derby which died at this place.

Grave and Traditions

On the mearing between Mounthall and Coradooey is a place called the Boys Grave. A pedlar is said to have been murdered and buried here, and the occupier of this part of the mountain asserts that his uncle, who is now dead, often saw at night the appearance of a man hovering about the spot; and as he was never, by any exertions, able to approach it, the people suppose that it was the spirit of the pedlar.

The hill where the trigonometrical station (called Lismullyduff in the townland of that name) is placed is supposed by the inhabitants to be a haunt of the fairies, and the sound of musical instruments and merriment often heard there.

Giant's Grave

The townland of Trusk and the lough are said to have been named after a giant whose grave is shown on the western side of the lough.

Under the surface of the bog near this place are found large stones laid at intervals like stepping [stones] in the ford of a river.

Mysterious Animal

A man named Byrne, who lives in a part of Trusk called Repentance, relates that there is in the lough a kind of amphibious animal as large as a young heifer. He has often seen its head above water and one summer's evening, as he and a boy were making hay by moonlight, he saw it coming from the lough towards them and ran home terrified.

The next evening his son, mowing grass beside the lough, saw it swim on shore to a dyke. He crept to the place in order to strike at it with his scythe, but its appearance affrightened him and he dared not venture. On seeing him, the animal plunged into the lake and has not since appeared; but when the lough is frozen, wild and tremendous howling is heard beneath the ice, which these people suppose to be the "dorhagh," as they call it.

Berwick Hall and Giant's Bed

Berwick Hall near Liscooley bridge is so named from Duke of Berwick's having rested there.

There is also a place called the Giant's Bed near the eastern extremity of Lough Mourne, in the townland of Crohonagh. No tradition exists respecting it.

Altar

There is a place in the townland of Meenagolan near the River Mourne called the Altar, which was used as such by a Roman Catholic priest named Dougherty who, about 60 years since, was parish priest of Termonamongan.

Carrickmagra

The townland of Carrickmagra is said to take its name from a giant called Magrath, who was killed on a rock situated in it which is still called Laught Ard or, in English, "the high monument."

Danish Forts

Throughout the parish of Donaghmore are many of the circular enclosures called Danish forts, presenting nothing unusual.

There is a tradition attached to one near the River Finn in the townland of Ballyarrell which relates that a church was once going to be built on the spot, but the structure was repeatedly thrown down by something in the shape of a goat that came out of the river.

Discoveries in Bogs

In the townland of Corgary a brass pot or cauldron was found under the bog in cutting peat. It is in the possession of Manus Byrne, pensioner from the 1st Regiment of Foot, and is used as a cooking utensil. There is no inscription on it.

A cake of tallow weighing about 5 lbs and several old iron implements resembling knives or razors were also found near the spot, at a considerable depth in the bog.

PRODUCTIVE ECONOMY

Castlefinn: Trades

Return of the trades etc. in the town of Castlefinn. [Table contains the following headings: trade or calling, number of employers, journeymen and apprentices, total number].

Shoemakers: 5 employers, 8 journeymen and apprentices, total 13.
Tailors: 4 employers, 8 journeymen and apprentices, total 12.
Painters: 3 employers, total 3.
Blacksmiths: 2 employers, 3 journeymen and apprentices, total 5.
Wheelwrights: 4 employers, total 4.
Weavers: 1 employer, total 1.
Carpenters: 3 employers, 3 journeymen and apprentices, total 6.
Bakers: 4 employers, 1 journeyman and apprentice, total 5.
Grocers: total 6.
Publicans: total 13.
Land surveyors: [blank].
Protestant clergymen: total 2.
Stonemasons: 4 employers, total 4.
Land agents: [blank].
Nailers: 1 employer, total 1.
Broguemakers: 3 employers, total 3.
Reedmakers: 2 employers, total 2.
Farmers: 4 employers, total 4.
Butchers: 2 employers, total 2.
Coopers: 2 employers, total 2.
Apothecaries: 1 employer, total 1.

Killygordon: Trades

Return of the trades etc. in the town of Killygordon.

Public houses 1, public houses and grocer's shops 3, grocer's shops 1, bakers 1, blacksmith's forges 2, blacksmiths 4, carpenters 5, shoemakers 4, tailors 6, weavers 12, butchers 4, tanners 4, nailers 2, post office 1, dispensary 1, doctors 1, cloth shop 1.

SOCIAL ECONOMY

Census and Enquiry in 1831

Statistical table of the parish of Donaghmore, as taken from census and enquiry made in 183[1]. [Table contains the following headings: name of townland, analysis of types of buildings and families, county cess [blank], name of landlord].

Allison Sessagh: 12 inhabited buildings, 25 dwelling houses and families, 6 outhouses, 1 uninhabited house, 19 total buildings; landlord Colonel Delap <Delop>.

Ardnagannagh: 6 inhabited buildings, 9 dwelling houses and families, 9 outhouses, 1 uninhabited house, 2 in ruins, 18 total buildings; landlord Revd Mr Hamilton.

Aviltygort: 13 inhabited buildings, 16 dwelling houses and families, 11 outhouses, 3 in ruins, 27 total buildings; landlord late Dr Gillespey.

Bahanbwee: 16 inhabited buildings, 19 dwelling houses and families, 14 outhouses, 1 uninhabited house, 5 in ruins, 36 total buildings; landlord Sir Alexander Stewart of Ards.

Ballybun: 35 inhabited buildings, 47 dwelling houses, 15 outhouses, 5 in ruins, 55 total buildings; landlord Mr Leckey.

Ballygunnigan: 13 inhabited buildings, 20 dwelling houses and families, 9 outhouses, 2 in ruins, 24 total buildings; landlord Robert Ferguson Bart.

Ballynaman: 11 inhabited buildings, 16 dwelling houses and families, 9 outhouses, 1 uninhabited house, 21 total buildings; landlord Mr McConkey.

Ballinacor: 48 inhabited buildings, 77 dwelling houses and families, 43 outhouses, 1 uninhabited house, 8 in ruins, 100 total buildings; landlords James Johnston Esquire, Mrs Scott and Miss Harvey.

Ballyarrell: 31 inhabited buildings, 44 dwelling houses and families, 19 outhouses, 6 in ruins, 56 total buildings; landlord Messrs Davidson and Beatty.

Bealalt: 21 inhabited buildings, 30 dwelling houses and families, 22 outhouses, 1 uninhabited house, 3 in ruins, 47 total buildings; landlord Sir Robert Ferguson.

Blairstown: 16 inhabited buildings, 30 dwelling houses and families, 10 outhouses, 2 uninhabited houses, 3 in ruins, 31 total buildings; landlord Counsellor Walker.

Breaghy: 3 inhabited buildings, 5 dwelling houses and families, 7 outhouses, 10 total buildings; landlord Colonel Delap.

Calhame: 23 inhabited buildings, 25 dwelling houses and families, 8 outhouses, 5 in ruins, 36 total buildings; landlord Sir Alexander Stewart.

Carnowen: 77 inhabited buildings, 82 dwelling houses and families, 67 outhouses, 3 uninhabited houses, 15 in ruins, 162 total buildings; landlord Robert Ferguson.

Carrick: 24 inhabited buildings, 34 dwelling houses and families, 21 outhouses, 1 uninhabited house, 3 in ruins, 49 total buildings; landlord Counsellor Walker.

Carrickashane: 12 inhabited buildings, 13 dwelling houses and families, 15 outhouses, 1 uninhabited house, 1 in ruins, 29 total buildings; landlord Counsellor Walker.

Carnadore: 7 inhabited buildings, 9 dwelling houses and families, 5 outhouses, 2 uninhabited houses, 14 total buildings; landlord Sir Robert Ferguson.

Carrickshandrum: 13 inhabited buildings, 20 dwelling houses and families, 5 outhouses, 1 in ruins, 19 total buildings; landlord Mr Montgomery.

Carrans: 41 inhabited buildings, 45 dwelling houses and families, 16 outhouses, 1 uninhabited house, 10 in ruins, 68 total buildings; landlord Mr Montgomery.

Carrickmagra: 55 inhabited buildings, 73 dwelling houses and families, 28 outhouses, 1 uninhabited house, 3 in ruins, 87 total buildings; landlord Lord Lifford.

Carricknamanna: 36 inhabited buildings, 41 dwelling houses and families, 44 outhouses, 8 uninhabited houses, 6 in ruins, 94 total buildings; landlord Sir Alexander Stewart.

Castlefinn: 41 inhabited buildings, 109 dwelling houses and families, 45 outhouses, 10 inhabited houses, 11 in ruins, 107 total buildings; landlords Dr Rogan and Captain Fox.

Cashellin: 11 inhabited buildings, 13 dwelling houses and families, 8 outhouses, 2 uninhabited houses, 2 in ruins, 23 total buildings; landlord Sir Robert Ferguson.

Cavan Upper: 25 inhabited buildings, 28 dwelling houses and families, 25 outhouses, 2 uninhabited houses, 2 in ruins, 54 total buildings; landlord Mr Hone.

Cavan Lower: 40 inhabited buildings, 43 dwelling houses and families, 36 outhouses, 3 uninhabited houses, 9 in ruins, 88 total buildings; landlord Mr Hone.

Cloonarrell, 19 inhabited buildings, 27 dwelling houses and families, 13 outhouses, 1 uninhabited house, 1 ruin, 34 total buildings; landlord Sir Robert Ferguson.

Cloughard: 5 inhabited buildings, 7 dwelling houses and families, 2 outhouses, 3 in ruins, 10 total buildings; landlord Sir Robert Ferguson.

Cooladawson: 12 inhabited buildings, 15 dwelling houses and families, 6 outhouses, 1 in ruins, 19 total buildings; landlord Mr Stewart.

Corcaum, 5 inhabited buildings, 6 dwelling houses and families, 3 outhouses, 1 in ruins, 9 total buildings; landlord Mr Stewart.

Cornabroag: 6 inhabited buildings, 7 dwelling houses and families, 3 outhouses, 2 uninhabited houses, 11 total buildings; landlord Rector Hamilton.

Correfrin: 23 inhabited buildings, 34 dwelling houses and families, 2 outhouses, 5 in ruins, 30 total buildings; landlord Sir Robert Beatson.

Corlea: 8 inhabited buildings, 9 dwelling houses and families, 7 outhouses, 3 in ruins, 18 total buildings; landlord Mr John Craig.

Coradooey: 9 inhabited buildings, 11 dwelling houses and families, 9 outhouses, 1 in ruins, 19 total buildings; landlord Mr Young.

Parish of Donaghmore

Corgary: 19 inhabited buildings, 24 dwelling houses and families, 10 outhouses, 3 in ruins, 32 total buildings; landlord Sir Robert Beatson.

Croonalaghy: 19 inhabited buildings, 28 dwelling houses and families, 17 outhouses, 2 uninhabited houses, 8 in ruins, 46 total buildings; landlord Dr Darby.

Crohonagh: 6 inhabited buildings, 7 dwelling houses and families, 3 outhouses, 3 in ruins, 12 total buildings; landlord Lord Lifford.

Curcullian: 9 inhabited buildings, 12 dwelling houses and families, 1 outhouse, 10 total buildings; landlord Lady Galbraith.

Demesne: 6 inhabited buildings, 8 dwelling houses and families, 6 outhouses, 12 total buildings; landlord John Finton Esquire.

Donaghmore Glebe: 8 inhabited buildings, 9 dwelling houses and families, 11 outhouses, 2 in ruins, 21 total buildings; landlord Rector Irving.

Dooghan: 8 inhabited buildings, 12 dwelling houses and families, 2 outhouses, 2 in ruins, 12 total buildings; landlord Colonel Delap.

Dreenan: 25 inhabited buildings, 42 dwelling houses and families, 9 outhouses, 7 uninhabited houses, 4 in ruins, 45 total buildings; landlord Sir Robert Beatson.

Drimfergus: 9 inhabited buildings, 11 dwelling houses and families, 6 outhouses, 1 in ruins, 16 total buildings; landlord Mr Delap.

Drimkennian: 9 inhabited buildings, 10 uninhabited buildings, 5 outhouses, 1 in ruins, 15 total buildings; landlord Mr Delap.

Dromore: 23 inhabited buildings, 35 dwelling houses and families, 15 outhouses, 3 uninhabited houses, 4 in ruins, 45 total buildings; landlord Mr Young.

Drummurphy: 16 inhabited houses, 18 dwelling houses and families, 17 outhouses, 1 uninhabited house, 2 in ruins, 36 total buildings; landlord Sir Robert Ferguson.

Drumeavish: 19 inhabited buildings, 25 dwelling houses and families, 12 outhouses, 3 in ruins, 34 total buildings; landlord James Johnston.

Dungorman: 15 inhabited buildings, 17 dwelling houses and families, 12 outhouses, 1 uninhabited house, 3 in ruins, 31 total buildings; landlord Sir Robert Ferguson.

Edenmore: 12 inhabited buildings, 13 dwelling houses and families, 14 outhouses, 1 ruin, 27 total buildings; landlord Mr Cockran.

Edenohill: 8 inhabited buildings, 12 dwelling houses and families, 9 outhouses, 1 uninhabited house, 4 in ruins, 22 total buildings; landlord Mr Delap.

Egglybaan: 6 inhabited buildings, 6 dwelling houses and families, 3 outhouses, 9 total buildings; landlord Mr William Causeland.

Garrison Hill: 9 inhabited buildings, 11 dwelling houses and families, 5 outhouses, 2 in ruins, 16 total buildings; landlord widow of the late Counsellor Scott.

Gleneely: 25 inhabited buildings, 38 dwelling houses and families, 17 outhouses, 2 in ruins, 44 total buildings; landlord Rector Hamilton.

Glencovit: 10 inhabited buildings, 11 dwelling houses and families, 7 outhouses, 4 in ruins, 21 total buildings; landlord Sir Robert Beatson.

Goland: 39 inhabited buildings, 59 dwelling houses and families, 19 outhouses, 1 uninhabited house, 8 in ruins, 67 total buildings; landlord Lord Lifford.

Gortachork: 14 inhabited buildings, 21 dwelling house and families, 7 outhouses, 1 uninhabited house, 2 in ruins, 24 total buildings; landlords Messrs McConkey and Doherty.

Gortfad: 8 inhabited buildings, 14 dwelling houses and families, 11 outhouses, 4 in ruins, 23 total buildings; landlord Revd Mr Colthurst.

Gortnamuck: 36 inhabited buildings, 48 dwelling houses and families, 13 outhouses, 1 in ruins, 50 total buildings; landlord Conolly Gage Esquire.

Grahamsland: 24 inhabited buildings, 42 dwelling houses and families, 5 outhouses, 3 in ruins, 32 total buildings; landlord Colonel Delap.

Killygordon: 52 inhabited buildings, 76 dwelling houses and families, 54 outhouses, 3 uninhabited houses, 1 in ruins, 110 total buildings; landlords Messrs Mansfield.

Killtown: 8 inhabited buildings, 8 dwelling houses and families, 8 outhouses, 2 in ruins, 18 total buildings; landlord Counsellor Walker.

Kilcadden: 9 inhabited buildings, 13 dwelling houses and families, 12 outhouses, 2 uninhabited houses, 1 in ruins, 24 total buildings; landlord Mr William Walker.

Kinleater: landlord Marquis of Conyngham <Cunningham>.

Knock: 19 inhabited buildings, 23 dwelling houses and families, 12 outhouses, 2 uninhabited houses, 33 total buildings; landlord Marquis Conyngham.

Knockrawer: 4 inhabited buildings, 4 dwelling houses and families, 3 outhouses, 2 uninhabited houses, 9 total buildings; landlord Marquis Conyngham.

Leaght: 37 inhabited buildings, 53 dwelling houses and families, 21 outhouses, 1 uninhabited house, 10 in ruins, 69 total buildings; landlord Mr Young.

Lisnabert: 3 inhabited buildings, 3 dwelling houses and families, 4 outhouses, 7 total buildings; landlord Colonel Delap.

Liscooley: 7 inhabited buildings, 7 dwelling houses and families, 6 outhouses, 2 uninhabited houses, 3 in ruins, 18 total buildings; landlord Counsellor Walker.

Lisnamulligan: 17 inhabited buildings, 25 dwelling houses and families, 9 outhouses, 7 in ruins, 33 total buildings; landlords Sir Robert Ferguson and Mr Chambers.

Lissmullyduff: 26 inhabited buildings, 37 dwelling houses and families, 29 outhouses, 4 in ruins, 59 total buildings; landlord Samuel Delap Esquire.

Longsessagh: 14 inhabited buildings, 18 dwelling houses and families, 9 outhouses, 4 in ruins, 27 total buildings; landlord Colonel Delap.

Magherareagh: 6 inhabited buildings, 6 dwelling houses and families, 12 outhouses, 1 uninhabited house, 19 total buildings; landlord Lady Galbraith.

Magherashanvalley: 11 inhabited buildings, 13 dwelling houses and families, 4 outhouses, 1 uninhabited house, 2 in ruins, 18 total dwellings; landlord Colonel Delap.

Magherybwee: 14 inhabited buildings, 15 dwelling houses and families, 16 outhouses, 1 uninhabited house, 2 in ruins, 33 total buildings; landlord Counsellor Walker.

Meenreagh: 19 inhabited buildings, 24 dwelling houses and families, 20 outhouses, 2 uninhabited houses, 4 in ruins, 45 total buildings; landlords Messrs Disney.

Meenlaugher: 18 inhabited buildings, 28 dwelling houses and families, 19 outhouses, 2 uninhabited houses, 1 in ruins, 40 total dwellings; landlord Sir Robert Ferguson.

Meenbog: 11 inhabited buildings, 12 dwelling houses and families, 3 outhouses, 4 in ruins, 18 total buildings; landlord Lord Lifford.

Meenahoney: 9 inhabited buildings, 12 dwelling houses and families, 8 outhouses, 2 in ruins, 19 total dwellings; landlord Counsellor Walker.

Meenagolan: 7 inhabited buildings, 7 dwelling houses and families, 5 outhouses, 5 in ruins, 17 total buildings; landlord Mr Delap.

Meenahenisk: 15 inhabited buildings, 24 dwelling houses and families, 11 outhouses, 1 uninhabited house, 3 in ruins, 30 total buildings; landlord Miss Harvey.

Monellan: 24 inhabited buildings, 30 dwelling houses and families, 19 outhouses, 2 uninhabited houses, 2 in ruins, 47 total buildings; landlord Mr Delap.

Mountain Park: 5 inhabited buildings, 7 dwelling houses and families, 4 outhouses, 1 ruin, 10 total dwellings; landlord Miss Harvey.

Mounthall: 22 inhabited buildings, 32 dwelling houses and families, 15 outhouses, 2 uninhabited houses, 6 in ruins, 45 total buildings; landlords Messrs Delap and Young.

Mullanbwee: 5 inhabited buildings, 6 dwelling houses and families, 8 outhouses, 2 uninhabited houses, 15 total buildings; landlords Messrs Lecky and Finton.

Mullaghanairy: 16 inhabited buildings, 26 dwelling houses and families, 9 outhouses, 1 uninhabited house, 6 in ruins, 32 total buildings; landlord Mr McConkey.

Mullingar: 5 inhabited buildings, 6 dwelling houses and families, 4 outhouses, 1 uninhabited house, 1 in ruins, 11 total buildings; landlord Sir Alexander Stewart.

Navenny: 27 inhabited buildings, 35 dwelling houses and families, 28 outhouses, 1 uninhabited house, 5 in ruins, 61 total buildings; landlord Marquis Conyngham.

Owenagaderagh: 5 inhabited buildings, 9 dwelling houses and families, 5 outhouses, 10 total buildings; landlord Mr Delap.

Raws Lower: 14 inhabited buildings, 19 dwelling houses and families, 5 outhouses, 1 uninhabited house, 2 in ruins, 22 total buildings; landlord Connolly Gage Esquire.

Raws Upper: 21 inhabited buildings, 29 dwelling houses and families, 11 outhouses, 2 in ruins, 34 total buildings; landlord Mr McCausland.

Rushyhill: 13 inhabited buildings, 22 dwelling houses and families, 9 outhouses, 3 in ruins, 25 total buildings; landlord Messrs Derby.

Sallywood: 12 inhabited buildings, 12 dwelling houses and families, 2 outhouses, 4 in ruins, 18 total buildings; landlord James Johnston.

Sessagh O'Neill: 18 inhabited buildings, 23 dwelling houses and families, 6 outhouses, 1 uninhabited house, 5 in ruins, 30 total buildings; landlord Marquis Conyngham.

Sessaghmore: 3 inhabited buildings, 4 dwelling houses and families, 3 outhouses, 6 total buildings; landlord Colonel Delap.

Scotland: 1 inhabited building, 1 dwelling house and family, 2 outhouses, 3 total buildings; landlord Counsellor Walker.

Parish of Donaghmore

Stranamuck: 4 inhabited buildings, 6 dwelling houses and families, 5 outhouses, 2 in ruins, 11 total buildings; landlord Lady Galbraith.

Tamnacrum: 10 inhabited buildings, 13 dwelling houses and families, 8 outhouses, 1 in ruins, 19 total buildings; landlord Miss Harvey.

Taughbuoy: 15 inhabited buildings, 18 dwelling houses and families, 2 outhouses, 2 in ruins, 19 total buildings; landlord Lord Lifford.

Tievebrack: 31 inhabited buildings, 44 dwelling houses and families, 12 outhouses, 1 in ruins, 44 total buildings; landlord Mrs Stanhope.

Tieranisk: 9 inhabited buildings, 13 dwelling houses and families, 7 outhouses, 2 uninhabited houses, 6 in ruins, 24 total buildings; landlord Mr Lecky.

Tieveclogher: 16 inhabited buildings, 20 dwelling houses and families, 15 outhouses, 1 in ruins, 32 total buildings; landlord Sir Robert Beatson.

Tiernagushog or Bickelstown: 8 inhabited buildings, 10 dwelling houses and families, 5 outhouses, 4 in ruins, 17 total buildings; landlord Sir Robert Ferguson.

Trusk: 28 inhabited buildings, 38 dwelling houses and families, 14 outhouses, 1 uninhabited house, 7 in ruins, 50 total buildings; landlord Marquis Conyngham.

Whitehill: 5 inhabited buildings, 7 dwelling houses and families, 1 outhouse, 2 in ruins, 8 total buildings; landlord Sir Alexander Stewart.

Table of Schools

[Table contains the following headings: situation, number of pupils subdivided by religion and sex, remarks as to how supported].

Ballyarrell: 4 Protestant males, 4 Protestant females, 9 Presbyterian males, 10 Presbyterians females, 11 Roman Catholic males, 3 Roman Catholic females, total 41; the teacher's name is Steven Maxwell, a Presbyterian. He estimates this school to be worth on the average 12 pounds per annum, which he receives from the scholars; he has nothing else to depend on.

Craig McLoughlin, in the townland of Gortachork: 42 Roman Catholic males, 24 Roman Catholic females, total 66; the teacher's name is Peter Murdock, a Roman Catholic. He has nothing to depend on but the scholars' payments, which he estimates to amount to 16 pounds per annum. He also boards with the scholars.

Monellan: 10 Protestant males, 20 Protestant females, 5 Roman Catholic males, 3 Roman Catholic females, total 38; the teacher of this school is Anne Jane Edwards, a Protestant. She teaches reading, sewing and knitting. The scholars get their education free, as the school is supported and patronised by the Revd Mr Delap <Delop> and his sisters the Misses Delaps. The tutor's salary by the year is 5 pounds.

Ballinacor: 34 Roman Catholic males, 23 Roman Catholic females, total 57; the teacher's name is Dennis McBrerty, a Roman Catholic. He is supported by the scholars; he estimates his school to be worth, on the average, 12 pounds per annum. He also boards with the scholars: he goes to each scholar day about.

Gleneely: 23 Roman Catholic males, 11 Roman Catholic females, total 34; the teacher's name is Alexander Craig. He is a Roman Catholic and is supported by the scholars; he estimates his school to be worth on the average 6 pounds per annum. He also boards with the scholars: he goes to each scholar day about.

Trusk: 28 Roman Catholic males, 17 Roman Catholic females, total 45; the teacher's name is Patrick Murley, a Roman Catholic. He is supported by the scholars; he values his school to be worth 10 pounds per annum. He does not board with the scholars.

Goland: 3 Protestant males, 2 Protestant females, 12 Roman Catholic males, 8 Roman Catholic females, total 25; the teacher's name is James McGowan. He is a Roman Catholic and is supported by the scholars. He teaches reading, writing and arithmetic. He charges for each quarter of a year: for reading 2s, writing 2s 6d, arithmetic 3s; he estimates his school to be worth in the average 10 pounds per annum.

Carrickmagra: 25 Protestant males, 16 Protestant females, 11 Presbyterian males, 4 Presbyterian females, 7 Roman Catholics males, 1 Roman Catholic female, total 64. The teacher's name is William Johnston; he is a Protestant. He receives 8 pounds per annum, also 1 acre of land and a house rent free from the Revd Robert Delap of Monellan, curate of the parish of Donaghmore. He also charges 1d per week from each scholar, which he estimates to be worth on the average 8 pounds per annum. He teaches reading, writing and arithmetic. He makes no difference in his charges for teaching any of the above branches. This schoolhouse was built at the expense of the above-mentioned clergyman in the year 1831; it cost 140 pounds.

Gortnamuck: 3 Protestant males, 2 Protestant females, 4 Presbyterian males, 3 Presbyterian females, 14 Roman Catholic males, 14 Roman Catholic females, total 40. The teacher's name is

William Gallagher; he is a Roman Catholic and is supported by the scholars. He averages his salary to 16 pounds per annum. He teaches writing and reading; he charges 2s 6d per quarter of a year for the former and 2s for the latter.

Drummurphy: 4 Protestant females, 10 Presbyterian males, 12 Presbyterian females, 2 Roman Catholic males, 2 Roman Catholic females, total 30; the teacher's name is Francis McClure, a Protestant. This school formerly was supported by the Kildare Street Society but at present it is not. The only advantage the teacher has is a house rent free and all the books etc. for instruction. He estimates his salary on the average to 14 pounds per annum. This schoolhouse was built at the expense of Sir Robert Ferguson.

Drummurphy: this school is taught by Mary Walker, a Presbyterian. She has nothing to depend upon but the children's payments, which are about 10 pounds per annum. She charges from 1s to 1s 6d per quarter. She teaches the females to sew. This school was under the Kildare Street Society, but since the government grant was withdrawn from it she receives no salary from the society.

Dreenan: 11 Protestant males, 9 Presbyterian males, 1 Presbyterian female, 45 Roman Catholic males, 22 Roman Catholic females, total 88; this school is kept in part of a dwelling. The teacher's name is Patrick Brisland. He has no other remuneration than what he receives from the scholars, which is about 2s per quarter from each; his yearly income averages about 13 pounds.

Castlefinn: 5 Protestant males, 1 Protestant female, 16 Presbyterian males, 6 Presbyterian females, 26 Roman Catholic males, 20 Roman Catholic females, total 74; this school is kept in a house of Dr Rogan's, which he gives to the teacher gratis to keep his scholars in. His name is Mr Hanagan; he has no other remuneration but what he gets from the scholars, which is from 2s 6d to 7d 6d per quarter from each. He teaches mathematics, book-keeping; he makes about 25 pounds per annum; he is a Roman Catholic.

Castlefinn: 5 Roman Catholic males, total 5; the teacher's name is Mr Dogherty, a Roman Catholic. He teaches in another person's house. He has no other remuneration but what he gets from the scholars, which is 15s per quarter from each; his yearly income averages from 24 pounds to 30 pounds.

Upper Raws: 3 Protestant males, 2 Protestant females, 12 Presbyterian males, 14 Presbyterian females, 4 Roman Catholic males, 4 Roman Catholic females, total 39. The teacher's name is William McClean; he is a Presbyterian and is supported by the scholars. He boards with the scholars and estimates the value of his school to be 9 pounds 15s per annum.

Grahamsland: 46 Protestant females, 40 Presbyterian females, 23 Roman Catholic females, total 109; this school is taught by Mrs Mary Mahaffey; she is a Protestant. She teaches reading, writing, sewing and knitting, and receives 12 pounds per annum from the London Ladies' Hibernian Society and is allowed quarterly premiums according to the number and proficiency of the pupils. She is also allowed to take from each pupil 1d per week from those that consider themselves able to pay it. This school is also supplied with books etc. from the society.

Grahamsland: 24 Protestant males, 7 Protestant females, 4 Presbyterian males, 3 Presbyterian females, 3 Roman Catholic males, 3 Roman Catholic females, total 44. The teacher's name is Robert Steele, a Protestant; he receives from the Kildare Street Society a house rent free, also books of instruction and 1 acre of land. He estimates the salary he gets yearly from the scholars to be worth on the average 7 pounds 10s 6d; he gets no money from the society.

Meenlaugher: 4 Protestant males, 3 Protestant females, 7 Presbyterian males, 6 Presbyterian females, 12 Roman Catholic males, 14 Roman Catholic females, total 46. The teacher's name is Hugh O'Donnell, a Roman Catholic; he is supported by the scholars. He does not board with the scholars; he estimates his salary to be on the average 12 pounds per annum.

Correfrin: 3 Protestant males, 1 Protestant female, 4 Presbyterian males, 17 Roman Catholic males, 6 Roman Catholic females, total 31. The teacher's name is Patrick Boyle; he is a Roman Catholic. He is not supported by any society but by the scholars. He estimates his salary to be worth on the average 10 pounds per annum; he also boards with the scholars.

Killygordon: 7 Protestant males, 10 Protestant females, 7 Presbyterian males, 39 Presbyterian females, 16 Roman Catholic males, 29 Roman Catholic females, total 108. This school is taught by Margaret Sterriot; she is a Seceder. She receives the sum of 13 pounds per annum from the Hibernian Society and about 2 pounds from the children, in all about 15 pounds per annum. The children learn to read, write and arithmetic; the females learn to sew. There were 2 schools taught in this schoolhouse till within a few months ago, and as soon as they can get a suitable master will be continued.

Dooghan: 2 Protestant males, 4 Protestant females, 6 Presbyterian males, 7 Presbyterian females, 9 Roman Catholic males, 7 Roman Catholic females, total 35. The teacher's name is John McKenny, a Roman Catholic; he is supported by the scholars. He values his school to be worth 9 pounds per annum; he boards with the scholars.

Upper Cavan: 1 Presbyterian male, 29 Roman Catholic males, 5 Roman Catholic females, total 34. The teacher's name is James Braceland, a Roman Catholic; he is supported by the scholars. He estimates his school to be worth on the average 12 pounds per annum; he also boards with the scholars.

Lower Cavan: 33 Protestant males, 71 Protestant females, 8 Presbyterian males, 6 Presbyterian females, 3 Roman Catholic males, 4 Roman Catholic females, total 125. The teacher's name is George Campbell, a Protestant; he is to receive a salary from the London Hibernian Society but he cannot say how much, as he is not more than one quarter teaching in this school. He receives from the scholars the sum of 6 pounds 5s per quarter. He charges from 1s to 2s per quarter: those learning to read and write 1s and those learning arithmetic 2s.

[Signed] I.I. Wilkinson, Lieutenant Royal Engineers, 18th April 1836.

Parish of Donegal, County Donegal

Memoir by Lieutenant W. Lancey, November 1835

Natural State

Name

This parish is usually spelt Donegal but sometimes Donegall. The peasantry pronounce it Dinnagall. It is said to have been one of the ancient strongholds or duns of the Gaille, from whence it is supposed to derive its name.

Locality

It is situated in the northern portion of the barony of Tyrhugh and is bounded on the west by the bay of Donegal and the parish of Killymard, on the north by Kilteevoge and Stranorlar, and on the east by Donaghmore and Termonamongan, and on the south by the parish of Drumhome <Drimholm>. Its extreme length is 9 miles and breadth 8 miles, contains 23,260 acres, 7,071 of which are cultivated, 14,447 uncultivated, 741 occupied by water and paid in 1835 210 pounds 1s 7d ha'penny to the county cess.

Natural Features

Hills

The northern part of the parish is very rough and mountainous, and is celebrated for the wild pass or Gap of Barnesmore which divides the Townawilly mountains by a great chasm through which the mail coach road passes. These granite mountains are 1,489 and 1,725 feet high on the right and left of the Gap and are a portion of a mountain range running east and west, dividing the country into 2 distinct districts; and in the adjoining parish of Killymard the highest point, at Glasscorns, attains the height of 2,213 feet.

The eastern boundary of Donegal lies on long slopes of subordinate hills falling towards the sea with narrow valleys, where the mountain limestone formation intervening, the ground is thrown up into numerous druims or backs succeeded by isolated elliptical knolls, some of which form islands of low elevation in the bay of Donegal.

Lakes

The principal lake connected with this parish is Lough Eske <Iasg>, 103 feet above the sea. It lies between it and Killymard, and contains 978 acres of water with a few small islands covered with wood, on one of which are the ruins of a castle which belonged to O'Donnell, the ancient proprietor. The northern end of this fine sheet of water lies in an amphitheatre of rocky mountains, the drainage of which it receives at its northern end and empties at the south by the River Eske, which flows under Donegal bridge. This lough will be more minutely described in the Memoir of Killymard. A table of the other loughs is inserted below. They present nothing worthy of notice.

List of Loughs

Contents of loughs in the parish of Donegal. [Table contains the following headings: name of townland, acreage of loughs, remarks].

Townawilly Mountain: Loughullanacrooney, 1 acre 2 roods 10 perches; Loughnacruche, 2 roods 26 perches; Loughillarmore, 5 acres 2 roods 16 perches; Loughnagrookgranagh, 1 acre 1 rood 30 perches; Loughaduire, 17 acres 1 rood 6 perches; Loughanwherein, 7 acres 3 roods 8 perches; Loughnagroocgranagh, 4 acres 3 roods 32 perches; Lough Barnus, 11 acres 8 perches; Lough Yellaghaleary, 1 acre 2 roods 3 perches; Loughadubh, 2 acres 1 rood 10 perches; Loughfadda, 3 acres 3 roods 24 perches; Loughnabreen, 3 roods 6 perches; Curragh lough, 1 rood 4 perches; Loughafachin, 28 perches; Lougherrabin, 2 acres 13 perches; Loughaminchin, 11 acres; Loughnacantagh, 3 acres 29 perches; Loughmhinanidh, 3 roods 5 perches; Loughnacruache, 1 acre 1 rood 2 perches; Hugh Boyle's lough, 22 perches; no.3, 3 roods; no.4, 1 rood 2 perches; no.5, 1 rood 33 perches; no.6, 30 perches; no.7, 2 roods 23 perches; no.8, 1 acre 2 perches; [total] 81 acres 22 perches.

Minambrock: Loughileive, 2 acres 1 rood 10 perches; Pool Dhu, 2 acres 1 rood 5 perches; Lough Pool Dhu, 1 acre 16 perches, 2 roods 38 perches to Tarmonamongan; Lough Michan, 4 acres 1 rood 10 perches; Loughnagoppag, 1 rood 36 perches; Lough Minambrock, 3 acres 2 roods 5 perches; lough no.14, 1 acre 1 rood 32 perches, part in Upper Keidue.

Upper Keidue: Lough Logan, 1 rood 34 perches; Loughnapaiste, 2 acres 3 roods 10

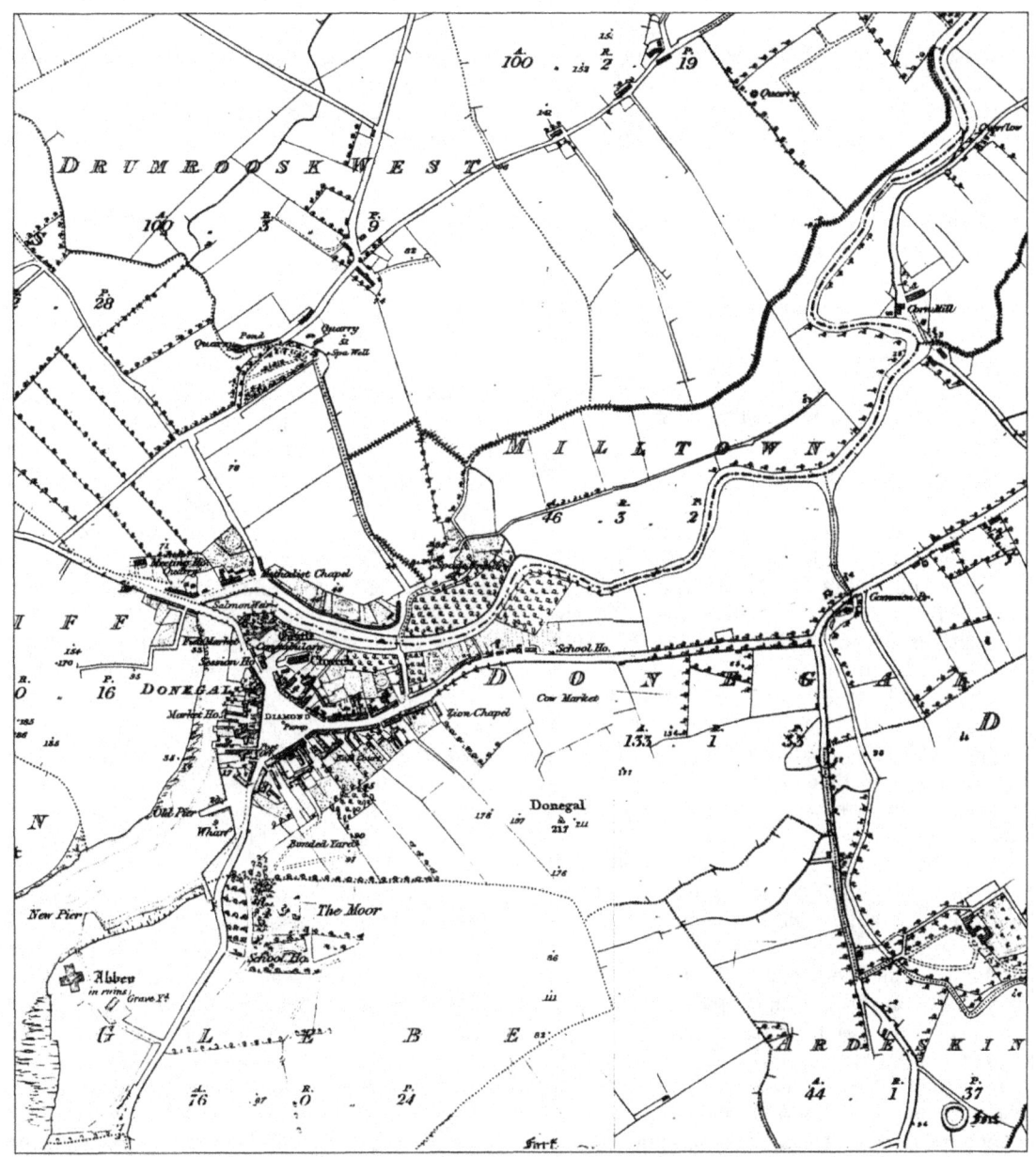

Map of Donegal town from the first 6" O.S. maps, 1830s

perches, 1 acre 10 perches in Donaghmore parish; Lough Chrohonagh, 2 acres 3 roods 32 perches; Loughnamodhu, 8 acres 8 perches, 1 acre 1 rood 2 perches in Donaghmore; Loughinnaghachola, 3 acres 1 rood 39 perches, 2 acres 3 roods 26 perches to Donaghmore and Termonamongan; Loughnaweelogue, 7 acres 17 perches, 2 acres to Termonamongan; lough no.51, 2 roods 29 perches; Loughnabrackbwee, 10 acres 12 perches; lough no.50, 3 roods 21 perches.

Coolenbuidh: Lough Golagh, 43 acres 3 roods; Lough Lughany, 4 acres 21 perches; Lough Slug, 9 acres 3 roods 2 perches; Lough Sallagh, 1 acre 12 perches; Lough Woollenleigh, 2 roods 15 perches; Lough Craig, 5 acres 3 roods 13 perches; Lough Coolenbiudh, 6 acres 36 perches.

Lower Keidue: lough no.52, 1 rood 13 perches.

Minadrin: Lough Minadrin, 1 acre 29 perches; lough [blank], 1 acre 12 perches.

Clachar: Loughatleave, 6 acres 15 perches; Lough Tahuia, 1 acre 2 roods 6 perches; lough [blank], 1 acre 2 roods 13 perches; Loughascatha, 2 acres 38 perches; Loch Lughany, 1 acre 3 roods 30 perches, part of; Lochnacairn, 32 perches, part of.

Loch Coille: part of Lough Sallagh, 9 acres 3 roods 28 perches, remnants in Drumhome; part of Coile, 1 rood 11 perches, remnants in Drumhome; part of lough no.11, 35 perches.

Lough Ray, 10 acres 3 roods 10 perches; Lough Creaghroe, 3 acres 2 roods 20 perches; Birch Hill lough, 2 acres 2 roods 30 perches.

Lough Eske, 970 acres 1 rood 2 perches, 503 acres and 32 perches in Donegal parish.

Total of water in parish, 741 acres 3 roods 27 perches; number of loughs 65, including Lough Eske.

Rivers

The principal river is the Currabla. It rises in the townland of Townawilly, about 960 feet above the sea, and, after falling over a rough and rocky bed for nearly 3 miles, it enters the Lough Eske and, at 2 and three-eighth miles, passes under a stone bridge in the townland of Corvin, where it is called the Eske and flows to the sea for 4 miles. The mouth of this river is within the tideway and is navigable for small craft to the bridge at Donegal. It is well adapted for machinery but is subject to floods in the flat ground just above the town.

The Drimminy river is a small brook which rises upwards of 1,000 feet above the sea, on the mearing of Strathnas and Leagafainne in the east of the parish, mearing with Drumhome, and flows to the west for 7 and a half miles and runs under the common bridge and, passing north of Donegal, falls into the River Eske.

The Lowerymore river flowing through Barnesmore Gap is a shallow stream. It rises in the north east mearing of Townawilly and flows over a rocky bed for 4 miles and empties itself at Corvin and Milton into Lough Eske.

The parish is well supplied with water and the streams generally flow over rough or rocky beds, and usually in a south and south west direction to the sea.

Bogs

There are considerable tracts of bog in the upper parts of Donegal parish and some fine turf banks in the valleys. The mountain bogs do not appear to contain much timber and even those in more sheltered situations have very little compared with other places. It has not been observed that the trees lie in any particular direction. The bogs appear to average 4 to 5 feet deep and in some instances they are not less than 7. Turf as an article of housekeeping is cheap in Donegal.

Woods

There are few trees in the county. Little planting has been put down and no remains of ancient forests are observable.

Coast

The bay of Donegal connected with this parish at low water is a sandy and muddy flat and is very insipid. At high tides the landscape is much improved. Cultivation is carried to high water mark but the whole, being of very low elevation, has nothing of that fine character which the coast possesses in the northern part of the country. At high water boats can land persons at any part of the shore, but at low tide in no convenient place but Donegal.

There are 2 islands in the south west of the parish, on one of which (formerly Rough Island but now St Ernan's) Mr John Hamilton has expended a considerable sum of money in building a large house and connecting the island with the mainland by a causeway. This causeway was completed in 6 weeks at an expense of 1,700 pounds. The channel of that part of the bay south of the island ran between Muckross and St Ernans.

The first attempt to turn its course and force it through a sandy bar south of the island failed and carried away the centre of the embankment. The second attempt was successful and had the effect of keeping up the water for 4 hours until the ebb tide leaving the sandy bar, the weight of water behind it opened a new channel.

Mr Hamilton has planted the island and laid it out in walks and parterres in a very ornamental manner, and the flowers, trees etc. appear to thrive extremely well.

Climate

A great deal of rain usually falls in Donegal, owing doubtless to the proximity of the Barnesmore range of mountains and its exposure to the Atlantic.

NATURAL HISTORY

Botany

No information: it has been remarked that wild flowers such as primroses, violets etc. are in pro-

Parish of Donegal

fusion around the town and in the neighbourhood of Donegal [insert note: on account of the limestone?].

Zoology

Hake, cod, ling, glassock, whiting, turbot, sole, flukes, herrings, sprats, lobsters, crabs, winkles, mussels are common in their seasons, with salmon and trout in the rivers. Foxes and badgers abound in the northern parts of the parish and hedgehogs, weasels and rats are common. Eagles are found in the Townawilly and Tyrone mountains, and kites, hawks and the usual common birds in the lowlands.

Geology

This district is composed of red granite in the Barnesmore hills, with quartz rock, quartz conglomerate, sandstone and mountain blue limestone intersected by green stone dykes descending to the sea. The limestone is the same as that of Ballyshannon and West Longfield but has fewer organic remains. Large boulders of granite containing from 30 to 40 cubic feet are constantly met with, even in the tops of the drums round Donegal. They lie between the sea and Gap of Barnes on the hills and in the valleys. These granitic stones are referred to [as] the Giants, 2 of whom are stated to have lived in the mountains of Barnes and, when disputing about a pipe they held in common and handed across the Gap, used to settle their differences by throwing stones at each other.

MODERN TOPOGRAPHY

Towns: Donegal

Donegal is 144 miles north east of Dublin, via Sligo and Longford, and is situated on the south west of the diocese of Derry and Raphoe, in the north west circuit, and parish of Donegal and province of Ulster. The town and suburbs lie at the mouth of the River Eske, on the mail road from Sligo to Londonderry, 32 miles from the former and 34 from the latter. It is nearly an equilateral triangle of 400 feet and, with its approaches, extends about 2,079 feet in the Derry and Mountcharles direction.

Its situation is very low, the buildings are generally good and have been much improved of late. The new church, the ancient castle, the river and old bridge, the green hills rising on 2 sides above the roofs of the houses, with the wharfs and shipping, give the town a respectable and varied appearance.

General History

Very little local information can be obtained on this subject. It now belongs to Lord Arran and was once held by Basil Brooke Esquire, who lived in the castle understood to have been founded by O'Donnell, the chief of Tyrconnell; see Antiquities.

Public Buildings

The new parish church was erected in 1826 by Mr Graham of Donegal and cost the parish 1,700 pounds. It is well built, of freestone, has a well-designed tower and spire, and does considerable credit to the architect. 400 persons can be accommodated in it in pews and half-gallery.

Zion chapel: The new Independent meeting house is just completed. It cost 350 pounds, can hold 200 persons in pews and side seats without galleries and is a very neat place of worship. It was designed and erected by the congregation by subscription.

The Methodist chapel is across the River Eske in Killymard parish. It was built in 1828, cost 140 pounds, can contain 130 on benches; is slated and has no gallery.

The Roman Catholic chapel is almost 2 miles from town, on the Derry road. The priest says mass in a room attached to his dwelling in the town every Sunday morning at 10 o'clock, to about 200 persons.

The Presbyterian house is in Drumhome parish, but the minister preaches occasionally in Donegal, in a room belonging to the market house.

The Seceders' place of worship is in the Killymard suburbs. It was erected in 1832, cost 300 pounds, has a house for the minister under the same roof, no gallery and can hold 250 persons in pews.

The Established Church Home Mission visits Donegal every month and a deputation from the Covenanting body once a year.

Court House

The court house was erected in 1833, cost 800 pounds. It is a plain building, freestone, accommodates the grand and petty juries, clerk of peace and office-keeper in separate rooms, having a bridewell with 12 cells in the basement storey.

Market House

The market house, now filled up for a barrack, is a substantial building consisting of 9 good rooms. It is the property of Lord Arran and was built about 45 years ago. It can accommodate 120 men.

Hotels and Inns

The principal hotel is kept by Mrs Dillon and is a large establishment, generally considered to be one of the best in this part of Ireland. It was built before the erection of the market house by Mr Devoul.

SOCIAL AND PRODUCTIVE ECONOMY

Schools

A ladies' school on a small scale, 2 schools under the Hibernian Society and the parish school at the Glebe gate, a quarter of a mile from town, are the only means afforded towards education in Donegal.

Description of Town

The town in the winter season, although the Diamond is swept every week, is far from being clean. It is partially paved and the whole is improving. No less than 6 extensive corn stores of freestone have been erected since 1825 near the wharf and a second pier head in 1833. The local jurisdictions are a manor court, which take cognizance of debts under 40s, and a quarter sessions holding by the barrister.

Markets and Fairs

Every Saturday is the Donegal market and the second Friday in every month is a fair. Grain, flax, cattle, sheep, pigs, eggs etc. are the principal traffic. No tolls are levied at present.

The town is tolerably well supplied with meat and poultry. There is a new market shambles and fish market in progress; few stall-fed cattle. The townparks let from 50s to 60s an acre, and in one or two instances the conacre ploughed and manured at 8 pounds.

Building Materials

Timber is imported from Norway and America. Freestone and lime are obtained from the adjacent country and slates from Bangor.

Insurances and Conveyances

There are 6 houses insured from fire but no life insurances made.

The public conveyances are the Derry and Sligo mails daily and an opposition day coach hence to Derry 3 times a week; a mail car to Killybegs daily and its opposition car; and a mail car to and from Ballyshannon daily. Mrs Dillon and Mr Stewart let cars and chaises and Mr McCormick post cars.

Dispensary

There is a surgeon and dispensary supported in the usual manner by private subscriptions and an annual grant from the grand jury. The number of patients relieved from the 5th January 1824 to 1835 was 1,075; the diseases for the most part being inflammation in the lungs, pneumonia, pleurites, influenza, diarrhoea, fevers, mostly of the typhoid type, constipation and dyspepsia.

Poor

There is no provision for the poor, aged or infirm, except the collections made in the public places of worship; neither have the people any public amusement.

Donegal is frequented by invalids in the summer season to drink the spa water which rises in the adjacent parish of Killymard, half a mile from town.

Parliament

Before the Union Donegal returned 2 members to parliament.

Port

Vessels require a westerly wind to enter the harbour and these winds generally prevail. There is a small bar at Dooran rock, but vessels of 400 tons can pass over it at high water. 3 of the pilots live at the Ship Ride, 2 miles from town, where vessels of 600 tons could lie in safety, 2 at Dooran rock below Mountcharles and 1 in Donegal.

There are no port dues and the pilotage is only 9d a foot in and 15d out. Vessels can load at the new pier 14 feet and the old 12 feet, which generally is sufficient for ships trading to this place.

There is no custom house but an officer is resident and a bonded yard in progress.

Imports and Exports

Timber, deals, slates, iron, flax seed, glass, coals, salt and cork are the imports, and grain the principal export, as butter, eggs and flax are generally taken overland to Derry or Strabane. The exportation of grain this last season was

6,451 quarters, all oats except 21 quarters of barley carried in 11 vessels to Gloucester, Southampton, Liverpool, London, Glasgow and Cork.

Vessels

The vessels belonging to the port are the brig *Zephyr*, 161 tons register, burden 214, now about to take passengers to America; the schooner *Susan Jane*, 85 register, 110 burden, both belonging to Messrs McDonald; and the *Blanch* schooner, 114 register and 150 burden, the property of Rankin and Co.

There is only 1 ship carpenter in town, but vessels are repaired with assistance from Derry. The people would willingly embark in a seafaring life if opportunities presented themselves.

The port is improving and it is hoped the Board of Works will give 100 pounds to buoy the harbour and otherwise advance its prosperity.

Public Buildings in the Parish

The Roman Catholic chapel, situated in the townland of Spierstown, was built in 1808, cost [blank] and can hold about 400 persons.

There is no Presbyterian place of worship in the parish: the people go to the Drumhome meeting house.

Gentlemen's Seats

The only one belongs to John Hamilton Esquire, situated in an island of 6 acres attached to Muckross formerly called Rough Island, now St Ernan's. [Insert addition: Note, Mr J.H. gave this island the name of St Ernan's from the name of a saint said to have resided in one of the neighbouring religious houses]. It was erected in 1828 (?), cost 3,500 pounds and is a commodious house handsomely fitted up with every convenience suitable to a wealthy family. The island is tastefully and judiciously laid out; fruit and flowers flourish in it, notwithstanding its great exposure; and from its natural position St Ernan's is a place well fitted for retirement.

The Glebe House, called the Moor, close to Donegal, was erected in [blank] at a cost of [blank]. It is a small square building near the town with a few fields and orchard pleasantly situated and commanding a limited view of the bay.

Bleach Greens and Mills

There are neither bleach greens or manufactories at present in the parish. A bleach green was once carried on in Clar Lough Eske. The mills are either corn or flax and are overshot, having wheels averaging 10 feet in diameter.

There are no disputes to prevent the erection of mills. They are situated as follows: Milton, Drimlecks, Clar Lough Eske, Druimcruach, Tullylusgain; 4 are corn mills, the fifth is appropriated to flax.

Communications

The mail road from Sligo to Strabane runs 11 miles through this parish and passes through the town of Donegal and Gap of Barnesmore. This road, being repaired with lime and granite, is tolerably good but might be easily made much better. Its breadth is about 35 feet and its expenses defrayed by the county.

The only 2 bridges worthy of notice are those over the Eske at Donegal and at Corvin. The latter was erected in [blank] by Mr Graham, cost [blank] pounds, and is a well-built structure of 5 arches. Donegal bridge was erected in the memory of man and is now going to be rebuilt.

A new road is in progress to Pettigo and generally the roads are not so well kept as they ought to be.

ANCIENT TOPOGRAPHY

Antiquities

Donegal Castle and the old ecclesiastical buildings to the south of the town are described on the next page.

In Ennis O'Donnell, in Lough Eske, are the remains of the foundation of a stronghold of O'Donnell. Nothing is now to be seen but the site of the building and a substantial high wall which embraces a large part of the island. The channel between the island and the main[land] is 15 feet deep. 2 old stones once belonging to the building in O'Donnell's Island are now in the wall of Mr Young's [sic] stables at Lough Eske Demesne, drawings of which will be seen in the Memoir of Killymard.

Drawings

Front elevation of Donegal Castle [showing Jacobean features, mullioned windows, towers], with dimensions of storeys; height of earlier storey [?] to top of chimney stack 39.7 feet, height of Jacobean addition 51.2 feet to top most tower.

[Detailed drawing of ornamented fireplace in Donegal Castle, giving coat of arms of the Brookes; second shield with Brooke coat of arms, scale 1 inch to 3 feet].

Donegal Castle

The fine old ruin of Donegal Castle, once the residence of the O'Donnells, the ancient chiefs of Tyrconnell, deserves particular notice. It is built at a sharp turn of the River Eske near its confluence with the sea. 2 sides of the castle are defended by the river, the others by a wall. At the entrance gate of this enclosure is a machicolated guardhouse of small dimensions.

The castle consists of an oblong keep or principal house nearly 60 feet high and stands 20 feet above the level of the river, having a wing extending to the south. The communication with the main body is through the wing close to the kitchen or hall which held the retainers of the house. You pass through a vaulted room supporting the state apartments of the castle, access to which is by a small, circular stone flight of steps. This vault is pierced with loopholes and probably was used as a chapel, and certainly was a place of considerable strength and security.

The state rooms lighted by large windows are 12 feet high and command a fine view of the abbey, the head of the harbour and all the approaches. They are now celebrated for their ancient chimney pieces, sketches of which may be seen in the *Dublin Penny magazine* for October 12th 1833. That of the chief room reaches to the ceiling and is a handsome and well-executed specimen of carving of fruit and flowers in coarse hard quartz sandstone after the fashion of James I, comprehending the arms of Brooke impaling Leicester and of Brooke only, put up about 200 years ago.

On the same floor are the remains of a doorway and a lesser chimney piece in the same style, but not so elaborately wrought. Above these were rooms occupied as dormitories for the family, whilst the wing 40 feet in height was inhabited by the servants and vassals. The angles of the keep were defended by machicolated towers about 9 feet square, one of which is in good preservation.

Carved stones are found in several parts of the building: in the machicolated towers, the circular doorway in the wing and 2 stone spouts near the large window in the gable. The stone frames of the windows are also well executed.

The roof having fallen, this ancient edifice is fast passing into decay. Its present proprietor, Lord Arran, lately restored in wood the principal window of the state room. Towards the river its walls are covered with ivy. It is now tenanted by large flights of rooks.

A very different state of things existed here 240 years ago. It was then the residence of Hugh Roe O'Donnell, the gallant and last scion of that illustrious race, the chiefs of Tyrconnell, descended from Conall Gulban, son of Niall of the Nine Hostages, monarch of Ireland. He was elected chief of his name by the different septs of the O'Donnells, O'Dohertys, O'Boyles, Macsweenys and others at the request of old Hugh O'Donnell, his father, and was inaugurated and proclaimed "the O'Donnell" on the 3rd of May 1592 (see antiquities of the adjacent parish of Killymard).

Hugh Roe is described as a person of great beauty and excelling in skill in feats of arms. After various attempts to emancipate his country from the dominion of England, in which he gained several victories, he was, with O'Neill, defeated at Kinsale on the 3rd January 1602 and, flying to Spain for assistance, died in September of the same year and was interred in the Franciscan monastery at Valladolid.

The territory of Tyrconnell being confiscated, the castle of Donegal, with 100 acres of land, fisheries, customs and duties from the castle to the sea, were granted to Captain Basil Brooke for 21 years from the 16th November 1610, afterwards for life on the 27th July 1620, and in fee for ever on the 12th February 1623. It continued in the possession of this family till [blank] and is now the property of Lord Arran.

The ground about the castle is kept as a garden and the old well about 20 feet deep was lately discovered and is now open.

Bridge

Close to the castle, and defended by it, stands the bridge, a modern structure but probably built on the site of the old one. At high tide Donegal Castle is safe from a coup-de-main from the Killymard side; at low water the river is fordable.

Donegal Abbey

Donegal is especially celebrated for the remains of its abbey, in which the Annals of the Four Masters were compiled in the 11th (?) century. A chapel, 1 or 2 gables, its cruciform foundation and a line of small circular arches, probably the remains of the cloisters, neatly and substantially executed, attest its extent and ancient respectability. No local history could be obtained. The sketch opposite shows the remnants of the east and south windows worked in compact blue limestone [drawing of windows with dimensions].

The second sketch exhibits the ruins of a modern church standing in the burial ground of the abbey, in which service was performed prior to the erection of the new one in Donegal [drawing, overall dimensions 80 by 32 feet].

2 drawings of tombs are added, 1 of the Bishop O'Gallagher of Raphoe who died in 1700, the other of Dean Marshall D.D., parish priest of Donegal [drawing of tombstones with coats of arms and other devices]. The Roman Catholics bury their dead in this graveyard.

Franciscan Friary

This ruin in Magherabeg [view of friary with dimensions, walls 30 feet high] is said to have been founded in the year 1474 by Odo Roe O'Donnell and his wife Penelope, daughter of O'Brian, Prince of Thomond.

2 sides of the rectangle in heavy, massive blue limestone are its only traces. The sketches on the other side exhibit 2 stones with devices taken from this building and preserved in St Ernan's garden [drawing of stones, showing views of beasts, 1835].

The greatest ignorance prevails with respect to these ancient religious houses, both among the gentry and peasantry, the want of which information is in some measure supplied by numerous sketches.

General Appearance and Scenery

The little town of Donegal, seen from the neighbouring rising knolls in connection with the harbour islands and bay at high tide, presents an interesting landscape. Its white spire, close to the lofty and ivy-clad keep of the ancient castle, with its river, bridge and shipping surrounded with green hills, tends materially to enliven the scene.

To the north of the parish, after a succession of small hills and fine valleys capable of yielding much produce, the country rises abruptly to the height of 1,725 feet on the west of the Gap of Barnes. The road through this chasm is extremely good, and had not this extraordinary deep ravine existed, the communication with the valley of the Finn would have been a laborious undertaking.

SOCIAL ECONOMY

Local Economy

The sea-coast and abundance of limestone are sufficient reasons for Donegal being a more prosperous place than it really is. The early settlers no doubt, from the name Dun-na-gaille, were induced to make it their place of strength from the advantages of the harbour, the lowlands in its neighbourhood and the refuge afforded in Lough Eske, the whole to the north being bounded by a lofty range of precipitous mountains.

The present race are improving fast. About 12 years ago none but the most common ploughs were used in this district and carts and drays were found only in the hands of the gentry. Through the exertions of Mr John Hamilton of St Ernan's, great improvements have been made in these matters. At present few cars are to be seen, and at the annual ploughing match of the Donegal Agricultural Society no less than from 10 to 16 iron ploughs, the property of farmers and driven with reins, usually contend for the prize.

Obstructions to Improvement

No legal disputes, ancient customs or gavelkind are met with. Run and dale have been discontinued. The principal hindrance to agricultural improvement is the prevailing habit of subdividing farms amongst a large family, leaving only perhaps from 1 to 3 acres for each child, whose numerous descendants are in consequence but half fed and not half clothed by day or night.

Local Government

There is no magistrate resident in the parish. The peace police consists of 1 sergeant and 4 men. An officer of the revenue police and 12 men are stationed in town and 1 coastguard. Petty sessions are held in the courthouse every fortnight, 3 magistrates being usually present. The crimes are of a common nature. Illicit distilling exists to a considerable extent. There are no military nearer than Ballyshannon, where infantry and cavalry are quartered.

Schools

There are 7 schools, situated in Ardaobhin, Donegal, Drumnaoil, in Muckross (2), Upper Ceide and Longafanine. One of these is the rector's school, 2 are under the Hibernian Society, 2 under the patronage of Mr John Hamilton and 1 under the Hibernian Society, teaching the Irish language.

Poor: see article Town.

Religion

The clergy are supported in the usual manner. The number of Church people are stated at [blank], Presbyterians, Seceders at [blank], Methodists at [blank], Independents at [blank], Roman Catholics at [blank].

Habits of the People

The cabins are built of stone, of 1-storey high, 2 rooms with glass windows. Some few are slated but they are generally thatched and are neither comfortable or clean. Their food is as usual potatoes, meal, milk, occasionally dry or salt fish and some meat according to their distance from absolute poverty. They have no public or national amusements or peculiar costumes.

Emigration

A few emigrate, but not so many this year as usual. Some go to England and Scotland for harvest.

Remarkable Events

The only remarkable person I have heard of connected with this parish is the woman who served on board of ship 2 or 3 years as a sailor, to whom the king has lately granted a pension of 10 pounds a year.

PRODUCTIVE ECONOMY

Spinning and Weaving

Spinning is very usual, but weaving has fallen into great neglect in this district in consequence of the decay of the linen trade. Donegal is not a cloth market and the few webs made are taken 14 miles to Stranorlar market.

Fairs and Markets

The fairs are held on the second Friday of each month, at which cattle, sheep and pigs are exhibited for sale but very few horses and those of an inferior kind. Yarn and flax is sold in abundance and all kinds of agricultural produce. The weights and measures are not yet the statute ones of the land.

Rural: Proprietors

The chief proprietors in Donegal are Lord Arran, Mr Johnston of Stranorlar, Mr J. Hamilton and Mr Crawford, the whole of whom are non-resident except Mr John Hamilton of St Ernan's. Lord Arran's agent lives near Monaghan and a deputy or overseer resides in the town. The usual size of the holdings is from 8 to 20 acres and numbers under 8 acres.

There are not many middlemen in this neighbourhood, but farmers let small portions of their lands to cottiers at exorbitant rates which are paid for generally by labour. Tenant rights are highly valued even without leases. The demand is so great for land that a farmer leaving for America can obtain for the goodwill of his place from 3 to 20 acres, not less than 10 pounds an acre, which is a common price.

Rents

The average rents vary from 10s to 30s, according to the value of the ground. The conacre is not extensively practised. The fields are generally well sized, especially near the town where quick fences prevail. There are no farms for examples to the poor nor is it believed they would profit by them did they exist, as they either have not capital to imitate their landlords or are inclined to believe it is "the weight of money" that makes their farms flourish.

Soil and Manures

The cultivated soil is cold and wet and lies generally on limestone. Seaweed is constantly used and compost for manure, when either can be had, but limestone hurts that land which lies on a calcareous substratum and seaweed binds it too much. Lime costs from 3d to 4d a barrel in town.

Implements of Husbandry

The implements of husbandry, it has been stated, have much improved these last 12 years. The slide car and wooden ploughs have given way to the Scotch ploughs and carts, and the first cartmaker established in Donegal, whom it was supposed would have soon been a bankrupt, died leaving no less than 60 orders for carts he had not time to complete. Oxen are not yet used in agriculture.

Rotation of Crops

The rotation of crops is generally thus: oats, potatoes or flax, oats and a constant repetition, to the ruin of the land.

Grazing and Cattle

There are few grass farms in this parish. Every farmer of respectability grazes a few cattle.

No improved breeds are kept. Everyone purchases the best he can get of the mixed breed found for sale in the markets.

Uses made of the Bogs

The bogs are grazed in summer and those who have none admit the cattle of their neighbours at so much per head, generally from 3s to 5s a sum [insert note: a sum means 1 beast, either a horse, ox or cow or heifer about 3 years old, and 6 sheep are equal to 1 sum]. From 3 to 6 pounds an acre are paid for permission to cut turf on bogs, tolerably convenient, but the tenants generally have leave to cut as much as they require for their own use.

Drainage: nothing has been done on a large scale. The farmers merely drain when they require it.

Plantations

There are no nurseries for young trees. The principal planting is in the townland of Upper Ceide and appears to grow tolerably well.

Sea-Coast

The seaweed is used for potato beds and is never burnt for kelp.

Fishing

There is no fishing worthy of notice connected with Donegal except the salmon-weir in the Eske river at the old castle in the town. The season commences about July and the weir, not being productive, lets for only 30 pounds a year.

General Remarks on Economy

The highest point cultivated in Donegal is in the townland of Lochcoill and the general height of the high cultivated lands about 400 feet above the sea. The lower lands afford great facilities for agricultural labour, lying on limestone hills with fine valleys and protecting each other from severe winds by reason of the general contour of that part of the country which, as already stated, is a series of elliptical knolls of low elevation. Seaweed, bog and compost are the usual manures.

The district is well watered and the port affords good security for vessels from 200 to 400 tons. The distance from the deep sea is too inconvenient for fishing speculations. The roads are well adapted to an improving district. Donegal is advancing rapidly in the scale of civilisation and during the memory of man has made very great progress.

A sea mark is about to be erected on the Dooran rock below Mountcharles, which will facilitate the making of the harbour in safety.

[Signed] William Lancey, Lieutenant Royal Engineers, 25th November 1835.

Replies by Andrew Hammond to Queries of North West Farming Society, October 1821

NATURAL STATE

Name and Locality

1. County Donegal, formerly named Tyrconnell from Connel Gulban, a descendant of Niall of the Nine Hostages, from whom the families of the O'Donnells spring.

2. Barony of Tyrhugh, from Aodha (Hugh), grandson of Cathbar, who was son to Donnell, from whom the O'Donnells took their name.

3. Parish of Donegal; Doonasarn or "fortress of ease" while under the dominion of the O'Donnell family. When this fortress was subdued by Captain Wilson, the commander of the northern division of Cromwell's army, he changed the name to Donegal or "the Protestant fortress," which name it still retains; the present incumbent, Revd William Hamilton.

PRODUCTIVE ECONOMY

Proprietors

4. Earl of Arran, non-resident, Joseph Johnston, David Crawford, John Hamilton Esquire and the diocesan schoolmaster (for the time being), resident. Earl of Arran's estate has 41 townlands, consisting of 2,316 acres of arable and 1,872 acres of mountain and bog. College manor, of which Joseph Johnston, David Crawford and John Johnston are proprietors, has in it 23 townlands, consisting of 2,974 acres of arable and 1,680 acres of mountain and bog. The diocesan schoolmaster of Raphoe is proprietor of the school lands of Townawilly. It has 12 townlands, consisting of 1,437 acres of arable and 5,390 acres of mountain and bog.

Farmers and Agricultural Methods

5. Farms are from 4 to 30 acres, enclosed with neat sod ditches. Those who have large farms cultivate them with the plough. The small farms are spaded. The opulent farmer, in consequence of his abundance of stock, amasses great quantities of stable and byre dung, and their manner of using it is so well known that it needs no comment. The

second class of farmers draw mud, with which they mix their summer manure and, by adding lime clay etc., are enabled to cultivate their farms much the same as the first class.

The third class of farmers, who perhaps have but one cow and are necessitated to sell their hay to pay their rent and their straw to pay the debts contracted for provisions, draws (if he has a horse) or carries mud, and by putting a quantity of it in the group of his little byre, every second night it is converted into good manure by the urine of his cow. What he cannot rot in this way he deposits in a shugh of standing water made for the purpose and, by adding stubble, rushes etc., he is thereby enabled to set a good quantity of potatoes. He does not spread the manure under the seed but kibs or prabbins them.

Kibbing is done 2 ways: the first method was to make a hole in the ground with a stick made for the purpose and drop the seed in it. But a better way is found out: the man digs fine shallow marks with his spade, in which the dropper deposits the seed. He then digs 5 more and throws the clay off the spade on the seed already dropped and so on till the dale is finished. When the fibres of the seed shoot forth (which could not extend so well otherwise), the manure is spread as thin as possible, set lightly, dressed neatly, and by shovelling heavily a good crop is expected.

Some neither set or kib but prabbin their potatoes: their method is as follows. The labourer trenches his dale in winter exactly the breadth of potato ridges. In spring he digs it down, leaving the former shugh (or furrow) for the middle of the ridge. After the ground is made level and harrowed or raked fine, the man agrees with a rich neighbour who must have 4 days' work for 1 of his horse and car. The poor man spends no idle time and the 1 day is nearly sufficient to get the manure to the middle of the dale.

He then makes the ridges as straight as possible and has a shallow creel which he slings over his right shoulder with a hay or straw rope, and it rests on the hollow of his left thigh. This creel he fills with manure and, as his little son or daughter drops the seed at a regular distance, he throws a handful of the manure upon the seed. This is called prabbing which, being set and shovelled the same as kibbing, potatoes produce a most excellent crop.

Improvements in Agriculture

As I am fully convinced that the North West Society have in contemplation the improvement of agriculture and bettering the condition of the poor, I shall only mention the exertions of poor farmers; and as I have begun the world in a farm of 8 acres without much stock, I am well acquainted with the progress which (by the blessing of providence) attend industry. The poor farmer, if he does right, sets his potatoes twice in the same dale. It will then produce a good crop of barley, and barley leavings produces by far the best flax; and good potatoes and flax ought to be the chief object of the poor man.

Crops

The regular succession of crops in cultivated ground ought to be 1st potatoes, 2nd barley, 3rd flax and then oats, hinting the ground and then shovelling the hintings neatly. The only improvement I have known is this: when there is an intention of letting it to grass by lightly scattering lime over the hinted ridges after the seed is sowed and before the hintings are shovelled, it will make a very great improvement in the grass. 20 barrels of lime, 32 gallons to the barrel, will be quite sufficient for an acre.

Cultivation

6. Poor farmers have their farms divided into parks of about 2 acres each, which they cultivate alternately. The general method is as follows: they open their ridges for the plough by coping, [which] is backing 2 sods of about 9 inches in breadth in a straight line from one end of the field to the other. These sods must be nicked only on the one side, which must close and form the centre of the ridge about 9 feet wide. This has a most beautiful appearance before the plough begins.

When the field is ploughed, it is found best to hint but not to break in the ground before the seed is sowed. After harrowing the field up and down, then shovel the hintings carefully and finish with the spade. NB Lea ground should be sowed thicker than cultivated ground.

24 stone of 14 lbs will be sufficient for an acre, plantation measure. This field will give 2 crops of oats before it requires manure, then, by taking only 1 crop of barley or oats after potatoes, it improves the soil every way and is certain of producing excellent pasture.

NATURAL FEATURES

Mountains

7. The principal mountains are Barnesmore whose stupendous height is truly astonishing,

Parish of Donegal

being little inferior to the Alps. The highest parts of the mountains are distinguished by the name of "croaghs," viz. Croagh Connalaih or "Connal's mount," Croagh Owenach or Owen's mount." These mounts were named after the proprietors of both counties: Tyrconnal (Donegal) or "Connal's country;" Tyr-Owen (Tyrone) or "Owen's country." These croaghs form Barn's Gap, through which the road leads from Donegal to Derry.

There is another gap through which the road leads to Killeter called Barn's O'Neally or "O'Neill's mountain," known by the name of Croagh Garrow or "the rough mount," Croagh Meen or "the smooth mount," with many others. These mounts are not cultivated but afford excellent pasture for sheep and young cattle.

Bogs

8. The principal bogs are Morismanon or "all turf," Tinny Cahil or "Cahel's fire," Clocher or "the stony bog" and Fien Dooh or "the black bog." There has been found abundance of oak and timber and blocks within 3 feet of the surface.

PRODUCTIVE ECONOMY

Plantations and Woods

9. There are several orchards in this parish but there is neither plantation nor nursery, which is a very great loss to the tenantry. If nurseries were encouraged by landowners and fruit and forest trees, hawthorns etc. given to the tenantry at a low price or gratuitously, it would enable the poor man to have regular and decent fences, pleasant gardens and would cause his hamlet to bear a respectable appearance, which is not the case at present in many places.

10. Every species of trees thrives well, but in general the alder, sycamore and ash thrive best.

Rents and Farms

11. Within the limits of the corporation the highest arable rent is from 2 pounds 10s to 4 pounds 10s per acre. In other parts land of the best quality sets from 1 pound to 1 pound 5s, middling from 12s 6d to 17s 6d and inferior from 7s 6d to 10s 6d, moory pasture from 2s 6d to 5s 6d and the highest 7s 6d per acre.

12. Turf bogs are in some places set at from 2 pounds to 4 pounds per acre; from a rood to half an acre is generally what is so taken. The tenantry of the Earl of Arran's estate pay no rent for their bogs, only at the rate of 1s per rood by way of trespass, as the mountain bogs are commonly grazed upon.

Enclosures

13. There is some improvement in tillage and enclosures. Formerly the farmer used to cultivate the most convenient part of his farm and enclose it whether regular or not. Now the farms are enclosed in neat parks of about 2 acres with straight regular ditches. The fences are for the most part furze mixed with broom which afford great shelter, but as yet there has been no improvement in the implements of husbandry. The old-fashioned plough, harrow and spade are the only farming utensils in use in these parts.

Fences

14. Single-sod ditches are now in use, sowed on the top with whin and broom seeds as already described, but the fence which I would recommend would be narrow double ditches, quicked with hawthorn on each side near the surface of the ground and on the top, alder, sycamore or ash. Alder would be preferable to any other description of trees in marshy ground.

Employment and Wages

15. Employment is more abundant in spring and harvest than in any other part of the year. What I would suggest as giving general employment would be reclaiming mountains as far as would be practicable, wherein thousands of acres could easily be made to become good arable meadow and pasture.

16. Good servant boys get 2 guineas for their half-year labour and middling boys 1 pound 10s; labourers 10d a day and their diet in spring and harvest.

Green Crops and Grasses

17. Green crops are not generally cultivated as they tend to impoverish the ground and not so good for pasture or meadow as the grass which grows naturally.

18. Artificial grasses are grown in some places, which are rye grass and what is called in these parts white grass.

Draining and Manures

19. Draining by surface is found to be the best method in some instances. Underdraining is used on particular occasions when it is found necessary.

20. Burning sods was the former practice of poor farmers. Their manner was to throw up the ground in nearly the breadth of potato ridges, then burn the sods in large fires, afterwards spread the ashes on the lea and set the potatoes, but the lime and clay is found to answer much better; see 6th query.

21. [Irrigation] In many parts the meadows have been watered, which answers in some particular cases.

Dairies

22. Every farmer's house is a dairy. There are none at present established in these parts.

Use of Oxen

23. Oxen are not used in husbandry, nor does it appear that it ever was the case in these parts.

Spade Husbandry

24. Spading is much in use. The ground is trenched in the winter about 4 feet broad and the shughs shovelled. These ridges are only dug down in spring and produce an excellent crop of oats or flax, as trenching this way effectually banishes annual weeds.

Grain Crops

25. Barley, potato oats and blanter are the only descriptions of grain sown in these parts. Barley and good oats are sold at 1s per stone and potatoes at 3d per stone of 14 lbs. Provisions are in general cheap.

Unit of Measurement

26. Earl of Arran's estate is measured according to the Irish plantation measure, most of the other estates according to the English acre.

Livestock

27. There has been a considerable improvement in the breed of black cattle, in consequence of some gentlemen having good bulls to whom the farmers have access with their cows, by which means the farmers are in the habit of rearing black cattle of a good description.

29. There has not been much improvement in sheep. As the large sheep are not at all adapted to the mountain grazing, their breeds not much desired.

30. There has been of late a great improvement in the breed of horses. The draft kind are most in use for agricultural purposes.

31. The swine are not improved, chiefly owing to the great number of ill-fed breeding sows which poor people keep, who generally sell their pigs from 2s 6d to to 3s 4d apiece, which has utterly destroyed their size, shape and general appearance.

Improvements in Stock

32. The farmer who occupies 4 acres generally keeps 1 cow, and so on in proportion to the size of the farm: 12 acres 3 [cows], 16 acres 4 cows; no farmer with less than 20 acres keeps 2 horses. As the sheep finds pasture on the mountains from April till October, there is no fixed rule respecting them. Every farmer keeps as many sheep as he thinks proper. If farmers would keep an enclosure of 1 rood and sow clover, he would thereby be enabled to keep an additional cow.

33. [Breeding] Horses and black cattle are greatly improved; sheep a little but swine much worse than they were 20 years ago; see query 31.

NATURAL FEATURES

Rivers

34. Townawilly, Eske and Drimminny are the only rivers of note in this parish.

Townawilly river rises in the mountains east of Croagh Connalagh and runs due south 3 miles, separating the parishes of Donegal and Stranorlar, then turns at the foot of Croagh Onagh and runs due west for 4 miles, then turns again and runs due north for 1 mile and empties itself in Lough Eske. The circuitous course of this river encloses 3 sides of the school lands of Townawilly, composing a tract of arable and mountain, consisting of 1,437 acres of arable and 5,390 acres of mountain and bog.

Eske is the next river. It leaves Lough Eske and runs due west, separating the parishes of Donegal and Killymard.

Drimminny river rises on the mountains near Croagh Garrow, runs due west for 2 miles then changes its course to west by north for a mile and a half, then turns west again and runs in that direction 1 and a half miles, separating Earl of Arran's estate from the college manor, turns again and runs north for half a mile, intersects the great road from Donegal to Derry, joins in conflux with the River Eske and both rivers thus form the channel of Donegal Bay which joins the western ocean.

Loughs

The only loughs of note are Eske, Tomlough, Lough Shig and Lough Leheny. Eske is well

Parish of Donegal

stored with salmon, trouts and charr. The other loughs are well stored with a species of trout called sainaghans. Donegal Bay is an excellent harbour for shipping which often produces herrings, cod, ling and glassan, and as the bay is due west of Donegal, the northern and southern shores produce abundance of sea manure which is peculiarly serviceable to farmers.

PRODUCTIVE ECONOMY AND NATURAL HISTORY

Mines

35. The torn and convulsed state of Barnesmore bespeaks some powerful effort of nature, in the strata of which such materials may constitute a cause. The layers of strata which are to be met with in this immense pile nearly 1,000 feet high are from granite to that of a coal formation on its side. This (I will venture to say) is as little known to speculators as that of Africa. The Earl of Arran sent a mine agent to view it and make an experiment, but the speculation was thought to be too expensive and the work was abandoned altogether.

Quarries

36. There are excellent freestone quarries [?] easily cut and very convenient, as they are near the main road.

37. There are several limestone quarries. The stone is of a beautiful blue colour, of a flinty nature and, when burned, is extremely white. 25 back-loads of peat will burn a ton weight of limestone, which will produce upwards of 50 barrels of slack lime.

Coal

38. Some coal has been found in the place already alluded to, in an argillaceous schistus of an inferior quality, and their better seams might be lower.

Mineral Springs

39. Several mineral springs have been found, both sulphureous and nitrous. They have been peculiarly useful in ulcerous and scorbutic disorders, and prejudicial only in pulmonic and consumptive cases.

Marl

40. Marl has been discovered, both of a calcareous and argillaceous kind; but in consequence of the difficulty of raising it, it has not been much used. The calcareous marl has been found useful when spread upon dry ground.

SOCIAL ECONOMY

Condition of the People

41. Although the inhabitants in general cannot boast much wealth, yet their domestic comforts are many. First, they are taught by the Gospel to provide things honest in the sight of all man; secondly, they are for the most part disposed to industry and economy. The only means which most of the farmers have of earning money is by the sales of the produce of their farms, such as barley, oats, oatmeal, butter and yarn. This they supply in paying their rent, taxes and debts, and if they have any to spare, they clothe themselves and their families.

Houses and Fuel

42. The houses are for the most part very neat, the limestone and turf being plenty. The farmers and cottagers in general whitewash them annually, particularly since the time that the typhus fever raged in this country.

In some cabins they have their bedsteads whitewashed with lime, water, and in most places the neighbours vie with each other in keeping their houses in repair. In some cases the landholder gives the poor tenants lime gratuitously, which serve as a stimulus to their exertions to cleanliness and decency.

43. The fuel is turf (peat), which are so plenty that tradesmen and labourers can buy them for 2d per load and a stack of 120 loads for 10s.

Food

44. The general food of the farming class of inhabitants is potatoes, bread, butter, milk, eggs and fish. Sometimes they have fleshmeat, which is considered a luxury. I have many times witnessed the domestic comforts of the poor farmer's table, consisting of potatoes, bread, butter and good milk, the bountiful donation of an all gracious God, in the participation of which great thankfulness was shown and more real happiness enjoyed than the children of luxury can possibly have an idea of.

45. The manufacturing class in general use more tea, fish, fleshmeat than the farmer, as they seldom keep any cows.

46. The labouring class can live as comfortable as the poor farmers, who are generally reduced in circumstances in consequence of high

Education

47. There is a general wish for education in *all* classes, and parents who are illiterate themselves embrace every opportunity of reaping its advantages by sending their children to school to receive instruction; and I am happy at being able to state that the blessing of education is not confined to one description more than another but all are partakers of the general good.

Cost of Education

48. The expense of education is now solely confined to the wealthy who send their children to a pay school. The children of the poor are all taught gratuitously and found in books, stationery, slates and pencils. There are 9 schools in this parish, including 1 female school, 1 parish school under Colonel Robertson's establishment, 2 pay schools, 2 Education Society free schools, 3 London Hibernian free schools and 1 female contribution school.

In these schools there are at present 156 pupils. Their classification etc. are as follows: in the alphabet class 65, spelling class 121, reading class 180, writing class 113, arithmetic class 73, making a total of 156. [Insert additional figures: males 317, females 239, [total] 552 [sic], Protestants 314, Roman Catholics 242]. Such are the blessed effects of the exertions of those benevolent societies established for promoting education and disseminating the Gospel.

Improvements

49. The difference is very observable in the state of the peasantry. Formerly the children of the poor were either strangers to education: now we behold the blessings of education, of cleanliness, of decency, of regularity and, above all, the glorious light of the Gospel of Our Lord, spreading their united influence over their native land. And it is a cause of great rejoicing to me to behold many worthy characters among the high and great who are anxious to promote the good cause and whose anxiety proceed from the true principle of good, namely that of love to God and a desire of bringing glory to His name.

Health

50. The inhabitants of this parish are at present healthy.

Friendly Societies

51. I regret to have to state that there are no friendly societies of any kind established here for bettering the situation of the poor.

MODERN TOPOGRAPHY AND PRODUCTIVE ECONOMY

Towns and Villages

52. Donegal is the only town in the parish. The villages are Stinsons, Clarr, Binlards, Clar Lough Eske, Drimbarren, Drimlaught and Townawilly.

Improvement: Premiums

53. The people in general have a turn for improvement, and in my opinion a small premium would greatly tend even to stimulate an industrious man to increasing exertion, such as a small sum of money by way of premium, a car, a plough, a harrow, a box barrow or even a spade. A few fruit or forest trees, hawthorns or any acknowledgment would not fail to encourage honest industry.

Practical Farmers

54. The farms to whom I would direct the attention of the North West Society as being active and skilful, and improving their several farms, are James Crawford Esquire, Donegal, Charles Dillon Esquire, Donegal and Andrew Hammond, Drumrat House near Donegal who, I am certain, will feel pleasure in communicating every possible information in their power.

PRODUCTIVE ECONOMY

Manufactures

55. The manufacture of linen is increasing in these parts.

56. There are only 2 mills connected with it in this parish.

Flax

57. The land is first ploughed and harrowed fine early in the season, afterwards ploughed and harrowed a second time, then the seed sowed and, if the ground is dry, a little lime is thinly scattered over the field. About 4 barrels to the rood is quite sufficient. Flax generally succeeds barley and is consumed in home manufacture. Seed is seldom saved.

58. Flax is sometimes prepared by mills but most by manual labour. Fire is always used in preparing it.

Yarn

59. Yarn is spun from 3 to 5 hanks yarn. A good spinner can earn about 2s a day.

60. Good coarse yarn sells from 1s 10d to 2s 2d per spangle, fine yarn from 1s 8d to 2s 2d per spangle. Some is used for home manufacture and some is sold for exportation.

61. Spinners in general grow their own flax.

62. A double wheel for spinning with both hands has not as yet been introduced in this neighbourhood.

63. Most manufacturers has the warp spun at home, purchases the weft in the market and prepares it himself. 12 lbs of [blank] and 2 lbs of soap is sufficient for boiling what yarn does a half web.

Yarn Greens and Webs

64. There are no yarn greens in this neighbourhood. The establishing of such greens would undoubtedly have the effect of facilitating and improving the manufacture.

65. Hall webs are manufactured in this neighbourhood. The set is from 10 and 3 to 13, price from 11d to 1s 3d. The markets: Stranorlar and Strabane.

Wool

66. There are no woollen manufactures in this neighbourhood.

67. Neither are there any wool staplers or sorters.

68. The wool is spun on the small wheel, but should a farmer's wife manufacture flannel for market, that spun on the large wheel would have the preference.

69. Some females knit stockings for those who may employ them, at which they earn about 3d a day, but there are none knit for sale in these parts.

70. Farmers used to practise shearing their sheep twice a year, but it was found not to answer and consequently is dropped altogether.

Cotton

71. There is very little cotton manufactured in this neighbourhood.

72. The description of what has been manufactured occasionally are gowns and petticoats which farmers' wives get wrought for their families.

Kelp

73. Kelp is manufactured in this neighbourhood.

74. Much improvement has been lately introduced in making it and, if encouraged, the manufacture could be extended, which would prove very lucrative.

75. The manufacturers who, in conjunction with others, are of ability to manufacture from 30 to 40 tons send their kelp to Liverpool and sometimes to Scotland. Others sell it to merchants at home. The common price is from 4s 6d to 5s 5d per cwt.

Fisheries

76. Herring and whitefish are the only kind of fisheries in these parts.

77. About 40 boats are usually employed in the fishery. They are not decked and are of about 4 tons burthen.

78. Herrings, cod, glassan, ling, whiting, mackerel are sometimes in great abundance. Fishermen often go 3 leagues to sea for whitefish, but herrings must be taken in the bay.

79. At a good fishing from 200 to 250 men are usually employed.

80. Fish are seldom cured for distant markets. Markets at 30 miles distance are supplied from our coast, viz. Derry, Strabane, Omagh, Enniskillen and the several towns within that extensive circle.

Improvements in Fisheries

81. The probability of improving the fisheries in these parts appears to me to be very uncertain. First, with respect to the herring fishery, and as it relates to codfish, ling, there being no banks such as Newfoundland, their settled situation must of course be kept precarious.

Composition of Memoir

However, as in all my answers I have only described what has come within my own knowledge, I shall be ever ready to submit to the superior judgement of others in their comments upon fisheries, manufactories and agriculture. [Signed] Andrew Hammond, 1st October 1821.

Parish of Drumhome, County Donegal

Note on Temple McMillighan by Lieutenant W. Lancey, December 1835

Ancient Topography

Temple McMillighan

The ruin of Temple McMillighan is situated near the boundary of West Trummon. It is said to have been erected at the same date with the castle of Donegal and its name is derived from McMillighan, a builder in the south who, hearing of the erection of Donegal Castle, proceeded with his men to the spot and made an unsuccessful application for employment, being supposed to be inexperienced.

It is said he left Donegal and at West Trummon, in order to show his skill, erected the shell of this building since called Temple McMillighan, which never was roofed. A sketch is added [signed] William Lancey, Lieutenant Royal Engineers, 30th December 1835. Requested to be added to the Memoir of the parish, [addressed to] Lieutenant Larcom.

East view of Temple McMillighan, situated in West Trummon near the western boundary [with dimensions of doorway, overall dimensions 24 feet 5 inches by 24 feet].

Answers to Queries of North West Farming Society

Natural State and Productive Economy

Situation and Proprietors

1st, Donegal; 2nd, barony of Tyrhugh <Tyragh>; 3rd, Drumhome; Robert Ball, clerk vicar.

4th. [Proprietors] Conolly, now Pakenham; Hamilton minors, Brownhall; Colonel Knox, Prehen <Preken>; John Hamilton, Coxtown; Joseph Johnson, Summerhill, Stranorlar.

Farms and Manures

5th. The farms average in general from 6 to 20 acres, enclosures marked by clay ditches very bad. The greater part of the parish not more than 4 miles from the sea, from whence they draw seaweed called leagh that detaches itself from foul grounds in the bay at certain seasons and is at other times forced off by high winds from the westward, by which large quantities are thrown in on the strand of Upper and Lower Murvagh, a space of 3 miles. The former strand belongs to the Glebe, the latter to the minors of Brownhall.

The farmers, either in person or with their several boys, attend by permission from proprietors with cars sometimes amounting to 200 and carry it away to their dunghills, and form a compost of lime, mud and seaweed which gives them a fine crop of potatoes, 1 of barley and 1 of oats.

Rotation of Crops

If the lands be new it will carry flax after the oats, but if long under tillage the plant of the flax is overpowered with weeds. The greatest improvement that could be introduced would be to have part of the farm under green crop, but the farms in general are too small and the occupiers cannot afford any portion to rest, and likewise there has been a custom, time immemorial, for the sheep of each townland to range at large as soon as the crop is taken off the grounds; and where there are no fences, this is an absolute bar to the cultivation of green crops.

I have a tenant who had little or no pastureland. I persuaded him to fence in a small garden and to sow clover, and from this he was enabled to feed a horse and cow and bedded them with sea-sand during summer. By the addition of the seaweed he collected he was enabled the next spring to plant 1 acre and half of potatoes and felt satisfied of deriving great benefit in the succeeding crops from the increased strength of the manure.

Grazing and Rabbits

6th. Pasture-lands are best for sheep in the neighbourhood of the town of Ballintra, where there is a light soil with limestone on the surface. Mr Hamilton of Coxtown holds the principal grazing farms in his hands, on which he feeds and breeds black cattle and sheep.

He holds a large rabbit warren from the minors of Brownhall, 300 acres, formerly very valuable pasturage but at present much injured by blowing sands. He generally kills 300 dozen of rabbits annually. Price now of skins from 6s to 7s per dozen. There is likewise a rabbit warren on the Glebe. I kill on an average about 150 dozen yearly. There is another warren in the parish, on the confines of Kilbarron, called Rossnoughlagh,

Parish of Drumhome

where are killed about 200 dozen annually on the Pakenham property.

Mountains

7th. The whole parish is mountainous except the space of 2 miles and a half in breadth and 6 miles and a half in length which runs along the sea-coast from the parish of Kilbarron to the parish of Donegal. This district has a level appearance as it is highly cultivated and is formed of small hills or hillocks with interjacent flats, in many of which are small lakes abounding with pike and roach.

The names of mountains are Fenmore, Owenbuy <Owenbery>, Croukagapple, Oughnadarnod, Shannagh and Meenacurreen and Copany. They are all pasturable and, from what I have observed in other parts of Donegal and Tyrone, few of them so high as to be within the region of cold fog inimical to the filling and ripening of grain.

Bogs and Moors

8th. Principal bogs and moors on the properties of Pakenham and Hamilton minor, and John Hamilton, Coxtown, and Joseph Johnson. Very fine timber found in the mountain bogs called bog firs; some sticks so large as to measure 2 tons. When planed it is fine in the grain and has the appearance of satin wood of a dark reddish colour. The farmers joist their floors with them and cut them into planks for boarding them. They generally lie from 8 to 10 feet below the surface of the ground.

In the district adjoining the sea there are old cut-out bogs where, with little difficulty, about 4 to 6 feet under the surface, they find roots of bog fir which is cut into bog wood, and from the quantity of turpentine contained in it, makes so good a light that they are enabled to spin by it in the farmers' houses at night.

Woods and Plantations

9th. No woods except at Brownhall. Most of the better kind of farmers in general have a small orchard stocked principally with apple trees; no nurseries.

Plantations: some at Brownhall and at Mr Hamilton's, Coxtown. At both places they thrive well. I have attempted to plant on the Glebe but, from proximity to the sea blast, they rather exist than thrive, except in a very few spots.

10th. [Thriving trees] Scotch fir, alder, beech, sycamore, timber, sally and poplar.

PRODUCTIVE ECONOMY

Rents

11th. I think from a guinea to 30s an acre is nearly the acreable rent of the district bordering the sea-shore. The rents on the Pakenham estates have been reduced one-fifth upon all leases made since a certain period. The rents of the remaining portion of the parish, which is mostly arable, green and moory pasture, average at from 15s to 18s per acre.

Charge for Turf

12th. The tenants who hold under the Pakenhams and Hamiltons pay nothing for turf bog, but Colonel Knox's tenantry, when they rent bog pay at the rate of 4 guineas per acre. The tenants on my glebe are allowed to cut their turf on the Pakenham property, as a remuneration for which they carry their grindable grain to a mill on the above property.

Improvements in Farming

13th. The principal improvement I observe in their farming is their improved use of the seaweed for manure. A few years since they laid it in ridges on the land and, after from 1 to 3 months, planted their potatoes. The consequence was their clay ground, naturally stiff, when they came to sow the following crop was so bound together that they were obliged to break it with flax breaks to render it fit for the seed. But now they gather their seaweed when opportunity offers, draw it to their potato ground and there mix it with bog, mud or clay, turn it over before spring and add a quantity of sea-sand or lime. From this process they derive great advantage in their succeeding crops.

Enclosures and Fences

[14th]. They have hardly any enclosures in their farms. Their crops are in dales and, where they have a patch of grass, they are obliged to put a herd's boy to watch their cow or horses.

The fences in the neighbourhood of Ballintra are mostly made of loose stones of a sufficient height to keep out sheep, broad at the base and ending with one stone on the top. In the country in general the fences are insufficient; ditches not of use to keep off any beast, which renders a herd-boy necessary in all cases.

The fences at present in use do not answer any purpose. In my opinion a good sufficient ditch well quicked would answer best.

Implements of Husbandry

The implements of husbandry are the Irish plough and small harrow and common cars with solid wheels. Some of the better description of farmers use carts and the improved cars with spoke wheels.

Employment

15th. There is nothing so much wanted as employment for the labouring poor. A farmer, who formerly employed 3 or 4 labourers, now contrives to steal in his harvest with 1 servant boy and the assistance of his family, consequently often suffering a great loss in his grain from not taking advantage of good weather in broken seasons.

The want of employment prevails at all seasons. I know nothing could remedy the evil but the expenditure of government money for public works, in forming embankments on arms of the sea to keep out the tide, whereby several hundred of acres could be brought into cultivation, now useless except for feeding a few straggling sheep.

An embankment was made on one of those arms by one of the Knox family. It answered the purpose for many years but from neglect it was carried away. From recent improvements in such works, I have no doubt they could be made permanent and effectual.

Wages

16th. A servant boy who lives in the farmer's house has 2 pounds 10s for half-year, the usual term time. Mowing is the only task work, about 4s 6d per acre. A common labourer is well satisfied with 8d a day and constant employment.

Green Crops

17th. In a very few places, owing to the winter pasturage of the sheep. Mr Millar, Ballintra, has 2 acres of clover and perennial rye grass. I have the same quantity.

18th. [Artificial grasses] No.

Drainage

19th. Very little draining attempted, in which case they make a very insufficient surface drain which, in a short time, fills up and increases the evil. Mr Hamilton of Coxtown and I have made a considerable extent of French or underdrains this year.

Burning for Manure

20th. Seaweed mixed with cow-house and stable dung, and mud with lime or sea-sand, form a compost scattered in small heaps through their potato land for the convenience of scattering in spring.

In the mountain skirts a considerable quantity of ground is burned every year. They score the ground early in spring into 6 feet ridges, allow the sods to remain until the first dry weather in spring, when they burn the ashes in heaps, scatter them and plant. The potatoes, being soft and juicy, answer well for seed, especially when brought to the low district. They afterwards sow a crop of oats and then let it out for grass, which it produces of a very improved quality.

21st. [Irrigation] No, nor have they many opportunities.

Farm Techniques

22nd. [Dairies] None.

23rd. [Oxen] No.

24th. [Spade husbandry] I have myself made use of it and I found it answered the purpose as well as ploughing. It takes from 20 to 30 men to dig an acre, according to the state it is in.

Grain Crops

25th. Wheat in small quantities by Mr John Hamilton, Mr Millar and myself. The climate and soil seem to suit it peculiarly well. I have grown on my glebe as fine a grain of wheat as I have ever seen. It does well after flax and limed.

No sale for wheat. Barley 1s per stone bought by the private distillers and fluctuates in price with the exertions of the gaugers. Oats middling in general, from want of renewal of seeds. I brought some Holland oats from Dublin and exchanged the produce of it with my neighbours for horse corn. The difference between the produce of this seed and the common oat of the country was very remarkable.

26th. [Unit of measurement] The Pakenham property by the Irish acre, all other lands by the English.

Livestock

27th. They are but indifferent from the want of good bulls. I think the introduction of a few good bulls would improve the breed of black cattle, as the farmers of this parish are in the habit of attending the fairs in Connaught and bring many good cows from thence.

28th. Sheep and black cattle from yearlings to 4 years old.

29th. In general, they are a bad description of Irish mountain sheep, but the landholders in the neighbourhood of Ballintra buy good sheep of a mixed breed, half English, half Irish, in Connaught, take the wool off them and sell them about November.

30th. A very bad animal 3 or 4 removes from some inferior blood horse. There is not a sire fit to give any mare to within 20 miles of this parish; 2 or 3 would be most useful.

31st. [Swine] Nothing but the common breed.

32nd. [Quantity of stock] I cannot ascertain.

33rd. [Improvements in breeding] None; I think they have within these 4 years deteriorated.

Rivers

34th. 3 small ones. Brownhall and Ballybulgan: these form a confluence near the sea and there is a small salmon fishery on them. The other river is called Tullygallon. Source of Brownhall river, Lough Ragh. Ballybulgan source, Lough Dowlagh-more, within 2 miles of Lough Derg. Tullygallon source, Owenbuy mountain from several small streams.

Mines and Minerals

35th. [Mines] None.

36th. Limestone and a freestone quarry at the village of Ballinakillew about 2 miles from Mullinasollis, where sloops of 100 tons burthen bring sea-coal and rock-salt to 2 saltworks, one worked by Mr John Hamilton, the other by a Widow Montgomery.

37th. Limestone in great abundance in almost every part of the parish, except immediately on the sea-coast, blue in colour and burned in general in small sod kilns except one built by Mr Hamilton, of lime and stone and of improved construction, burned with turf; price about 4d per barrel.

38th. [Coal] None.

Mineral Springs and Marl

39th. One of a sulphureous quality, component parts nitre and sulphur, very much resembling in taste the Donegal and Lucan spa but not so strong; has fallen into disuse.

40th. [Marl] In many places but not used, calcareous.

SOCIAL ECONOMY

Condition of the People

41st. In general they live comfortably except the labouring poor. They are in general industrious, supported principally by the yarn and linen, and occasionally by fishing.

Houses and Fuel

42nd. In general the farmhouses are in good repair, cleanly and have every comfort.

43rd. Turf plenty but distant. About 35s to 40s per hundred when at home. A hundred and half an average consumption for each farmhouse. A hundred is 24 car-loads of 5 measures to the gauge <cage>.

Food

44th. [Farmers] Oatmeal and potatoes and milk; meat occasionally, not used as generally as formerly.

45th. [Manufacturing class] No such description distinct from farming class.

46th. [Labourers] Potatoes, milk, fresh and dried fish.

Education

47th. A general wish for learning. The poorest labourers' children can read. Does not appear confined to any description.

48th. 18d a quarter each scholar; but there are 6 Hibernian schools where they are educated gratuitously and 4 schools on the Pakenham property, the schoolmasters of which schools receive 5 pounds per annum. The schoolmasters are under an obligation to charge only 5d per quarter each scholar. There are besides 11 Sunday schools, where they are taught gratis on Sundays, and 15 pay schools.

49th. [Improvements] A very marked one: the yeomanry and peasantry are by far the most civilised and most obedient to the laws I have ever met.

Health

50th. Deaths very few, considering the population. Rheumatism and occasional typhus the prevalent complaints.

Friendly Societies

51st. A dispensary, a very useful institution.

Towns

52nd. Ballintra, Laghey, Lackan and Ballinakillew and Mullinasollis.

Improvements

53rd. I think in general they have a spirit for improvement. How it would be best excited I do not feel myself adequate to advise.

54th. [Practical farmers] Mr Hamilton, Coxtown; Mr Millar, Ballintra; Mr Coghran, Ballymagrorty; Mr George Thompson, Drumhome; Mr John Cobourn, Ballymagrorty.

Productive Economy

Manufactures

55th. [Linen manufacture] Increasing.

56th. 6 scutch mills, of very bad description and defective machinery.

Flax

57th. They generally plough the land twice which has had a crop of potatoes, barley and oats, and sow their flax so late as the 12th of May. This lateness of sowing flax is caused by the people of this neighbourhood waiting to purchase their flax seed at a fair held in Donegal on the 5th of May, where it is brought to from Derry. If a cargo or two were brought to Ballyshannon or Donegal at an earlier time in spring, it would greatly benefit this neighbourhood as flax sown late never has the same produce as what is sown about the 20th of April.

The farmer and grower generally put it through all the necessary processes of watering, spreading, drying, bleaching and scutching, either at the mills or by hand, scutching at home and spins it at home, either by the family or servant maids, and makes it into linen either by his son or journeyman or self. No seed saved except in very few instances.

Preparation of Flax

58th. In general by mills, but by the poorer description of people by hand scutching which saves the expense of mill, 6s per hundred, and gives a greater proportion of clean flax from a given quantity than the mill, and less severe on the fibre; dried by fire in all cases.

Yarn

59th. 3 and half to 4 hanks, 2d ha'penny a day if the flax be good but not so much in general from purchased flax, as great fraud is practised by flax dealers in making it up for market.

60th. [Price of yarn] From 17d to 22d; some used for home manufacture, the greater part manufactured by the poor solely in market to buyers from the Lagan and from Armagh, Lurgan and north east. Ballintra yarn much esteemed from the good colour, owing to the nature of the water.

Cultivation of Flax

61st. The farmer and small landholder grow their own flax. The labouring poor are obliged to go to market for their flax, where they are subject to great imposition as before remarked.

Preparation of Yarn

62nd. [Double wheel] No.

63rd. [Yarn] Buys it at the market. Green gives it a half bleach, which costs him 20d for alkali and his own labour bleaching, spooling and warping.

Bleach Greens

64th. No bleaching greens. A green would be useful as the ground is unfit in many places and water bad in others.

Size of Webs

65th. The Coleraine web, consisting of warp 3 hanks and half and weft 4 hanks, and wrappering of 2-hank yarn.

Wool

66th. Yes, blankets and flannels, 6 cuts out of the lb.

67th. [Wool staplers] No.

68th. Now the small wheel.

Knitting

69th. They knit a good deal of stockings for sale in this neighbourhood. Most of the knitters have emigrated from the Rosses; have about 8d per day if good knitters.

70th. [Shearing of sheep] No.

71st and 72nd. [Cotton] None.

Kelp and Fisheries

73rd. No kelp in this parish.

74th to 76th. In the bay which bounds this parish to the west there has been occasionally a great herring fishery. There is turbot from June

Parish of Drumhome

until October; cod, haddock, ling, gurnet, grey and red mackerel, whiting from May until August. They are taken with eels on long lines from a sailing boat, kept under smart way. They keep on the foul rocky ground covered with seaweed.

77th. [Fishing vessels] 2, on the bounty; smacks, 16 tons burthen.

78th. [Common fish] Described before. Fishermen go 15 or 16 miles to the herring fishery. They go 8 or 10 miles to fish for cod, haddock, ling and hake, which they take with standing lines.

79th. [Numbers employed in fishing] When there is a great fishery, the whole population of the sea-coast of the parish go off to it. There are 2 boats constantly employed fishing when the weather will permit.

80th. [Curing of fish] None but for herrings, which cadgers or carriers drive to Fermanagh, Tyrone and Cavan, and sometimes to Armagh.

Parish of Glencolumbkille, County Donegal

Replies by John Ewing to Queries of North West Farming Society

NATURAL STATE

Situation and Extent

1. The parish of Glencolumbkille, in the diocese of Raphoe, contains 48 townlands. Its greatest length from north to south about 7 miles and its breadth from east to west 5.

NATURAL FEATURES AND NATURAL HISTORY

Soil and Mountains

Soil: very rocky towards the mountains, the valleys fertile. Mountains are numerous but 3 are very high, viz. Slieve League and Slieve-a-tory extending from east to west, and Glen Lough mountain from north to south west.

Rivers and Lakes

2. Rivers, each called Glen river. One runs nearly through the centre of the parish from east to west into the Atlantic, where it forms a small bay called Glen bay. The other of the same name runs nearly from north to south into Teeling bay, where there is a herring and salmon fishery.

The lakes are very numerous but small, generally named after the townlands in which they are situated.

Coast

The coast is very bold, rugged and precipitous, was much frequented by smugglers but this has been greatly cramped of late by the coastguards who have 3 stations in this parish.

There are no plantations, not 1 tree in the parish.

Mines and Minerals

2. No mines or minerals hitherto discovered. Stones of various kinds: limestone in abundance and some quarries of coarse slate.

ARTIFICIAL STATE

Modern Topography

3. No modern buildings, no towns, no gentlemen's seats; the scenery an alternate succession of rocks, mountains and improvable valleys; no inn. Roads horribly bad: not a perch of good road in the parish.

ANCIENT TOPOGRAPHY

Church and Castle

4. No ancient building except the church. The time of its erection I cannot ascertain. There are the remains of an old castle on the mountain called Slieuve-a-liegue near Teeling.

SOCIAL ECONOMY

Food and Health

5. The food of the inhabitants chiefly potatoes and fish, not much oatmeal. Milk and butter pretty plenty, fuel invariably turf or peat.

Diseases are mostly of the scorbutic class. Fevers not more prevalent than in other parts of Ulster. Inhabitants not remarkable for longevity or the contrary.

Character and Language

6. From what I as yet know of them, I would say that the inhabitants are quiet, peaceable and inoffensive. There is neither lawyer, attorney, magistrate or policeman in the parish.

All the inhabitants speak Irish. All the Protestants and some of the Roman Catholics speak the English language, which is fast increasing since the establishment of the coastguards, who in general don't speak Irish.

Amusements

Christenings, marriages, wakes and funerals are very numerously attended, more so than in any other part of Donegal I am acquainted with. They are seldom attended with any unpleasant riots.

Stations in Glencolumbkille

The traditions respecting Columbkille are very numerous indeed but in general too ridiculous to mention. In a valley extending from Glen bay about 2 miles into the interior, from west to east, are 7 stones from 5 to 7 feet high and about 18 inches broad inscribed with crosses and circles. They are held in very high veneration by the Roman Catholics, who perform stations at them on Sundays and holy days.

St Columb's House and Bed are shown here, as also his well, the water of which the people

Parish of Glencolumbkille 65

think is possessed of great virtue in healing diseases of every kind. There is a stone of very particular use in curing headaches which must be lodged every night in St Columb's Bed, but is generally taken off every morning through the parish. I was not fortunate enough to see it though I called twice, but each time it was out on duty.

Education

7. Children are generally employed in taking care of cattle. Education here is very far back indeed. There is a school on Robertson's foundation which is numerously attended, another where the master is paid entirely by the pupils. The London Hibernian and Kildare Street Societies had a school here, but during last winter the pupils were withdrawn. I now hear they are about to return to the school again.

No libraries or manuscripts.

Religion

8. The tithes are very low, but there is an old church near which a new one is shortly to be erected. No Roman Catholic chapel nor meeting house, no Protestant Dissenters in the parish.

PRODUCTIVE ECONOMY

Ploughs and Crops

9. There are very few ploughs here.

The crops are in general put down with the spade, the rotation as follows: potatoes, barley, oats or flax, potatoes.

Livestock

The breed of horses small but hardy, and well fitted to the soil; black cattle and sheep numerous but of a small breed; pigs increasing fast.

General Economy

No fairs or markets in the parish. Wages from 10d to 1s per day.

10. Tradesmen neither numerous nor good.

Flannel is the only manufacture; from this and butter and young cattle the rents are mostly paid.

11. [Rents] To this number I can say nothing as yet.

Improvements

12. The first steps to be taken for the improvement of this parish is to make roads or at least a road into it.

At present a wheel car with half a load could not enter the parish on any side whatever. People from the interior cannot come in here for flannel, butter or fish. The latter is most abundant on the coasts but the natives have no encouragement to take them. Strangers can't drive them off by land and there is no safe landing place for boats except at Teeling, which is the eastern boundary of the parish.

Quays built at Malinbeg, Malinmore, Glenbay or Purt [Port] would be of infinite advantage to this district.

MEMOIR WRITING

Composition of Memoir

I have got such scanty information for your society that I am almost ashamed to send it to you. However, what I do send is accurate; and if I can, when established here, procure any more particulars worth notice, I shall forward them to you. [Signed] John Ewing.

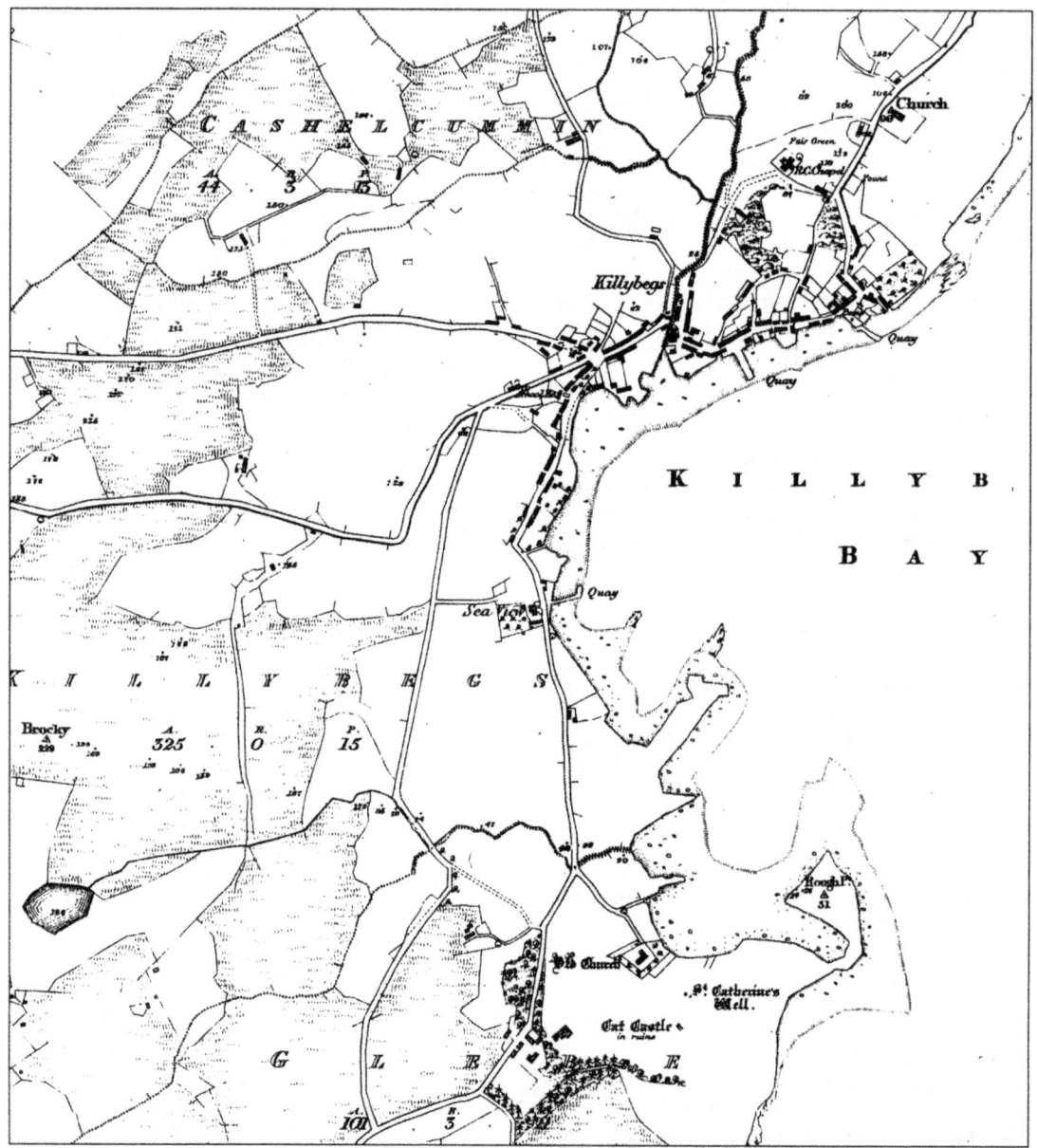

Map of Killybegs from the first 6″ O.S. maps, 1830s

Parish of Inishkeel, County Donegal

Replies by John Barrett to Queries of North West Farming Society

NATURAL STATE AND PRODUCTIVE ECONOMY

Name and Proprietors

In the county of Donegal, baronies of Bannagh and Boylagh, and diocese of Raphoe; present incumbent the Revd John Barrett.

4. The names of the different landed proprietors are the Marquis of Conyngham, the Bishop of Raphoe, Mr Murray and Mr Hamilton. The Bishop of Raphoe's property is leased to Colonel Pakenham; no proprietor resides.

Extent

There are 151 townlands. It is impossible even to guess at the number of acres of arable, mountain and bog, a very small portion of the parish having been surveyed. The parish is about 22 miles long and averages about 7 miles in breadth. By much the largest portion of the parish consists of bog, loughs and mountains. The society will form a more correct idea of this parish from a fact lately learned: a part of Lord Conyngham's estate containing 1,000 acres was last year leased for 12 pounds per annum.

Farms and Crops

5. Farms differ more in size in this parish than can be easily conceived by those more conversant with more happily circumstanced countries. From the fact I stated in answer to no.4, the very inferior value of some descriptions of land is evident; yet near to the sea land lets frequently for 30s per acre, and I paid 2 guineas per acre. It is therefore utterly impossible to say what is the general size of farms so as to convey to the society the most accurate information; in the best inhabited districts near to the sea-shore, I think about 4 acres of arable land, independent of pasture, is the general size of farms.

There are large districts totally unenclosed; when there is any cultivation, the usual enclosure is a bad mound composed partly of stones and partly of sods, merely to answer for the one season. The cattle during the winter being permitted to roam at large, destroying the wretched fences now in use, they must be consequently made anew each successive spring.

The usual mode of cultivation is with the spade and, instead of a harrow, a heavy rake is used to cover the grain when sowed. In the farms bordering on the shores the usual succession of crops is: first potatoes, followed by barley, then oats or flax; in the mountainous districts barley is never sown, oats follow potatoes and I have often seen 3 and 4 successive crops of potatoes, occasioned from the want of manure. In our very sandy district rye is sown, which answers well. Wheat would grow in many places, but there are no flour mills within 30 miles, and the prevalence of illicit distillation induces the farmer to prefer the sowing of barley.

Improvements

I conceive that were a skilled Scotch farmer induced to settle in this parish, conversant in the reclaiming of moors and bog, much good would result from it. I say Scotch, their climate and soil having a greater affinity to ours than the English. I think that draining and lime might be used with invaluable benefit.

6. I would advise pasture-lands to be occasionally tilled and tillage lands to be occasionally converted into pastures, which is not practical in this parish from the farmer's being unequal to the expense of fencing his pasture-grounds. The pasture-lands in the parish consist entirely of natural grasses and almost uniformly require draining.

NATURAL FEATURES

Hills

7. To enumerate the mountains and hills would be an Herculean labour, this parish abounding so in them that I think they occupy one-fifth part of the parish. They are in general pasturable to their limits, but rarely capable of cultivation.

Bogs

8. The entire of this parish is interspersed with moors and bogs that I know of no inhabitant 1 mile distant from fuel. The society will have an idea of the extent of bog when I state that in my opinion the arable land does not constitute the one-hundredth part of the parish.

Timber is found in the bogs in great abundance, usually fir and oak, the former in general of an admirable quality, but the latter is so liable to warp that it cannot be used where it may be liable to the least heat; timber generally lies from 4 to 10 feet deep.

I only once saw a piece of bog yew. I employed a cabinetmaker to make a table of it. It is of a most beautiful dark colour and of the finest grain imaginable, but of so hard a texture as to render it very difficult to be wrought into furniture.

The preserving quality of bog is strongly exemplified in the preservation of butter and tallow, which I have seen found in bogs at a depth so great as to induce [me] to think that it has been there for some centuries.

Woods and Plantations

9. There are neither woods, orchards, nurseries or plantations in this parish, and I know from experience they would all thrive. I planted a few pear, apple and plum <plumb> trees which produce most abundantly.

In former times it is evident that this country abounded in woods. Were the tracts now covered with underwood enclosed, in 30 years they would return twentyfold to the proprietor more than they now yield, by affording a scanty browsing to a few famished sheep.

10. I have found sycamore to thrive best in the most exposed situations, and ash in the least exposed ones. My respected friend and neighbour, Major Nesbitt of Woodhill in Killybegs parish, has planted an extensive orchard, a number of shrubs and forest trees of all kinds, and they all thrive most admirably.

Productive Economy

Rent

11. The highest acreable rent for the best arable land is about 2 pounds, for middling about 25s and for inferior about 9s. The highest acreable rent for green pasture is about 10s and for moory pasture about 1s; from that rent they fall gradually to about 1s 4d per acre, and many thousands of acres in this parish, in their present [state?], are not worth even that small sum.

Charge for Turf

12. The sum paid for permission to cut a dark of turf, that is, as much as 3 men can cut in a day, varies from 1s 8d to 2s 6d. The landlord receives no rent for bog.

Improvements and Fences

13. There have been no improvements as to tillage and enclosures and implements of husbandry recently made.

14. The fence commonly used is a mound of earth, which must be made anew annually. In the stony districts a badly built dry wall is made; I would recommend what is usually called a double ditch, that is, a mound of earth with a dyke on either side; and I would advise the planting either side of the mound with whitethorn. The dykes would drain the land and the thorn edge would afford useful shelter in our northern climate.

Employment

15. In spring it is almost impossible to procure labourers, all being employed in the planting of their own potatoes; at all other times of the year it is very easy to procure labourers. In all other parts of Ireland which I have known, harvest time is that when labour is at the highest price. In this parish our crops are small and our situation renders emigration to England in the harvest season impracticable.

To give general employment I would recommend the establishment of manufactures, of which the parish is almost totally destitute. Premiums might be advantageously offered for the apprenticing of children to trades. The usual custom at present is, when there are 6 sons, the father divides the already too scanty farm into 6 parts, and thus creates 6 families of beggars, instead of apprenticing 5 of his sons to trades and giving his farm to 1.

Wages

16. An able manservant's wages average about 5 pounds per annum, a maidservant's about 2 pounds 10s per annum. Labour is uniformly performed by the day; the usual price 6d per day and food. I give to my labourers 10d a day without food.

Green Crops and Grasses

17. I never saw a green crop in this parish.

18. I never saw a field of artificial grass but with myself. I frequently sow red clover, but I derive little benefit from it, occasioned by the incessant trespassing of the numerous flocks of sheep roaming without a shepherd.

I would recommend premiums for the sowing of turnip seed, for which burnt bog is the very best soil. Were the farmers of this parish induced to stall-feed sheep on turnips, the benefit arising from the quantity of manure such a practice would produce is incalculable.

19. [Drainage] Almost universally surface draining.

Parish of Inishkeel

Manures

20. In the districts bordering on the sea-shore seaweed is almost the only manure used. From its producing a greater weight of potatoes on a given surface than any other manure known here, they use both the seaweed thrown in by the tide and that cut from the rocks. In the inland districts stable and cow-house dung, usually mixed with bog or mud, is used.

Burning of the soil is very little used here. When it is practised, the ground is cut into the shape of small sugar loaves, dried and burnt in heaps. I have never myself practised this species of agriculture. Those who practise it in the neighbouring parish of Inver speak very highly of it and have assured me its produce is equal to dung.

As to lime, it is never used as manure here; why, I cannot tell. In many parts of this parish adjoining my residence the substratum is limestone. I am induced to think lime would not answer on a soil so circumstanced. The farmers in the parish of Stranorlar use lime very much as a manure and, what is singular, they draw their limestone a considerable distance from a district in this parish abounding in moors and bogs where undoubtedly lime would answer very well, and yet I have never been able to prevail on one of my parishioners to try the effects of lime.

Irrigation

21. I never saw a watered meadow in this parish. Some years since Mr Stewart of Stranorlar brought a person from Scotland skilled in the watering of meadows. I learn from the gentlemen in the neighbouring districts that the advantages have been very great. Indeed I have seen wonders performed by irrigation in different parts of England.

Dairies

22. There are 2 small dairies in this parish and I have reason to think that they answer very well.

Use of Oxen

23. I never saw oxen used in husbandry in the county of Donegal, except by myself. I always have 2: they answer very well. They plough <plow> and harrow, and bring home my turf. I never shoe them.

Spade Husbandry

24. In this parish spade tillage is almost exclusively used, from the small size of the farms and the consequent inability to purchase ploughs. I therefore cannot speak of its comparative merits or defects in this district, but in my opinion plough tillage is far superior. I conceive spade tillage totally impracticable on a farm of the rent of 1,000 pounds per annum; and I was assured lately by a gentleman of veracity that in the lowlands in Scotland 5,000 pounds per annum is not an unusual rent.

Grain Crops and Provisions

25. Barley and oats are the only descriptions of grain in the parish. From the universal practice of illicit distillation, grain sells much higher in this parish than in many other parts of Ireland.

In former years illicit whiskey sold for 7s per gallon and barley was then 2s 10d per stone. During some years past it has partaken of the universal depression of prices. Barley is now sold at 1s per stone and oats at 9d.

Provisions are generally dearer here than in other parts of Ireland. The causes I conceive to be an overabundant population, bad husbandry, small farms and the great consumption of grain in illicit distillation. Were it not for the importation of provisions from the province of Connaught, this parish would very frequently be in danger of starving.

Unit of Measurement

26. I have resided constantly in this parish for the last 19 years and I never saw or heard but once of a surveyor employed. The measurement of land, I learn, is computed by what is called the plantation acre, containing 7 yards to a perch.

Livestock

27. A small breed of black cattle is usually raised in this parish, which I conceive well adapted to the soil and climate.

28. In general black cattle from 1 to 4 years old, the soil being adapted to the rearing of young cattle but not to fattening.

29. A small breed of sheep well adapted to soil and climate. The mutton is delicious, much of the quality of the celebrated Welsh mutton.

30. Horses are little used for agricultural purposes, except for the carrying of sea and other manures. They are of a small kind, produced between the Irish and the Scotch, a number of the latter being annually brought into this country. I have one of that description now in my possession, on which I have frequently rode 50 miles in one day.

31. The swine are not large but well shaped, and probably better adapted to the scanty fare of the poor farmers of this district.

Quantity of Stock

I have no data from whence I could give even a remote guess of the quantity of stock of each description in this parish. I should imagine that cattle imported from Scotland would tend to improve the present breed and would thrive well, but this suggestion comes not from myself who have never visited Scotland. Importing large English cattle would be absurd: I could not, in a range of 4 parishes, procure grass to fatten an ox of about 5 cwt.

Improvements in Breeding

33. I do not think that any improvements have been made in the breeds of horses, black cattle or sheep in this parish for the last 20 years. In pigs I have perceived a substitution of the short-legged for the long-legged Irish breed.

NATURAL FEATURES AND NATURAL HISTORY

Rivers and Lakes

34. There are 2 principal rivers. The River Onea runs from Lough Fea due west and empties itself into the sea at Loughros <Louris> bay. Gweebarra <Gubbara> river takes its rise in Lough Barrow and falls into the sea at Gweebarra bar in a westerly direction. There are salmon fisheries in both these rivers and the fish are of a most excellent quality but not very abundant.

This parish, like all mountain districts, abounds in loughs; by much the largest are Lough Finn and Lough Barrow.

Coast

Dawris is an excellent harbour. The Church Pool is extremely safe in the summer months but not during winter. The shore abounds in creeks but, lying on the great Atlantic, none safe.

There are 2 ferries between this parish and Lettermacaward for people only; the cattle must swim. I live very near the seashore. I have not seen or heard of any peculiar productions.

Mines

35. Some years since a silver mine was discovered in the townland of Glenamohill in this parish. An English miner pronounced it to be very rich. It has never been worked: I believe this has been occasioned by the minority of Mr Hamilton of Brownhall, the proprietor. I think the quarry about 5 miles from the sea.

There was an iron mine in the parish of Killybegs some years since, I have been told a very rich one. On the death of the late Colonel Conyngham the working of it ceased. I think it evident from the tinge of the mountain streams that almost all the mountains contain iron ore, but whether they would answer the expense of working, I am unable to solve.

Lime and Slate Quarries

36. The parish abounds in limestone quarries, very easily wrought, many very conveniently situated for exportation, but I never heard of any being exported. Indeed very little limestone is raised, as the inhabitants don't raise it as a manure, and all convenient to the shore prefer the digging for shells of cockles, mussels and oysters, from the superior facility of burning them, to be used in buildings. The lime produced is of a whiteness superior to that from limestone, but requires less sand to constitute good mortar.

I hear there are many slate quarries, most of them convenient for exportation. They are of a very durable quality but, from their thickness and consequent weight, require a stronger roof than English slates. This, I presume, prevents their exportation in large quantities, for they are sold as low as 1 pound 10s per 1,000.

37. The colour of the limestone is uniformly blue. It is easily burned; it is always burned with peat. When sold 126 quarts of sleaked lime bring 5d.

38. No species of coal have ever been found in this district.

Mineral Springs

39. There are many sulphurous and [?] still springs in this parish, but the only celebrated one is in the townland of Dawris, near to the shore. It is of a strong sulphureous quality and has much benefitted the few who used it in scrofulous complaints. It appears to partake much of the flavour of the Harrowgate spa, as far as I can recollect, many years having elapsed since I visited it.

Marl

40. I have made diligent enquiry and I find that no marl has ever been discovered in this parish.

Parish of Inishkeel

Social Economy

Condition of the People

41. From what I have already stated, it is evident that the situation of the inhabitants as to domestic comforts is very bad. I think their want of industry may be attributed to their want of a stimulus to their exertions, no resident gentry, not a man possessing the fee of a single acre of land living in the parish.

When the wretched cottager has planted his potatoes, he rests from his labours till the period of digging them. From that period till spring little labour is done; for in many parts of this parish there are none who want to hire a labourer. Add to these causes the facility of procuring another, cheapness of illicit whiskey, many domestic comforts are not to be expected.

Many things combine to render the inhabitants of this parish less comfortable than our English neighbours. I resided for many years in England. I think our want of manufactures is the primary cause: few, very few, are the means of earning money in this parish; but when by servitude at home or in Scotland (whither many go annually) a small sum of money is earned, it is expended on the purchase of a farm from some of those who annually emigrate to America. They then marry and entail misery on a large family.

Houses and Fuel

42. The general conditions of farmhouses is bad, that of cottages wretched; the want of cleanliness is the more obvious defect.

43. The only fuel used is turf. The inhabitants have it in great abundance. I believe I am the only person who does not possess the right of turbary. I consequently [purchase] at the rate of 1 pound for 120 measures of turf, each measure being 4 feet long, 21 broad and 2 and a half deep.

Food

44. [Farmers] Potatoes, milk, butter, eggs, salted fish, oaten bread, on Sundays probably salted beef or poultry, but I am sorry to add there are very few of that description in this district, not 100.

45. There cannot with propriety be said to be a manufacturing class.

46. [Labourers] Potatoes with milk for 4 months, potatoes with only salt too frequently for the remaining 8 months.

Education

47. There is a strong and general inclination for education in all classes, but the object is often defeated by the poverty of the parents, obliging them to keep their children at home for agricultural purposes, and thus they frequently forget what they have learned.

48. The expenses of each of the classes is the same: for arithmetic, reading and writing about 3s 6d per quarter; for reading and spelling only, 2s 6d per quarter. There are 10 schools in this parish.

49. [Improvements] I have not observed any.

Health

50. The peasantry are in general a healthy race, the only general exception is what is usually termed the King's Evil; the prevalence of that disorder I conceive to arise from their intermarrying in the same district. The cure applied to it by me is seaweed worn as a poultice. I have not often found it to fail if accompanied with sea bathing.

Some years since the typhus fever raged here, as I believe it did in every district of the kingdom. I conceive it arose in many instances from want of cleanliness. I found tartar emitic applied in the early stage of the disease of great use; when application to me was long delayed, the disorder generally proved fatal.

51. [Friendly societies] There are none.

Modern Topography

Towns

52. The only town is Glenties; the principal villages are Narin and Cloghboys. I know of no other consisting of 20 houses contiguous.

Productive Economy

Improvements

53. The people in general are shrewd and intelligent, and did they enjoy the advantages of more favoured districts, I doubt not but they would be equally intelligent. I conceive small premiums as encouragements would operate powerfully to that desirable end.

Practical Farmers

54. I cannot answer this question as I could wish. The largest farm in this parish is tenanted by a person who can neither read or write. The most intelligent agriculturist in my neighbourhood is Mr Babington; his address near to Donegal.

Linen Manufacture

55. I think rather increasing.

56. [Bleach greens] None.

Flax

57. The land is dug as for corn. It is then carefully clodded, that is, all large lumps are gathered. It generally succeeds the barley crop. Part is consumed in home manufacture, but by much the greater part is sold in the neighbouring districts and sent to Derry, I presume for exportation.

Preparation of Flax

58. The process is this: after pulling, the flax is permitted to remain for 2 days stacked; it is then steeped in water. When sufficiently wilted, it is spread; it is taken from the field on which it was spread, when dry. It is then placed on a wicker hurdle, fire being placed underneath to dry it. It is then laid on a hard floor and broken by manual labour, generally of 2, who alternately strike it with an instrument called a break, a flat piece of timber about 1 foot long by 4 inches broad and 3 inches deep; a handle about 4 feet long is inserted into it. The flax is then sent to a mill worked by water, to be scutched. This latter operation is sometimes performed by women by manual labour, which prepares it for the wheel.

Linen Yarn

59. The usual grist is 4 hanks to the spangle, produced from a lb. of hackled flax. A spinner earns on an average about 3d per day.

Price of Yarn

60. Yarn has varied very much in price during the last 10 years. I have known it sold for 4s 4d per spangle; the present average price is 1s 7d per spangle. A small proportion is used in home manufacture.

61. In general the spinners purchase the flax.

Preparation of Yarn

62. The double wheel is not known in this parish.

63. I know of no linen manufactured for sale in this parish: a few manufacture for their own use. The farmer sends his yarn prepared for the loom to the weaver, and by weaving for him per yard the weaver earns his subsistence.

Yarn Greens

64. There are no yarn greens in the neighbourhood. The method to establish a linen manufactory, I conceive, would be for one of the great proprietors to build a village expressly for the purpose and introduce weavers from other districts.

Quality of Webs

65. The very little linen manufactured for sale is of a very coarse description; not 5 pounds' worth is annually sold. It is sold at about 5d per yard in the markets of Ardara and Glenties. The set about 6 hundred.

Woollen Manufacture

66. More than half the woollen cloth used is the manufacture of the parish. It is usually about 1 yard wide and would, if sold, produce about 5s per yard. I have very rarely seen any sold. The few weavers weave linen and woollen indiscriminately. A large proportion of the labouring class buy second-hand clothes sold in all the neighbouring market towns by auction.

Mills

67. [Wool staplers] There are none. There is 1 tuck mill for thickening cloth in the parish. I believe there are very few in the neighbouring districts, as I have frequently met with persons bringing cloth to it from the neighbouring parishes.

Use of Wheel

68. Usually on the small wheel, because more can be spun in a day on it than on the large wheel, although they are aware that the latter produces the softest and the best yarn.

Knitting

69. In the districts neighbouring the sea-shore the females are universally employed in spinning linen yarn. In the mountainous parts of my parish they knit woollen stockings, and on an average the knitters earn about 5d per day. The neighbouring district of Rosses is celebrated for its knitting of woollen stockings.

Cotton

71. and 72. [Cotton and description] There is none.

Kelp

73. There is some manufactured in this parish.

74. No improvements in the manufacture of kelp have been adopted in this parish. In the

Parish of Inishkeel

neighbouring district of Rosses I learn that a Mr Rogers has obtained a patent for the building of kelp-kilns in which wreck [wrack] taken from the sea can be converted into kelp. On the contrary, with us it must be spread to dry and as much labour expended to fit [it] to be burned as in saving hay; and a similar process of cooking it. A small premium for the erection of kilns, on Mr Rogers' plan, would, in my opinion, be a judicious use of the funds intended to ameliorate the condition of the poor in this district.

75. The kelp manufactured in this district is usually sold in Ballybofey at about 3s 4d per cwt, a distance from where it is burned of 22 miles. It is carried on the backs of horses, each horse carrying about 3 cwt. Carts or cars they have none.

Fisheries

76. In answering the queries respecting the fisheries, I do speak of the vessels which come from other districts and who obtain the bounty granted by parliament. On that subject I beg leave to recommend to the society to apply to Captain Nesbitt, Woodhill near Ardara, a very intelligent gentleman and who has the superintendence of the fishery on this coast.
Very little fish is taken in this district.

77. [Boats employed] Only a few small boats. My table is usually supplied with fish taken by a curragh, a species of boat composed of wickerwork and covered with a horse's skin.

78. Cod and pollock. If the weather be not very fine, no boat will venture from the shore. When the sea is extremely calm, they will go 4 leagues from the land, aware that were a wind off land to arise, America is the nearest shore.

79. Not more than 30 are employed, and from my answer to 78 it is evident that even that small number are only employed in the summer months.

Curing of Fish

80. None are cured for distant markets and there is no market to which fresh fish could be sent to produce adequate compensation.

Improvements in Fisheries

81. I have no hesitation in saying that the fisheries in this district could be greatly improved, but it is a question whether, from the remoteness of this district from towns, or a large population, an adequate reward could be procured for increased exertion.

Within 1 mile of the shore, near to my house, there is a bank abounding with turbot and sole, yet I never saw one at my table caught in this parish. I learn that herring have been, of late years, frequently on this coast, but were not taken for want of nets. I hope Lord Mountcharles' bounty in generously supplying his tenants with flax gratis will in future supply this defect. [Signed] John Barrett.

Parish of Kilbarron, County Donegal

Replies by Robert Ball to Queries of North West Farming Society

NATURAL STATE

Situation, Proprietors and Extent

1–3. County of Donegal, barony of Tyrhugh, diocese of Tyrhugh, parish of Kilbarron; Revd Robert Ball, incumbent.

4. Colonel Pakenham Conolly holds the fee simple, estate of all this parish, with the exception of 5 townlands containing about 1,000 acres belonging to Trinity College, but a great proportion of the parish is held under Colonel Conolly in perpetuity at low rents by Counsellor Johnston and Dickson, Messrs Atkinson, Tredermisk [Tredermich], Coane.

The parish contains about 10,000 plantation acres of arable land and 6,000 acres of mountain, with some bog interspersed in the mountain.

PRODUCTIVE ECONOMY

Farms and Crops

5. From 5 to 20 acres. Ditches in some few cases but in general dry walls.

Lea grounds are for the most [part] laid down with potatoes, which are succeeded by 2 crops of oats and in some cases barley is put down next after the potato crop. Flax is also raised after grain, very often in poor grounds, but in [every?] case in large quantities. The land is capable of improvement by the introduction of clover and turnips.

Grazing

6. A large portion of the pasture-lands are high grounds on a limestone bottom, with a soil too thin in general to admit of cultivation but affords good pasturage.

NATURAL FEATURES

Hills

7. The mountain of the parish lies all in the eastward part of it and extends from the River Erne to its northern extremity. These mountains are not high but are very barren. There are no very elevated hills and all capable of cultivation.

Bogs

8. There are now no other bogs in the parish but what those mountains contain. A little fir and oak timber is found in them, at from 6 to 9 feet deep.

Woods and Plantations

9. Colonel P. Conolly planted a few acres of those mountains 7 or 8 years ago, which are the only woods in the parish; a few orchards in an infant state and very small, never exceeding a rood of ground.

10. [Thriving trees] Fir, sycamore, birch and ash.

PRODUCTIVE ECONOMY

Rents

11. Highest acreable rent 3 pounds, middling 2 pounds, inferior 1 pound to 12s, for mountain 2s to 3s. Some town fields near Ballyshannon let from 5 to 6 guineas per annum.

12. [Charge for turf] 4 pounds to 4 guineas per acre in the mountain. All Colonel Conolly's tenants have had a portion of bog free until lately.

Improvements in Farming

13. No general improvements in tillage. Potatoes are in very few instances lately put in by the plough in loose soil. No material improvement in either fences or implements.

Fences

14. Walls are very generally used for fences, except when ditches are advantageous to the grounds. We would recommend ditches fenced with stones and thickly planted with quicksets.

Employment and Wages

15. Employment is abundant in spring and harvest, but not at all so in the other seasons of the year. Encouragement to the fisheries and the opening of a canal from Ballyshannon to Belleek: see answer 81st.

16. Servant man from 5 pounds to 6 pounds yearly, labourers 1s to 1s 3d a day.

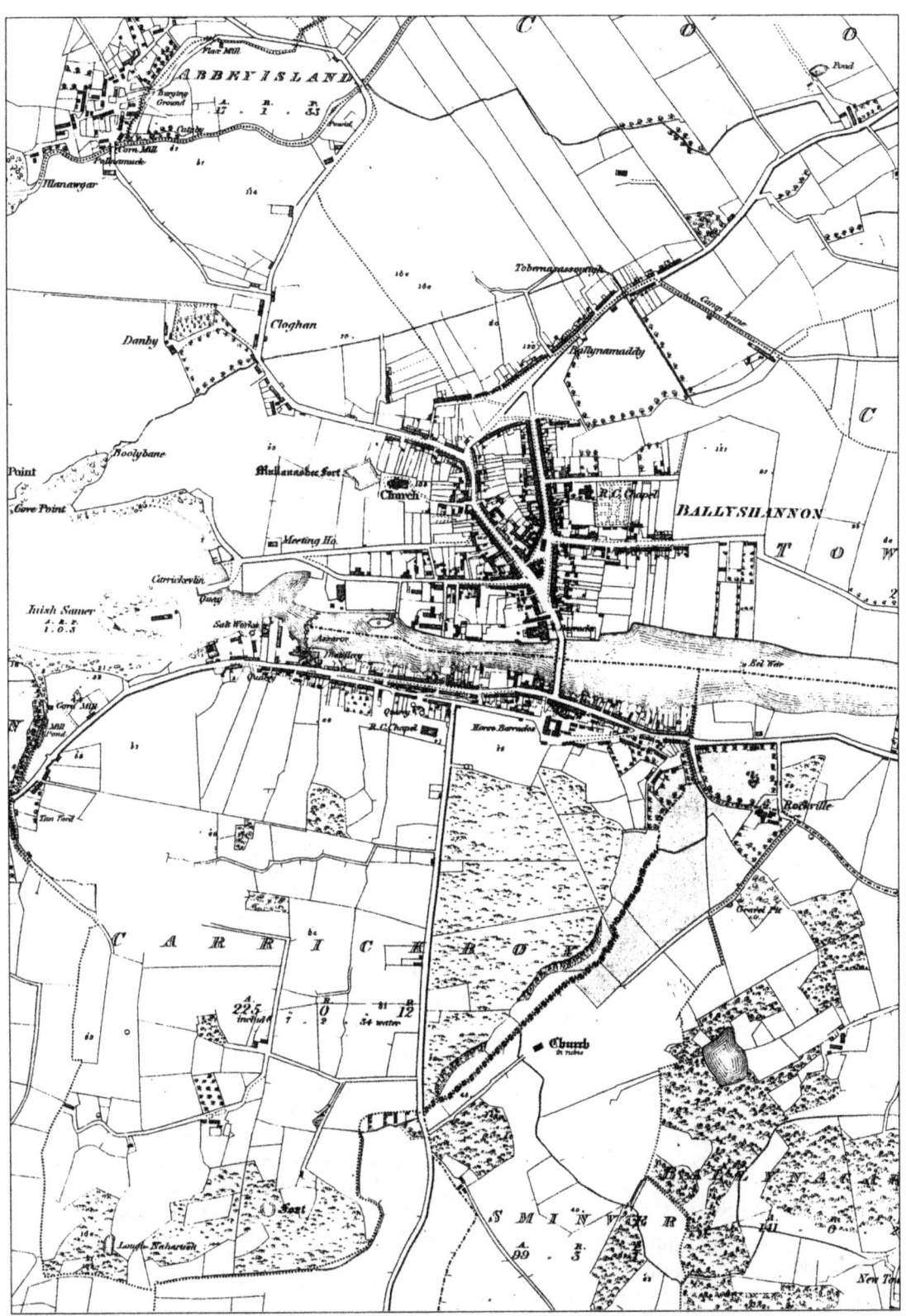

Map of Ballyshannon from the first 6" O.S. maps, 1830s

Green Crops and Grasses

17. [Green crops] Very little; very small spots of clover are sown. A little encouragement would introduce it more generally.

18. [Artificial grasses] A little rye grass in some few instances, on being laid down for meadow.

Draining and Manures

19. Surface draining in general.

20. A compost of dung, clay and mud is very generally used. On breaking in lea ground for potatoes, scoring and burning is very generally practised. This will give 2 or 3 very good crops in general, but in order to improve the ground further, manuring is absolutely necessary afterwards. The above mixture with the addition of lime or sea-sand is very beneficial.

21. [Irrigation] Not generally.

Farm Techniques

22. [Dairies] There are none.
23. [Oxen] No.
24. [Spade husbandry] It answers well and is used of necessity on rocky soils.

Grain Crops

25. Oats for the most part, some barley. Oats and barley are 10d to 1s per stone, meal 12s per cwt, potatoes 3d per stone.

26. [Unit of measurement] Irish plantation acre.

Livestock

27. [Cattle] Long-horned Leicestershire.

28. Exclusive of milch cows and horses used in husbandry, there are some sheep fed and a few cows fattened.

29. [Sheep] The old native breed, but the Leicestershire has been introduced in some cases with advantage.

30. Common draught horses. Those crossed with ponies are in some instances preferred and commonly kept by the farmers.

31. [Pigs] Leicestershire.

Number of Livestock

32. Of black cattle probably 2,000, horses 700, sheep 2,000 to 3,000. As this parish is rather a tillage district, few general experiments in the management or improvement of stock have been adopted. The introduction of a few good Leicestershire bulls, to be let to service at a cheap rate, would have a good effect and the breed of sheep could also be improved by the use of good Leicestershire rams.

33. Very little improvement in sheep and somewhat more considerable in swine has been accomplished within 10 or 15 years last past.

NATURAL FEATURES

Rivers and Lakes

34. The River Erne from Belleek to Ballyshannon is the only river of any note.

A few mountain lakes, some of them producing trout, bream, perch, eel and pikes.

Coast

A sea-shore extending from the bar of Ballyshannon to the mearing of the parish of Drumhome, being an extent of nearly 3 miles. It is bold and rocky throughout, producing wrack and other marine productions. The harbour of Ballyshannon and 2 very indifferent creeks which afford shelter in their present states.

NATURAL FEATURES AND NATURAL HISTORY

Mines and Minerals

35. None have been actually discovered though there are certainly some iron mines in a part of it.

36. Limestone are the principal quarries, some of it of a very good quality.

37. [Limestone] Blue, burned with peat. Expenses of burning 3d ha'penny per barrel.

38. No coal has been discovered.

39. [Mineral springs] A good deal of chalybeate spa; very little used.

40. Marl is found in a good many places but very rarely used. It is of a calcareous quality.

SOCIAL ECONOMY

Condition of the People

41. The number of poor is very considerable. Industrious habits are gaining ground progressively. Labourers and mechanics in and near the town of Ballyshannon apply their [?] earnings to their daily support. Those in the country parts generally raise some potatoes and in some cases a little flax.

Houses and Fuel

42. The number of comfortable farmhouses bear a very small proportion to those that are

Parish of Kilbarron

otherwise, either as to repair or interior comforts.

43. [Fuel] Peat, which is inconvenient to the inhabitants on the sea-coast; 30s per 100 barrels is the general price at the bogs.

Food

44. [Farmers] Potatoes with milk and butter.

45. [Manufacturing class] The same in general.

46. [Labourers] Potatoes with milk or salt fish, if anything.

Education

47. Education is much more general than it was a few years ago. The Protestants avail themselves of the advantages held out by public institutions for that purpose. The Roman Catholic clergy oppose the plan of education as adopted by those institutions, but the whole of the children of that persuasion receive more instruction from education than they did a few years ago.

48. There are a number of schools established under the bounty of those institutions where children are taught free. Farmers and mechanics pay 8s to 10s yearly for instructing their children in spelling and reading, and from 10s to 20s for writing and figures. There are about 10 schools in the whole parish.

49. The morals of the lower order are manifestly improved within the last 20 years, which improvement is progressing.

Health

50. [Health] Good: the most prevalent disease is rheumatism, occasioned by the moisture of the atmosphere.

Friendly Societies

51. None except some instructions given in knitting and sewing to destitute female children by some young ladies in Ballyshannon.

MODERN TOPOGRAPHY

Towns

52. The town of Ballyshannon: the villages of Mobuy and Kildoney, the hamlets of Carricknahorna, Behy, Tullyhork, Knather, Cortia and Lisahully.

PRODUCTIVE ECONOMY

Improvements

53. A disposition for improvement does in some degree exist. There is very little planting of any kind of timber or fruit trees. All the fruit consumed in the parish is brought from the counties of Fermanagh and Cavan. If an extensive nursery was established to furnish the different kinds of fruit and forest trees at a cheap rate, a spirit of improvement would be thereby excited and the parish benefitted.

54. [Practical farmers] John Tredermisk and Thomas John Atkinson Esquires.

Linen Manufacture

55. Increasing in consequence of the establishment of a linen market in Ballyshannon last year.

56. [Bleach greens] None except 2 flax mills.

Flax

57. Most commonly by 2 ploughings after barley or oats, and does tolerably well. By far the greatest part spun and sold in yarn for exportation. No seed saved of any account.

58. [Preparation of flax] Some by mills and some by manual labour. It is all prepared with drying by fire.

Linen Yarn

59. The flax is spun to 2 and a half to 3 and a half hanks to the lb.; tow 1 and a half to 2 hanks. Spinners cannot now earn more than 1d ha'penny per day.

60. Coarse yarn 18d, fine 18d to 20d; all mostly sold for exportation.

Provision of Flax

61. Farmers raise their flax but the labouring class are principally supplied by flax brought from the barony of Raphoe.

62. [Double wheel] It never was used here.

63. [Preparation of yarn] The weavers generally get it spun and prepared themselves; the expense of preparing the yarn is about 5s for each web of 52 yards.

Yarn Greens

64. There are now no greens for either cloth or yarn, though there are many excellent situations for bleach greens; and the waters of the River Erne, as well as some other small rivers and lakes

in the parish, possess excellent qualities for bleaching. A bleach green which was worked at Carrangartin near Ballyshannon has been discontinued.

Quality of Webs

65. Coleraine webs and some wrappers, the set 10 to 11 hundred for the Coleraines, price 11d ha'penny to 13d ha'penny per yard. The only market is that of Ballyshannon.

Woollen Manufacture

66 and 67. [Woollen manufactures and staplers] There are none.

68. All the wool spun in this parish now is done in the small wheel. The use of the large wheel is discontinued.

69. There are no stockings knit for sale.

70. [Shearing of sheep] They have not [any].

Cotton Manufacture

[In a different hand] 71 and 72. None.

Kelp Manufacture

73. [Is kelp manufactured?] It is.

74. There has been no improvement in the manufacturing of it lately introduced. The manufacture of it could be greatly extended.

75. There has been no export of it for several years past. The sales has been confined to what was used for the purposes of bleaching and soap manufactures, and since the one bleach green which was in the parish has been given up, the sales are confined altogether to a soap manufactory in Ballyshannon; price from 2s 6d to 3s 4d per cwt.

Fisheries

76. Beside the salmon and eel fisheries of the River Erne, the west side of this parish is washed by a part of the bay of Donegal, by which it might enjoy the advantage of sea fishing if it were not for the want of places of security for boats or vessels.

77. Not more than 6 or 7 boats of from 2 to 2 and a half tons burthen, very seldom employed.

78. Herrings and a variety of whitefish and shellfish. Boats cannot go out and come in unless in very fine weather. When out they ply in the bay, inside St John's Point and the Point of Mullaghmore, county Sligo, and sometimes in Teeling bay.

79. From 40 to 50 persons work their boats when they do go out, which is very seldom.

80. None of the fish taken by them are cured for distant markets. The town of Ballyshannon affords a very considerable consumption for fresh fish. It is supplied from the north side of the bay.

Improvements in Fisheries

81. The fishery in this parish is thus limited from the want of a place of security for the boats and vessels necessary to be employed in it. The port of Ballyshannon is extremely difficult of access. It cannot be entered but in fine weather and with a fair wind; beside[s] it is rather too remote from the sea to enable the fishermen to attend it daily, if they could even get into it with safety.

There are 2 creeks already mentioned on the coast, one at Kildoney and the other at Coolbeg, both situated at a little more than 2 miles from Ballyshannon. Boats are drawn up in both these places occasionally but cannot rise at either for want of shelter. A small sum laid out in the improvements of the seas to enable boats to ride with some degree of safety would be attended with very great advantage to the parish and neighbourhood, so far as to relate to the benefit to be received from the sea fishing.

The contiguity of that place to the town of Ballyshannon, and from thence to the counties of Fermanagh, Leitrim and [blank], would always ensure an unlimited demand for fresh fish at all seasons of the year and would certainly induce a great portion of the inhabitants to avail themselves of the bounties now given by the government for the encouragement for this branch of trade. Next to have a canal made from Ballyshannon to Belleek, to open navigable communication with the interior, there is nothing would be so beneficial to this neighbourhood.

We have every reason to hope that a proper presentation would be the means of getting from government such a grant as would accomplish the improvement of their 2 creeks, and the advantage to the parish [would] be incalculable.

Parishes of Killea and Taughboyne, County Donegal

Replies by I. Grier to Queries of North West Farming Society, October 1821

MEMOIR WRITING

Memoir Writing

Statistical survey of St Johnston district, addressed to the Right Honourable Sir G.F. Hill Baronet, Vice-President of the North West Society of Londonderry.

Sir,

When your high and dignified station is considered and the good nature with which you condescend to be a vice-president of a philanthropic society, not only to promote the welfare of that city (Londonderry) for which you are representative, but also to search out and relieve the wants of all classes in the 3 north west counties of Ireland, what pen can be silent that is qualified to forward even the weakest philosophic hint to that institution, the information of which is so eminently conducive to the improvement of agriculture, arts and sciences, and that tends in the ultimate to the happiness and well-being of all mankind.

Stimulated from such condescension, I assume the honour of subscribing myself, right honoured sir, your most obedient, most humble servant [signed] I. Grier.

To write a correct account of even the smallest district requires an equal knowledge of agriculture, manufactures and mechanics, with literary research and accurate observation, as what it would to do it on the most extended scale: the one, like natural philosophy, which describes the phenomena of bodies in the aggregate; the other, like chemical, which is more pervading and treats of that various operations of their elementary or component parts.

Had those statistical queries been of Lanarkshire in Scotland, where I resided some years with open eyes and ears to their unrivalled improvements, I might have had a better chance for a premium and not been like an eastern statue, with my fingers on my mouth, indicating now rivalship; and had I not used the freedom of writing for them, the anxiety of the good-natured Revd Mr Law and William McClintock Esquire would have been left unsatisfied till a future period.

In hopes that this, although incorrect, will better apologise for my ignorance of the barony of Raphoe than a silent pen, also from my volubility in casting a mite into so useful a treasury, I therefore present it to the mercy of the humane and enlightened North West Society of Londonderry.

GEOGRAPHY OR NATURAL STATE

Situation and Extent

1. County Donegal.

2. St Johnstown district, extending along the west of the River Foyle from Robert Beatson Esquire to the parish of Lifford or half a mile above the ferry of Carrickmore, which is 7 miles in a direct line nearly due south with an obtuse angle through Cralindoes by the south end of Birnorhill to the parish of Raymoghy <Rye>, where it takes a curvilineal to Port lough, comprehending the summits of north and south Dough's hill, then bounded by the road leading from Fort Stewart to Derry.

This district comprehends a semicircular surface of 21 Irish miles, containing 13,289 acres, 260 farmers, 2,600 cattle, 569 horses, 2,800 sheep, 1,040 swine and a population of 3,600 inhabitants, 600 tradesmen, 265 of which being weavers.

3. Parishes: part of Killea and Taughboyne. Incumbents: the Revd Mr Law <Laid> and Revd Mr Bowen.

Proprietors

4. The Earl of Wicklow, Marquis of Abercorn, Robert Beatson Esquire, William McClintock Esquire and some other small proprietors and freeholders.

Townlands

1st Bellugarry, 2nd Mullinean, 3rd Breckfield, 4th Killdrum, 5th Garshiney, 6th Cloon, 7th Munreagh, 8th Cornecanmon, 9th Churchtown, 10th Lustade, 11th Dunmore, 12th Prospect Hill, 13th Carrigans <Carrigane> (a village), 14th Cocktown, 15th Dunnycally, 16th Cloughfin, 17th Derrymore, 18th Castle-third, 19th Tibber, 20th Clashygawan, 21st St Johnstown (a village),

22nd Rockfield, 23rd Castletown, 24th Killgort, 25th Kinnycally, 26th Trintaugh, 27th Linuthraive, 28th Ardaugh, 29th Moncan, 30th Drummanan, 31st Burthall, 32nd Tullyowen, 33rd Whitehill, 34th Mount Gavelin, 35th Carrickmore, 36th Crackdoos, 37th Binion.

The quantity of land in Irish measure 13,289 acres, in English measure 13,557 acres, of which 10,000 acres are arable, 3,000 are pasturable and the remainder are mountain and bog.

PRODUCTIVE ECONOMY

Farms

5. The general size of farms are from 16 to 100 acres, with a few exceptions. The enclosures are banks or ditches covered with furze or brambles, and in some places both. The method of cultivation is not uniform nor regular.

The description of crops are potatoes, oats, barley and flax which, if there were a proper system adopted and crops put down in rotation, there is not the least doubt that the whole district might be considerably improved.

Grazing

6. Pasture-lands are often the arable left out lea in rotation, especially in inland farms. Mountain farms have their pasture separate from the tillage land. Also, some of the lowland ones, when they have much heath or swamps and by draining the latter and planting the former, the occupier would soon be amply repaid for his trouble.

NATURAL FEATURES

Hills

7. Binion's and Dough's hills are the only mountains or hills in the district. The former is pasturable all over and cultivated even in the summit; the latter is rather barren towards the top. However, I have seen cows on it frequently and, although it rises 400 feet above the level of the sea, both oats and potatoes are raised to within a very little of its apex. In this there is a valley betwixt 2 prominences which could easily be converted into excellent meadow, with a very little levelling and draining; and what an acquisition would it be in a situation when not any other good soil for the like is to be found.

Bogs

8. The principal bogs are Killgort, Trintaugh, Monean, Carrinan, Monreagh, Comecannaman, Tyrioddy, Mullinan and Cookstown. The moors are dispersed tracts round the bogs. Timber is found in them all, principally bog fir which is mostly used for fuel. However, one of the best logs I ever saw was lifted in Carrickmore this season at the usual depth (where most of it is found), viz. 10 to 12 feet.

Woods and Plantations

9. Woods none. Orchards many but small; almost every town contains one or two. Nurseries none, the want and loss of which are felt more than understood.

Plantations: I may say none. However, Robert Beatson Esquire, Revd Mr Law and William McClintock Esquire have some very good timber growing on their respective properties at Cloon and Mullinan. I have seen also very nice and valuable plantings.

10. Oak, larch, Spanish chestnut, birch, sycamore, elm, ash, pine, birch, turkey sallow all thrive very [well].

PRODUCTIVE ECONOMY

Rents

11. The highest acreable rent of each description of land: of the best from 3 pounds to 4 pounds sterling, of the second from 1 pound to 2 pounds and of the third from 10s to 1 pound sterling; the moory pasture at about 2s 6d or 3s per acre, some of which rates so high as 5s.

12. Though turf bog be plenty in this district, still it is very valuable; and whether the landlord receive any rent for it or not, I will not take on me to say. Yet some of the tenants pay very smartly for it. I am informed that whether they cut turf or not, they must pay 1s per pound sterling of duty. One farmer of respectability told me that he paid 13 pounds sterling annually to his agent for what he called bog room or the liberty to cut what turf served his own family.

Improvements in Agriculture

13. Improvements undoubtedly are making rapid progress in this district. Iron ploughs after the Scotch make are now generally used here, and many of our intelligent farmers are drilling their potatoes.

Summer fallowing: Revd Mr Law of Killive has done great justice to a park of old weedy ground and, although rather a porous than a retentive substratum, it has received much benefit from a complete fallow in 1819. I hope this example will be followed by all who wish to clean their grounds of anomalous growth of weeds.

Enclosures, I am sorry to state, are not making so great progress as they ought. I understand that the 2-hand hoe and 3-pronged grape as used in Scotland have found their way here, nor will the early adopters of them have any cause to respect their credibility in this respect. The proper tokens of good husbandry, viz. liming, charging and watering, are now almost universally practised, and rolling after the seeds are sown is likewise attended to.

I could wish that deep ploughing and, in some situations, transversely and diagonally were had recourse to in dry porous soils; such (as practised in Lanarkshire in Scotland) a plan the winter rains and snows tend much to enrich, instead of impoverishing reclining and sandy soils.

Fences

14. The description of fence used by the intelligent and those of circumstance is either hawthorn hedges or stone walls; but the other class must be content without any fence or let the useless, I may say pernicious, banks of mud or manure which their forefathers had raised remain, many of which betwixt cultivated land and crop are 6, 7 or 8 yards asunder. Surely such a stupid waste of land, and that probably of the best quality, stands highly reprehensible.

Between St Johnstown and Carrigans, although in as good land as any in the parish, we find these vast banks of rich loam covered with whins and brambles which, if the latter were burned and the former scattered over the shallow places of fields, better and cheaper fences could be easily raised.

Along the highway it is so much higher than the cultivated lands; no fences required but merely to fence it up and to sink an 18-inch trunk; and by setting some whitethorn, this would keep their land dry, preserve much lost land, enrich the rest and at the same time secure travellers from the danger of being swallowed up alive in the deceitful and illegal trenches.

In meadows or swampy tracts open drains are to be recommended. In this situation it is to be understood that shelter is unnecessary and often hurtful, and when scouring such drains instead of raising ditches, as they are usually called, the stuff being of a fertile quality ought to be preserved for manure.

In mountainy situations shelter by planting ought to be the only object in view when about to fence. The Scotch fir answers well for shelter, and what is denominated the living hedge in the county Tyrone demands the attention of farmers. This fence is raised at once by planting of 4-year old quicks in a double bank 2 feet high, a trunk on each side and the stuff cast up constitute the bank.

However, where stones can be easily procured, I would recommend them as the most secure and permanent fence: witness Mr Scott's of Mullinan, the 2 of William McClintock's Esquire of Dunmore and Prospect Hill. Many other kinds of fences are in use and recommendable: the dead fence, the armed fence etc.

Employment

15. In this district employment is neither abundant nor regular. During good weather, in harvest or spring, it is the reverse: none may be idle who wish to be employed. But the great evil is: at least 8 months out of 12, one-half of the weaving classes at home, without earning 1s, except when called a day now and again on particular occasions. And in my opinion this is the grand source from whence all evils arise to which they are exposed; and had we a remedy for this deleterious enemy, idleness, heavy cesses for securing against felony, burglary etc., for enlarging prisons and establishing extra police etc., would be happily found unnecessary.

My plan for giving general employment is by establishing public works, not by neglecting agriculture which shall be hinted at in another place; and as much of costly labour could be equally well executed by females, I would hunt them all out to the fields who are only killing time at their wheels.

Wages

16. The general wages of servants during the half-year is from 2 pounds to 3 pounds sterling and maids from 10s to 1 pound. Labourers per day can be had costnet, viz. not boarded, for 10d per day throughout the year. On harvest, tolerable good wages may be had per day; from 1s to 1s 3d with victuals is the usual rate. On winter and summer they are for little or nothing. I had an excellent spadesman in my garden for the mere trifle of 5d a day.

Green Crops

17. Green crops, potatoes excepted, are not generally cultivated here and as the soil can be

excelled by none for turnips, I [find it] strange much why they are not more universally sown. Mr Andrew Mason has a small quantity. They look extremely well and I hope his plan of labour will soon become universal.

Artificial Grasses

18. Artificial grasses are sown here; rye with a mixture of clover and sometimes rib grass is put down. I am sorry to state that the cultivators of them do not agree in their reports. Mr Hutchinson from much experience has quit sowing any kind of grass, assuming that his farms, when left lea, can produce a better crop of natural than any artificial grass he has tried. This shows plainly that his lands are not kept in good order when so many weeds spring forth when left out.

It would not be amiss to try tuscan, sain foin, chiacary, especially the first as fine reports are given of its productiveness in Scotch husbandry; and as it answers transplanting and retentive in rich soils, many parts of this district would undoubtedly grow great crops of it.

Draining

19. Draining by surface and underdraining are both done here. Meadows and some spongy soils require to be drained by surface and fine clays and irregular springs require covered drains. Mr Hugh Stephenson of Lignatheau has very much improved a cold and wet farm by a number of well-planned drains.

Manure

20. The general kinds of manure are dung, sometimes itself, at other times compounded with various composts, viz. loam, lime, shells and vegetables, all which answer very well.

Clay or soil is frequently burned for manure, and were it not that it raises quantities of potatoes which are our staff of bread, I would almost condemn every kind of soil burned for manure, or in other words, the burning of any kind of soil to bring in the land; as it is for this intent it is generally practised. And let others say what they may, in the ultimate it never fails to injure the aftercrops for many years.

If any part be too deep and deaf, mixing it with red or sandy till answers the purpose much better than burning. The vegetable sward, whether it be heath, bent, rush or sprit, when decomposed makes good manure, but when burned the most nutritious particles are volatilized, dispersed and wafted through the atmosphere. The component parts of one vegetable does not require to be analysed to afford nutrition to another but merely fermented, and this itself would not be carried to the highest point; but more of this hereafter.

Experience may have taught the most obtuse farmer who has been in the habit of burning the sward that it requires a considerable time before the fertility of the soil can be recovered, even although it be ever so well manured. Hence the propriety of leaving out lea after such labour and either sowing or planting grass to prepare it for aftercropping.

In mountainy places the poor certainly provide for their families a supply of victuals, when not provided with the means to purchase them; and as remarked above, were it not for this circumstance, the plan of burning for manure would be incompatible with good husbandry. Those who have no need for having recourse to the above expedient but merely to reduce barren lands to a fertile state would be much home at their purpose by covering the swards with various composts of different soils, which can be easily found in almost every field by raising the subsoil; and if lime, marl, shells and seaweed can be found, so much the better; then watering above, winter and summer, will soon, without any other labour, mollify and fertilize the most stubborn ground.

Irrigation

21. The practice of watering meadows is laudably adopted in every part of this district, yet in this appearingly simple labour, much might still be done to improve and procure larger and better crops of hay. Most farmers follow the same notion of letting the water on at November to either dam or circulate at pleasure all winter, and without theory or observation are satisfied from experience. Sometimes they miss and at others they hit a good crop. Nor am I acquainted with one point in agriculture less understood than meadow watering.

The main ends which ought to guide us in this delicate point of farming are to destroy the roots of some vegetables and afford nutriment to others. When water runs rapidly over the sward, it may answer the first but at the expense of the second, for thereby those roots which have a slender texture and hold are carried from the seat of growth. Consequently sprit and other strong grasses are able to stand while the slender ones are destroyed, and by letting a small quantity of water remain at rest, and probably a chalybeate, the damage is still greater by absorbing oxygen from the atmosphere; and from its assiduous and corroding quality, the tender blade suffers more, being entirely decomposed.

The plan most proper to adopt is to put plenty of water on, the softer and muddier the better, and let the meadow be either drained or not. Neither of the above evils can occur. It must be understood, however, that the water, instead of being let off, ought to be on the sward when the 2 main objects will be afforded, viz. decomposition and nutrition. The roots of sprits and rushes, having more carbon than the other grasses, are more easily rotted in the organized state.

Hence our observation establishes this theory: in trenches and margins of lakes and ponds of water, when covered the whole winter, produce most grass, yes, and that of a proper quality, especially for black cattle, without a mixture of moss, sprit, rush or any other unnecessary weeds. Instead of letting the water run off, as is usually the case on April, May, it is to be prevented from running on; and what is on, at this period, ought to be evaporated by the rays of the sun, when a complete covering of rich glutinous matter is left to nourish the ensuing crop which, if judiciously managed, excels all other manure for the natural grass of the soil.

22. No dairies have been established here in my time.

Spade Tillage and Oxen

23. Spade tillage is practised and answers very well. My opinion, however, is that much might be done with the plough to a better purpose, particularly with regard to potato culture and hinting. It may be remarked here that when light land is shallowly ploughed, no other substitute can equal hinting.

24. Oxen are not much used in husbandry.

Grain Crops

25. The different sorts of grain sown are oats, barley and wheat. More wheat might be put down, as the soil answers extremely well for it. Oats sell at from 8d to 9d per stone, barley has got up to 1s or 1s 2d per stone and potatoes to from 3d to 4d per stone. 8 of such stones make one hundred of 112 lbs. Provisions in general have been very low priced during all the seasons, but appears from the uncertainty of our harvest to look up a little.

26. Land is generally computed by Irish measurement.

Livestock

27. The black cattle, which farmers are in the habit of rearing, are of the middle size.

28. The description of stock kept on pasturelands is mostly young cattle, oxen and sheep.

29. The description of sheep is of the middle size. They answer the climate very well. Still, a larger description might do just equally well and be of considerably more benefit.

30. The description of horse in agricultural use is various. The higher order of farmers indeed have horses adequate to the task, but the other order have a small weak animal neither able for plough nor cart.

31. The description of swine is likewise of the middle size.

Livestock and Improvements

32. As in query 2nd, the quantity as nearly as can be calculated by 6 intelligent persons are as under: black cattle 2,600, horses 569, sheep 2,800, swine 1,040, amount 7,009.

The improvements having respect to soil and climate: it suggests to me that our climate is not so cold nor our soil so barren that would make us afraid to improve every description of stock. Robert Beatson Esquire has brought some beautiful cows of Ayrshire breed, nor have I any doubt from the number of them that are frequently sold in different parts of the north of Ireland but our indulgent landlords shall soon see their fertile soils as well improved with regard to stock as any other in a more favourable climate.

Improvements in Breeding

33. Being only a few years resident in this parish, I can say little to the improvement during the last 20 years. Yet from what I can learn, the farmers had as good horses 20 years back as what they have yet; and if we value them according to their agility, much better. Other kinds of stock have been considerably improved.

NATURAL FEATURES

Rivers and Loughs

34. The River Foyle, being our only one, rises from various subterraneous crevices in Barnesmore <Bainesmore>. When collected, forms a considerable rivulet at the foot of the mountain and although the natural course and final discharge be north by east, yet it necessarily takes many irregular and serpentine windings.

Loughs: 1, Port lough.

Coast

Harbours: 2, St Johnstown and Carrigans; creeks: many, Dunalong and Carrinmore; shores: none but the beach, which is covered except when the tide is out or low water.

Peculiar production: salmon, trout etc., eel on some parts of this beach or shore. Excellent manure might be procured at Tullyown, Mountgavelin, Carrumon, St Johnstown and almost the whole length of the district. It lies plentifully, although I do not know of one individual that leaves it off for that purpose. It is of a tough argillaceous quality intermixed with many carbonaceous fossils.

NATURAL HISTORY

Mines

35. No mines are open here, yet iron appears to be very plentiful as I have seen many large pieces of ore aggregated with both argillaceous and other classes. Whether the reason of them being not known, or for want of ingenious men to set out such works afoot, or whether we could procure iron from Sweden and Holland cheaper than this would be manufactured, I cannot say. Still, such undertakings would turn out ultimately to the advantage of those who are in want of employment.

Quarries

36. We are as well accommodated with quarries in this district as what other parts are, lime, slates, stones and, I presume, coal in abundance; nor would we wish a more convenient situation for exporting our slates from Doughill by Mr Marshall and Mr Alexander. Lime from Crackadoos by Mr Smith and brick by Mr Semple and Mr Alexander are too well known and valued in Londonderry to require any comment, all being only 2 short miles from St Johnstown harbour.

The 2 latter are much nearer Carrickmore <Carricmon>, when they can be as easily boated; and did we wish to give employment for our poor, might not a pottery and crockery manufacture be established here, when this district can compete with any other in the north west, of argillaceous clay (it being the only ingredient necessary)?

Limestone

37. Limestone, colour bluish grey, is plentifully found at Crackadoos. Quality: it is nearly a pure carbonate of lime; however, other substances are present in considerable proportions. Its hardness is semi-inclining to soft; specific gravity scarcely 2.5. It is found massive and irregularly stratified, and in connection with other secondary strata. It loses from 25 to 30 per cent in burning, of its weight. As turbary is very convenient, it is burned with peat at very little expense. It can be purchased at the kiln for sometimes so low as 8d per barrel and mostly at 10d.

Coal

38. No coal mines are yet opened here. Still, I am of opinion this most useful of all fossils may be raised, from what indications I am able to make in mineral waters; and I am not out of the opinion but we may yet find abundance of employment from this simple article for all, and more men than our district can produce.

Mr Hamilton told me he found a piece of coal in his farm, and by the manner it burned it was bituminous, as a quantity of bitumen or resin was produced as it burned, or as Lord Dondonnells terms it, tar coal. When exhaling much smoke and flame at first and afterwards burning with only a clear reflection towards the end; some term it pitch coal.

Be this as it may, I spent the most of a day with Mr Hamilton through his farm trying to procure a small piece but in vain. Could such a valuable discovery be found so near the River Foyle, would it not be an inestimable treasure, affording employment to a numerous population of poor in St Johnstown and at the same time saving the inhabitants of Derry and Strabane of some thousands sterling annually for fuel?

Mineral Springs

39. Mineral springs are numerous in this district. 2 only are famed for their wonderful cures, one of which at Cloughfin, 5 miles from Derry and 1 mile from St Johnstown, about 10 yards off the west side of the road.

I have been at some pains analysing this water and from the quantity of oxygen which it attracts from the surrounding atmosphere, it is quite evident that iron is the predominant principle, hence the term chalybeate may be given; and that it also contains sulphuriated hydrogen there is not the least doubt or circumstance truly worthy of prosecution, for thereby we might find some of that valuable fossil sulphur. I have drank often of this water and can affirm that it is an excellent tonic and at the same time has a diuretic effect, as its qualities naturally indicate.

The most evident ingredient in the other well at Kinnycally is carbon or carbonate of lime, it having an acidulent taste and sparkles when poured out of one tumbler into another. Whether it will redden the infusion of such I cannot say. Still we may infer that it ought to be recommended to such as are troubled with acid in the stomach, and more particularly to those who are deficient in that most useful and permanent principle (lime) in their bones.

Marl

40. Some say marl has been found in this district. I have tried where they said it lay, but none appeared to me. There is no doubt but by tracing the vein of this compound earthy clay, some marl might be had as it appeared to have a mixture of this useful fossil, and if found it would be of the carbon kind. Still, I am afraid that no compact marl will be discovered here for any useful establishment further than for manure.

SOCIAL ECONOMY

Condition of the People

41. The situation of the inhabitants in general, compared with that of other districts, is superior in many respects, nor is there another district, all things considered, that can compare with this for domestic comforts and conveniences, disposition to industry, but I must stop at the means of earning money; as to the mode of employing it, I can say nothing as we have it not.

Houses and Fuel

42. The condition of farmhouses is tolerable, but nothing to what I hope they will yet be either for repair or cleanliness etc. Some of the upper class of them have acquired a little taste in this respect. They are still behind what I have seen in many parts of Scotland.

43. Fuel is remarkably plentiful in this neighbourhood most commonly high. I have not seen it so reasonable as at present: turf can be had at 1s 8d to 2s per cage or creel.

Food

44. The general food of farmers are potatoes, meal, beef, bacon, milk and butter, and frequently fresh herrings and other fish; seldom salmon.

45. The manufacturing class nearly the same.

46. The poor or labouring class that cannot keep a cow live miserably; very rarely, if [ever?], they can get above potatoes and herrings, and that often 3 times per day.

Education

47. So far as I am acquainted, education is happily embraced by all who have it in their power; and although a certain description of professors does not for conscience sake attend public schools promiscuous with others, yet I am informed Sunday evening schools and even weekly meetings are regularly attended for the promotion of literary knowledge. I am rather inclined to think the intention of these meetings is to establish in religious principles.

In conclusion to this query, we may safely say that the education is principally confined to the higher order who see beauty and admire its charms.

48. Education in the upper class of this neighbourhood is 1 guinea per quarter for classics and half a guinea per quarter for English; yet many of the higher branches of English rate as classics. The next class pay from 5s to 10s per quarter and the third class from 2s 6d to 5s per quarter.

49. [Improvements] Yes, the observable difference in the state of the peasantry, in consequence of the more general difference of education, is manifest; and its effects are such that time never shall be able to efface them.

Health and Common Complaints

50. I have often remarked that this is the most healthy season I have ever witnessed. Few diseases in this district of any kind that has a mortal tendency are prevalent. The only common complaints I am consulted in are toothache, rheumatism and psora or itch, and, although lamentable, few who understand the latter distemper are applied to for cure, as most of the common and even some of the very respectable people rest contented with this contagious malady in their families for many years, may I say, ages.

One says oh! it's the effect of oat bread, another says salt herrings is the cause, and a mother ascribes this heat in the blood to the teething of her child, all which cases are merely nominal without having any foundation in truth. Therefore few medical gentlemen are consulted to destroy this contagious virus.

Although rheumatism is always ascribed to cold, which we cannot deny, but it either directly or indirectly brings on this complaint, nevertheless from judicious management, the extremes of heat and cold may be undergone without affecting the constitution.

Although toothache be almost overlooked by therapeutic writers, yet it demands the attention of every professor of the healing art; and although the pretended cures of this distressing disease are many, the most of them just know as much physiology as the pen that censors them. The remote causes of toothache is whatever impairs the nervous system locally or generally considered, and this cause acts either by irritation or compression or both. Hence all scouring of the gums with stimulating medicines, instead of removing or preventing, never fail to increase and render the constitution more susceptible of the complaint.

Where the absorbents overbalance the exhalants, accumulation of superfluous fluids compresses the nervous effluvia and stops the circulation in those non-elastic parts of the face, hence the acute pains which are felt in the temples, cheek-bones and lower jaw, in comparison to what are felt in the more muscular parts.

During the warm weather in summer, more people were complaining of wandering pains, particularly the lean and nervous, which they called rheumatism, than were in the midst of winter. Not a day passed without some person asking for flies to blister certain pains, which when in the face was toothache and when in other parts was rheumatism; nor would they be prevailed on but blister they would. The effect was adding fuel to the flames.

True cause: when being exposed to the strong rays of the sun without exercising, a preternatural quantity of calorie was imbibed and accumulated, which accounted for the disagreeable warm sensation felt in such circumstances and the enormous quantity of electricity which is conducted through the medium of the atmosphere from positive clouds to the earth, it being negative during very warm seasons. Consequently the animal system being impregnated with these pervading and excoriating fluids which, when not neutralised by drink nor yet carried off by perspiration, why should we [find it?] strange that the human body would be tortured even to the inflammatory points?

Nor are these instances wanting on record when the body was excited to inflammation and explosion from such causes. Experience may have taught those who have been exposed to the rays of the sun, even through windows, that such pains are not rheumatic but the unquestionable effects of electricity and calorie. The only preventative is exercise and vegetable acids, hence the necessity of sour fruits and buttermilk when thus diseased.

Friendly Societies

51. Friendly societies are not established here for bettering the condition of the poor. The reason is obvious, being so near Derry and Strabane, where our generous and opulent are not backward in casting in their portions into charitable institutions. Still, societies of various kinds are much wanted amongst us.

MODERN TOPOGRAPHY

Towns and Villages

52. Towns: none; villages: 3, St Johnstown, Carrigans and Newtown Hamilton.

PRODUCTIVE ECONOMY

Means to Improvement

53. All, so far as I am acquainted, have a turn for improvement; and how such a spirit could be best excited has cost me many hours' study during these 7 years. At one time I was of the opinion that giving rewards to those who would commit most of the sacred Scriptures to memory in a limited time gained the ascendancy, and as there is in them an attracting charm to allure the mind from every kind of vice, I concluded that undoubtedly the premium of a faithful donor would not be withheld in granting other necessaries.

Upon a second reflection I found that, although this might lay the basis of economy and decorum which must proceed all happiness here and hereafter, still something else is wanting to excite a spirit of industry without which we are worse than infidels, as the apostles says "those who will not provide for those of their own house are."

Again I was led to believe, and am still of the same opinion, that without education all other methods to encourage industry in Ireland must vanish like a nightly phantom, as it teaches not only how to earn but how to lay out. A fool may do the former, but a wise man can only do the latter to advantage. I had almost said the want of gratuitous seminaries for educating the poor was a stigma on British government which America, the different parts of Europe and even the more unenlightened nations can boast of.

It is truly with reluctance I state anything that would hurt the feelings of an individual. Much less am I inclined to cast a slur on that government which stands unrivalled on the globe we inhabit. It is not necessary that all mankind be classic scholars but that a knowledge of natural, mechanical, experimental and chemical philosophy is absolutely useful in every department of life; and where a seminary of these sciences is established in every respectable town for teaching gratis such important branches, at what a height of improvement would our Irish genius soon arise. Yes, would they not soon be bright constellations in this reflecting isle?

I recommend also that all parish schoolmasters be versioned in these branches, who should at proper intervals lecture their pupils in their intended occupations. If this mode of instructing were once set on foot, what a flourishing people would a small loan from government soon make. As otherwise we, the lower order, are a set of illiterate Irish blockheads laughed at by the Scotch, condemned by the English and directed by the sons of our fathers beyond the Atlantic.

I have seen an Irish student, when not having the means to enter a member of an honourable institution, when his master had been previously enrolled, throw himself down on the ground and pull the hair out of his head. The reason of this distraction was because he had corrected and prepared his master's thesis for examination, who passed and was admitted by paying 150 pounds sterling, the usual admittance. Still, since that time I feel for a *persevering genius*.

Practical Farmers

54. The number of active and spirited farmers in this district are numerous. As to their intelligence I can say little, not being much acquainted. However, the Revd Matthew Heron of the Hall, Mr Hugh Stephenson of Lignathraw, Mr John Alexander of Drummanan, Mr Scott of Mullinan, Mr Hunter of Tullyown, Mr McFarland of Cloon and Mr Samuel Marshall of Tibber are all active and intelligent farmers. Others have made great improvements lately, which are owing principally to their indulgent landlords, Mr Andrew Mason of Killdrum, Mr Joseph McPherson and Mr William Elliott of Cloughfin, and this farm, the occupier of it I do not know, it lies immediately above Robert Beatson Esquire, I imagine he is a Mr Mills, and Mr David McClean, all have done much to the farms.

Linen

55. [Linen manufacture] is nearly at a stand these 3 or 4 years back, but much decreased from what it was for 20 years previous.

56. The number and extent of millworks are many and great, no less than 20 mills are in this limited district of 21 miles: Mr Stephenson of Lignathraw 1, Mr Alexander of Drummanan 1, Mr Alexander of Kinnycally 1, Mr Shaw of Kinnycally 1, Revd Mr Cunningham of Castletown 1, Mr McClean of St Johnstown 1, Mr Gallagher of Carrigans 1, Mr McPherson of Killdrum 1, Mr MacFarland of Cloon 1, Mr Marshall of Tibber 1, Mr Laid of Cross 1, Mr Mackin of Lishill 1, Mr Roger of Ginsurry 1, Mr McPherson 1, Mr Mills 1, Mr Caldwell of Killdrum 1, Mr Culbert of Killdrum 1, Mr Pinkerton 1, Mr Gallagher of Port Lough 1, Mr Levins of Brickfield 1, 21 in all. Probably some others may have escaped my notice.

Flax

57. The lands intended for flax are generally ploughed early, then harrowed and ploughed again before the seeds are put down, which is either in barley land or the second crop after lea. Some put down their flax the next crop after potatoes, which I do not recommend; neither is it so certain as the second crop after them. Part is consumed at home but a greater part is still exported.

Preparation of Flax

58. Flax is usually prepared by mills and fire is always used in preparing it which, with steeping, this might to more advantage be omitted. For what purpose is flax steeped but to fructify the stalk. To accomplish this it must undergo the first stage of fermentation, which might be as well and better executed without any water save what it retains when pulled, and the wetter so much the better, than by building and covering it in large piles; the parts will be much sooner decomposed than the corticle or ruddy fibre.

And were this plan once adopted, what immense labour would be saved and what a healthy atmosphere would we have. Otherwise were it not for the equinox gales and heavy rains which immediately follow, we would be exposed to deleterious, pestilential vapours, the sure and never failing parent of mortal typhus.

And all that is necessary to be attended to in thus preparing flax for mill manufacture is to keep it from being exploded when the temperature rises high which, if the weather be not wet, may be done by throwing a little water over now and again about the 4th, 5th and 6th days.

Yarn

59. The usual grist which yarns are spun to is from 3 to 6 hanks in the lb. and the tow from 1 to

2 hanks in the lb. The daily wages which a diligent spinner can earn per day is very trifling, not more than 3d or 4d at the outside.

60. The price of fine yarn is from 3s 4d to 3s and coarse from 1s 6d to 2s per spangle, the most of which is sold for exportation.

61. Spinners generally grow their own flax.

Spinning Wheels

62. The double [wheel], which has been introduced into this neighbourhood but not with such success as what it has met in Scotland. Mrs Stephenson of Lignathraw says it has no advantage over the single.

Preparation of Yarn

63. The manufacturer generally works here on a very limited scale. He goes to market and purchases the making of what he calls a web, being 52 yards; this, at 2s 6d a spangle, amounts to 2 pounds 10s, allowing 20 spangles to the web, bleaching stuff besides his own trouble 2s 6d, which is done in mornings and evenings, so that time is not taken up in bleaching except 1 day to boil and another to swift and a third to warp.

Say 4 days are expended in a lb. at 4s, bleaching stuff 1s 6d, first cost 2 pounds 10s, to the weaver 1 pound 2s 6d, what one web stands the manufacturer 4 pounds 1s; suppose he sells at 1s 10d per yard, 4 pounds 15s 3d, manufacturer's profit 14s 3d. But as the weaver is mostly the owner, his profit is considerable.

Yarn Greens

64. Only 1 small yarn green is in this neighbourhood. It belongs to Miss Pinkerton of St Johnstown. She is making well by it and would she adopt the new methods of bleaching, she would have at least 4 turns of her money for every one, which would be a very handsome profit itself. I have often advised her to try it and offered to put her on the proper plan, assuring her against hurting the texture of the thread in the least.

Wool

66 to 69. Woollen manufacture: none.

70. Our farmers, especially Mr Hugh Stephenson, have tried to shear his sheep twice in the year which, owing to the uncertainty of our climate, did not answer well.

71 and 72. Cotton manufacture: none.

73 to 75. Kelp manufacture: none.

Fisheries

76. The description that are taken in Foyle river are salmon, trout and eel.

77. The number of vessels usually employed are from 7 to 8, of from 5 to 20 tons burden, and a few small boats.

78. This fishery has in former years sent an immense quantity to Liverpool, which is the principal town exported [to]. The distance from shore is not calculated upon, as the river is but of a narrow breadth.

79. The number of persons employed are from 70 to 80 men.

Curing of Fish

80. Derry and Strabane are supplied with fresh fish from this river, or at least the surrounding inhabitants get their fresh fish here during the summer months plentifully, and many of them are so well up to curing them that they have what they call cured salmon all winter round.

81. And are capable of being improved by preserving the pregnant fish also in their proper season.

Queries and Answers on St Johnstown

MEMOIR WRITING

Memoir Writing

Appendix containing preliminary and miscellaneous remarks. The reason why I present this under the title of St Johnstown district is because this is my place of residence and the most notable part in it. And the reason why I have comprehended nearly 2 parishes and not confined my survey to one is because I am not acquainted so well in the parish as what I am in this district, my business calling me through some parts of it every day.

NATURAL STATE AND PRODUCTIVE ECONOMY

Situation

3. The parishes of Killea and Taughboyne are separated by a small serpentine rivulet which rises or has its source at Port lough and empties itself at Carrigans into the Foyle, on which are 5 flax mills and 1 corn mill. This last, with an elegant flour mill, are the property of Mr McClintock of Dunmore, and as the baronies of Raphoe and Inishowen are peculiarly adapted for wheat, it is

lamentable such beautiful houses and machinery should be idle and that when the persons formerly employed are in a state of starvation for want of employment.

Proprietors

4. Whether there are more landed proprietors in this district than the Earl of Wicklow, Marquis of Abercorn (a minor), Robert Beatson Esquire, Revd Mr Law, the 2 Messrs McClintocks and the Lord Bishop of Raphoe, I cannot say. One circumstance I know, that it is happy for all the tenants of the 4 last-mentioned gentlemen that they mostly reside in this district; and did the 2 non-residents find it convenient to stop occasionally here, it would still add much to our prosperity.

Farming Methods

5. Lands well enclosed, are half cultivated. In mountainous situations small parks well hedged with whitethorn have an excellent effect in producing bountiful crops, as well as preserving them from destructive winds. In low and wet lands draining is the principal object which demands our attention, and when well executed other fences are unnecessary. In Scotland a description of oats is much famed for not having a bosom prickle.

The usual plan of kibbing potatoes is erroneous. Instead of merely covering the seed, they are frequently put forth 5 or 6 inches deep. Laying them on the manure in some places is still worse, especially if it be acidulous, which acts too powerfully and decomposes their semina before sufficient stems be produced. The generality of farmers recommend having the brows of the ridges when shovelling uncut down, the good intent of which is more than counterbalanced by affording weeds to grow plentifully at the expense of the potato crop. One of the greatest errors by the cultivation of potatoes is being not particular in selecting and cutting their seed.

Early put down potatoes never ought to be kept for seed, nor ought the cut or two next the base ever be put down. During 10 years' observation I do not recollect to see a good stalk grow from the base or tangle end. When large none but the rose or apex of them and when small this apex never ought to be cut longitudinally through the centre as is always the case.

I have tried them in drills, lazy beds, whole and cut, large and small, wet and dry manured, and after careful observation I give the preference to whole seed in drills if early, but cut seed answers equally well if late; and the dung always put on and covered immediately in its strength before its volatile parts be dissipated.

It is to be recommended and remembered that a little earth must be put between the seed and manure, otherwise its oxygen will act too powerfully and ferment it too soon. I have taken 18 stones of potatoes of 18 yards square in drills and 14 of the same quantity of land in lazy beds; and as they were dug in August, when they were not nearly at their growth, at 6d per stone, the drilled ones amounted to 144 lbs per acre, the other to 112 lbs; in favour of the drill 32 pounds sterling per acre.

Letting cattle run at random on heavy retentive soils never fails hurting the ensuing crop, and exposing dry, porous, sandy land to the same winter pasture adds much to its advantage. For thereby water remains in their tracts and absorbed, which would otherwise be evaporated or run off. It is also improved by consolidation whereas wet ground is materially injured by it.

Pasture-Land

6. Liming pasturing-land if wet, and watering it if dry, will improve it materially. Between Carrigans and Port lough is a vast tract of deep swampy soil which is not worth more than 5s per acre, and by proper culture would soon be worth as many pounds. A great number of acres are unreclaimed at the north western side of Binion hill, truly worthy the attention of the proprietor, and lime is found on the spot and requires no other manure save shelter, which the living fence and Scotch fir would answer completely.

NATURAL FEATURES

Bogs

8. The timber found in Mullenan and Monreagh is mostly fir roots, which are of great service to those who live convenient as they are a substitute for both candle and fuel. When the turf has been cut off they are exposed, so they require no trouble to lift them.

Plantations and Trees

9. If nurseries were regularly planted in this neighbourhood they would stimulate our farmers, who are encouraged by long leases to ornament this delightful country for the future benefit of a rising offspring.

10. To say absolutely what description of trees thrive best in many parts of the district would

require one versant in the science. Many parts have no description of trees growing on them whatever. We find at the gentlemen's seats, who reside on their respective properties, this attention inverted, as they have set a good example in this, as every department, of useful [practice], although neglected husbandry.

PRODUCTIVE ECONOMY

Rents and Farms

11. Although the farmer knows the value of most of his lands, still in mountainous parts he occupies many acres he does not know how much it stands him per acre, nor is it necessary he should.

12. As I am not very well acquainted how landlord and agent settle the affair of turf bog between themselves and the Crown, it being a royal claim, I know, still, that out-tenants pay some places at the rate of 8 pounds sterling per acre and at others 10s per acre. This is what I pay for it to Mr Marshall of Tibber. How he comes to be entitled to let it, I cannot tell.

Fences

13. The description of fence I would recommend is various, accordingly to the situation. Stone walls in some, hawthorns in others and open drains in others, as remarked at query 13th. Mr Gallagher of Carrigans or Dunmore Lodge has some very beautiful hedges which, if they were put down at the height they stand, I would call them the lining hedges or fences.

Enclosures

14. Mr Scott of Mullenan ought to get the preference in this district, the landed proprietors excepted, for beautiful, regular and permanent enclosures. I know of no place or plan that would afford regular and permanent employment except by setting manufactories on foot, not only here but in every other part of the kingdom, and let the nation take a certain farmer's advice.

His maxim is not to lay out money for what he can have at home and to draw in as much as possible by disposing of what he can conveniently spare. Therefore while other farmers are purchasing poultry, eggs, fruit and paying tradesmen for making clothes, shoes, farming utensils etc., he is disposing of all these articles to his neighbours. Consequently, whilst they are in distress for want of money, he is termed the banker of the town, and my wish is that Ireland would take a lesson from this illiterate but preternatural philosopher.

We have in our island the necessaries and luxuries of life for a much more numerous population than what it yet contains; and were a heavy duty levied on all imported articles, to be contributed amongst the ingenious manufacturers here of the said articles, might not such a plan have a good effect in lifting us to the same level of our now dependent, imperial kingdom?

Wages

16. Such is the deplorable situation of our poor that I have known servants offer their services for their victuals. What exertion ought this create in every humane breast, to afford relief to an industrious and spirited people?

Green Crops

17. The reason why, in my opinion, green crops are not cultivated to any extent here is because the benefit of such culture is not known. I have seen beans, peas, carrots, parsnips, cabbage, turnips etc. cultivated in different parts of Scotland, and which not only afforded good nourishment for cattle, sheep, horses, swine etc. but at the same time enriched the soil very materially. In some well-enclosed parks peas might, as I have done in a small garden, be put down in potato trenches and turnips after the early ones are dug out. I have produced good crops both ways.

Artificial Grasses

18. Although artificial grasses are laudably sown, still our natural ones, if well managed, would be nothing inferior to the best of them. Not only our natural white clover seed or poor shamrock might be procured in abundance and sown, which by 20 per cent excels our red artificial grass, but our foreen might be planted with little expense or trouble on rich clays by merely scarring those trenches when it grows plentifully and scattering the stuff over them. Thus in a few years of this description a crop of the most nourishing [kind] may be had off even the most barren ground. I have known it crop between 20 and 30 feet in 4 months.

Timothy grass is another of great importance. I know a park or two where scarcely any other is to be found, and although the soil be wet and poor still it grows to great perfection. Robert Young, wheelwright, sowed some of this kind of hay at 2 pounds 16s in Londonderry when others, appearingly as good hay, did not exceed 2 pounds 10s per ton. I understand that it excels most other grasses for horses, a singular fact that this seed weighs much heavier than any of our artificial ones.

It may be remarked that alkaline lees never fail to produce abundant crops of almost every kind of grass. As ashes, whether of soil or vegetables, have the same effect, might not some of our useless banks of earth that are mock fences round our meadows be burned for this purpose and spread either by themselves or mixed with other composts amply reward the husbandman's trouble?

Drainage

19. At query 19th I have remarked that open drains are principally left in meadows. How far this is absolutely right remains a question. If water ought to lie a considerable depth to afford nutriment and prevent from souring, underdraining certainly has the preference as thereby the trouble of irrigation along the margin of the drains is prevented.

Manures

20. We have found out in this district the praiseworthy method of raising potatoes by compound and scarring turf mould or moss as it is called. Still, this manure might be much improved from what it generally is by mixing it with various other clays in a moist situation, frequently excusing [exposing?] its undersurface to atmospheric light, calorie and electricity, which would greatly improve its quality, the absorbing oxygen etc. Many people, I observe, put themselves to very unnecessary trouble and expense by leaving this mire home and in the space of 6 months just drawing it back to where it came from.

Irrigation

21. Meadow watering must be managed according to the soil, situation and season. Soft soils require less water than dry ones. In reclining situations much irrigation becomes necessary during frost and searching weather; on [in] February and March an abundance does much good.

Farm Techniques

22. Dairies established here, and properly managed, would pay well.

23. Oxen might, with great propriety, be used in husbandry, being not so expensive as horses.

24. [Spade husbandry] In mountainous situations it cannot be dispensed with.

25. [Grain crops] As this undoubtedly is a grand soil for wheat, no sufficient apology have I heard for not putting it down more generally.

26. I believe bishop and college lands are computed by English measurement.

Livestock

27. The black cattle reared by farmers might be improved.

28. [Most common] Principally young stock.

29. Our own breed of sheep, if fed on turnips as in Scotland, would grow much larger.

30. Our agricultural horse is scarcely strong enough.

31. We have a very good description of swine.

32. For the quantity of stock: most farmers have too many for them to be well fed in either winter or summer; the loss is more than what is known.

33. [Improvements] Not so much in proportion as what have been made in some other districts in the country.

NATURAL HISTORY

Porpoises

34. A number of cowan or porpoises has been seen.

Minerals and Mines

35. As iron is still of more importance to us year after year, we ought to strain a point by establishing manufactures of this kind.

36. Enforcing the good effects of lime cannot be too often repeated for cold and retentive soils.

37. When burned, our lime is a good white.

38. I intend, when the springs are completely opened, to make a general research for coal.

39. [Mineral springs] When provided with delicate tests, I intend not only to analyse the waters of this [district] but those of all the barony of Raphoe, and tell their compound parts accurately for the benefit of the public.

40. As much as is said about marl in other parts of those parishes I will soon prove that, which will be the first good weather, if spared.

SOCIAL ECONOMY

Condition of the People

41. The mode of employing money is for the absolute necessaries of life.

42. As my business too frequently obliges me to visit the poor cottager, I can safely say the [houses are] cold, filthy and miserably small.

43. One happiness which the mountain inhabitants enjoy is a plentiness of fuel.

Food

44. As at query 44th, food of farmers is plenty and healthy.

45. Manufacturers' food is exactly the same as farmers'.

46. Few of the opulent know how wretched our poor class are fed, nor would I believe did I not too often see it, for which I lament.

Education

47. The general wish for education is the same. The late Revd Mr Pemberton got Sunday schools established and which his successors, the Revd Messrs Bowen and Law of Killea, are conscientious in affording every possible encouragement. They are not above visiting themselves and seeing that useful and lasting morals be faithfully inculcated in the minds of the numerous youth who attend them.

48. Would prefer teachers to be encouraged by giving a certain salary per annum. Education would not be so expensive as it is at present.

Improvements from Education

49. Yes, the difference in the state of the peasantry is such in consequence of the diffusion of knowledge that when lately passing over the west part of Binion, I found a poor cowboy with his Testament, behind a ditch, perusing the 23rd Psalm. On asking him what he was doing, replied "preparing his task for the evening school."

Health

50. I doubt our ensuing winter will not be so wholesome as the summer, in consequence of the great exposure of the labouring classes to these heavy rains.

Friendly Societies

51. Friendly societies, news rooms, meetings and circulating libraries are much wanted for promoting knowledge, harmony and love.

MODERN TOPOGRAPHY

Towns and Villages

52. St Johnstown contains 260 inhabitants, Carrigans 200 and Newtown Hamilton 80.

PRODUCTIVE ECONOMY

Improvements

53. By established quarterly fairs at St Johnstown would have a good [effect] in enabling its inhabitants to pay their rent.

Practical Farmers

54. Revd Mr Heron is a very scientific farmer and, I am confident, would be a useful correspondent. Mr Hugh Stephenson stands high in the farming scale and is anxious to have established here a branch of society for promoting husbandry. Referred to 54 in the queries.

Linen Manufacture and Mills

55. I understand that more linens are manufactured here than what were last season.

56. From the great quantity of flax that is raised in this district, 3 mills have been built in it this season. Might they not be so constructed as to prepare the flax for the spinning wheel?

Flax

57. A number of people find, especially on dry, sandy, light soils once ploughing, and that immediately before putting down the seed, answers better the farmer than the former custom of twice ploughing.

58. It is to be remembered that when fermenting flax to fructify the stalk, it must be securely covered; and if not wet when pulled, to sprinkle every row of sheaves, as they are built, with water.

Yarn

59. As both spinner and weaver find more profit arising from fine than from coarse yarns, farmers ought to consider this when procuring their seed; and some kinds of it grow finer than others and flax is in general too thin sown.

60. Our coarse yarns are mostly sold for exportation.

61. Spinners sometimes grow and sometimes purchase their flax.

62. [Double wheel] It would not be amiss; give the double wheel some further encouragement here.

Preparation of Yarn

63. We are far behind other parts, even in Ireland, in manufacturing yarns. The fly shuttle is scarcely

known amongst us. I am creditably informed that 1 man or woman, the weaver as I have seen them do in Scotland, can make more cloth in the same time than 4 of our weavers with the hand shuttle.

Linen manufactures on a small scale ought to be established that would give employment for 10 to 20 men. The expense would be most trifling.

64. Bleach greens would undoubtedly have a very good effect in the district.

65. The usual description of linen manufactured here is from 11 to 16 hundreds; price of the former about 1s 5d per yard and of the latter 2s 4d or 2s 6d per yard.

MEMOIR WRITING

General Remarks

These solutions and observations, being written in much haste on Friday and Saturday last, were intended to be corrected immediately and done in a better hand; but an unavoidable circumstance occurring has prevented that intent. It being now after 1 o'clock I, although with reluctance, am obliged to forward them as they are, hoping this will, in some reason, apologise for the errors of my pen. I am, [I. Grier], 31st October 1821.

Parish of Killymard, County Donegal

Memoir by Lieutenant W. Lancey, January 1836

NATURAL STATE

Name

Killymard is probably derived from *coill* "a wood" and *ard* "high portions;" portions of it betoken the remains of an extensive woodland country and large natural woods still exist on the bank of Lough Eske.

Locality

This parish is in the county of Donegal and barony of Banagh, and lies immediately west of the parish of Donegal, on the right bank of the River and Lough Eske, and forms the most eastern part of the northern shore of Donegal Bay.

Its extreme length north and south is 11 and a half miles, breadth 9 miles; contains 28,230 acres, of which [blank] are arable and pasture, [blank] acres mountain, bog and waste and 677 water. Its eastern boundary is common to the parish of Inver, its northern is surrounded by Inishkeel and Kilteevoge.

NATURAL FEATURES

Hills

The granite hills on the north of Killymard are very rugged and bold. They rise at Glascorns to the height of 2,202 feet above the sea and are the continuation of the Barnesmore range, running nearly north east and south west. The summits of these hills possess little or no verdure. In point of wildness and natural grouping they are striking and, when viewed in connection with Lough Eske, present a beautiful landscape.

The lower part of the parish towards the sea falls in long slopes until near the coast, where isolated elliptical hills are formed. This, however, is the most western part of this peculiar formation and the drims are larger and fewer than those of Donegal and Drumhome <Drimholm>, with broader valleys.

A small but conspicuous hill of this nature, half a mile west of the Killymard suburbs of Donegal, commands an extensive and varied landscape and is supposed to be the place of inauguration of the chiefs of Tyrconnell (see Antiquities). Note these chiefs were crowned at Doon rock in Kilmacrenan.

Lakes

There are many lakes, a table of which is subjoined. Lough Eske is the principal sheet of water in the district near Donegal and is divided between that parish and Killymard. It lies at the foot of the range of hills already mentioned, its northern portion being surrounded by the highlands, its southern by flat. The height of its water varies with the seasons; its extreme level may be taken at 103 feet. It is said to be 20 fathoms deep. Its north western shores are greywacke, the opposite point of limestone. Islands of [?] both rocks occur. They are very little elevated, the highest being that of O'Donal, 8 feet above the water.

This lake receives the drainage of the mountains at its northern end and empties itself by the River Eske at the south, and contains 978 acres of water.

Table of Loughs

A list of the loughs in Killymard parish.

Part 1: Lough Skennagh, 3 acres 3 roods 16 perches, part of; lough no.1, 1 rood 19 perches; Lough Minaghuis, 2 acres 26 perches; Lough Annairgia, 10 acres 2 roods 18 perches; Lough Cribbrit, 9 acres 1 rood 30 perches, 3 acres 3 roods in Inishkeel; lough no.4, 13 perches; lough no.5, 2 roods; lough no.6, 17 perches; lough no.2, 21 acres 2 roods 24 perches; Lough Magrabeg, 4 acres 2 roods 38 perches, part of.

Part 2: Loughanameathog, 2 acres 1 rood 3 perches; Loughcraw, 1 rood 4 perches; Loughcrunnabrows, 1 rood 13 perches; Loughcrongormard, 2 roods; Loughamhaisil, 22 perches; Loughanabrac, 1 acre 30 perches; Loughnagcrapangom, 2 roods 35 perches; Lougheascartha, 7 acres 2 roods 30 perches; Loughanabracbuey, 8 acres 3 roods 3 perches; Loughanabracbutha, 4 acres 2 roods 16 perches; lough no.17, 2 acres 24 perches; Loughnagcolum, 2 acres 35 perches; lough no.19, 6 perches; Lough Cam, 10 acres 3 roods; Lough Migrealor, 1 acre 2 roods 30 perches, part of, and Lough Astura; lough no.22, 1 acre 6 perches; lough no.23, 1 acre 3 roods; lough no.40, 13 acres 1 rood 8 perches; Loughanacullane, 1 acre 3 roods; Land lough no.25, 2 acres 3 roods 13 perches; Land lough no.24, 2 acres 1 rood 24 perches; Loughadhairuigh, 4 acres 3 roods 18

Parish of Killymard

perches; Lough Mhairin, 1 acre 3 roods 24 perches; Loughamellain, 3 acres 7 perches; Loughfadda no.30, 3 roods 24 perches; Lough Bhelsheid, 68 acres 3 roods 8 perches; lough no.32, 26 perches; Loughfadda no.33, 2 roods 21 perches; Loughnagerraigeach, 2 roods 26 perches; Loughnamhasnugh, 1 rood 9 perches; Loughamillain, 1 acre 2 perches; lough no.39, 1 rood 19 perches; lough no.37, 1 acre 26 perches, part of; lough no.38, 2 roods 22 perches, 1 rood 30 perches in Kilteevoge; Lough Croughanara, 13 acres 1 rood 8 perches; Loughadubh, 1 acre 12 perches.

Part 4: Loughavaddy, 1 acre 1 rood 13 perches; Lough Banachuir, 13 acres 2 roods 30 perches; lough no.25, 2 acres 3 roods 13 perches; lough no.24, 2 acres 1 rood 24 perches; Lough Eske, 978 acres 1 rood 32 perches, 503 acres 32 perches in Donegal parish.

51 loughs, containing 677 acres 2 roods 21 perches.

Rivers

The River Eske is the largest in the parish. It flows from the lough to Donegal Bay in a south west direction for 3 and a half miles, is about 66 feet broad and [blank] feet deep. It meets the tide at the town of Donegal but is only navigable to the bridge at O'Donnell's Castle. Its bed is for the most part rocky and rough. Its waters are used for machinery and at certain seasons overflow the low ground to the north of Donegal.

There are some brooks in Killymard flowing from the north to the sea, draining the higher lands. Their waters are inconsiderable but on the whole the parish is naturally well drained. The fall of the East Duanan, 111 feet high, is in Ednigal on the parish mearing of Donegal. This cataract is inconsiderable except in such seasons.

The Mare's Tail in Struthail is a series of steep rapids tumbling over rocks and always presenting a white line of foam.

Mineral Spring

There is a spa in the townland of Druimros, close to Donegal, over which a pump-room has been erected this season with 2 baths. It is said to be useful in bowel and cutaneous complaints, and is frequented in the summer for these and other diseases.

Bogs

The bogs are chiefly situated in the middle district of the parish, the southern parts being cultivated and the northern, mountain and rocks. The remains of bog timber are not very frequent. The turf is deep but not of good quality. Nothing worthy of remark is known in connection with the bogs of this parish.

Woods

A considerable portion of natural wood is found on the right bank of Lough Eske, amounting to about [blank] acres, and traces of woods are observable in other parts of the parish. Little good timber is met with; at present it is principally birch with some ash.

Coast

This parish, it has been stated, lies on the north coast of Donegal Bay. The land is low, terminating usually in abrupt, gravelly and rocky banks about 20 or 30 feet in height. An extensive and hard strand is left dry at low water. The line of coast is much indented and forms 2 bays at Rivlin and Drimgunna which are left dry at ebb tide.

There are 3 islands. The only one of consequence is Baillewbhuil. It lies off the town of that name and is a green elliptical knoll of 87 feet in height. South west of it is a long narrow point of land terminating in a similar knoll 64 feet in height called Green Island, which shoots in the harbour and affords shelter to the anchorage which lies east of it called the Ship Ride.

Climate

The climate of Killymard is moist and wet. The sea on the south of the high range of mountains on its north easily accounts for the great quantity of water that falls in this and the adjacent parishes.

NATURAL HISTORY

Zoology

Botany and natural history: no information.

Salmon frequent Lough Eske but not in large numbers, as its waters are evidently not well adapted for spawning (see Zoology, Memoir of Templecarn).

The fish usually pass though the lake and are caught in the mountain fords by torchlight in the months of harvest. Trout are common in the River Eske and the mountain loughs. The usual sea-fish described in the Memoirs of Donegal are common also to Killymard.

Badgers, foxes and hedgehogs, with the usual common animals, are also found in Killymard.

Eagles, kites, herons and the usual common birds are found in this district. Widgeon are common in the bay in the winter season but are seldom shot.

Pigeon house in Lough Eske Demesne [hexagonal shape, with dimensions].

Geology

The northern mountains of Glascorns, Blue Stack etc. are granite, on whose bases lie quartz rock and greywacke succeeded by blue limestone. The greywacke is quarried for millstones. The lime is also used for common purposes, but is not so good or so extensively raised as in Drumhome parish.

The whole is a primitive country whose hills and valleys run in the usual direction of the county Donegal, from north east to south west, with dykes of greenstone which, however, are much scarcer here than in Fanad and Inishowen.

MODERN TOPOGRAPHY

Towns

The western suburbs of the town of Donegal lie across the River Eske in this parish (see Memoir of Donegal).

Public Buildings

These consist of the new church, the Roman Catholic chapel, the Seceders' and Methodists' houses. The 2 latter were described in the Memoir of Donegal, as they form a part of that town.

The new parish church in the townland of Ballydivit is built of freestone and was erected by Mr Graham in 1829 at a cost of 900 pounds, fitted to contain 240 persons in pews and is a neat building.

The Roman Catholic chapel in Haugh was built in 1799 at a cost of 500 pounds. It has lately been repaired and can accommodate 1,000 persons.

Gentlemen's Seats

Mr Brooke of Lough Eske Demesne, Mr Steel of Rosalongan House, Dr Swan of the Cottage and the rector are the principal residents in Killymard.

Mr Brooke's demesne is the only one of consequence and it is on a limited scale. It lies south east of Lough Eske. The house is a whitewashed building of common dimensions to which excellent offices have been lately added, and improvements and alterations are constantly taking place.

Ruins in Lough Eske Demesne, Mr Brooke's: [drawing of ruined castle, with dimensions].

Mr Brooke has let the woods of Grianans on the coast of the lough to Mr Ray who, it is said, intends to build a residence there for his family.

Other Seats

Rosalongan House is a neat small place commanding a view of part of the bay and town of Donegal. It is a whitewashed and slated house.

The Cottage is a small place opposite St Ernan's Island in the townland of Summer Hill. It occupies the ground of an old abbey and is a retired spot.

The rectory appears to be a substantial house on the shore of Edrim glebe. There is nothing particular about it. It was erected in 1817 at an expense of 600 pounds.

Mills

The mills are situated in the townland of Lough Eske Demesne (now in ruins), Druimghornan and a spade mill in Milltown. The corn mills are overshot, having small wheels averaging 8 to 10 feet. This branch of profit has fallen into comparative decay since the exportation of corn to England and Scotland.

Communications

The principal road in Killymard is from Donegal to Mountcharles, thence to Killybegs bay and the Rosses. This communication is a very indifferent one. It is badly repaired and the constant traffic, especially in the herring season, usually destroys it for the rest of the year (see Fishing). The other roads in Killymard are generally hard and dry, the materials to the north being of a better description.

There are no bridges of consequence to be described. The county pays for their repairs, as well as for the roads.

ANCIENT TOPOGRAPHY

Abbey

A small part of the wall and the old well of an old abbey in the cottage and grounds in Summer Hill still exist. This is said to have belonged to O'Boyle, whose 3 sons Owen, Hugh and Connel gave names to 3 districts: Tyrone, Tyrhugh and Tyrconnell. This abbey is pleasantly situated close to high water mark, on a rocky bank 20 feet above it, and stood on the manor of Baillewbhuil, which gave name to the townland and island adjacent.

Parish of Killymard

Castle

A small remnant of a castle is met with in the grounds of Lough Eske Demesne, occupied in the memory of man by one Knox but now fallen into total decay. No accounts were obtained of its ancient history. It consists of a corner wall and 2 arches pierced with loopholes. In Mr Brooke's yard are 2 stones built up in the wall originally brought from the ruin in O'Donnell's Island, sketches of which are below.
 [Sculpted sheila-na-gig.
 Engraved slab with inscription WF, IM 1621].

Old Church

The old church stands on the sea-coast south west of the Glebe House, in a detached part of Edrim glebe about 25 feet above high water mark. Its situation is well chosen, commanding a fine prospect of the bay. Service has been discontinued in it almost 3 years and transferred to the new church, which stands in a wide valley and is much better adapted to the convenience of the mass of the people.

Forts

Old forts are met with in the townlands of Ballydivit, Druimstibhlin, East Druimros, Mullachs and Summer Hill. They present nothing new to the observer, being similar to the same class of antiquities in other districts.

Doonan Rock

At Doonan rock, half a mile west of Donegal, common report states the chiefs of Tyrconnell were inaugurated. The ceremony was to kill a white ox and make him into soup in a large cauldron, in which the chief was seated up to his chin. His prerogative was to lap the soup whilst his sept were only permitted to drink it.
 The Doonan rock is a spot well adapted to such a purpose. It rises to a table of greenstone rock and is a conspicuous object from the surrounding country.
 Note: The above is supposed to be true at Donegal, but the place of inauguration was in Kilmacrenan.

Modern Topography

General Appearance and Scenery

The north eastern part of Killymard possesses interesting scenery. The loughs, the woods, the mountains combine to form some striking views. An extensive devastation has apparently taken place in the strata and immense masses of rocks are tumbled about in all directions. Towards the northern boundary granite mountains, precipitous with little that is green on them, bound the view. A deep valley, of which the Gray Mare's Tail waterfall forms a conspicuous object, is worthy of notice.
 To the sea large tracts of grasslands, with a tolerable belt of arable, thickly studded with farmhouses and small villages surrounded with trees, form a varied landscape backed by the ocean or arm of the sea which forms the bay, having the shores of Donegal and Drumhome in the distance.
 The eastern side of the parish is rough and wild. The valleys are large and well watered, the Eske flowing through a cultivated district of considerable width. The cottages are frequently whitewashed and the parish as a whole is above the usual mean in general appearance and scenery.

Social Economy

Early Improvements

The advantages of the harbour and sea-coast are probably amongst the chief reasons of this district being populous. It was in ancient times the residence of the sept of O'Donnells, which gave way to the mixed people who now inhabit it. The Protestants are numerous and, as usual, are settled in the cultivated lands. The others occupy the hill country.

Progress of Improvement

No prevailing family names are known, no system of means is taken to improve the civilisation of the people except the erection of schools, and that is chiefly confined to the labours of Mr John Hamilton, whose exertions to evangelize and improve the people are of a marked and unusual nature.
 There are no legal disputes or tenures which at present obstruct improvement, and capital and resident landlords are the things required to make Killymard a flourishing agricultural country.

Local Government

2 magistrates reside; they conduct their judicial business in Donegal (for information under this head see Memoir of that parish).
 The poor receive medical assistance from the establishment in Donegal.

Schools and Poor

There are 7 in the parish, 6 of which are free. The seventh is supported by the scholars; the average attendance is 280 daily.

No provisions for them except the collection at the public places of worship.

Religion

The clergy are supported in the usual manner. The numbers of Roman Catholics in the parish are 3,059, Protestants 1,598, Presbyterians 141.

Habits of the People

Their cottages are stone, thatched, some whitewashed, a few slated, consisting of 2 rooms with small glass windows and as usual not overclean. There are neither peculiar customs or any mark in the character of this people to notice. They appear to be much the same as the rest of the peasantry of Donegal.

Bealtinne is still kept up. They make and drink plenty of whiskey, with which they associate almost everything in life, whether good or evil. Fishing is nearly unknown amongst them. Their food and dress are of the usual very common kind, but it is said they are improving in civilisation.

Very few persons, comparatively, emigrate at present.

PRODUCTIVE ECONOMY

Weaving and Spinning

Weaving is quite given up except for domestic uses. Hand-spinning is common and pays well at present, although a woman does not earn more than 3d a day.

Millstones

Mrs Walker of Donegal rents all the millstone quarries in the parish. They are found in the townland of Attlilou. She pays the quarrymen 27s 6d apiece for 5-feet stones delivered at "the style," a convenient spot on some adjacent road for carrying them away.

2 men will furnish a stone a week, from whose wages the expense of bringing them from the quarry to "the style" must be deducted. They hire 11 men at 15d a day each to assist them and the 13 are able to leave 6 stones daily at the appointed place. The old price was 12 guineas a pair. At present Mrs Walker will transport them to Milltown in Tullyaughnish for 5 (see that Memoir).

The texture of the stone is good and, as the trade has fallen into decay by the great exportation of corn, Mrs Walker is now exporting millstones to Liverpool and America.

Fairs and Markets

There are none in Killymard. Donegal is the usual market and fairs are occasionally held in Mountcharles.

Rural: Proprietors

The chief proprietors are the Marquis of Conyngham, Mr Murray, who resides in Scotland, Mr Brooke, Mr J. Hamilton. The Earl of Arran has only 1 townland.

Mr Murdock is the agent to the marquis, Mr Babbington of Bonny Glen in the parish of Inver is the agent to Mr Murray.

The size of the holdings vary from 6 acres to 30, held under the head landlord at rents varying from 10s to 25s an acre. The farmhouses are much the same as in other places. No farms are kept as examples to the people.

Agricultural Practices

The soil is wet and cold, manured with lime, compost and seaweed. The custom of burning land does not prevail, except in bringing mossy ground into cultivation. The improvement in implements of husbandry has extended to Killymard equally with Donegal and adjacent country. The slide car is seldom seen. Good Scotch carts and common wheel cars are usual.

Rotation of Crops

This is little understood. Potatoes, corn and a little flax, repeated as often as the land will bear them, is the usual method.

Grazing and Irrigation

The farms are not exclusively devoted to grazing, yet there are more grassland[s] in Killymard than generally met with in the cultivated districts of the north. Irrigation and artificial grasses are not valued. Drains are partially used and, with the exception of the lands on the sea-coast and one or two favoured spots, neatness and good fencing are not much thought of.

The rate of servants' wages are the same as usual, about 50s to 60s the half-year with board and lodgings.

Cattle

There are no peculiar breeds of cattle. The mixed breeds purchased at fairs, comprising crosses of old Irish, Devon and [blank], are common.

No good horses for quick work are likely to be got. Those for slow work are tolerably good in appearance. A large supply of pigs are purchased in this and the adjacent parishes, and driven through Donegal for exportation at Derry. Poultry is not cheap and abundance of eggs are forwarded weekly for the Derry steamer.

Green feeding and stall-fed cattle are not practised. A small breed of asses is common.

Uses made of Bogs

The bogs are grazed in the summer and extensively cut for fuel. Coal is imported at Donegal but not generally purchased by the agricultural classes.

Planting

Nothing of this kind is met with except on a very small scale. Mr Brooke has planted some few acres in belts to embellish his estate. Oaks, particularly ash and birch, flourish on the bank of Lough Eske and much land in Killymard might be profitably stocked with trees.

Sea-Coast

The small supply of seaweed on this shallow coast is the only thing of agricultural value connected with it, unless its sand which, it is believed, is seldom used by the farmers.

Fishing

This branch of profit is not followed by the people of Killymard to any great extent. The chief herring fishery is at Killybegs. The season commenced in 1835 on the 14th of January, when the fish were sold for 10s a 1,000 at the boats (the long 1,000 equals to 10 times 120). No less than 470 carts and cars passed through the town of Donegal and the parish of Killymard on the 27th January.

The fish were sold about this time at 15s a 1,000. 500 boats were employed and it is said that the people of Killybegs cleared in 1834 not less than 10,000 pounds, and that the daily demand this season is 2,000 pounds. A car takes away 2,000 or 2,500, at an average of 12s 6d. On one occasion reports state there were nearly 1,000 carts and cars waiting the return of the boats.

Decked vessels from Dublin and Liverpool are also employed in the fishery. The town of Donegal is kept in complete confusion night and day, and the atmosphere is burdened with the smell of herrings during the season.

Remarks on Cultivation

The rage for arable land and cultivation of grain has not yet altered the appearance of Killymard so much as it has other parishes. Large sweeps of grasslands are yet met with. The upper and wild valleys yield good coarse herbage for young cattle and there is considerable short pasture for mountain sheep. The highest point cultivated, 960 feet, is in the townland of Minaguishmore. [Insert addition: Cultivation has been carried to 771 feet in Cruachanargoid and 850 feet in Leacthrom].

Mr Brooke is peopling a large valley in the town[land] of Eagluis which, in some years hence, will doubtless much alter its aspect, as it is easy to drain and, although high, is accessible and sheltered.

The average elevation of the higher cultivated cornlands is about 400 feet. Tracts extensive enough to employ considerable capital and the energies of its proprietors exist in Killymard for planting pasture and sheep-walks.

General Remarks on Improvements

The parish receives the advantage of the harbour of Donegal and is sheltered to the north and west by high lands from injurious winds. There is plenty of lime and fuel, some seaweed and many sites for mills. The roads, though generally not good, have materials at hand to render them excellent. The general style of the district is varied, with hill and dale succeeded to the north by long ridges, the tails of the rugged mountains which occupy its extremity.

Finally, Killymard, Donegal and Drumhome, forming the head of Donegal Bay, are 3 parishes susceptible of being brought to a highly cultivated state and form at present an interesting and tolerably advanced civilised district.

DIVISIONS

Townlands

No local divisions more extensive than townlands are known to exist in Killymard. [Signed] William Lancey, Lieutenant Royal Engineers, 2nd January 1836.

Replies by John Foster to Queries of North West Farming Society, October 1821

NATURAL STATE AND PRODUCTIVE ECONOMY

Situation and Proprietors

County of Donegal, barony of Banagh, diocese of Raphoe, Revd William Smith, incumbent.

Alexander Murray [crossed out: Smith] of Broughton in north Britain, Esquire, proprietor of a large estate in this county and principal proprietor of this parish. This gentleman is a non-resident, having only visited his estate once since he came into possession, at which time the leases granted by his father, the late James Murray Esquire, had expired. The lands were then set for 21 years and the life of the Duke of Clarence, and the tenants have since anxiously looked for the return of Mr Murray, with the hope of deriving certain benefits from him, but hitherto they have not been gratified with his presence. His agent is Murray Babington Esquire.

The representatives of the late James Hamilton of Brownhall, Esquire; the heir of this estate is now of age, a period much looked forward to by the tenantry, but 'tis feared that his residence on his estate would be very partial.

The representative of the late Thomas Young Esquire; was a resident till his death. His widow since that period has been a non-resident.

A very small part of the Marquis of Conyngham's estate is in this parish. Lord Mountcharles has for the last 3 years resided about a month or 6 weeks annually and on some occasions the marquis and his lady have honoured the country with their presence.

A part of the Earl of Arran's estate is this parish. His lordship is a non-resident and his lands are enormously high rented, but in other respects he is an indulgent landlord.

The glebe lands comprise the remainder of the parish, the greater part of which are occupied by Mr Smith, the present incumbent, and a Mr Donlevy of Donegal, who has a poor distressed tenantry in his proportion.

Townlands and Extent

The townlands are 49 in number and contain 729 houses, 4,125 inhabitants, 4,979 acres arable and green pasture, 8,860 acres bog and mountain and are under the following denominations and proprietors.

Table of Townlands

[Table contains the following headings: name of townland, analysis of land type, number of houses and inhabitants].

Alexander Murray's Esquire: Croghenerragate, 20 acres arable and green pasture, 804 acres bog and mountain, 7 houses, 34 inhabitants.

Meenaguirk, 25 acres arable and green pasture, 414 acres bog and mountain, 4 houses, 26 inhabitants.

Cronkeeran and Atidirigh, 341 acres arable and green pasture, 464 acres bog and mountain, 7 houses, 210 inhabitants.

Gortlosky and Owenbwee, 64 acres arable and green pasture, 170 acres bog and mountain, 10 houses, 70 inhabitants.

Meenatagart, 10 acres arable and green pasture, 95 acres bog and mountain, 2 houses, 9 inhabitants.

Meenamuldarg, 14 acres arable and green pasture, 83 acres bog and mountain, 3 houses, 11 inhabitants.

Drumgun, 50 acres arable and green pasture, 4 houses, 22 inhabitants.

Drimmark, 87 acres arable and green pasture, 10 acres bog and mountain, 7 houses, 50 inhabitants.

Fosters Court, 100 acres arable and green pasture, 13 houses, 107 inhabitants.

Drumkeenan, 210 acres arable and green pasture, 30 acres bog and mountain, 23 houses, 143 inhabitants.

Summer Hill and houses, 150 acres arable and green pasture, 26 houses, 161 inhabitants.

Ballyweel, 160 acres arable and green pasture, 14 houses, 62 inhabitants.

Rerhie, 57 acres arable and green pasture, 8 houses, 47 inhabitants.

Doonan, 150 acres arable and green pasture, 23 houses, 145 inhabitants.

Ballydivittbeg, 110 acres arable and green pasture, 17 houses, 50 inhabitants.

Drimgoman, 160 acres arable and green pasture, 25 houses, 151 inhabitants.

Drimroosk, 183 acres arable and green pasture, 19 houses, 113 inhabitants.

Drimnahoo, 73 acres arable and green pasture, 7 acres bog and mountain, 6 houses, 36 inhabitants.

Munacally, 105 acres arable and green pasture, 15 acres bog and mountain, 10 houses, 46 inhabitants.

Damland, 20 acres arable and green pasture, 2 houses, 19 inhabitants.

Newtown, 258 arable and green pasture, 32 acres bog and mountain, 22 houses, 114 inhabitants.

[Totals]: 2,247 acres arable and green pasture, 2,124 acres bog and mountain, 282 houses, 1,626 inhabitants.

Heirs of the late James Hamilton Esquire: Heney, 200 acres arable and green pasture, 65 acres bog and mountain, 26 houses, 149 inhabitants.

Ballydivittmore, 100 acres arable and green pasture, 10 acres bog and mountain, 44 houses, 305 inhabitants.

Drimslavlin, 88 acres arable and green pasture, 12 acres bog and mountain, 10 houses, 50 inhabitants.

Clenborin, 50 acres arable and green pasture, 50 acres bog and mountain, 13 houses, 64 inhabitants.

Lacrum and Golands, 255 acres green pasture and arable, 135 acres bog and mountain, 27 houses, 128 inhabitants.

Orbegg, 120 acres arable and green pasture, 250 acres bog and mountain, 23 houses, 141 inhabitants.

Altito, 100 acres arable and green pasture, 300 acres mountain and bog, 21 houses, 133 inhabitants.

Haugh, 165 acres arable and green pasture, 100 acres mountain and bog, 29 houses, 152 inhabitants.

[Totals]: 1,078 acres arable and green pasture, 822 acres bog and mountain, 191 houses, 1,122 inhabitants.

Heirs of the late Thomas Young Esquire: Lough Eske, 128 acres arable and green pasture, 20 acres mountain and bog, 10 houses, 61 inhabitants.

Drimmeenenagh, 146 acres arable and green pasture, 12 houses, 68 inhabitants.

Drimacarry, 180 acres arable and green pasture, 13 houses, 70 inhabitants.

Friary and Island, 120 acres arable and green pasture, 30 acres bog and mountain, 21 houses, 117 inhabitants.

Grennans, 100 acres arable and green pasture, 395 acres bog and mountain, 18 houses, 110 inhabitants.

P. Ward's farm, 30 acres arable and pasture, 5 houses, 31 inhabitants.

Burn's Mountain, 30 acres arable and green pasture, 140 acres bog and mountain, 7 houses, 32 inhabitants.

Iglish, 30 acres arable and green pasture, 1,300 acres bog and mountain, 4 houses, 34 inhabitants.

Shruhill, 50 acres arable and green pasture, 2,250 acres bog and mountain, 6 houses, 34 inhabitants.

Doughro, 10 acres arable and green pasture, 1,090 acres bog and mountain, 3 houses, 25 inhabitants.

Edergill, 25 acres arable and green pasture, 360 acres bog and mountain, 9 houses, 34 inhabitants.

Townawarragh, 36 acres arable and green pasture, 4 houses, 18 inhabitants.

Sonar's Gate, 30 acres arable and green pasture, 10 acres bog and mountain, 7 houses, 34 inhabitants.

[Totals]: 915 acres arable and green pasture, 5,595 acres bog and mountain, 119 houses, 658 inhabitants.

Estate of the Marquis of Conyngham: Beef Park, 40 acres arable and green pasture, 15 houses, 78 inhabitants.

Glen and Scrawhill, 68 acres arable and green pasture, 11 houses, 56 inhabitants.

Glencoagh and town, 40 acres arable and green pasture, 74 acres bog and mountain, 4 houses, 27 inhabitants.

[Totals]: 148 acres arable and green pasture, 74 acres bog and mountain, 30 houses, 161 inhabitants.

Earl of Arran's estate: Mullins, 56 acres arable and green pasture, 30 acres bog and mountain, 26 houses, 134 inhabitants.

Ralph Spence Phillips Esquire: Drimcliff, 45 acres arable and green pasture, 2 houses, 11 inhabitants.

Revd William Smith: Upper and Lower Glebe, 321 acres arable and green pasture, 160 acres bog and mountain, 28 houses, 143 inhabitants.

Mr Donlevy, Donegal: Upper and Lower Dromore, 169 acres arable and green pasture, 55 acres bog and mountain, 51 houses, 270 inhabitants.

Summary of Estates

Recapitulation of estates and proprietors: Alexander Murray Esquire, 2,247 acres green pasture and arable, 2,124 acres bog and mountain, 282 houses, 1,626 inhabitants.

Heirs of Mr Hamilton, 1,075 acres green pasture and arable, 822 acres bog and mountain, 191 houses, 1,122 inhabitants.

Heirs of Mr Young, 915 acres green pasture and arable, 5,595 acres bog and mountain, 119 houses, 658 inhabitants.

Marquis of Conyngham, 148 acres green pasture and arable, 74 acres bog and mountain, 30 houses, 161 inhabitants.

Earl of Arran, 56 acres green pasture and arable, 30 acres bog and mountain, 26 houses, 234 inhabitants.

R.S. Phillips, 45 acres green pasture and arable, 2 houses, 11 inhabitants.

Revd Mr Smith, 321 acres green pasture and arable, 160 acres bog and mountain, 28 houses, 143 inhabitants.

Mr Donlevy, 169 acres green pasture and arable, 55 acres bog and mountain, 51 houses, 270 inhabitants.

[Totals]: 4,979 acres green pasture and arable, 8,860 acres bog and mountain, 729 houses, 4,129 inhabitants.

PRODUCTIVE ECONOMY

Size of Farms

The farms in this parish are generally in size from 3 to 20 acres, badly enclosed, in many places with clay ditches, some of which are quicked with hawthorn but more without any. In other parts of the parish the enclosures are made wholly with dry, built, stone walls, but the method of cultivation is truly wretched, owing principally to the small size of the farms and deficiency of capital in the farmers.

Rotation of Crops

The first crop is potatoes, on which depends the vital interest of the parish; therefore 'tis a crop cultivated with much attention. The next in succession is barley, if the land is sufficient to produce it; if not, potato oats is put down in its stead. If the potato is sufficient to yield barley, a crop of potato oats follow it and then a crop of flax, and possibly a crop of the old blanter oats will then be attempted, but the last never pays the expense of seed and labour.

An alternate green crop is never attempted, nor are grasses sown except in some few instances by the gentlemen of the country, on which occasion rye grass with a small proportion of clover are what are generally laid down.

The pasture-lands of this parish are generally wet and produce a sour, hard, one-pointed grass. They are uniformly the refuse of the farm, but much might be done for their improvement if properly drained and that they got top dressing with lime, clay and shells.

Limestone can be obtained in no extreme of the parish, but the great difficulty arises from a scarcity of turf and the great distance they have to be drawn.

NATURAL FEATURES

Mountains

The principal mountains of this parish are Doughro, the highest, Iglish, Shruhill, Edergill and Owenbwee. Many parts of these are barren, others tolerably and some remarkably pasturable, but none capable of cultivation. They are wholly under stocks of black cattle, sheep and oats during the summer months, and wasted in the winter owing to their bleak and exposed situations. Small veins reaching to the skirts of the mountains are cultivated and that with potato crop only.

Bogs

Timber is sometimes found in the bogs, from 5 to 10 feet from the surface, some black oak and some fir of 8 to 10 inches square in short pieces. Frequently large roots of the latter are met with, which are of much service in saving candles to the industrious spinner after night. The wood of Lough Eske, the only one in the parish, formerly contained about a 150 acres of well-grown timber but within the last 20 years it has been reduced to about 130.

The parish contains about 20 orchards, no nurseries but there are a few acres of thriving young plantations belonging to Mr Foster of Fosters Court, in which ash and sycamore appear to be coming best forward in the dry land and alder <elder> in the moist soils.

PRODUCTIVE ECONOMY

Rents

The highest acreable rent in this parish for the best arable land is a part of the estate of the Earl of Arran near the town of Donegal and set at 3 pounds 10s per acre, good arable at 40s, inferior 20s and from that down to 10s and 6s, [?] grass and moory pasture from 6s to 1s per acre.

Turf bog is in general free to the tenants in this parish, but when they cannot obtain a sufficient supply from the landlord, they are charged in the church and glebe lands from 4 pounds 10s to 3 pounds 10s per acre.

Tillage and Fences

Some improvements in tillage are observable, more particularly about the top and lands and skirts of the mountains, where limestone is obtainable, but in the implements of husbandry none are apparent.

The best description of fence, where the lands are dry and stones are attainable, are stone walls, but in wet lands a double ditch with a deep trench in each side of the ditch, sown with broom or furze or quickset closely with hawthorn, forms the best fence and affords a shelter which is of the utmost consequence both to the crop and grazing cattle. The prevailing winds in autumn, being from the north west, are most destructive to the potato crop. Fences of this description assist in draining the lands.

Employment

Employment is not abundant except in spring and autumn, but in some instances it might be created. Situated about half a mile from the town of Donegal, and adjoining the farm of Fosters Court occupied by the writer, there is an acre of the bay or large shoal covered by the sea at high water to the depth of 7 feet from the channel's edge, and that gradually lessening in depth as it approaches the shore. This space contains about 100 acres and its bottom is a deep rich glar. It is embraced by 2 headlands distant from each other about 30 perches and in all the extent of land by which it is surrounded 1 very small stream of water only empties itself into it.

By reclaiming this tract of land, meadow of the best quality would be produced. Invaluable from its contiguity to the town of Donegal, independently of the services it would render the navigation by deepening the bay and in erecting the rampart and forming the conductor for the fresh water, much general employment could be given to the industrious poor and that during the summer months when their privations are greatest and wants the most distressing.

The community of this neighbourhood would also derive a further advantage from the carrying on of such improvements during the months from July and August. Mendicity is very prevalent in this parish and, by employing the sturdy mendicants or any of his family that would be capable of wheeling a barrow, his or their earnings would afford a sufficient support and thereby release the parish from expense and importunity; and in the event of such employment being rejected by the mendicant resorting to this place (numbers being attracted here from all directions owing to the facility and plenty in which shellfish are procured), the parishioners might very conscientiously withhold their accustomed alms.

An extension of this system of reclaiming land and affording general employment might be found entered into if, on a more minute investigation, the object would be found answerable.

Near the church of Killymard there is a spacious inlet of the sea covering probably 200 acres. The depth at high water where the embankment would take place is about 6 feet and the embankment must extend about 35 perches. Its bottom is composed principally of a wet sand with small proportions of glar surrounding the small creeks near the shore. The rivers empty themselves into it.

Wages

Wages of labourers in this parish is from 40s to 50s the half-year, and when the labourer supports himself 10d to 13d a day.

Green Crops

Potatoes and flax are the only green crops. A crop of turnips is never thought of by the small farmer, nor does he ever adopt the sowing of grasses or laying down his land for grass when in heart, but takes crop after crop as long as it will yield any, when it will be either manured again for potatoes or left waste for grazing.

Manures and Irrigation

Surface grazing is generally what is practised, owing to the stiff cold till on which the soil of this parish runs, it being as retentive in its nature as a bottle, but in veins where the blue clay is mixed gravel-covered drains are sometimes used.

Clay and new lands are frequently burned for manure, but latterly it is found better only to scald the clay and not reduce it to ashes, by which means the soil is not so much impoverished and the ensuing crops more productive. The scalded clay is broke fine on the ground and assisted with a small portion of wispy dung or seaweed, when it will yield a good crop of potatoes. But when deep moss or rough moory pasture is burned, it is generally made in small fires and reduced to ashes, when it will produce an excellent crop of potatoes and an equally good [crop] of potato oats; and if the land thus reclaimed were laid down with artificial grasses when in heart, the advantage would be very obvious.

The system of watering meadows has never been more than partially adopted in this parish and now seems in equal measure given up.

Dairies and Oxen

A few dairies have been established and seem to offer well, in being more productive than any previous efforts of tillage on the same farms, taking into consideration the present prices of butter and grain, townland Ballyweel.

Oxen are not used in husbandry.

Spade Husbandry

Spade tillage alone is practised and is found to answer well. The lands in this parish are so stiff and cold that any efforts to plant potatoes with the plough, it is feared, would prove pointless. The writer experienced this in its fullest extent.

Grain Crops

The descriptions of grain grown in this parish are barley, potato oats, black and brown oats, and the old blanter. This last, when harvest turns out unfavourable, is apt to turn out most productive, not being so liable to shell in the handling as the other sorts; but in the event of a good harvest the potato oats is the most abundant.

The prices last season were barley 13d to 9d a stone, potato oats 10d to 9d and the other sorts 9d to 7d per stone; and this year no sales have as yet been made, but it is supposed the prices will not vary much from last year.

Provisions

Butter at present, fresh from 5d to 6d ha'penny per lb., firkins 1st quality 7d to 2d, 6s per cwt less, potatoes 3d per stone, beef 3d to 4d ha'penny per stone, mutton 3d ha'penny to 5d, tallow 5d per lb., hides 3d ha'penny to 4d and oatmeal 12s to 3s per cwt.

Land

The measurement of land is generally computed by the Irish plantation acre of 7 yards to the perch.

Cattle

The black cattle reared in this parish are generally of a small degenerate race, but we are so much beholden to our Connaught neighbours for the supply of a more generous and larger breed, which are brought here annually at the age of yearlings. With these, the greater part of the inland stock farms are supplied, and they turn out well, but the bleak mountains are generally stocked with the small breed of the country.

Sheep

We also get from Connaught a larger breed of sheep for the inland farms, but the mountains retain the hardy small kind whose flesh is remarkably sweet and their wool tolerably fine, resembling pretty much the breed they have in Wales.

In the parishes of Glen and Kilcar, west of this county, the inhabitants purchase in Connaught yearling wethers of a large size and fine wool and, after keeping them on 1 or 2 years, they are repurchased in some cases by the original seller, frequently at first cost, and taken back to Connaught, the Glen men considering themselves tolerably remunerated for their grazing by the fine wool they produce, which affords employment to the females in the manufacture of flannel and stockings.

Horses

The horses in use for agricultural purposes are various indeed: in the mountains the small Raghrey and Scotch shelty, both hardy and well adapted to any trifling ploughing and harrowing of the deep soft moss lands and carrying turf from the soft turf banks. Amongst the farmers are a wretched description of horses not calculated for husbandry; some are half-racers got out of the dwindles of that class on the worst sort of mares; others got by long-legged, empty-carcassed half-drafts that don't in any of their points bear shape or resemblance to a useful horse for agricultural purposes.

Much is wanting to benefit the breeder and parish and barony in general: a compact stallion of the Suffolk breed and a strong, large, well-shaped Scotch Mull stallion; if these were obtained and mixed with the best of our mares, our present race of non-effective horses would soon become extinct and in their [place] would be raised a strong, active and hardy race of horses, patient of labour and calculated for draft and every other purpose of farming pursuits.

Pigs

The swine bred in this parish are generally of a large size but rather of a [?] ribish shape and difficult to fatten until past 2 years old, at which age they become valuable, weighing from 28 to 24 score. Latterly there has been some pains taken to cross the breed by mixing them with a handsome and more compact breed brought from Ballinasloe. The produce are likely to answer well for, notwithstanding that they are not just so large yet, being of a round handsome shape, are more valuable and will fatten when a year old to from 14 to 18 score.

Numbers of Stock

The exact quantity of each description of stock in this parish is: horses 423, cows, bullocks and heifers 2,519, sheep 1,542, swine 525, mules and asses 25, goats 243.

Improvements in Horses

With all due deference the writer submits to the North West Farming Society the following as his slender opinion of the most likely method to create improvements and prevent a degeneracy of the race thus to be raised in the above descriptions of stock.

Horses for agricultural purposes, he has already suggested, should be raised from a stallion of the Suffolk punch breed, in selecting which a competent judge should be employed, not only to ascertain the exact proportions of the horse's frame but to procure him hardy in constitution and colour and not of an overgrown size, a medium being best adapted to the purpose of soil and climate.

Also a Mull stallion from Scotland; the latter cannot be too large or strong, if well proportioned; and as they are uniformly hardy in colour and performance, and are only deficient in spirit, this would be fully imported to their produce when mixed with the Irish Raghery and the present race of half-bred gallopers now so prevalent.

By placing such horses central in each barony and leasing them free of expense to the farmer, and holding at a small premium for the best produce when yearlings, the farmers would vie with each other in sending their best mares to obtain the premium. In the course of a few years the premium to be discontinued, when the society would fully obtain their object in propagating a good breed of this nobly useful animal.

The writer begs further to observe that by creating a charge, however small, for the service of each horse, so blind to his own interest is the small farmer of this country that if he could procure a sire at 1s less expense, no matter of what description, the horse of the society would be rejected and their object, of course, defeated.

Other Stock

A couple of bulls of the largest and most improved breeds and a few rams of the description and finest fleeces, placed also central in each barony, would be productive of the desired effect. Small premiums for the best quality of wool would soon put us on a footing with our Connaught neighbours; and lastly a small acreable premium for thoroughly enclosing and bringing into tillage coarse green pasture and moory rough ground that had never been cultivated, and laying it down, after being twice under potato crop, with artificial grasses would the more effectually tend to improve the pasture and thereby prevent degeneracy in the stocks thus raised.

Very few improvements, except with the gentlemen and a few of the more wealthy farmers.

NATURAL FEATURES

Rivers and Lakes

The principal, and only, river of note in the parish is the Eske, which takes its rise from the mountains of Edergill and, running south about 1 mile, empties into Lough Eske near the residence of Thomas Young Esquire, from whence it takes its course in the south west direction and falls into the sea near the town of Donegal, where it washes the ruins of the old castle formerly the splendid seat of the O'Donnell family.

The source of the River Foyle is said to be from a lough in the highest mountain of this parish called Doughro where, running in an east north east direction for about 3 miles, empties into the River Finn near Fintown.

Lough Enerrigate or "the lough of the silver hill" is also said to be the source of the Inver water. This water, at a short distance from the lough, issues down an immense precipice at Shreehill mountain, forming what is called "the Grey Mare's Tail," from the white foam it produces contrasted with the black and grey appearance which that hip of the mountain exhibits, and, not infrequently, carrying with it in its passage in the rainy season stones and rocks of a ton weight.

From the Grey Mare's Tail it takes a north east direction until it empties itself into the Eany water when, running south for about 6 miles, it falls into the sea at Inver near Whitehill, the beautiful seat of the Revd Mr Montgomery, washing the walls of the old church of Inver in the passage.

Lough Meenaguirk, on the mountain of the same name, and Lough Eske are the only remaining loughs in this parish, the former well stored with red trout and the latter beautifully diversified with small wooded islands north of the great road leading from Barnes mountain to Donegal. Besides the red trout, this lough produces trout of a most exquisite quality called char, as well as excellent salmon.

Coast

The harbour of this parish, called the Green Island or Ship Ride, is situated about 2 miles west of the town of Donegal, inside a great gulf or straits called the Haussons, and is well known as a place of perfect security for vessels of 500 tons to lay at anchor. It is the only harbour from Killybegs to Donegal; there are a few small creeks between the harbour and town of Donegal for the reception of fishing boats.

The tide ebbs to a narrow channel for the distance of about 3 miles from the quay of Donegal, leaving the strand firm and dry, from whence are obtained during the summer months black cockles, innumerable mussels, clams and razor-fish, food of the utmost importance, a necessary of life to the poor and labouring classes of the community. The farmer is also much benefitted by procuring vast quantities of shells which are found in deep strata about 2 feet from the surface of the dry strand, but latterly, in consequence of the great efforts to obtain this manure, it has been nearly exhausted; and from whatever source it was originally supplied, the strands do not seem to be filling with it again.

It is worthy of observation that the majority of the shells obtained in this way are oyster-shells, of which fish we have not one on the coast. As a substitute for this manure, the farmers have in some instances resorted to what is here called glar, with which the shores near the small creeks is surrounded. This is obtained with considerable labour and, when dry and mixed with mud, is used as a manure for the potato crop.

NATURAL HISTORY

Mines

2 mines have been discovered, one of coal, in this parish, the other a silver mine at a place called Townawilly in the parish of Donegal, both in the estate of the Earl of Arran. His lordship has a miner engaged for making discoveries of this description, but he only resided for about a year and has been discontinued, and nothing done since in working either of the mines.

Quarries

In this parish, in the estate of the late James Hamilton and Thomas Young Esquire, are millstone quarries. They are at present rented by a lady in Donegal who exports annually about 40 pair of stones. The quality of the stones is most excellent, being freestone mixed with whin and peculiarly adapted for corn mills. The quarries are well situated for exporting their produce, being only 2 miles from the town of Donegal, with a good road to its quay.

In the adjoining parish of Inver, near the town of Mountcharles, is also a most extensive and excellent freestone quarry well situated for exportation, being within half a mile of the sea, to which there is a good road and falling ground. Considerable quantities of this stone have been sent to Castle Coole, the seat of the Earl of Belmore, and Sir James Galbraith Bart made use of a portion of it in his building at Castletown.

Limestone

Limestone plenty in the townland of Lough Eske, [at] the extreme of the parish; its colour is a rich blue with a vein of a good quality and very productive. The usual method of burning it is with turf, and the expense about 40s for each 100 barrels of about 25 gallons each barrel.

Mineral Springs

There is a sulphurous spa in the parish, near the town of Donegal, famous for its anti-scorbutic and diuretic qualities, and much frequented during the summer months by persons afflicted with such disease, on whom it has effected many signal cures.

Marl

Marl has been discovered and used in some instances as a surface manure for pasture. Its effect for the first year has been considerable in producing a luxuriant growth of fine grass, but the second year wholly unproductive owing, I suppose, to the want of proper attention in conveying off the sour surface water and keeping the land properly drained. It has been found in the moss and clay land, at about 4 feet from the surface, and generally of a calcareous or living nature partially mixed with shells.

SOCIAL ECONOMY

Condition of the People

The domestic comforts of the lower order of farmers who comprise the bulk of the population in this parish are but few and their conveniences fewer. With every good disposition to industry, they are almost all fishers, to the frequent injury of their farming pursuits.

Parish of Killymard

The great means they look to towards the payment of one half-year's rent, at least, is the profits that arise to them from the herring fishery; and in this they are as frequently disappointed as successful. If the harvest fishing fails their case then becomes truly calamitous, as from the small size of the farms in general, they do not afford more than a subsistence for their families; and in order to pay the landlord, the crop is no sooner safe thatched in the stackyard than it must be brought to the [?] flail, and from thence to the market and sold for whatever the purchaser chooses to offer, and not unfrequently the seed for the ensuing crop is disposed of in this manner.

The unfortunate small farmer has then his potato crop to subsist on, with possibly some milk but more probably none; and this fare, with some salt and an occasional herring, forms the entire support and luxuries of his table. If a winter fishing sets in, he is enabled to purchase nets and seed his ground, otherwise he must go into arrear with his landlord until the following harvest fishing enables him to pay or else he be turned out and go beg.

The more extensive farmer on the coast, who depends wholly on his agricultural pursuits, may probably so far embark on the fishing as to have a boat and a share of nets. This does not interfere with the necessary attention to his farm, and if a good fishing takes place it is a certain source of gain to him; if not, he gains some assistance towards the support of his house.

Houses and Fuel

The conditions of the houses of this class of farmers is in general neat and clean, with some internal comforts. They have a sufficiency, without a profusion, of fuel which can be purchased from 3d to 5d per back-load.

Food

Their food consists of potato, herring and some dried cod or hake <heak>, stirabout, flummery, milk, oatbread and occasionally bacon with saltpork and poultry. Their butter is made up for sale which, with sheep and heifers, are sold to make up the rents.

The food of the manufacturing class is generally the same of the better farming class, but that of the poor labouring class is principally potatoes and salt but sometimes buttermilk or a herring.

Education

There seems to be a general wish for education amongst all classes, the expense of which is very moderate for reading, writing and arithmetic, which is all that the bulk of the farming Protestant population aim at.

There are 7 schools in this parish, 2 of which are Hibernian and 3 share Mr Robertson's donation. The Roman Catholic parishioners will not admit of their children going to the former schools, owing to their making use of the New Testament and committing it to memory, a diffusion of which knowledge their spiritual pastors deem contrary to their religious tenets.

Health

The general state of the country is healthy, except in the spring and autumn when fever is apt to occur, occasioned by the change of temperature, heats and colds.

Friendly Societies

No friendly societies of any kind have been established but barony dispensaries have, for assisting the poor with proper medicine and attendance in the event of accident or disease.

MODERN TOPOGRAPHY

Towns

There are no towns in this parish; the principal villages or hamlets are Ballyweel, Doonan, Ballydivit, Altilo and the Mullins, containing from 15 to 20 houses each.

PRODUCTIVE ECONOMY

Improvements

The people seem all anxious for improvement and, in my humble opinion, if the North West of Ireland Society lay open to them a well-regulated system of husbandry, such as in their knowledge and thorough information they must be enabled to procure, and hold out some small premium as an encouragement, the aspect of this country and situation of its inhabitants will in a few years be much benefitted.

Practical Farmers

The name of the farmers in this parish who are most likely to be useful correspondents to this society are Andrew Faucett, Revlin, Donegal; Alexander Davis, Drimroosk, Donegal; Andrew

Crummer, Drimroosk, Donegal; Andrew Pery, Drimroosk, Donegal.

Linen Manufacture

The linen manufacture in this parish is rather diminishing than increasing. An inspector properly qualified is much wanted for the baronies of Banagh and Boylagh, there being none from Donegal to Glenhead.

One flax mill only in this parish.

Cultivation of Flax

Land in preparation for a flax crop is generally ploughed in November, December or January, as the season answers. It remains in that state until seed time, the latter end of April or the beginning of May, when it is well harrowed and the weeds and roots carefully gathered. It is then ploughed a second time and, before sowing the seed, gets a third ploughing. It is then lightly broke in with the harrow, that none of the seed may be too deeply buried between the furrows, then hinted in narrow ridges and carefully harrowed up and down. The flax crop frequently succeeds that of barley, except when the land is good and mouldy, in which cases oats succeed the barley and then flax.

The entire of the flax grown in this parish is consumed in home manufacture, independently of quantities purchased in Ballybofey and its adjoining markets. For the last 2 years great efforts have been made to save the seed, or the greater part of it, and that produced from Riga or Dutch seed is found to answer tolerably well.

Preparation of Flax

In some cases the flax is prepared for manufacture by manual labour, but where the growing is more extensive by mills, and it is the usual system to use fire in preparing it. Within the last year 1 millstone has been erected in this parish for breaking flax, previously to its been sent to the scutching mill, and is hoped that this saving of manual labour will be more generally adopted. In some instances where the spinner has to purchase flax, it will be spun to 5-hanks yarn, but the general grist is spangle yarn.

Yarn and Earnings

The spinner can only earn from 1d ha'penny to 2d a day. The general grist of tow yarn is from a hank to 16 cuts out of the lb. The present price of yarn is from 17d to 22d per spangle for exportation, but for home manufacture the weaver will give 2s for good bunches. The poorest sort of spinners are obliged to purchase their flax but the better sort grow it.

Wheels and Looms

The double wheel has not been introduced in this parish nor in the barony, that the writer has heard of. The manufacturer uniformly prepares the yarn for the loom himself. The cost of preparation is about 5d per spangle.

Yarn Greens

There are no yarn greens established in this neighbourhood, but no doubt can be entertained that the establishing of such would much facilitate the manufacture. At present the manufacturer, after purchasing yarn for his web, must remain idle for 10 days until it is boiled and prepared for the loom, and from want of capital is not able to purchase a further supply for another web until the first is made sale of. He is thus put idle for 10 days more, whereas if greens were established and the yarn always in readiness the manufacturer would be enabled to furnish 2 webs for market in the same space of time that he can now produce 1 only.

Note: Mr Alexander Davis and Mr Andrew Crummer of Drimroosk near Donegal live convenient to the Eske river, the water of which is the best in this parish for bleaching. They are in the green yarn trade and would willingly embark on establishing yarn greens if encouraged by the society.

Quality of Webs

The descriptions of linens usually manufactured in this neighbourhood are coarse wrappers and Coleraine webs: the price of the former from 6d to 6d ha'penny and the latter 1s to 1s 4d per yard. The markets are Stranorlar weekly and Ballyshannon every second week.

Wool

The woollen manufactures in this neighbourhood are confined to three-quarter wide blue and grey cloth, sold at from 3s to 4s 6d per yard, and three-quarter wide flannels, from 14d to 18d per yard. The manufacturing of this last is more extensively carried on than that of the cloth and is frequently sold in quantities, both in the markets of Strabane, Ballyshannon and Londonderry.

Wool staplers or sorters are not known in this neighbourhood. Wool is spun both on the large and small wheel; the former is preferred. Females knit quantities of woollen stockings for sale and earn from 2d to 4d a day.

The shearing of sheep twice a year is practised in the mountains to afford employment to the females in the winter season, when they do not grow any flax, and is not attended with any bad effect to the sheep; but the system is not practised by the inland farmer.

No cotton manufacture in this neighbourhood.

Kelp

Kelp is not manufactured in this parish, but in the adjoining parishes of Inver and Killaghtee, about the shores of Dooran and St John's Point, considerable quantities are made. The manufacture could be much extended if encouragement was held out and improvements in the system introduced, but the market of Donegal, to which it is principally sent, does not afford more than 3s per cwt; when sent to Ballybofey from 4s 2d to 5s is obtained and speculators purchasing within 2 or 3 miles of the shore when manufactured give from 2s 6d to 3s for exportation.

Fisheries

The fish taken in the neighbourhood are principally herrings. The number of vessels or boats at present belonging to the parish and employed in fishing are 26; their dimensions from 18 to 19 feet keel, 8 to 8 and a half feet beam and about 3 and a half feet in the hold, carrying from 3 to 4 tons. The description of fish taken in the months of August, September and October are called harvest herring. They are generally small in size but remarkably fat and well shaped, more particularly those taken in August.

Those taken in the months of December or January are called winter fish. They are much larger in size but not so fat or well proportioned as the harvest herring. They are taken in quantities of from 1,000 to 20,000 between the setting and rising of the sun, and in pursuit of them the fishermen sometimes go to sea from 6 to 10 miles, but they are more frequently taken in the different bays and shoals on the coast.

Almost at all times when the weather is moderate, but more particularly in frosty calm weather, whitefish of various kinds are taken, viz. cod, hake, ling and glassen in plenty and some few small haddock and turbot, but I don't know that at any time they have been cured for exportation. They are generally dried and made use of in local consumption, and when haddock and turbot are procured in plenty they are taken by backload carriers to the markets of Donegal, Ballyshannon, Strabane and Derry.

Employment in Fishing

The number of persons employed as fishermen in the boats belonging to this parish amount to 156, but along the coast in this barony the number may be estimated at 2,184 and boats 364. Our herrings cured last winter have been shipped for Sligo, Ballina, Newry, Belfast and Dublin.

Improvements

The village of Ballyweel in the parish, situated on the bay 1 mile west of Donegal, is an excellent harbour for the boats to shore at and make sale of their cargoes, having the indispensably necessary accommodation for the fishermen of space to spread and dry their nets, but unfortunately the quay is totally broken away and not a vestige remaining. The building of a new quay, or procuring funds from government for that purpose, and it would be but an inconsiderable expense, is an object not unworthy [of] the notice of the society.

And were the present difficulties lessened which are thrown in the way of persons obtaining the drawback on salt expended in curing herring, as well as the premiums for saving them in barrels, the fisheries would unquestionably be benefitted and much employment would be created for coopers as well of gutters of herring. But the custom house and coast officers throw so many obstacles in the way of recovering such drawback and premiums, the latter requiring in some cases to have the herring produced at their places of residence for inspection, that many who would otherwise embark in the business are deterred from the unnecessary trouble they must encounter in order to be successful. [Signed] John Foster, 5th October 1821.

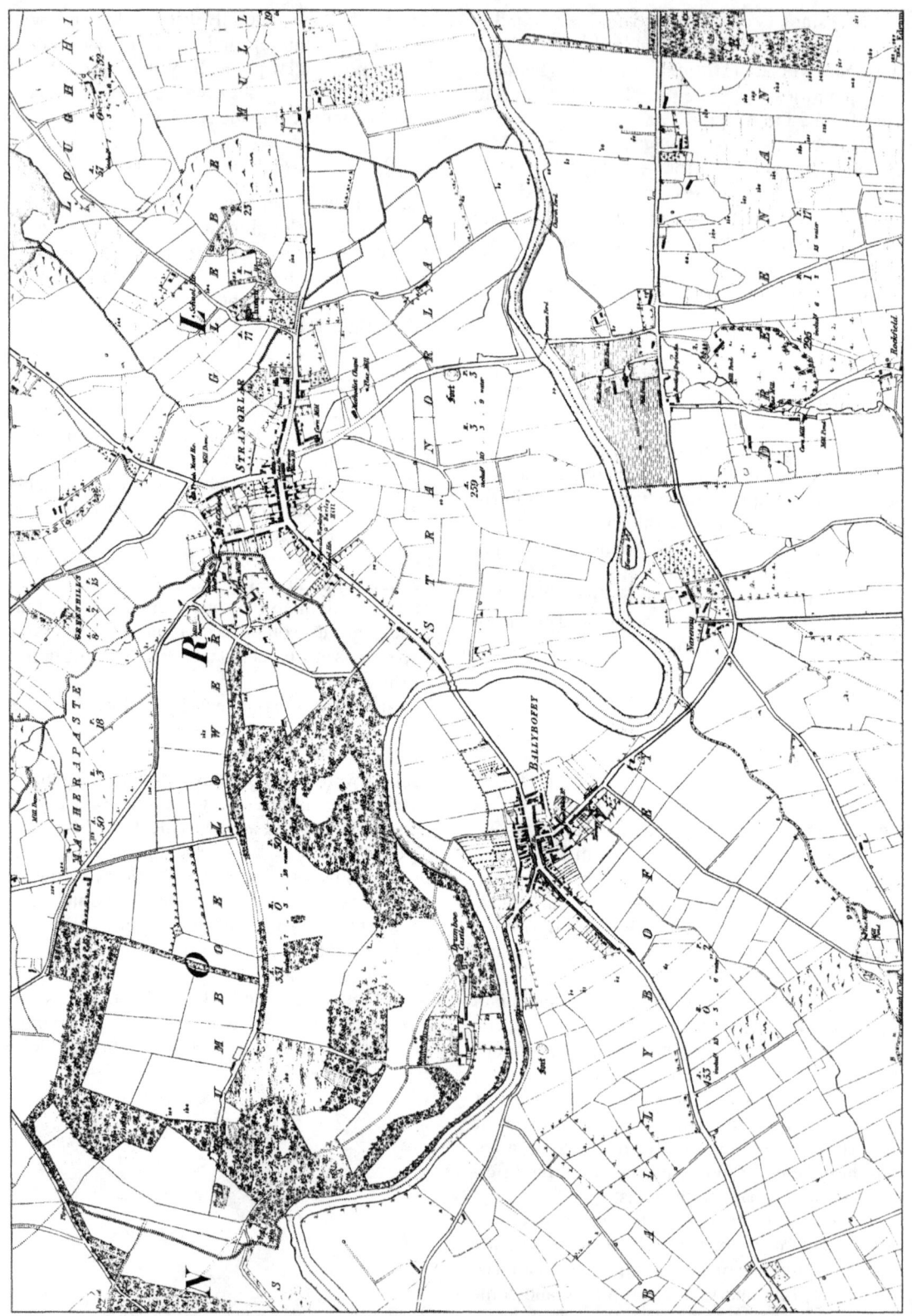

Map of Ballybofey and Stranorlar from the first 6" O.S. maps, 1830s

Parish of Kilteevoge, County Donegal

Statistical Report by Lieutenant I.I. Wilkinson

NATURAL STATE

Name

Kilteevoge <Kilteevogh>: this name is usually pronounced as it is written and is said to be derived from the Irish *Cill Taobog* or in English "the church of Teeboge." There is a tradition that a virgin named Teevoge Nee Divenny founded the church which stands in the glebe at Ballybotample.

Locality

The parish of Kilteevoge is situated in the county of Donegal, in the barony and diocese of Raphoe.

It is bounded on the north by the parishes of Convoy and Conwal, on the west by the parish of Inishkeel and on the south and east by the parishes of Killymard, Donegal and Stranorlar. It occupies the western extremity of the barony of Raphoe.

Extent: the outline of the parish is irregular. Its greatest length from north to south is about 11 miles and its greatest breadth from east to west about 10 miles, comprising an area of [blank] acres nearly. These are divided into [blank] denominations or townlands.

NATURAL FEATURES

Hills

The parish of Kilteevoge is a wild mountainous district. The principal mountains are Gagin, rising to the height of [blank] feet above the sea; Altnapaste, rising to 1,199 feet; and in the portion of the parish north of the River Finn, Arbatt, 938 feet, Altlaghan, 840 feet.

Rivers

The Finn traverses the parish of Kilteevoge for about 8 miles. It is unnavigable, flowing in a rocky channel with numerous fords and gravel beds formed during the heavy floods to which it is subject.

The Reeland river joins the Finn nearly in the centre of the parish and a considerable number of smaller streams throughout its course, some of which appear tinged with iron ore. No other springs of a mineral nature have been discovered. The parish is in general well supplied with water.

Bogs

The parish of Kilteevoge is well supplied with bog, in which a considerable quantity of timber, chiefly fir and oak, occurs imbedded. It is generally used for fuel but the large logs, some of which sell as high as 3 pounds, are also used for roofing houses and forming axle-trees for the wheels of corn and flax mills.

MODERN TOPOGRAPHY

Towns

There is no town situated in the parish but a considerable number of small villages.

Public Buildings: Church

The parish church is situated in the glebe of Ballybotample and is said to have been originally erected by a virgin named Teevoge Nee Divenny. It was rebuilt in the year 1774, partly by the Board of First Fruits and partly by the parishioners. It contains seats for about 250 persons

The Glebe House adjoining was built in the year 1779 by the late Revd Mr Butt.

The Roman Catholic portion of the inhabitants usually bury in the churchyard.

CATHOLIC CHAPELS

In the townland of Brockagh the building of a Roman Catholic chapel was commenced in 1799. The walls still remain but it never was roofed (though divine service was performed in it till the present chapel was built), on account of a dispute amongst the parishioners respecting the situation, which was considered too high up Glenfinn. There is an altar near it which was used periodically until the year 1799.

The present chapel is situated in the townland of Killtyfergal. It was built in 1825 by subscription from persons of all persuasions and will hold about 800 persons.

The parish priest has a curate to assist him, the Roman Catholic parish comprising also that of Stranorlar. His emoluments are estimated at 200 pounds per annum.

Mills

There is a corn and flax mill in the townland of Kinnaderry. The corn mill is of about 16 horsepower, the diameter of the wheel 12 feet, its breadth 2 and a half feet and the fall of water 9 feet. It will grind about 20 barrels of meal in 12 hours.

The flax mill is of 10 horsepower, the diameter of its wheel 10 feet, the breadth 1 foot 8 inches and fall of water 6 feet. Both these wheels are breast shot.

The mills are let to Michael Martin, with a farm of about 41 acres of land, at a yearly rent of 46 pounds 13s.

Communications: Roads

The main road from Stranorlar to Fintown passes through the parish for about [blank] miles, parallel to the River Finn. It is not much used and therefore is in tolerable order, but the same road near Stranorlar is in a very bad state, as are the by-roads leading to the mountains.

Bridges

There is but 1 bridge over the Finn river in the parish, which crosses at Cloughanmore on the road to Ballybofey <Ballyboefay>, and the [so] called Reeland bridge from a small river of that name which falls into the Finn near it. The inhabitants assert that no bridge built in any other place could withstand the torrent of water in the winter.

Natural Features and Modern Topography

River Finn and Fisheries

The River Finn from Ballybofey to this place is in general about 4 to 5 feet in depth, having several shallow fords where the depth of water is usually from 2 to 3 feet. There is a salmon leap on the river close to Reeland bridge. It is about 25 feet high and the scenery, with the bridge, extremely picturesque.

The fishery belongs to Sir Charles Style and the fish are usually taken by means of a net fastened to a hoop, through which they leap.

Gentlemen's Seats

Cloughan Lodge, the residence of Sir Charles Style, is situated on the road from Stranorlar to Fintown. It is surrounded with thriving and ornamental plantations of fir, beech and alder, and commands a very romantic view of Glenfinn and the adjacent mountains.

The residence of Sir Charles Style is of the greatest benefit to his neighbourhood and has materially assisted in repressing the illicit distillation which was carried on to a considerable extent. He is a magistrate of the county.

Cloughan Lodge is the only gentleman's seat in the portion of the parish north of the River Finn.

Social and Productive Economy

Dispensary

The Kilteevoge and Stranorlar dispensary is supported one-half by private subscriptions and the other by a grant from the grand jury of the county. The medical attendant is Surgeon Davis of Stranorlar; his salary is 75 pounds per annum. Monday is the day of attendance in Stranorlar and Saturday in Kilteevoge each week. Between 1,400 and 1,500 persons are annually relieved.

Farms

A considerable portion of the land in the parish is mountain pasture and bog. The extent of the farms consequently varies very considerably: some are so small that they do not exceed 2 acres (Cunningham), while others comprise 400.

Crops and Manures

They produce oats, flax, potatoes and hay, in one or two spots some barley. The land yields on an average 150 stone of oats to the Cunningham acre, which will sell in August on the ground (the money to be paid before Christmas) for from 5 to 7 pounds the Cunningham acre.

The quantity of land under potatoes is almost entirely dependent on the quantity of manure the cultivator may have for the purpose, perhaps one-third of the arable land in most cases.

The manures used are chiefly lime, compost of lime and bog, earth and dung.

Rents

The highest rate at which land is let in this parish is 25s the Cunningham acre, but very little at that rate.

Fairs

Fairs are held at Cloughan-beg, free of all tolls and customs, on the 1st of February, 19th of May, 25th August and 19th November, principally for the sale of cattle, yarn and drugget.

Parish of Kilteevoge

Manufactures

The manufacture of linen and yarn was very considerable. Until the last few years it was carried on in the houses of individuals and not by means of a general manufactory. Coarse drugget, woollen cloth and worsted stockings are still manufactured to some extent.

Population

The census ordered to be taken by government in 1822 was very imperfectly done. The number of houses returned were 677, with an amount of population 3,735 inhabitants. I should estimate the number of dwellings at not less than 900 and the average number of inhabitants in each at 5 and a half. This would make the amount of population a little short of 5,000, nor should I consider it overrated at that.

Of this population, there are of Protestants 147 families, average 808 individuals; 10 families of Presbyterians, average 50 persons. There is no return of Roman Catholics but they may be estimated at 4,142, as including the rest of the population.

Population of Kilteevoge from census 1834: members of the Established Church 933, Roman Catholics 3,587, Presbyterians 56, total 4,576.

Schools

There are 2 schools in the parish on Robertson's foundation, 1 at Welchtown and 1 at Altnapaste, 78 scholars; and 1 Sunday school (Sunday School Society), 38 scholars on the average.

Labour

A day labourer in this parish receives 10d per day, for turf-cutting 1s and for mowing 18d without diet. Agricultural servants are hired by the half-year at from 2 to 4 pounds, boarded and lodged.

County Cess

The amount of county cess levied in this parish for the 5 years has varied from 350 pounds to 390 pounds per annum. For this account of the parish of Kilteevoge I am indebted to Sir Charles Style Bart.

Advowson

The Dean of Raphoe appointed a perpetual curate for the duties of this parish. The present value of the living is about 140 pounds per annum and was attached to the deanery of Raphoe.

The parish has been erected into a rectory entire by an act of council pursuant to a clause in the Church Temporalities Bill.

Sir T. Charles Style pays the tithe for all the tenants on his estate and gives great encouragement to them to keep their houses clean etc., and has granted to the poorer sort 2 pounds each for whitewash etc.

NATURAL HISTORY

Geology

The parish of Kilteevoge is a primitive country. The soil never continues of the same stratum, either far or deep. In places are to be met with rock crystal, quartz, mica slate, granite, limestone in detached rocks, pyrites, lead and iron ore.

The streams flowing from the north into the River Finn appear to be strongly impregnated with iron.

There is an excavation in the townland of Welchtown called an old silver mine, which was opened by the agent of the late Sir Charles Style in 1775 with miners from England, but no silver is said to have been procured. The ore was transported on horses' backs as no road existed at the time. The leading road from Stranorlar to Fintown now passes within [blank] of the place.

The excavation extends about 30 yards, cut out of the rock, and the roof is in some places upwards of 6 feet high, the passages in general about 5 feet wide. [Signed] I.I. Wilkinson, Lieutenant Royal Engineers.

SOCIAL ECONOMY

Table of Townlands

Statistical table of the following townlands north of the River Finn in the parish of Kilteevoge, as taken from census and enquiry made in 183[4]. [Table contains the following headings: name of townland, analysis of population and dwellings, name of landlord].

Arbatt, 10 inhabited buildings, 14 dwelling houses and families, 11 outhouses, 21 total buildings; landlord Sir Charles Style.

Altlaghan, 26 inhabited buildings, 38 dwelling houses and families, 12 outhouses, 3 in ruins, 41 total buildings; landlord Sir Charles Style.

Ballybotample, 6 inhabited buildings, 11 dwelling houses and families, 11 outhouses, 17 total buildings; landlord Sir Charles Style.

Ballynatone, 9 inhabited buildings, 10 dwelling houses and families, 20 outhouses, 1 in ruins, 30 total buildings; landlord Sir Charles Style.

Brockagh, 17 inhabited buildings, 23 dwelling houses and families, 10 outhouses, 1 uninhabited house, 2 in ruins, 30 total buildings; landlord Sir Charles Style.

Cloughanbeg, 8 inhabited buildings, 11 dwelling houses and families, 12 outhouses, 2 in ruins, 22 total buildings; landlord Sir Charles Style.

Cloughanmore, 6 inhabited buildings, 6 dwelling houses and families, 6 outhouses, 1 uninhabited house, 1 in ruins, 14 total buildings; landlord Sir Charles Style.

Corlecky, 22 inhabited buildings, 32 dwelling houses and families, 21 outhouses, 3 in ruins, 46 total buildings; landlord Sir Charles Style.

Cullagh, [blank]; landlord Sir Charles Style.

Deregnalore, 8 inhabited buildings, 9 dwelling houses and families, 1 outhouse, 1 in ruins, 10 total buildings; landlord Sir Charles Style.

Gallwooly, 13 inhabited buildings, 17 dwelling houses and families, 18 outhouses, 5 in ruins, 36 total buildings; landlord Sir Charles Style.

Glebe, 1 inhabited building, 1 dwelling house and family, 4 outhouses, 5 total buildings; landlord Revd Mr Ramsay.

Killtyfergal, 20 inhabited buildings, 27 dwelling houses and families, 28 outhouses, 1 in ruins, 49 total buildings; landlord Sir Charles Style.

Kinnaderry, 16 inhabited buildings, 23 dwelling houses and families, 18 outhouses, 1 uninhabited house, 35 total buildings; landlord Sir Charles Style.

Lettershamboe, 1 inhabited building, 1 dwelling house and family, 1 outhouse, 2 in ruins, 4 total buildings; landlord Sir Charles Style.

Letterbrick, 24 inhabited buildings, 24 dwelling houses and families, 13 outhouses, 1 in ruins, 38 total buildings; landlord Sir Charles Style.

Meenbog, 2 in ruins, 2 total buildings; landlord Sir Charles Style.

Meenenamph, 1 inhabited building, 1 dwelling house and family, total 1 building; landlord Sir Charles Style.

Meenahorna, 4 inhabited buildings, 5 dwelling houses and families, 2 outhouses, 6 total buildings; landlord Sir Charles Style.

Meengilcharry, 17 inhabited buildings, 24 dwelling houses and families, 5 outhouses, 22 total buildings; landlord Sir Charles Style.

Monienahasragh, 1 inhabited building, 1 dwelling house and family, 4 outhouses, 5 total buildings; landlord Sir Charles Style.

Tullytrasna, 1 inhabited building, 1 dwelling house and family, total 1 building; landlord Sir Charles Style.

Welchtown, 19 inhabited buildings, 23 dwelling houses and families, 27 outhouses, 1 uninhabited house, 4 in ruins, 51 total buildings; landlord Sir Charles Style.

Total: 230 inhabited buildings, 322 dwelling houses and families, 224 outhouses, 4 uninhabited houses, 28 in ruins, 486 total buildings.

Schools

[Table contains the following headings: situation, number of pupils subdivided by sex and religion, remarks as to how supported].

Welchtown, Protestants 10 males, 9 females, Presbyterians 1 male, 5 females, Roman Catholics 5 males, 6 females, total 36 pupils; the master of this school receives a salary of 8 pounds 6s from Robertson's fund, 2 pounds from the Dean of Raphoe and 9 pounds from the scholars, making in all the sum of 19 pounds 6s per annum. He charges each scholar the sum of 1s 6d per quarter. They learn reading, writing and arithmetic. His name is James Witter, a Protestant.

Arbatt, Roman Catholics 18 males, 2 females, total 20 pupils; this school is taught in one of the dwelling houses. The master has nothing to depend upon but the children's payments, which amount to about 4 pounds per annum. He charges each scholar the sum of 1s per quarter. They learn reading, writing and arithmetic. The master's name is Michael Ivers, a Roman Catholic.

Altaghan, Protestants 3 males, 2 females, Roman Catholics 76 males, 14 females, total 95 pupils; this school is taught under the Hibernian Society. The master receives on an average the sum of 6 pounds per annum from the society and about 12 pounds from the children, making in all about 18 pounds per annum. They learn reading, writing and arithmetic. The master's name is John Ivers, a Roman Catholic.

Glebe, Protestants 7 males, 1 female, Roman Catholics 18 males, 4 females, total 30 pupils; the master's name is Charles Hume, a Protestant. He teaches his scholars reading, writing and arithmetic, and charges them from 1s to 2s per quarter. He estimates his yearly salary at about 6 pounds a year. He has no benefit from any society.

Parish of Leck, County Donegal

Statistical Report by Lieutenant I.I. Wilkinson, January 1836

NATURAL STATE

Name

The name of this parish seems to be derived from the Irish, which signifies "a stone or slate." This district of country is stony and slates in particular are procured from it. This also occurs in the parish of Leckpatrick near Strabane.

Locality and Divisions

The parish of Leck is situated in the county of Donegal, in the barony and diocese of Raphoe. It adjoins the town of Letterkenny and is bounded by the parishes of Raymoghy <Ryemoaghy>, Raphoe, Convoy, Conwal, Aghanunshin and Lough Swilly.

Its greatest length from north east to south west is about 7 miles and its greatest breadth from north west to south east about 4 miles, comprising an area of nearly 10,481 acres of land and 259 acres of water.

The parish of Leck is divided into 39 denominations; the principal proprietors are Colonel Pratt, Sir Edmund Hayes Bart, the Dean of Raphoe and Captain Dobson and J. Stewart Esquire.

NATURAL FEATURES

Hills

The parish of Leck is a hilly tract of country, descending in ranges from the mountain called Mongorry towards Lough Swilly. The valleys have the same general direction from south west to north east. The hills are not distinguished by name from the townlands in which they are situated, with the exception of the range in the townland of Dooballagh where, nearly in the centre, is a remarkable rock called Craignasiguart or in English "the priests' rock," which rises to 672 feet above the sea, and the south west extremity of the same range which rises to 781 feet nearly and is called "the herd's seat." Both these summits have trigonometrical stations erected on them.

Rivers

The River Swilly, which bounds the parish on the north, is the principal stream connected with it. This river rises in Glen Swilly and, about 15 miles from source, enters Lough Swilly. The tideway extends as far as Ballymacool or about 2 miles above Letterkenny, and at high water the river is navigable for boats of from 20 to 30 tons burthen as far as the bridge at the old town of Letterkenny, and for vessels of 300 tons as far as Port Ballyrean immediately below Letterkenny.

Within the tideway the bed of the river is soft mud, above it becomes gravelly and rocky. An embankment is formed from Big Isle to Ardahee whenever it becomes necessary to protect the adjacent grounds from high tides and freshets.

There is a good supply of water from numerous streams and springs, some of which are deeply tinged with bog iron. None else of a mineral kind have been discovered.

Bogs

The principal bog in the parish is in the townland of Dooballagh, from whence and from Glenkeiran in the parish of Raphoe the inhabitants are generally supplied with turf. Very little timber occurs imbedded in these bogs. The average depth of turf is from 4 to 7 feet. Its price at Letterkenny is about 4s a cart-load. Occupiers of land pay for all turf cut beyond the proportion assigned to their holding, at the usual rate of 4 pounds an acre.

The bogs are grazed at seasons, and when they are cut out for good arable land in later years, much of the turf has disappeared; and in many places where formerly great plenty of fuel was had on moderate terms, a scarcity is already beginning to be felt.

Climate

In the mountain part of the parish seed time is about the 1st April and harvest about the 1st October. In the lowlands seed time and harvest are about a fortnight earlier. The climate is in general mild and moist.

MODERN TOPOGRAPHY

Towns

The old town of Letterkenny is merely a village situated on the right bank of the River Swilly, opposite the new town which is usually distinguished by the name Letterkenny. There are numerous villages throughout the parish which the inhabitants call towns, though they do not in general contain more than from 6 to 12 houses. These villages generally bear the name of the townland in which they are situated and hence perhaps they are designated towns.

Public Buildings: Church

The parochial church is situated near the Swilly river, at the north east extremity of the townland of Old Town. People assert that it was built in the year 1335 or 1336 and used as a Roman Catholic chapel. The founder is unknown. It contains accommodation for about 150 persons.

Catholic Chapel

There is a Roman Catholic chapel in the townland of Coachmill, built in the year 1817 at an expense of about 150 pounds to contain about 300 persons. It is not used at present. The Roman Catholic inhabitants of the parish usually attend the chapel at Letterkenny.

Mills

There is a corn mill and kiln in the townland of Pluck belonging to Sir Edmund Hayes, whose tenants are bound in their leases to have their corn ground there at the rate of the 25th grain; other persons are charged the 35th. There are also a few flax mills for scutching, but of a very middling sort and not sufficient for the yearly increasing growth of the article. They are usually turned by the same stream that is applied to the oatenmeal mill, one of which is generally under the same roof with them.

SOCIAL ECONOMY

Local Government

A police force consisting of 1 constable in the townland of Aghliard, principally for the purpose of protecting a farm, the property of Sir Edmund Hayes, from which the original tenant was ejected for non-payment of rent. Intimidation has been used to prevent any other person occupying it, the house once pulled down and cattle haughed at several times. Another tenant has, however, taken possession of the farm this year (1835), but the inhabitants are apprehensive of some outrage being committed on him.

MODERN TOPOGRAPHY

Gentlemen's Seats

Rockhill, the property and residence of J.B. Stewart Esquire, is situated in the townland of that name about 2 miles to the westward of Letterkenny, on the road to Fintown and Dungloe <Dunlo>. The mansion commands an extensive and beautiful view and is ornamented with pleasure ground and plantations of fir, ash and oak.

Drum Lodge in the townland of Druminny was built by Sir Edmund Hayes for his own accommodation in visiting his estate and receiving rents. It is at present occupied by Mr John Wilson, master of Druminny school.

Swilly View in the townland of Lurgybrack was built at an expense of about 400 pounds by the occupying tenant, Mr Gallagher of Letterkenny.

Communications

The main road from Letterkenny to Londonderry and to Lifford passes through the parish of Leck for about 4 miles. It is of sufficient breadth but by no means well laid out or kept in good order.

The road from Letterkenny to Fintown, which passes through the parish for about 3 miles, is better in these particulars.

The crossroads from Letterkenny to Convoy, Raphoe and Stranorlar are very hilly and in places very bad.

The roads are made and repaired at the expense of the county by grand jury presentment.

SOCIAL ECONOMY

Habits of the People: Cottages

The general style of cottages, which are buildings of stone and thatch (some few are slated), 1-storey high, consisting of 2 rooms with each 1 small glass window, is dirty and comfortless.

Food and Fuel

The food among the lower classes is generally potatoes, buttermilk and salt herrings with oatmeal occasionally. The fuel is turf.

Longevity and Marriage

The number in each family is on the average 7 and many of the cottagers attain to the age of 70: in the adjoining parish of Conwal is an instance of a woman who can read without spectacles at the age of 109. The marriages are early: the men at 23, the women at 18.

Amusements and Traditions

Fires on St John's Eve and those dedicated to other saints were customary but are now discontinued. There are neither clan marches nor funeral cries, nor any peculiarity of costume.

Parish of Leck

Migration

Many go to England at harvest time, leaving their wives and families, who are provided for during their absences by the produce of a conacre of potatoes which is usually set for their support.

Productive Economy

Rent and Tithe

The cottiers generally pay rent in labour. Tithe is paid by an acreable composition, which varies according to the quality of the land.

Farms and Rents

The farms in the lowlands usually consist of 15 acres, at a rent of 25s per acre; in the mountains of 50 acres, at a rent of 3s per acre. They are generally held on lease of 31 years or 3 lives. The farm buildings are bad and any repairs are done by the tenant.

Model Farm

Colonel Pratt's steward, who resides on his estate, has a farm in his own hands. He instructs the people and has made great improvement. Under his direction some barren moor has been converted into valuable pasture by means of irrigation. French drains are also used. There is but little forced grass.

Soil and Manures

The soil in the greater part of the parish is cold and bad.

Farmyard manures, shells from Lough Swilly and limestone, which is abundant and burnt with turf, are the manures employed. Burning the ground does not prevail.

A boat-load of sea wreck 5 tons, cost 10s 6d and manures half a rood. A boat-load of shells from Fort Stewart costs 6s per 4 and a half tons, and about 5 loads manure an acre. A barrel of lime costs 11d and an acre requires about 30 barrels of 3 bushels each. A barrel of limestone requires about a pack of turf, 6d, to burn it into lime. These are the prices of the old town of Letterkenny.

Livestock

The hills are considered too cold for sheep-walks. Horned cattle, usually of the Irish breed, are preferred. The fences are good.

An improved breed of horse is desirable. They are generally small and bad, though this may in some degree arise from their being worked much too early and poorly fed.

On a farm of 20 acres will generally be found 2 horses, 4 cows, 2 pigs, 15 geese and ducks.

Implements of Husbandry

There are few slide or wheel cars, carts and drags are in general use, 2 horses in a team.

Wages

The wages of a farm manservant are from 4 pounds to 6 pounds a year with board and lodging.

Fairs and Markets

Neither fair nor market is held in the parish. Those to which the people generally resort are Londonderry and Letterkenny.

Agriculturist

Sir Edmund Hayes has lately engaged, at considerable expense, a Scotch agriculturist to instruct his tenants.

Social Economy

Religion

According to the government census take in 1834, the population of the parish, distinguishing each religious persuasion, was as follows: Established Church 384, Roman Catholics 2,441, Presbyterians 1,420, total 4,245.

The benefice was a perpetual curacy attached to the deanery of Raphoe but has lately been separated. The incumbent, the Revd Mr Chambers, received from the dean, to whom the rectorial, vicarial tithes were paid, a residence with about 25 acres of glebe land attached to it in the townland of Corranagh and also the tithe of 4 townlands, namely Curragh, Bunagee, Corranagh and Druminny.

The parish has been erected into a rectory entire by an act of council pursuant to a clause in the Church Temporalities Bill.

The Presbyterian portion of the population attend divine service at the meeting house in Letterkenny.

Ancient Topography

Antiquities: Castle

In the townland of Ardahee, on the right bank of the River Swilly about 2 miles west of

Letterkenny, the foundation of a castle, one of the strongholds of the O'Donnells, is still shown. This fortress was called Castle Solace or "the castle of light" and is said to have derived its name from the great light that appeared from it when taken and burnt by the English in June 1650.

It was built in the year 1540 by Shane O'Donnell, an Irish chieftain, and in 1641, while held by his grandson Phelemy Rua O'Donnell, was besieged by Cromwell and partly destroyed.

In the month of June 1650 a battle was fought before Castle Solace between the parliamentary forces and the king's troops, in which the latter were defeated; and most of the officers made prisoners are said to have been killed in cold blood by order of Sir Charles Coote, though they received quarter when taken.

The castle was cannonaded from Conwal Brae (at that time a town with a monastery) about a mile distant and totally destroyed. Some of the garrison, though badly wounded, effected their escape to the house of a woman named Cromwell, who received and sheltered them, in gratitude for which a silver cup was given her by one of them on his departure. This cup is said to be still in the possession of the Chambers' family.

There is a tradition that the castle would have held out had not a maid belonging to O'Donnell discovered to the besiegers the best point of attack. Scarcely a vestige now remains, the stones having been used for building and other purposes.

Forts

There are several of the circular enclosures called Danish forts and also some subterraneous passages built and covered with large stones. They extend about 20 feet and are similar to those found under the parapets of the forts. Nothing remarkable, as far as I could learn, has been discovered in them.

Mass Rock

Mass is supposed to have been performed in times past at the rock called Craignasiguart in the townland of Dooballagh.

SOCIAL ECONOMY

Census in 1835

Statistical table of the parish of Leck, as taken from census and enquiry made in 1835. [Table contains the following headings: name of townland, analysis of population and dwellings, name of landlord].

Ardahee, 3 inhabited houses, 5 families, 3 outhouses, 6 total buildings; landlord Revd William Boyd.

Aghliard, 21 inhabited houses, 29 families, 2 in ruins, 22 outhouses, 45 total buildings; landlord Sir E. Hayes Bart, M.P.

Ardaganny, 13 inhabited houses, 18 families, 7 outhouses, 20 total buildings; landlord Colonel Pratt.

Ballyboe, 7 inhabited houses, 9 families, 1 in ruins, 5 outhouses, 13 total buildings; landlord Colonel Pratt.

Ballyconally, 6 inhabited houses, 8 families, 5 outhouses, 11 total buildings; landlord Widow Humphrey.

Bunagee, 9 inhabited houses, 18 families, 1 in ruins, 5 outhouses, 15 total buildings; landlord Colonel Pratt.

Calhame, 8 inhabited houses, 14 families, 1 in ruins, 4 outhouses, 13 total buildings; landlord Colonel Pratt.

Carrygally, 5 inhabited houses, 8 families, 9 outhouses, 14 total buildings; landlord Colonel Pratt.

Coachmill, 5 inhabited houses, 8 families, 1 in ruins, 8 outhouses, 14 total buildings; landlord Colonel Pratt.

Corranagh, 21 inhabited houses, 31 families, 16 outhouses, 37 total buildings; landlord see of Raphoe.

Crieve Glebe, 14 inhabited houses, 20 families, 8 outhouses, 22 total buildings; landlord see of Raphoe.

Crieve Smith, 23 inhabited houses, 27 families, 1 in ruins, 4 outhouses, 28 total buildings; landlord Mr Bartley.

Cullian, 10 inhabited houses, 15 families, 2 in ruins, 3 outhouses, 15 total buildings; landlord Colonel Pratt.

Curragh, 6 inhabited houses, 9 families, 3 in ruins, 5 outhouses, 14 total buildings; landlord Colonel Pratt.

Dooballagh, 37 inhabited houses, 49 families, 1 in ruins, 12 outhouses, 50 total buildings; landlord Sir E. Hayes Bart, M.P.

Drimnahoagh, 20 inhabited houses, 30 families, 4 in ruins, 23 outhouses, 47 total buildings; landlord government.

Dromore, 19 inhabited houses, 30 families, 1 in ruins, 23 outhouses, 43 total buildings; landlord Captain Dobson.

Drumgregan, 2 inhabited houses, 3 families, 1 outhouse, 3 total buildings; landlord Captain Dobson.

Druminny, 11 inhabited houses, 14 families, 4 in ruins, 15 outhouses, 30 total buildings; landlord Sir Edmund Hayes Bart, M.P.

Drumardagh, 9 inhabited houses, 11 families, 1 in ruins, 14 outhouses, 24 total buildings; landlord Sir Edmund Hayes Bart, M.P.

Farsetmore, 1 inhabited house, 1 family, 5 outhouses, 6 total buildings; landlord Captain Dobson.

Fycorranagh, 5 inhabited houses, 7 families, 2 in ruins, 3 outhouses, 10 total buildings; landlord Colonel Pratt.

Glenoughty, 18 inhabited houses, 28 families, 11 outhouses, 29 total buildings; landlord Colonel Pratt.

Glentillade, 11 inhabited houses, 16 families, 6 outhouses, 17 total buildings; landlord Colonel Pratt.

Knockbrack, 24 inhabited houses, 45 families, 20 outhouses, 44 total buildings; landlord Sir E. Hayes Bart, M.P.

Lismonaghan, 7 inhabited houses, 8 families, 4 outhouses, 11 total buildings; landlord Colonel Pratt.

Lurgy, 7 inhabited houses, 14 families, 1 in ruins, 14 outhouses, 22 total buildings; landlord Sir E. Hayes Bart, M.P.

Lustillian, 27 inhabited houses, 41 families, 4 in ruins, 19 outhouses, 50 total buildings; landlord Sir E. Hayes Bart, M.P.

Lurgybrack, 3 inhabited houses, 4 families, 5 outhouses, 8 total buildings; landlord Sir E. Hayes Bart, M.P.

Magherabwee, 19 inhabited houses, 32 families, 6 in ruins, 12 outhouses, 37 total buildings; landlord Sir E. Hayes Bart, M.P.

Old Town, 20 inhabited houses, 42 families, 5 outhouses, 25 total buildings; landlord Revd Mr Fenwick.

Pluck, 11 inhabited houses, 15 families, 3 in ruins, 8 outhouses, 22 total buildings; landlord Sir E. Hayes Bart, M.P.

Raan, 25 inhabited houses, 33 families, 4 in ruins, 11 outhouses, 40 total buildings; landlord Colonel Pratt.

Rockhill, 10 inhabited houses, 11 families, 1 in ruins, 12 outhouses, 23 total buildings; landlord John Stewart Esquire.

Rossbrackan, 10 inhabited houses, 18 families, 1 in ruins, 13 outhouses, 24 total buildings; landlord Mr Law.

Scribly, 7 inhabited houses, 10 families, 10 outhouses, 17 total buildings; landlord Colonel Pratt.

Trainavinney, 4 inhabited houses, 7 families, 8 outhouses, 12 total buildings; landlord Sir Edmund Hayes Bart.

Trimragh, 6 inhabited houses, 12 families, 1 in ruins, 14 outhouses, 21 total buildings; landlord Sir Edmund Hayes Bart.

Woodpark, 4 inhabited houses, 5 families, 2 in ruins, 1 outhouse, 7 total buildings; landlord Colonel Pratt.

Total average in the parish: 468 inhabited houses, 705 families, 48 houses in ruins, 373 outhouses, 889 total buildings.

Schools

[Table contains the following headings: situation, number of pupils subdivided by religion and sex, remarks as to how supported].

Druminny, Protestants 18 males, Presbyterians 23 males, Roman Catholics 30 males, total 71. This school is still kept under the Society for Promoting the Education of the Poor of Ireland, Kildare Place, Dublin; and though the government grant has been withdrawn from the society, it is the determination of the patron and parents of the children to adhere to it, as no other system could possibly give so general satisfaction. The salary on an average may be about 10 pounds or 12 pounds per annum. The teacher's name is John Wilson.

Druminny, Protestants 4 females, Presbyterians 20 females, Roman Catholics 11 females, total 35. The females in this school are instructed in the several branches of reading, writing, arithmetic and needlework, according to the Kildare Place Society system of instruction. The yearly income from the scholars is about 6 pounds and 4 guineas from the patron, Sir Edmund Hayes, in all amounting to about 10 pounds 4s. The teacher's name is Ellen Russell.

[Insert note: Both schools are in 1 house but in different apartments].

Old Town, Protestants 8 males, 7 females, Presbyterians 8 males, 4 females, Roman Catholics 11 males, 5 females, total 43. The master of this school receives a salary of 11 pounds 1s 6d from Colonel Robertson's Fund. He also receives the sum of 8 pounds from the scholars. There are but few of them pay him, not more than 15 or 16; the rest are poor and taught free. The teacher's name is Mr Hamilton Doggan; he is a Protestant.

Curragh, Roman Catholics 5 males, 17 females, total 22. The master of this school has nothing to depend upon but the children's payments, which is about 6 pounds 12s per annum. He charges each scholar the sum of 1s 6d per quarter; he makes no difference, he charges them all alike. His name is Mr Neal Boyle, a Roman Catholic.

Fycorranagh, Presbyterians 4 females, Roman Catholics 3 males, 3 females, total 10. The teacher of this small school is merely a lad. His name is William Martin, a Roman Catholic, and is supported by the scholars. This school only commenced this day and he, the teacher, had only 10 scholars at 1s and 10d each per quarter of a year. They were all little children commencing to learn the alphabet. 30th March 1835.

Magherabwee, Presbyterians 17 males, 6 females, Roman Catholics 15 males, 4 females, total 42. The teacher's name is James Clee, a Roman Catholic, and is supported by the scholars. He averages his salary to be value to 16 pounds per annum, and besides the above salary he boards with the scholars. He goes to each scholar day about. He teaches reading, writing and arithmetic. For reading he charges 2s per quarter of a year, for writing the same and for arithmetic he charges 3s 6d per quarter of a year.

Lustillion, Presbyterians 4 males, 4 females, Roman Catholics 10 males, 6 females, total 24. The teacher's name is John McShane, a Roman Catholic, and is supported by the scholars. He averages his salary to value 12 pounds per annum. He does not board with the scholars. For writing he charges 2s 6d per quarter of a year, for reading 1s 8d and for arithmetic 3s 6d.

[Signed] I.I. Wilkinson, Lieutenant Royal Engineers, 27th January 1836.

Correspondence between Lieutenants T.A. Larcom and R. Fenwick

MEMOIR WRITING

Letters concerning Lagan

My Dear Fenwick [crossed out: Waters].

Do you know a district near Letterkenny called the Lagan? Whereabouts is it, and in what parish? Yours, Thomas A. Larcom, 18th June 1835.

The Lagan is situated in the parishes of Leck, Raymoghy <Ryemoghy>, in the barony of Raphoe. It commences at Letterkenny port bridge and reaches to Newtowncunningham. Its boundaries are indefinite. It is in Lieutenant Wilkinson's work. [Signed] R. Fenwick, Lieutenant Royal Engineers, 19th June 1835.

Parish of Raphoe, County Donegal

Statistical Report by Lieutenant I.I. Wilkinson, February 1836

Memoir Writing

Letter to Lieutenant Larcom

Strabane, February 24th 1836.
My Dear Larcom,
I have not kept a note of the usual contents of Raphoe parish. Would you be good enough to have it inserted in the accompanying Memoir? Yours very truly I.I. Wilkinson.

Natural State

Name

Raphoe: this name is said to be derived from "the rath or fort of the foe," meaning a position occupied by the Danes near the Tops windmill, where there is still a circle of large upright stones, about 20 in number, supposed to be druidical. In the centre was a cairn or vast heap of stones now removed to form fences near the spot.

County Cess

1826, 878 pounds 16s 4d ha'penny; 1827, 1,192 pounds 13s 3d 3 farthings; 1828, 1,473 pounds 5s 6d; 1829, 1,453 pounds 7s 1d farthing; mean annually, 1,249 pounds 10s 6d 7 farthings.

Locality

The parish of Raphoe is situated in the county of Donegal, in the barony and diocese of Raphoe. It is bounded on the north and north east by the parishes of Leck and Raymoghy <Ryemoaghy>, on the east by the parish of Taughboyne, on the south by the parishes of Clonleigh and Donaghmore, and on the west by the parish of Convoy. It is nearly in the centre of the barony.

Extent and Divisions

The outline of the parish is very irregular, its greatest length from south west to north east about 8 and a half miles and greatest breadth from south east to north west about 6 and a quarter miles, including an area of 13,000 acres nearly.
These are divided into 62 denominations, of which the proprietors are the Lord Bishop of Raphoe principally, the Marquis of Abercorn, Mr Hawksworth, Mr Verschoyle, William Rea Esquire and the Dean of Raphoe.

Natural Features

Rivers

The Burndale river is the only one in the parish and forms for about 2 and a half miles its boundary with the parish of Donaghmore, presenting nothing remarkable.
The Swilly burn is the principal brook, dividing Raphoe from Clonleigh for about 2 miles. There are many smaller ones. No mineral springs have been met with.

Mountains

The highest mountain in the parish is Mongorry, rising to nearly 937 feet. The top (on which is a trigonometrical station, a pile of earth and stones) is barren. There are many smaller hills.

Bogs

The principal bogs are in Mongorry, Ballyholy and Glenkeerin. Turf is sold at Raphoe per barrel at the rate of from 4d to 5d. The timber usually found in turf bogs is scarce.

Modern Topography

Towns: Raphoe

Raphoe, situated nearly in the centre of the parish, on the direct and shortest road between Londonderry and Ballyshannon and distant about 12 miles from the former place, is the only town, but there are numerous villages.
Raphoe is a bishopric and, till the year 1834, the residence of the bishop was at the palace adjoining the town. In the autumn of that year, by the death of the Right Revd William Bissett and according to the provisions of the Irish Church Temporalities Bill, the superintendence and patronage of the see was annexed to the bishopric of Derry and the revenue arising from rents and renewal fines, together with the amount of rent to be obtained by the setting in perpetuity of the palace and mensal lands, became payable to the Board of Ecclesiastical Commissioners.

Gentlemen's Seats: Palace

Immediately in the vicinity of the town of Raphoe stands the palace, commanding an extensive view

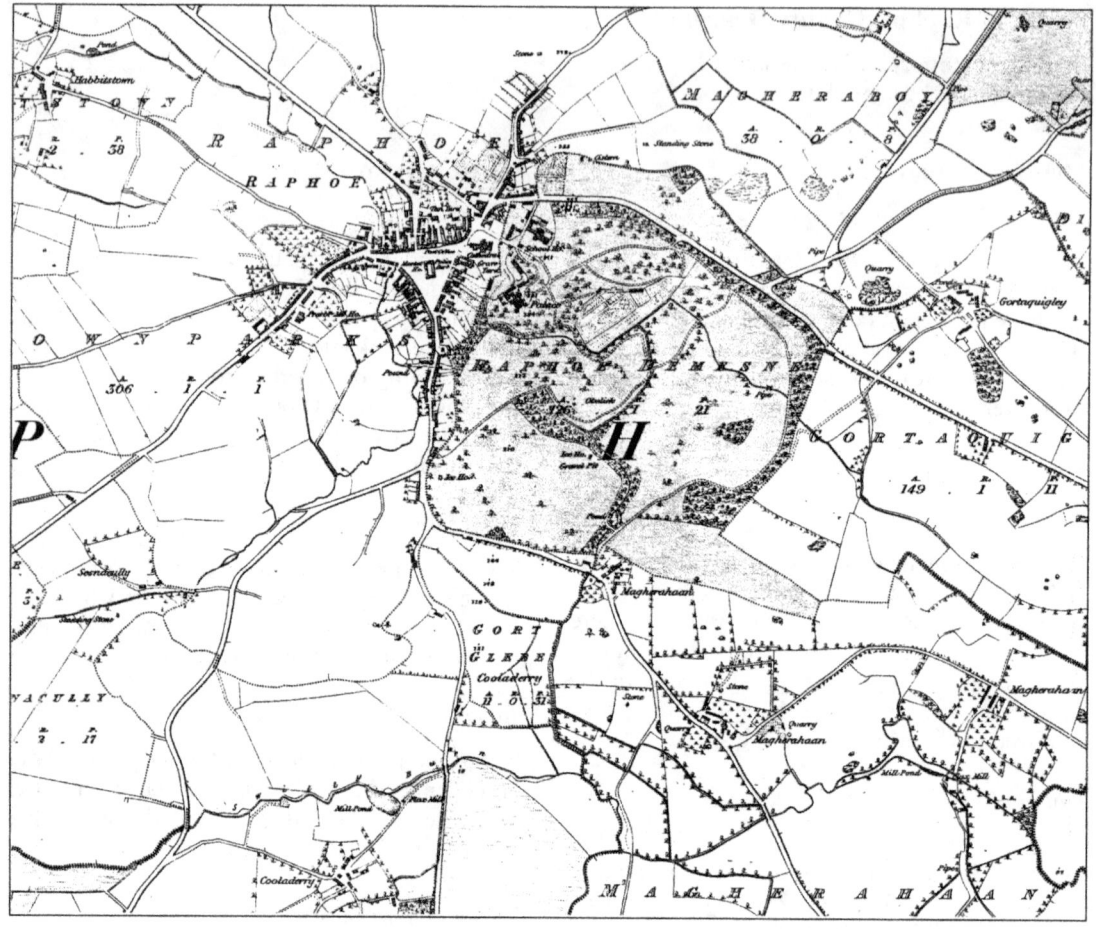

Map of Raphoe from the first 6" O.S. maps, 1830s

of the surrounding country. It is evidently a building of much antiquity. I could not obtain any authentic account of the date of the original building, but from an inscription which is cut on a stone inserted in the wall of the north east tower, and of which the following is a copy, it would appear that 4 towers, one at each angle of the building, were erected between the years 1636 and 1637 by Bishop John Leslie: "Jo Leslius Eps Rapot imum posuit lapidem 17 Maii 1636 supremum 19 Aug 1637 translat suae 5."

The last bishop, Dr William Bissett, soon after his elevation to the episcopal bench, much improved the house by re-roofing and slating it. He also added parapet walls and gave it the appearance of a castle by adding minarets.

The offices are very excellent and appear to have been re-roofed at the same time with the dwelling house. The demesne is extensive and well laid out with pleasure grounds. There are many fine old trees, ash and sycamore, in the ground and about 200 yards from the house, on the south side, stands a pretty cut-stone obelisk about 16 feet high, on which is the following inscription: "In grateful memory of the loyalty, spirit and, it is hoped, the friendship of the Raphoe Corps, by which under God this place was protected when surrounded by robbers, murderers and rebels in the year 1797. This was erected by Bishop Hawkins."

The removal of the residence of the bishop has been a severe loss to the town and neighbourhood, where formerly every charitable institution was mainly supported by his bounty and the quantity of employment given to labourers and mechanics by the liberal expenditure of a considerable income was very great. The revenues are now entirely withdrawn from the place whence they are derived, and however the annexing this bishoprick to another see may profit the establishment in the main, certain it is that the town and neighbourhood of Raphoe have suffered an irreparable injury from it.

There are good gardens with greenhouses and hothouses which are set with the grounds by the year to a neighbouring farmer till a permanent tenant can be obtained for the house and demesne.

Deanery

To the north of Raphoe, and about half a mile from the town, on left of the road to Londonderry, is the Deanery House, a commodious modern building well placed on a rising ground and pleasantly situated in a well-planted demesne. Some of the trees are of considerable growth and many very large ones appear to have been cut down in the times of former deans. The quantity of mensal land is about 270 acres, which the present dean occupies.

Green Hills

To the south west, and about 2 miles distant from Raphoe, is Green Hills, the seat of Captain William Fenwick, formerly the residence of the late Charles Nesbitt Esquire. There are here some thriving plantations and there is an air of comfort and evidence of the residence of the proprietor on his property in the immediate vicinity.

Public Buildings: Cathedral

The cathedral, which very little merits the appellation, is a low irregular building with a tower and short slated top which hardly deserves to be named a spire. It is said to have been built in the 11th century on the ruins of an old abbey. It is used as a parish church and has for many years been in a very wretched state of repair.

I understand the late bishop offered a very considerable sum as a subscription to induce the late Board of First Fruits to repair this church, but it has hitherto been left in a disgraceful state. It is calculated to contain a congregation of 1,000 persons.

Royal School

Adjoining the bishop's demesne, and divided from it by a wall, is the Royal School of Donegal. It is a plain modern building apparently well constructed for the purpose it is intended for. On the western front is an inscription as follows: "Schola regia Donegalensis, 1737."

This school was endowed by royal grant in 1608 with 302 acres of land. The Commissioners of Education now pay the master 400 pounds in lieu of the rents arising from the lands with which the school was originally endowed.

Widows' House

The widows' house in the town, a neat house 2-storeys high, originally founded by Bishop Forster in 1752 and endowed by him with 200 pounds per annum for the maintenance of 4 widows of clergy of the diocese, repaired by the present primate, Lord [blank] Beresford while Bishop of Raphoe.

Library

The diocesan library, which was founded by Bishop Forster, now occupies the eastern wing of the Royal School. The collection of books was the bequest of Dr Hall, formerly Vice-Provost of Trinity College, Dublin. They were rebound at the expense of Dr Bissett, the last bishop.

Meeting House

The Presbyterian meeting house was built about 50 years since by the parishioners. It cost about 300 pounds and accommodates about 850 persons.

SOCIAL ECONOMY AND MODERN TOPOGRAPHY

Temperance Society

A temperance society has been established at Raphoe for the last 3 years, consisting of about 300 members who meet quarterly. It has neither increased nor diminished in number lately. The people are (generally speaking) temperate.

Dispensary

There is a dispensary, supported by subscription. Captain Fenwick, as the treasurer, contributes 40 pounds per annum, and should the subscriptions fall short of this sum, he himself subscribes the amount deficient. The grand jury of Donegal grant an equal sum to the subscriptions. The salary of the medical attendant, Dr McClintock, is therefore 80 pounds per annum, out of which a dispensary is provided.

Schools

Bishop Forster, among several schools erected by his bounty, also founded one at Raphoe for 20 boys, who were to be clothed, instructed and afterwards put out to trades. No trace of this school at present discoverable, though it is particularly made mention of in the *Irish ecclesiastical register.*

Market House

The market house is built in the centre of the town, in an open space where the fairs etc. are held. Petty sessions are held in the market house every fortnight on Saturdays. The sitting magistrates are Captain Fenwick of Raphoe, John Beirs Esquire of Leslie Hill, Captain Humfrey of Cavanacor and Mr Taylor, sub-inspector of police (stipend 200 pounds per annum).

PRODUCTIVE ECONOMY

Farms and Crops

The size of the farms varies from 10 to 30 Cunningham acres but there are some from 30 to 150. They produce potatoes, oats, barley, flax and hay in some farms to [a] considerable extent, and in some farms wheat in small quantities. The quantity yielded per acre of potatoes 960 stone, barley 6 barrels, oats 80 stone, flax 2 and a half cwt of cleaned flax, hay 2 tons, wheat 6 barrels. This may be the average but some lands yield much more abundantly.

The value of the crops on the ground per acre (Cunningham) is: of potatoes 9 pounds, of barley 6 pounds, of oats 3 pounds, of flax 5 pounds, of hay 3 pounds and of wheat 7 pounds. Potatoes generally occupy from 2 to 3 roods in a farm of 10 acres, in one of 30, about 1 acre and a half.

Rents: the land lets from 10s to 25s per acre.

Fairs and Markets

There are 4 fairs held in Raphoe, on the 1st May, 22nd June, 27th August and 4th November; and 5 markets for the sale of cattle, held the first Saturday in each month from December to April. There is also a weekly market on Saturdays.

The tolls were let by the bishop, Dr Bissett, to Attorney Wilson, who lives there still, for standings on the street or in the market house, at a rate of from 1d to 3d, according to the size, and also for meal and potato sacks both on fair and market days.

The fairs are well supplied with cattle of all kinds. In the summer fair of 1833 the people assembled and drove their cattle past the toll collectors, who were also knocked down and beaten. No tolls upon cattle have since been levied.

The old market house was taken down by Bishop Bissett and a new one built on its site in the year 1826. It cost about 200 pounds, appropriated from the tolls. The people, however, consider the old one better adapted for the purposes of a market house.

Manufactures and Labour

Linen is manufactured in a very small quantity. There are no fisheries.

Labourers' wages vary from 9d to 12d per day without diet, with diet from 5d to 8d. Their diet is potatoes and buttermilk and sometimes without milk, meal porridge or stirabout, potatoes and herrings, sometimes butter but rarely.

ANCIENT TOPOGRAPHY

Antiquities

In this parish are several of the ancient mounds called generally Danish forts, though no tradition exists respecting them.

A remarkable circle of large stones, at a place called the Tops, resembling druidical remains; the stones are from 4 to 7 feet in height.

An old graveyard is in the townland of Beltany.

There are also in the townland of Ruskey some ancient stones called the Druids Altar; nothing is known respecting it.

Cathedral

The cathedral is said to have been founded by St Columbkill and the only alteration made in it at the Reformation is supposed to have been lowering the roof of the tower. It was called "the Church of St Union [Eunan]," in whose name all writings are done. A large cross is said to have stood in the cathedral and to have been removed to Omagh in the 15th century.

In the cathedral is the following inscription on the monument of Bishop Forster: "This stone only shows that under ye holy table lie the mortal remains of Nicholas Forster, 27 years bishop of this diocese. He died ye 5th of June 1743 aged 79. What he was, let gratitude tell. May his successors imitate him."

Vault House

It is said that there stood a convent of Franciscans about 2 chains west of the cathedral, near

Parish of Raphoe 125

Graveyard

The Close, where Captain Fenwick resided, was once a graveyard and bones have often been dug up there.

Battle Burn

The Danes are said to have encamped at the village of High Trench and the Irish at that of Low Trench in the townland of Glenmaquin, previous to an action which took place between them, and from which the stream near these villages derives its name of the Battle burn. A great number of bones have been dug up along the banks of this stream.

NATURAL HISTORY

Geology

The geological features of the parish are entirely of the primitive class, the prevailing rock, micaceous schist. Limestone of a good quality is found on parts of the parish in abundance. No mineral veins have been discovered.

SOCIAL ECONOMY

Population

From the government census taken in the year 1834, the parish of Raphoe having contained: 1,149 members of the Established Church, 2,730 Roman Catholics, 2,552 Presbyterians, total 6,431.

Number of baptisms entered in Raphoe parish, registry from March 21st 1827 to March 21st 1830: births 182, marriages 23, burials 42.

Table of Townlands

Statistical table of the parish of Raphoe, as taken from census and enquiry made in 1835. [Table contains the following headings: name of townland, number of buildings and families, landlord].

Aghnakeeragh, 2 inhabited buildings, 2 dwelling houses and families, 2 outhouses, 2 in ruins, 6 total buildings; landlord see of Raphoe.

Ardvarnock Glebe, 8 inhabited buildings, 17 dwelling houses and families, 9 outhouses, 17 total buildings; landlord see of Raphoe.

Beltany, 20 inhabited buildings, 30 dwelling houses and families, 2 uninhabited houses, 16 outhouses, 5 in ruins, 43 total buildings; landlord see of Raphoe.

Ballyholy Near, 8 inhabited buildings, 13 dwelling houses and families, 1 uninhabited house, 5 outhouses, 5 in ruins, 19 total buildings; landlord Counsellor Schoales.

Ballyholy Far, 21 inhabited buildings, 29 dwelling houses and families, 1 uninhabited house, 16 outhouses, 38 total buildings; landlord Counsellor Schoales.

Black Repentance, 9 inhabited buildings, 9 dwelling houses and families, 3 outhouses, 2 in ruins, 14 total buildings; landlord Mr Mehaughney.

Boggagh, 13 inhabited buildings, 16 dwelling houses and families, 7 outhouses, 20 total buildings; landlord see of Raphoe.

Breahead, 6 inhabited buildings, 6 dwelling houses and families, 6 outhouses, 1 in ruins, 13 total buildings; landlord Revd Mr Scott.

Broadlee, 8 inhabited buildings, 14 dwelling houses and families, 4 outhouses, 1 in ruins, 13 total buildings; landlord Marquis of Abercorn.

Burnside, 6 inhabited buildings, 6 dwelling houses and families, 1 uninhabited house, 7 outhouses, 1 in ruins, 15 total buildings; landlord Revd Mr Scott.

Carrickbrack, 5 inhabited buildings, 5 dwelling houses and families, 6 outhouses, 11 total buildings; landlord Dr Rogan.

Cooladerry, 12 inhabited buildings, 13 dwelling houses and families, 7 outhouses, 4 in ruins, 23 total buildings; landlord see of Raphoe.

Coolaghy, 7 inhabited buildings, 7 dwelling houses and families, 9 outhouses, 3 in ruins, 19 total buildings; landlord Marquis of Abercorn.

Coolaghy Glebe, 1 inhabited building, 1 dwelling house and family, 3 outhouses, 4 total buildings; landlord see of Raphoe.

Common, 28 inhabited buildings, 38 dwelling houses and families, 1 uninhabited house, 5 outhouses, 5 in ruins, 39 total buildings; landlord Counsellor Stokes.

Craigs, 8 inhabited buildings, 12 dwelling houses and families, 7 outhouses, 15 total buildings; landlord see of Raphoe.

Creggan, 17 inhabited buildings, 19 dwelling houses and families, 4 outhouses, 21 total buildings; landlord Mr Scott.

Cottown, 9 inhabited buildings, 12 dwelling houses and families, 1 uninhabited house, 4 outhouses, 14 total buildings; landlord see of Raphoe.

Deerpark, 9 inhabited buildings, 13 dwelling houses and families, 9 outhouses, 4 in ruins, 22 total buildings; landlord Robert Montgomery Esquire.

Difflin, 2 uninhabited houses, 1 in ruins, 3 total buildings; landlord see of Raphoe.

Drimoneny, 4 inhabited buildings, 5 dwelling houses and families, 6 outhouses, 10 total buildings; landlord see of Raphoe.

Drumnabratty, 4 inhabited buildings, 5 dwelling houses and families, 2 outhouses, 6 total buildings; landlord Marquis of Abercorn.

Doorable, 12 inhabited buildings, 20 dwelling houses and families, 4 outhouses, 16 total buildings; landlord Counsellor Schoales.

Figuart, 12 inhabited buildings, 14 dwelling houses and families, 12 outhouses, 5 in ruins, 29 total buildings; landlord see of Raphoe.

Flemingstown, 10 inhabited buildings, 16 dwelling houses and families, 5 outhouses, 15 total buildings; landlord Robert Montgomery Esquire.

Glenkeerin, 26 inhabited buildings, 33 dwelling houses and families, 1 uninhabited house, 5 outhouses, 32 total buildings; landlord Sir E. Hayes Bart, M.P.

Glenmaquin Lower, 32 inhabited buildings, 44 dwelling houses and families, 18 outhouses, 50 total buildings; landlord see of Raphoe.

Glenmaquin Upper, 18 inhabited buildings, 23 dwelling houses and families, 6 outhouses, 24 total buildings; landlord see of Raphoe.

Gortaquigley, 7 inhabited buildings, 7 dwelling houses and families, 7 outhouses, 6 in ruins, 20 total buildings; landlord see of Raphoe.

Gort Glebe, landlord Dean of Raphoe.

Gort of Cooladerry, landlord Dean of Raphoe.

Gortnest, 4 inhabited buildings, 6 dwelling houses and families, 3 outhouses, 7 total buildings; landlord see of Raphoe.

Kabbitstown, 6 inhabited buildings, 7 dwelling houses and families, 4 outhouses, 10 total buildings; landlord late Mr Abram of Dublin.

Kiltoal, 17 inhabited buildings, 21 dwelling houses and families, 1 uninhabited house, 12 outhouses, 3 in ruins, 33 total buildings; landlord Messrs Hawksworth and Verschoyle.

Lismontigley, 9 inhabited buildings, 13 dwelling houses and families, 4 outhouses, 1 in ruins, 14 total buildings; landlord Bishop Alexander.

Lisnoble, 2 inhabited buildings, 2 dwelling houses and families, 1 outhouse, 3 total buildings; landlord see of Raphoe.

Magherabwee, 1 inhabited building, 1 dwelling house and family, total buildings 1; landlord see of Raphoe.

Magherahee, 16 inhabited buildings, 18 dwelling houses and families, 25 outhouses, 1 in ruins, 42 total buildings; landlord Captain Fenwick.

Magherahan, 11 inhabited buildings, 12 dwelling houses and families, 1 uninhabited house, 13 outhouses, 1 in ruins, 26 total buildings; landlord Mr Carson.

Magheestown, 11 inhabited buildings, 17 dwelling houses and families, 5 outhouses, 1 in ruins, 17 total buildings; landlord Counsellor Schoales.

Magherasollus, 17 inhabited buildings, 24 dwelling houses and families, 1 uninhabited house, 17 outhouses, 35 total buildings; landlord Counsellor Smiley.

Milltown, 5 inhabited buildings, 10 dwelling houses and families, 10 outhouses, 15 total buildings; landlord see of Raphoe.

Mountain Park, 11 inhabited buildings, 17 dwelling houses and families, 3 outhouses, 14 total buildings; landlord Mr Finton.

Mongorry, 4 inhabited buildings, 4 dwelling houses and families, 1 outhouse, 2 in ruins, 7 total buildings; landlord Counsellor Smiley.

Muntertinney, 27 inhabited buildings, 38 dwelling houses and families, 10 outhouses, 1 in ruins, 38 total buildings; landlord Lady Galbraith.

Mullaghfin, 9 inhabited buildings, 15 dwelling houses and families, 3 outhouses, 1 in ruins, 13 total buildings; landlord see of Raphoe.

New Row, 2 inhabited buildings, 6 dwelling houses and families, 1 in ruins, 3 total buildings; landlord see of Raphoe.

Raphoe Demesne, 3 inhabited buildings, 3 dwelling houses and families, 16 in ruins, 19 total buildings; landlord see of Raphoe.

Raphoe Townparks, 75 inhabited buildings, 283 dwelling houses and families, 7 uninhabited houses, 174 outhouses, 13 in ruins, 269 total buildings; landlord see of Raphoe.

Ruskey Lower, 7 inhabited buildings, 8 dwelling houses and families, 1 uninhabited house, 2 outhouses, 2 in ruins, 12 total buildings; landlord Counsellor Macklin.

Ruskey Upper, 49 inhabited buildings, 56 dwelling houses and families, 3 uninhabited houses, 24 outhouses, 3 in ruins, 79 total buildings; landlords Messrs Verschoyle and Mansfield.

Oakfield Demesne, 12 inhabited buildings, 12 dwelling houses and families, 7 outhouses, 1 in ruins, 20 total buildings; landlord see of Raphoe.

Sessnacully, 2 inhabited buildings, 2 dwelling houses and families, 1 uninhabited house, 3 total buildings; landlord see of Raphoe.

Shannagh, 5 inhabited buildings, 6 dwelling houses and families, 4 outhouses, 1 in ruins, 10 total buildings; landlord see of Raphoe.

Parish of Raphoe

Slieveboe, 8 inhabited buildings, 10 dwelling houses and families, 5 outhouses, 1 in ruins, 14 total buildings; landlord Counsellor Schoales.

Stranorlaghan, 3 inhabited buildings, 5 dwelling houses and families, 1 in ruins, 4 total buildings; landlord see of Raphoe.

Tops, 8 inhabited buildings, 9 dwelling houses and families, 1 uninhabited house, 13 outhouses, 2 in ruins, 24 total buildings; landlord see of Raphoe.

Tops Demesne, 1 inhabited building, 1 dwelling house and family, 5 outhouses, 6 total buildings; landlord see of Raphoe.

Tullydonnel Lower, 5 inhabited buildings, 9 dwelling houses and families, 2 uninhabited houses, 1 in ruins, 14 total buildings; landlord Mr Montgomery.

Tullydonnel Upper, 9 inhabited buildings, 12 dwelling houses and families, 1 uninhabited house, 6 outhouses, 5 in ruins, 21 total buildings; landlord Mr Montgomery.

Tullyvinney, 14 inhabited buildings, 16 dwelling houses and families, 11 outhouses, 25 total buildings; landlord see of Raphoe.

Winneyhaa, 9 inhabited buildings, 14 dwelling houses and families, 5 outhouses, 2 in ruins, 16 total buildings; landlord Mr Scott.

[Totals]: 684 inhabited buildings, 1,086 dwelling houses and families, 29 inhabited houses, 583 outhouses, 89 in ruins, 1,385 total buildings.

Table of Schools

[Table contains the following headings: situation, number of pupils subdivided by religion and sex, remarks as to how supported].

Town of Raphoe: Protestants 54 males, 14 females; Presbyterians 31 males, 9 females; Roman Catholics 12 males, 8 females; total 128. This is called the parish school. Messrs Andrew and William Walker are the teachers, both Protestants. It was built about 60 years ago at the expense of the Right Revd Dr Oswald and cost about 70 pounds. The teachers live in it. There is about 30 perches of a garden attached to it. The house and garden are worth about 7 pounds per annum. There is 12 pounds Irish currency per annum left to the school by the late Colonel Robertson. They teach reading, writing and arithmetic. They charge the scholars from 3s 3d to 2s per quarter. Their yearly income averages about 40 pounds.

Town of Raphoe: Protestants 8 males, 2 females; Presbyterians 5 males, 8 females; Roman Catholics 3 males, 1 females; total 27. Mr and Miss Barclay teach these schools in the same house but in different apartments; they are Protestants. They have no remuneration but what they get from the scholars. Mr Barclay keeps a classical school. He charges from 10s to 16s per quarter. He says his yearly income averages 50 pounds. Miss Barclay teaches sewing, reading, writing and arithmetic. She charges from 5s to 8s per quarter. She says she is worth, by her school, 30 pounds per annum.

Town of Raphoe: Protestants 6 males, 1 female; Presbyterians 5 males, 1 female; Roman Catholics 11 males, 6 females; total 30. The teacher is Mr James Galbraith; he is a Protestant. He has no other remuneration but what he receives from the scholars. He teaches book-keeping, arithmetic etc.; his terms are from 3s 4d to 5s per quarter. His yearly income averages about 30 pounds.

Town of Raphoe: Protestants 1 male, Presbyterians 3 males, 4 females, total 8. Miss Cunningham teaches this school; she is a Presbyterian. She teaches sewing, reading, writing etc. She has no remuneration but what she gets from the scholars. She charges 3s per quarter. She makes about 6 pounds per annum.

Town of Raphoe: Protestants 6 females, Presbyterians 17 females, Roman Catholics 2 females; total 25. This schoolhouse was built by Bishop Beresford, but is now rented from Captain Fenwick (to whom the late Bishop Bisset left it) by Mrs Pitcairn who teaches in it; she is a Protestant. She teaches sewing, flower work, reading, writing, arithmetic etc. She has no remuneration but what she receives from the scholars. Her terms quarterly are from 7s 6d to 10s 6d. Her yearly income averages about 40 pounds.

Lack Hall in the townland of Common: Protestants 6 males, 5 females; Presbyterians 10 males, 4 females; Roman Catholics 6 males, 7 females; total 38. This school is kept in a place called Lack Hall in the townland of Common. The teacher's name is Samuel Topping. He is a Protestant and has 1s 1d ha'penny per day pension, having been in the army for some time. He keeps the school in his own house. He gets 1d ha'penny per week from writers and 1d per week from spellers, readers etc. He has no other remuneration. He makes about 4 pounds per annum for teaching.

Creggan: Protestants 1 male, 3 females; Presbyterians 37 males, 12 females; Roman Catholics 7 males, 7 females; total 67. This schoolhouse was built by the people of the neighbourhood on a kind of common or rock. It cost about 30 pounds. The teacher's name is William Pinkerton; he is a Presbyterian. He has no other remuneration but what he gets from the scholars (except that he pays nothing for the schoolhouse), which is 1s 8d per quarter from each, amounting to about 10 pounds per annum. He teaches reading, writing and arithmetic.

Beltany: Protestants 5 males, 4 females; Presbyterians 11 males, 7 females; Roman Catholics 4 males, 2 females; total 33. The teacher's name is Mr McClintock; he is a Presbyterian. He has a house and about 30 perches of ground and 8 pounds a year from the Society for Discountenancing Vice, all worth about 11 pounds per annum. He has not received any money from the society for the last 12 months and thinks they have discontinued giving it, as they intimated to him sometime ago would be the case on account of their funds being nearly run out. He gets from 1s 8d to 2s per quarter from each scholar. He teaches reading, writing and arithmetic. His emoluments are (in all) about 17 pounds or 18 pounds per annum.

Ballyholy: Presbyterians 27 males, 12 females; Roman Catholics 2 males, 1 female; total 42. The school of Ballyholy was placed under the New Board of National Education and, from some reasons which I have not been able accurately to ascertain, the grant to this school has been withdrawn.

It is said that the Roman Catholic priest on one occasion turned out the children of his communion, to the number of between 30 and 40, from this school and the reason alleged for his doing was that the Bible was admitted to be read by the scholars. The Revd W.D. Killan, the Presbyterian minister, under whose immediate superintendence and patronage the school is placed, has published a statement of the whole circumstances of the school from [when] under the National Board, but I have not been able to procure a copy of his pamphlet. Some outrage has been lately committed by persons unknown in breaking the windows of the schoolhouse.

The Ballyholy school is at present under the care of the Synod of Ulster. They are to pay the master, William Craig, a Presbyterian, a yearly salary, the amount of which is not yet known. He is also to be paid by the scholars: farmers' children for spelling and reading 2s per quarter, writing 2s 6d and arithmetic 3s; cottiers' children for spelling and reading 1s 1d per quarter, writing and arithmetic 1s 7d ha'penny. Since their school came under the Synod of Ulster, the parents of Roman Catholic children will not allow them to attend.

Trades and Occupations

A list of the trades and of persons of other calling in the town of Raphoe.

Publicans 13.
Grocers 6.
Tailors: 10 employers, 18 journeymen, 6 apprentices, total 34.
Carpenters: 6 employers, 1 journeyman, 2 apprentices, total 9.
Coopers: 2 employers, total 2.
Reedmakers: 1 employer, total 1.
Nailers: 2 employers, total 2.
Blacksmiths: 5 employers, 1 journeyman, 2 apprentices, total 8.
Whitesmiths: 2 employers, 1 apprentice, total 3.
Cabinetmakers: 3 employers, 2 journeymen, 1 apprentice, total 6.
Slaters and plasterers: 2 employers, 2 journeymen, total 4.
Shoemakers: 13 employers, 7 apprentices, total 20.
Weavers: 6 employers, total 6.
Bakers: 4 employers, 3 journeymen, total 7.
Gardeners: 1 employer, total 1.
Apothecaries: 3 employers, total 3.
Protestant ministers 3, Presbyterian ministers 1.
Painters and glaziers: 2 employers, total 2.
Wheelwrights: 3 employers, 2 journeymen, total 5.
Saddlers: 1 employer, 1 journeyman, 1 apprentice, total 3.
Curriers and tanners: 2 employers, total 2.
Butchers: 8 employers, total 8.
Sawyers: 2 employers, 2 journeymen, 1 apprentice, total 5.
Hacklers: 3 employers, total 3.
Chandlers: 1 employer, 3 apprentices, total 4.
Basketmakers: 1 employer, total 1.
Blue dyers: 1 employer, total 1.
Chainmakers: 2 employers, total 2.
Wool hatters: 3 employers, total 3.
Attorneys: 3 employers, total 3.
Skindressers and capmakers: 1 employer, total 1.
Thatchers: 3 employers, total 3.

[Signed] I.I. Wilkinson, Lieutenant Royal Engineers, 24th February 1836.

Replies by John Toner to Queries of North West Farming Society, April 1823

Parish of Raphoe

NATURAL STATE

Locality and Extent

The ancient and well-known parish of Raphoe lies on the south eastern side of the county of Donegal, having for its boundaries the parishes of Leck and Raymoghy on the north, and the parishes of Taughboyne and Lifford on the east, and the parishes of Donaghmore and Stranorlar on the south, and the parishes of Glenfin and Conwal on the west, being, by the nearest computation, from the east to the west 12 miles in length and upon an average 4 miles in breadth, making 48 square miles in the whole.

NATURAL FEATURES

Mountains

The western end of the parish is a little mountainous or, in other words, moorlands, where young cattle and sheep thrive amazingly well. The moors and mountains are well stored with hares and moor-fowl, where sporting gentlemen in former times amused themselves hunting with hounds, the net or the gun in a space of land 4 miles long and 4 miles broad, in all 16 square miles and upwards.

The mountain at the western extremity, namely Kark, is greatly broken up on the southern side and produces fine crops of oats and potatoes, with excellent grazing for young cattle.

Lakes and Rivers

On the northern side of the mountain there is a lake called Loughdale, well stored with fine trout, out of which Burndale rises and runs round the northern end and then turns to the south, and is joined by another that comes down along the southern side of the mountain. It is called Kark burn and the two, when together, form a little river and, with many windings and turnings, it comes along southwards, dividing the little moors and mountains into 2 equal parts nearly, until it comes on to the leap of Drumkeen.

It is full of very good trout but no salmon at all go above the leap, the fall is so great.

Surface and Soil

Leaving the moors and mountains on the west and coming on to the lowlands, there one will see an open, a spacious, pleasant and fine country, but it would be doing injustice to the inhabitants of the mountains near the lowlands without remarking [on] their improvements which are very great, considering the hardship which they endure and labour under. They have drained ditches, broken up and reclaimed barren ground beyond conception, and, much as they have done, there is far more to be done if they were able to employ men to assist them.

Burndale River

As the Burndale comes through the mountains, the rivulets and other streams falling into it swell it up so that it becomes a little river; and as it runs along, it turns its course to the south through the middle of the parish, having on its banks on every side nearly as good land as is to be desired, limestone, turbary, fountains with excellent water, pure air and pleasant verdure.

Crops

The fields produce excellent crops of potatoes, oats, barley, flax and meadow, turnips and clover, and in many parts excellent wheat, if the land be rightly prepared.

Hills

On the southern side of the parish there are 3 little mountains, to wit Knockagarron, Mullaghagarry and Libado. Knockagarron is reclaimed all over where it could be reclaimed and there is but the half or a part of Mullaghagarry in this parish. The other half on the western side is in the parish of Stranorlar and in Mr Stewart's demesne, which he has beautifully ornamented with planting all over the mountain. He also built a lofty spire at our march, on the top of which objects might be described at a great distance.

Further south of that is Libado, rising out of a deep valley at the west end and, gradually ascending to a great height, stretches along a good length through the townlands towards the north east. There was, it is said, a slate quarry there but of what quality is not now known.

East Side of Parish

Coming around from that mountain and proceeding on eastward one will see open and pleasant country from the outside of the parish into Burndale, in the midst of which is to be seen the seat of the Revd Charles Nesbitt which is both splendid and beautiful, as is all the country to the end of the parish. The further down, the more delightful all along the banks of Burndale until it passes into the parish of Lifford.

Coming round the eastern side upon the verge of the parish, one would be enraptured to look at the fields, the enclosures and the different crops which are to be seen in the summer season of the year, as if nature intended that place to be one of its beautiful ornaments of grandeur.

Thence passing round to the lofty mountain called Mongorry, one will see that great mountain rising out of deep valleys on all sides and gradually up to a great height, said to be the highest mountain in the country. It was once a great turbary but now the turf is worn off and the mountain reclaimed and broken up by the rent-holders.

MODERN TOPOGRAPHY

Town of Raphoe

The next thing to look at is the beautiful town of Raphoe, which gives title to the diocese, the barony and the parish. They are all named by it. It stands on a beautiful plain on the eastern side of Mongorry mountain, in the form of an equiangular triangle having 3 equal sides and, as it were, 3 equal angles.

The houses are beautifully arranged, spacious and handsome. The street is wide, well paved and very clean. In the middle of the street stands a clever market house and shambles.

They have 4 fairs in the year and a weekly market every Saturday; besides in the winter season there is a great monthly market every fourth Saturday equal to any fair.

Residence of Prelates

The bishop's palace stands on the eastern side of the town, in a pleasant demesne containing groves, serpentine walks, plantations and every other variety to please the human mind.

A little distance to the north east of the palace is the residence of the dean, in the midst of an enclosed demesne full of groves and plantations with grand fields all beautifully walled round. Both places indicate as if Heaven itself had designed the place and situations for the use of the pious servants of the Lord.

Cathedral

At the north eastern angle of the town stands the cathedral church, with a lofty steeple decorated with a grand clock and every other requisite fitted to the episcopal see.

School

Near the church stands the diocesan schoolhouse, wherein the sciences are taught by eminent teachers. There are other inferior schools in the town for the lower orders of the people.

Meeting House

Besides the church there is a Dissenting meeting house in the south western end of the town. It is filled with a decent congregation.

Communications

The great road from Derry to Donegal passes through the town, another to Strabane from Letterkenny passes through it, one to Castlefinn and another to Killygordon. A traveller passing over Mongorry mountain to Letterkenny would see the whole parish all over and the great part of the county.

Deer Park and Castle

Passing on westward, one will see the remains of a deer park and the remains of an old building said to be a castle, where an ancient family dwelt in former times at a place called Tulleystonal. It lies on the northern side of the road leading to Convoy town.

Covenanting Meeting House

Drawing nearer to Convoy, a little to the left of the great road and on the road from Convoy to Castlefinn, there is a new meeting house built by Covenanters. They have a burying place there also for their dead.

Convoy Town

Entering into Convoy town, there is an ancient meeting house and burying place well enclosed, where a decent congregation assemble at divine worship; and in the middle of the town, a little to the right or northern side, stands a handsome Roman Catholic chapel which, with a large burying place, is beautifully enclosed. Opposite to that, on the southern side of the street, there is a new church a-building, all which beautifies the town very much; and at the western end of the town stands the dwelling of Robert Montgomery Esquire, a gentleman of great respectability and highly esteemed.

He is the successor of the famed Captain Alexander Montgomery, late of Conway [Convoy?], who made great improvements in his time by planting and enclosing in Greenfield, where the dwelling now stands, and in Drumgumerland, a large demesne where he kept his livestock which is now greatly enlarged by his successor, who has planted in such a manner from Greenfield to Drumgumer-land and along the road to Glesly bridge westward, and even purchased land on another estate near to his dwelling in order to beautify it by planting, so that in the course of a little time the whole country may be compared to a spacious forest.

Ancient Topography

O'Donnell's Castle

Coming on along the road, and drawing near to the south western end, one will see the stump of an old castle said to have been inhabited by an ancient family of the O'Donnells before the confiscation of Ulster, and that they were in possession of a vast tract of land. There was, it is said, a nunnery near the castle, and about half a mile west of it is the place which they call a little monastery, where some pious men led a retired life and where there was a large burying place, the remains of all of which may be seen to this day.

Social Economy

Population

According to the returns relative to the population of this parish made in the year 1821, the spiritual land of the parish contained 5,071 souls, including men, women and children, and the temporal lands contained 5,078, making in the whole 10,149. Of the men, some are landholders, some tradesmen, some labourers and some dealers. Jobbing, that is to say, buying and selling cattle, is much practised even by farmers. Weaving, or the linen trade, has the lead of any other. It is said that the manufacturing of woollen will be revived again.

Migration and Labour

The poor labouring men, for want of employment, are often obliged to go to England and to Scotland to look for work, and on their return report that they never saw in England or Scotland as good land as is in their own country, if it were laboured and manured as theirs is and in the same manner. Now what a pity it is that labouring men are obliged to be labouring in other countries and such good land in their own.

If the leading gentlemen of our country in their wisdom and goodness would lay out some ways and means whereby the labour would be kept at home, it would cause our country to flourish in time and promote the prosperity of our community in general hereafter.

Productive Economy

Extent and Capacity of Parish

As the parish is 12 miles in length and upon an average 4 in breadth, that is 48 square miles, each square mile being 320 perches long and 320 broad; multiplied into each other makes 182,400 square perches which, divided by 160, the square purchase of an acre, gives 640 acres of ground in a square mile; consequently 640 acres multiplied by 48, the number of square miles in the parish, produces 30,720 acres of ground in the parish of Raphoe.

And considering the moors, mountains and inland grazing, the one-third of that number may, very justly, be allowed for the grazing of cattle, which comes to 10,240 acres, leaving 20,480 acres for tillage or labour; that again divided by 10,149, the number of inhabitants, gives 2 acres 3 perches nearly to each of them and even the child upon the breast. Again allowing 3 acres upon an average for a sum of grass, that is to divide 10,240 by 3, produces 3,413 and a third sums grazed between cows, horses and sheep.

Now, gentle reader, I have given you a concise statement of the parish. To be treating about the different crops and other productions would not be else but imposition, because most crops are put down by speculation and the farmer very often deceived. Therefore, I think it the most proper and the surest plan to treat of things just as they stand.

If I should be required, at any future time, to make a return of crops or the like, what would [it] be but supposition. I now take my leave of you and if my feeble efforts meet your approbation, it will be highly gratifying to your very humble servant, [signed] John Toner, Maughracorran, 5th April 1823.

Parish of Raymoghy, County Donegal

Statistical Report by Lieutenant I.I. Wilkinson, January 1836

Natural State

Situation and Extent

The parish of Raymoghy is situated in the county of Donegal, in the barony and diocese of Raphoe.

The outline is irregular: the greatest length is 7 miles from north to south, the greatest breadth is 5 miles from east to west, comprising an area of 15,189 acres nearly.

Divisions and Boundaries

The parish of Raymoghy is divided into 62 denominations. The principal proprietors are the Marquis of Abercorn, the Marquis of Londonderry, Earl of Wicklow, the Revd John Leslie. A portion of the parish also belongs to the see of Londonderry and Raphoe. The townlands of Upper and Lower Mondooey are annexed to the institution at Raphoe for the support of the widows of Protestant clergymen.

The parish of Raymoghy is bounded by Lough Swilly and the parishes of All Saints, Taughboyne, Raphoe and Leck.

Natural Features

Surface and Produce

There is a considerable portion of unclaimed land in the parish, but the remainder is highly cultivated and produces wheat, oats, barley, flax and potatoes, and is considered one of the most productive parts of the county Donegal.

The higher part of the parish, namely the townlands of Dooish Upper and Lower Mondooey, Kincraigey and Highbanks, do not produce much barley and very little wheat or flax. Cultivation is carried to the height of [blank] feet above the sea.

To sow an acre will be required from 16 to 18 stones of oats and that acre will produce from 120 to 144 stones; average price this year is 10d per stone. From 14 to 16 stone of wheat will be required to sow an acre and the return will be from 120 to 160 stones; average price this year 11d per stone.

From 10 to 12 stones of barley is required to sow an acre and produce will be from 168 to 210 stones; average price 10d per stone.

Flax seed costs from 12d to 14d per gallon, and to sow an acre with Dutch seed will require 36 gallons and with Riga or American flax seed 28 gallons. The acre will produce from 4 to 6 cwt, which is worth this year from 3 pounds 5s to 3 pounds 15s per cwt. Flax has sold better in the Irish markets this year than it has done for several years on account, as it is supposed, of the failure of flax crops in Holland.

The farmers who sowed their land with flax this year (1835) have reaped considerable profit. For instance, a man holding an acre of land at 1 pound 5s, including rent, tithe and county cess (and there is not much land in the parish of Raymoghy higher charged), and supposing that to labour and sow that acre would cost 1 pound 5s more, amounting to 2 pounds 10s, the value raised would be on the average 17 pounds 10s, leaving a profit of 15 pounds.

To sow an acre of potatoes requires from 16 to 18 measures and the produce will be from 110 to 140 measures, each measure containing 8 stones of 14 lbs each. The average price of potatoes this year is 2d per stone. Seed time is generally from the 16th March to the 16th April and harvest time from the 18th September to the 16th October throughout the parish.

Quality of Land

The best land in the parish is near Manorcunningham, near which a large portion of excellent land has been redeemed from Lough Swilly. This land requires at present no manure and produces larger crops of wheat, barley and oats than any other in the parish.

Manures

There is a valuable bank of shells and sand in the lough near this place which is used for manure. 4 boats are generally engaged throughout the year transporting these shells up the small river between the parishes of Leck and Raymoghy to Connaghan's bridge. The farmers purchase it at the rate of 5s for each boat-load, generally about 7 tons in weight.

These shells are acknowledged by experienced farmers to be superior to lime. 2 stout experienced men are required to manage each boat, as it is necessary to load the boats during the period of low water and make their passage to the point where the load is to be discharged with the flood tide.

Lakes and Rivers

There are no lakes in the parish but a number of small streams and springs. It is well supplied with water. No mineral springs have been discovered, unless those tinged with bog iron should be considered such.

MODERN TOPOGRAPHY

Towns: Manorcunningham

Manorcunningham, situated on the high road from Londonderry to Letterkenny, is the principal town or rather village in the parish.

2 fairs are held on the 7th July and 6th November annually, but they are not of much repute; few sales are effected. There is a post office, 2 grocer's shops and 2 public houses.

Public Buildings

The parish church adjoins Manorcunningham. It was built in the year 1792 at the cost of 540 pounds, partly defrayed by government, partly by general subscription. The ruin of a former church is situated near the village called the Shades of Raymoghy. There is a burial ground attached to each.

Close to Manorcunningham is a Presbyterian meeting house built in 1746 at the expense of the congregation. It will contain 700 persons and cost 600 pounds. The minister, the Revd John Browne, receives 40 pounds per annum from the hearers; the regium donum is 50 pounds.

In the townland of Errity there is a new meeting house for Seceders from the Presbyterian congregation. It is designed to contain 800 people and the cost is estimated at 600 pounds. Revd James Rentoul receives 70 pounds from his hearers per annum; the regium donum is 100 pounds.

There is a new Roman Catholic chapel building in the townland of Drimochill by contract at 247 pounds 10s. It is intended to contain 700 persons and is built so cheap on account of no pews or carpenter's work being required.

The Roman Catholic parish comprises Taughboyne, All Saints and Raymoghy. The priest receives from each farmer 5s annually and from each cottier or person holding no land 2s 6d; there are also fees.

Mills

There are 3 corn mills in the parish. That in the townland of Milltown belongs to the Earl of Wicklow, whose tenants are bound in their leases to have their oats ground there at the rate of the 30th grain. Other persons are only charged the 35th grain.

The mill in the townland of Glensmill belongs to the Marquis of Abercorn and the other, in the townland of Corkey, to the Revd John Leslie. Their regulations are the same as Lord Wicklow's.

There are many flax mills. The charge for cleaning flax is 5s per cwt or 1d ha'penny per lb.

NATURAL FEATURES

Bogs

In the parish of Raymoghy the bog is scarce and turf of course being dearer than usual, the blacksmiths do not use charcoal made from turf in their forges, though fuel of this kind would generally be preferred.

The inhabitants of Manorcunningham procure turf from Dooballagh in the parish of Leck. No timber worth mentioning has been found in the bogs.

Woods

There is a natural wood in the townland of Kincraigey of about 20 acres in extent. The trees are principally birch, alder, ash, holly, hazel and oak, too much crowded to attain a larger size than about 2 feet 6 inches in circumference and 28 feet in height. The wood is held under the Revd John Leslie at a rent of about 12s an acre and the trees sold to the country people for rafters, gates etc.

About 10 pounds has been made this year (1835) of the wood by the cutting the oak. The bark is sold to the tanners, chiefly in Letterkenny.

About 5 acres of the original extent of the wood has been cleared at an expense of about 12 pounds an acre, leaving it ready for crops. This land has proved considerably better than the adjoining. The process of clearing is still going on and it is intended to cut down the whole wood.

SOCIAL ECONOMY AND MODERN TOPOGRAPHY

Advowson

The living of Raymoghy is distinct and in the gift of Trinity College, Dublin. The tithe composition was valued at 700 pounds per annum, the glebe at 200 pounds, total 900 pounds.

Balleaghan Abbey and Raymoghy old church.

Glebe House: Sharon

There is also a good glebe house (situated in the eastern part of the parish) called Sharon. It was the only gentleman's residence in the parish but there is another lately built in the townland of Corkey and occupied by John Beers Esquire, a magistrate, the nephew and representative of the Revd John Leslie, who holds an estate in the parish. It is supposed to have cost 600 pounds and is called Leslie Hill.

Temperance Society

A temperance society has been established about 2 years at Manorcunningham; it consists of about 200 members. There is also a juvenile temperance society consisting of 160.

ANCIENT TOPOGRAPHY

Antiquities: Churches

In the townland of Balleaghan, at the place called Ballyboe, is the ruin of an abbey or church (with a burial ground attached) in which is a tombstone bearing date 1651.

In the graveyard attached to the ruin of another church near Manorcunningham there is no tombstone of a prior date to 1698. This ruin is situated in the townland of Raymoghy and was the parish church before the present edifice was built. There is no inscription on it by which the date of erection can be traced.

Balleaghan Abbey

In the eastern corner of Balleaghan Abbey, near the steps, the great grand-uncle of the present

Parish of Raymoghy

Lord Londonderry is said to be buried. The family do not bury there now.

The abbey itself is supposed to have been founded previous to the tenth century (as also that of Raymoghy). They were both friaries of the same order, but what particular order is not known and were built by 2 masons or architects, brothers called McDegeney. The heads of these men are carved in relief upon the stonework forming the large window in the eastern gable.

The building was of greater extent than the walls still remaining, but the northern portion has been removed and the stones used for some cottages under which a cellar with a well in it is still existing and has been seen by an old inhabitant of the place. This cellar is at present covered up but the occupying tenant of the farm, Mr Alexander, intends opening it.

Burial Pits

About 100 skulls have been dug up in a place about 3 yards square, and pits about this size filled with bones are numerous near the abbey. These pits are supposed to contain the remains of the slain at a battle said to have been fought in the 14th century at a place near Connaghan's bridge, on the Strabane and Letterkenny road, between 2 Irish chieftains and their followers, in which the slaughter was so great that the water of the Lough Swilly from thence to Balleaghan Abbey was tinged with blood.

There is a tombstone in the abbey inscribed to Thomas Cunningham, 17th March 1651, the Cunningham arms and a death head and crossbones carved on it.

Tombstone

In the old church of Raymoghy is a tombstone near the south gable inscribed "to wit heer lieth the body of the Revd Moses Davis, rector of Raymoghy, who died the 30th January 1712 in the 52nd year of his age." The Davis family still bury there.

Drawings

Balleaghan Abbey, showing decorated east window and south wall, with central door and 2 windows each side.

Old church of Raymoghy, showing east window and south wall, with end door and 2 windows.

Lagan Well

In the townland of Drimochill, close to the village of Ringsend, is a well called by the inhabitants the Lagan Well, near which tradition relates that a giant named Lagan died and from whom the parish derives its popular name of the Lagan. The inhabitants use it to designate themselves and sign their names, as for instance "William Cohoun, Laganier."

Danish Forts

There are several of the circular enclosures called Danish forts, and also caves extending a short distance about 20 feet underground and formed similarly to the flagged passages which are frequently formed in the parapets of the forts. They are supposed to have been made or used by smugglers for concealing contraband goods.

NATURAL HISTORY AND PRODUCTIVE ECONOMY

Rocks and Building Materials

The parish of Raymoghy is a primitive country mica or talc slate. The prevailing rock, limestone, is very abundant: a vein runs from Dooish to the townland of Raymoghy. It is nearest to the surface and principally raised in the townlands of Sallybrook, Grawkey, Tullybogley and particularly Raymoghy, where the process of raising and burning is constantly going on. The burnt lime is sold at the rate of 10d per barrel, each barrel containing 32 gallons.

Roofing slates are also procured and the adjacent country supplied. The quarries are on that side of Dooish hill situate in Taughboyne, though it obtains the name of the Lagan.

The slates are in size from 2 feet 4 inches to 7 inches in length and from 4 to 12 inches in breadth, and are sold at the best at 1 pound 10s per 1,000, the second rate, of the same size but worse colour being tinged with iron ore, at 1 pound 2s 6d. They are much inferior in quality to the English slates, which latter are sold in the stores at Londonderry per ton of mill slates at 3 pounds 5s and of rag slates at 2 pounds 17s 6d. They are from 3 feet to 2 feet 6 inches in length and 23 to 20 inches in breadth and average 170 to the ton.

The Lagan slates are sold by Mr Alexander of Trentagh in the Marquis of Abercorn's estate and Mr Marshall of Tubber, held under Andrew Ferguson Esquire of Burt.

Social Economy

Table of Townlands

Statistical table of the parish of Raymoghy, from census and enquiry made in 1835? [Table contains the following headings: name of townland, population subdivided by religion and sex, number of houses and other buildings, details of looms and weavers, size of farms, rent, tithe, cess, name of landlord].

Ardnadittion: Church of England 6 males, 6 females; Roman Catholics 2 males, 3 females; population 17; 4 inhabited houses, 4 outhouses, 8 buildings; 1 loom, 1 weaver; size of farms 62 acres, rent 52 pounds; tithe 2 pounds 12s, cess 7 pounds 10s; landlord Marquis of Londonderry.

Ballylawn: Church of England 20 males, 19 females; Roman Catholics 61 males, 71 females; population 171; 24 inhabited houses, 1 ruined or uninhabited house, 13 outhouses, 38 buildings; 2 looms, 2 weavers; size of farms 8 to 65 acres, rent 14s to 1 pound 8s 4d; tithe 23 pounds 8s 10d, cess 42 pounds 3s 9d; landlord Marquis of Londonderry.

Ballyleven: Church of England 15 males, 21 females; Roman Catholics 12 males, 9 females; population 57; 9 inhabited houses, 2 ruined or uninhabited houses, 1 outhouse, 12 buildings; size of farms 36 to 42 acres, rent 18s to 1 pound 6s 3d; tithe 12 pounds 9s 4d, cess 21 pounds 10s; landlord Revd Mr Ball.

Ballyboe: Church of England 25 males, 27 females; Roman Catholics 8 males, 6 females; population 66; 7 inhabited houses, 6 outhouses, 13 buildings; size of farms 7 to 30 acres, rent 7s 6d to 9s; tithe 4 pounds 14s, cess 6 pounds; landlord Mr Cohoun.

Balleaghan: Church of England 25 males, 34 females; Roman Catholics 21 males, 27 females; population 107; 12 inhabited houses, 5 ruined or uninhabited houses, 11 outhouses, 28 buildings; 2 looms, 2 weavers; size of farms 3 to 74 acres, rent 12s 6d to 1 pound 8s 5d; tithe 15 pounds 7s 11d, cess 28 pounds 10s 6d; landlord Marquis of Londonderry.

Big Isle: Roman Catholics 4 males, 4 females; population 8; 1 inhabited house, 2 ruined or uninhabited houses, 2 outhouses, 5 buildings; size of farms 130 acres, rent 1 pound 9s 4d; tithe 10 pounds 14s, cess 10 pounds; landlord Marquis of Londonderry.

Carrickballydooey: Church of England 19 males, 17 females; Roman Catholics 16 males, 24 females; population 76; 9 inhabited houses, 1 ruined or uninhabited house, 3 outhouses, 13 buildings; 1 loom, 1 weaver; size of farms 6 to 30 acres, rent 7s 6d to 1 pound 6s 8d; tithe 7 pounds 8s 8d, cess 14 pounds 12s 10d; landlord Mr Cohoun.

Carrickballydooey Glebe: Church of England 2 males, 2 females; Roman Catholics 2 males, 1 female; population 7; 1 inhabited house, 2 ruined or uninhabited houses, 1 outhouse, 4 buildings; size of farms 40 acres, rent 27 pounds; tithe 2 pounds, cess 3 pounds 15s; landlord Archdeacon Ussher.

Carricknamart: Church of England 87 males, 93 females; Roman Catholics 28 males, 30 females; population 238; 32 inhabited houses, 5 ruined or uninhabited houses, 15 outhouses, 52 buildings; 6 looms, 6 weavers; size of farms 4 to 50 acres, rent 5s 10d to 18s; tithe 16 pounds 11s 2d, cess 19 pounds 6s; landlord Revd John Leslie.

Castleblaugh: Church of England 13 males, 20 females; Roman Catholics 31 males, 30 females; population 94; 11 inhabited houses, 11 outhouses, 22 buildings; 3 looms, 3 weavers; size of farms 4 to 67 acres, rent 7s to 1 pound 6s 3d; tithe 10 pounds 7s 10d, cess 8 pounds 8s; landlord Earl of Wicklow.

Castledooey: Church of England 62 males, 64 females; Roman Catholics 38 males, 51 females; population 215; 29 inhabited houses, 1 ruined or uninhabited house, 20 outhouses, 50 buildings; 15 looms, 15 weavers; size of farms 3 to 59 acres, rent 8s 5d to 19s; tithe 18 pounds 10s 8d, cess 21 pounds 6s 6d; landlord Marquis of Abercorn.

Corkey: Church of England 44 males, 34 females; Roman Catholics 16 males, 20 females; population 144; 16 inhabited houses, 13 outhouses, 29 buildings; 11 looms, 4 weavers; size of farms 5 to 60 acres, rent 11s 6d to 16s 8d; tithe 18 pounds, cess 21 pounds 8s 6d; landlord Revd John Leslie.

Cottage: Church of England 2 males, 8 females; Roman Catholics, 8 males, 8 females; population 26; 3 inhabited houses, 6 outhouses, 9 buildings; size of farms 50 acres, rent 24 pounds; tithe 4 pounds 4s 8d, cess 6 pounds 6s; landlord Earl of Wicklow.

Dooish: Church of England 106 males, 104 females; Roman Catholics 22 males, 21 females; population 253; 33 inhabited houses, 1 ruined or uninhabited house, 29 outhouses, 63 buildings; 7 looms, 7 weavers; size of farms 12 to 115 acres, rent 7s to 1 pound 1s 10d; tithe 28 pounds 3s 8d, cess 23 pounds 4s 9d; landlord Marquis of Abercorn.

Drain: Church of England 24 males, 20 females; Roman Catholics 2 males, 3 females;

Parish of Raymoghy

population 49; 7 inhabited houses, 1 ruined or uninhabited house, 9 outhouses, 17 buildings; 6 looms, 6 weavers; size of farms 17 to 30 acres, rent 9s 7d to 1 pound 11d; tithe 8 pounds 10s 3d, cess 18 pounds 12s; landlord Marquis of Londonderry.

Drimochill: Church of England 28 males, 26 females; Roman Catholics 49 males, 62 females; population 165; 22 inhabited houses, 2 ruined or uninhabited houses, 17 outhouses, 41 buildings; 8 looms, 8 weavers; size of farms 8 to 34 acres, rent 8s to 1 pound; tithe 13 pounds, cess 20 pounds 4s; landlord Revd John Leslie.

Drumatoland: Church of England 33 males, 38 females; Roman Catholics 77 males, 76 females; population 224; 26 inhabited houses, 12 outhouses, 38 buildings; 6 looms, 6 weavers; size of farms 9 to 55 acres, rent 6s 2d to 18s 6d; tithe 12 pounds 6s, cess 14 pounds 2s 10d; landlord Marquis of Abercorn.

Drumbarnet Upper: Church of England 15 males, 14 females; Roman Catholics 17 males, 11 females; population 57; 7 inhabited houses, 10 outhouses, 17 buildings; 2 looms, 2 weavers; size of farms 65 to 66 acres, rent 10s 4d to 10s 6d; tithe 5 pounds 6s 10d, cess 7 pounds 7s 2d; landlord Earl of Wicklow.

Drumbarnet Middle: Church of England 11 males, 7 females; Roman Catholics 11 males, 8 females; population 37; 4 inhabited houses, 6 outhouses, 10 buildings; size of farms 11 to 23 acres, rent 12s 3d to 1 pound 2s; tithe 4 pounds 16s 8d, cess 7 pounds 6s; landlord Earl of Wicklow.

Drumbarnet Lower: Church of England 16 males, 10 females; Roman Catholics 7 males, 10 females; population 43; 6 inhabited houses, 10 outhouses, 16 buildings; 1 loom, 1 weaver; size of farms 15 to 49 acres, rent 7s 11d to 19s 7d; tithe 9 pounds 4s 5d, cess 12 pounds 19s 6d; landlord Earl of Wicklow.

Drumcairn: Church of England 34 males, 50 females; Roman Catholics 23 males, 22 females; population 129; 15 inhabited houses, 5 ruined or uninhabited houses, 20 outhouses, 40 buildings; size of farms 5 to 71 acres, rent 7s 4d to 1 pound 5s; tithe 19 pounds 15s 1d, cess 27 pounds 14s; landlord Mr Marshal.

Dunduff's Fort: Church of England 26 males, 25 females; Roman Catholics 14 males, 7 females; population 72; 9 inhabited houses, 12 outhouses, 21 buildings; 4 looms, 4 weavers; size of farms 26 to 50 acres, rent 8s 8d to 12s 6d; tithe 13 pounds 2s 9d, cess 14 pounds 19s 4d; landlord Earl of Wicklow.

Errity: Protestants 28 males, 14 females; Roman Catholics 9 males, 1 female; population 52; 9 inhabited houses, 3 ruined or uninhabited houses, 12 outhouses, 24 buildings; 2 looms, 2 weavers; size of farms 22 to 45 acres, rent 8s to 17s 6d; tithe 11 pounds 18s, cess 21 pounds 19s; landlord Revd John Leslie.

Errity Churchland: Protestants 5 males, 3 females; Roman Catholics 9 males, 12 females; population 29; 2 inhabited houses, 1 ruined or uninhabited house, 2 outhouses, 5 buildings; size of farms 36 acres, rent 30 pounds; tithe 1 pound 14s, cess 4 pounds; landlord Bishop of Raphoe and Derry.

Galdonagh: Protestants 62 males, 66 females; Roman Catholics 37 males, 44 females; population 209; 24 inhabited houses, 1 ruined or uninhabited house, 27 outhouses, 52 buildings; 7 looms, 7 weavers; size of farms 40 to 66 acres, rent 11s to 14s 6d; tithe 18 pounds 19s 2d, cess 23 pounds 15s; landlord Marquis of Abercorn,

Galdonagh Glebe: Protestants 27 males, 35 females; Roman Catholics 36 males, 30 females; population 128; 23 inhabited houses, 1 ruined or uninhabited house, 9 outhouses, 33 buildings; size of farms 6 to 40 acres, rent 7s to 12s 6d; tithe 12 pounds 12s 8d, cess 15 pounds 13s 9d; landlord Archdeacon Ussher.

Grawkey: Protestants 44 males, 49 females; Roman Catholics 9 males, 12 females; population 114; 15 inhabited houses, 2 ruined or uninhabited houses, 13 outhouses, 30 buildings; 3 looms, 3 weavers; size of farms 7 to 50 acres, rent 12s to 17s 6d; tithe 15 pounds 1s, cess 31 pounds 16s; landlord Marquis of Londonderry.

Grawkey Glebe: Protestants 14 males, 12 females; Roman Catholics 3 males, 1 female; population 30; 4 inhabited houses, 5 outhouses, 9 buildings; 5 looms, 4 weavers; size of farms 5 to 15 acres, rent 10s 6d to 17s 6d; tithe 3 pounds 13s, cess 5 pounds 10s; landlord Archdeacon Ussher.

Highbanks: Protestants 4 males, 5 females; Roman Catholics 1 male; population 10; 2 inhabited houses, 1 outhouse, 3 buildings; size of farms 51 acres, rent 12 pounds; tithe 1 pound 5s 8d, cess 2 pounds 10s; landlord Marquis of Londonderry.

Hunger's Mother: Protestants 15 males, 13 females; Roman Catholics 6 males, 9 females; population 43; 7 inhabited houses, 2 uninhabited or ruined houses, 4 outhouses, 13 buildings; 2 looms, 2 weavers; size of farms 80 acres, rent 40 pounds; tithe 4 pounds, cess 3 pounds 6s; landlord Earl of Wicklow.

Killyverry: Protestants 17 males, 23 females; Roman Catholics 19 males, 17 females; population 76; 14 inhabited houses, 1 ruined or uninhabited house, 9 outhouses, 24 buildings; size of farms 7 to 59 acres, rent 12s 6d to 1 pound 6s 3d; tithe 16 pounds 17s, cess 21 pounds 7s; landlord Earl of Wicklow.

Kincraigey: Protestants 13 males, 10 females; Roman Catholics 57 males, 55 females; population 135; 16 inhabited houses, 1 ruined or uninhabited house, 11 outhouses, 28 buildings; 1 loom, 1 weaver; size of farms 7 to 55 acres, rent 5s to 18s; tithe 10 pounds 17s 10d, cess 13 pounds 11s; landlord Revd John Leslie.

Labadish: Protestants 39 males, 33 females; Roman Catholics 36 males, 48 females; population 156; 13 inhabited houses, 3 ruined or uninhabited houses, 14 outhouses, 30 buildings; size of farms 2 to 72 acres, rent 13s 5d to 1 pound 1s; tithe 18 pounds 6s 3d, cess 30 pounds 3s 10d; landlord Revd John Leslie.

Lisclamerty: Protestants 26 males, 25 females; Roman Catholics 69 males, 57 females; population 177; 21 inhabited houses, 5 ruined or uninhabited houses, 12 outhouses, 38 buildings; 7 looms, 7 weavers; size of farms 4 to 50 acres, rent 1s 9d to 8s 6d and 17s 6d; tithe 15 pounds 7s 10d, cess 19 pounds 16s 3d; landlord Mr Ramsey.

Lismochry: Protestants 57 males, 57 females; Roman Catholics 14 males, 19 females; population 147; 20 inhabited houses, 6 outhouses, 26 buildings; 8 looms, 8 weavers; size of farms 12 to 40 acres, rent 4s 9d to 1 pound 1s 5d; tithe 13 pounds 12s 1d, cess 15 pounds 16s; landlord Marquis of Abercorn.

Magherybeg: Protestants 25 males, 25 females; Roman Catholics 42 males, 51 females; population 143; 17 inhabited houses, 4 uninhabited houses, 14 outhouses, 35 buildings; size of farms 2 to 25 acres, rent 9s 9d to 1 pound 4s; tithe 10 pounds 16s 10d, cess 20 pounds 6s; landlord Messrs Sanderson and Chittick.

Magherymore: Protestants 6 males, 10 females; Roman Catholics 7 males, 7 females; population 30; 4 inhabited houses, 1 ruined or uninhabited house, 4 outhouses, 9 buildings; 1 loom, 1 weaver; size of farms 9 to 18 acres, rent 1 pound 5s; tithe 4 pounds 14s 8d, cess 11 pounds 5s; landlord Mr Sanderson.

Maybin: Protestants 7 males, 10 females; Roman Catholics 3 males, 2 females; population 22; 3 inhabited houses, 4 outhouses, 7 buildings; size of farms 24 acres, rent 19 pounds 2s; tithe 4 pounds 4s, cess 5 pounds 12s; landlord Earl of Wicklow.

Manorcunningham: Protestants 54 males, 59 females; Roman Catholics 63 males, 46 females; population 222; 26 inhabited houses, 9 ruined or uninhabited houses, 12 outhouses, 47 buildings; 3 looms, 3 weavers; size of farms 2 to 25 acres, rent 13s to 1 pound 13s 4d; tithe 8 pounds 1s 8d, cess 28 pounds 17s 2d; landlords Messrs Sanderson and Chittick.

Manorcunningham Churchland: 2 ruined or uninhabited houses, 2 buildings; size of farms 2 and a half to 16 acres, rent 16s 8d to 1 pound 1s; tithe 4 pounds 3s 10d, cess 9 pounds 6s 6d; landlord Bishop of Raphoe and Derry.

Manorcunningham Churchland Isle: 1 ruined or uninhabited house, 1 building; size of farms 34 acres, rent 75 pounds; tithe 5 pounds, cess 5 pounds; landlord Bishop of Raphoe and Derry.

Minneyhaughley: Protestants 40 males, 26 females; Roman Catholics 10 males, 10 females; population 86; 9 inhabited houses, 3 ruined or uninhabited houses, 5 outhouses, 17 buildings; 3 looms, 3 weavers; size of farms 6 to 50 acres, rent 8s 6d to 1 pound; tithe 13 pounds 13s 9d, cess 23 pounds 14s; landlord Mr Ball.

Minneymore: Protestants 32 males, 44 females; Roman Catholics 52 males, 55 females; population 183; 26 inhabited houses, 15 outhouses, 41 buildings; 5 looms, 5 weavers; size of farms 6 to 64 acres, rent 14s 6d to 1 pound 6s 10d; tithe 13s 4d, cess 17s 6d; landlord Earl of Wicklow.

Milltown: Protestants 20 males, 13 females; Roman Catholics 4 males, 2 females; population 39; 4 inhabited houses, 1 ruined or uninhabited house, 4 outhouses, 9 buildings; size of farms 30 to 33 acres, rent 17s 7d to 1 pound 2s; tithe 5 pounds 1s, cess 5 pounds 19s; landlord Earl of Wicklow.

Monclink: Protestants 26 males, 29 females; Roman Catholics 21 males, 24 females; population 100; 12 inhabited houses, 11 outhouses, 23 buildings; 1 loom, 1 weaver; size of farms 5 to 32 acres, rent 6s 2d to 1 pound 2s 8d; tithe 11 pounds 4s, cess 8 pounds 7s 10d; landlord Captain Stewart.

Mondooey Upper: Protestants 53 males, 59 females; Roman Catholics 20 males, 21 females; population 153; 23 inhabited houses, 4 ruined or uninhabited houses, 14 outhouses, 41 buildings; 5 looms, 5 weavers; size of farms 12 to 55 acres, rent 4s 2d to 11s 6d; tithe 8 pounds 5s 6d, cess 10 pounds 11d; landlord: clergymen and widows of Raphoe.

Mondooey Middle: Protestants 24 males, 25 females; Roman Catholics 9 males, 6 females;

population 64; 11 inhabited houses, 6 outhouses, 17 buildings; size of farms 5 and a half to 100 acres, rent 4s 4d to 12s; tithe 9 pounds 9s 3d, cess 8 pounds 9s 6d; landlord Earl of Wicklow.

Mondooey Lower: Protestants 13 males, 17 females; Roman Catholics 13 males, 17 females; population 60; 10 inhabited houses, 2 outhouses, 12 buildings; 1 loom, 1 weaver; size of farms 25 to 46 acres, rent 11s 6d to 14s 6d; tithe 6 pounds 3s 8d, cess 7 pounds 13s; landlord: clergymen and widows of Raphoe.

Plea Isle: Roman Catholics 5 males, 2 females; population 7; 1 inhabited house, 2 ruined or uninhabited houses, 3 buildings; size of farms 41 acres, rent 82 pounds; tithe 7 pounds 17s, cess 5 pounds 10s; landlord Mr Chittick.

Ruskey: Protestants 56 males, 41 females; Roman Catholics 81 males, 92 females; population 270; 37 inhabited houses, 11 ruined or uninhabited houses, 15 outhouses, 63 buildings; 16 looms, 16 weavers; size of farms 5 to 40 acres, rent 3s to 15s and 1 pound 4s 10d; tithe 19 pounds 12s 1d, cess 27 pounds 7s 4d; landlord Revd John Leslie.

Raymoghy: Protestants 68 males, 66 females; Roman Catholics 24 males, 28 females; population 186; 18 inhabited houses, 5 ruined or uninhabited houses, 17 outhouses, 40 buildings; 6 looms, 6 weavers; size of farms 3 to 52 acres, rent 13s 6d to 1 pound 13s 6d; tithe 24 pounds 6s 9d, cess 39 pounds 9s 6d; landlord Bishop of Raphoe.

Raymoghy Glebe: Protestants 4 males, 3 females; population 7; 1 inhabited house, 1 building; size of farms 6 acres, rent 6 pounds; tithe 10s, cess 14s; landlord Archdeacon Ussher.

Rylands: Protestants 61 males, 47 females; Roman Catholics 17 males, 10 females; population 135; 19 inhabited houses, 1 ruined or uninhabited house, 20 outhouses, 40 buildings; 6 looms, 6 weavers; size of farms 11 to 63 acres, rent 7s 7d to 1 pound 5s 9d; tithe 19 pounds 7s 2d, cess 23 pounds 10s; landlord Marquis of Abercorn.

Sallybrook: Protestants 7 males, 6 females; Roman Catholics 4 males, 1 female; population 18; 2 inhabited houses, 4 outhouses, 6 buildings; size of farms 49 acres, rent 64 pounds; tithe 4 pounds 1s 7d, cess 6 pounds 3s; landlord Earl of Wicklow.

Sharon Glebe: Protestants 16 males, 14 females; Roman Catholics 7 males, 7 females; population 44; 6 inhabited houses, 3 ruined or uninhabited houses, 7 outhouses, 16 buildings; landlord Archdeacon Ussher.

Sheskinapoll: Protestants 18 males, 17 females; Roman Catholics 9 males, 12 females; population 56; 8 inhabited houses, 5 outhouses, 13 buildings; 2 looms, 2 weavers; size of farms 20 to 42 acres, rent 5s 3d to 9s 2d; tithe 3 pounds 7s 6d, cess 3 pounds 16s; landlord Marquis of Abercorn.

Terherrin: Protestants 11 males, 10 females; Roman Catholics 12 males, 16 females; population 49; 8 inhabited houses, 1 ruined or uninhabited house, 6 outhouses, 15 buildings; 2 looms, 2 weavers; size of farms 30 to 42 acres, rent 8s 4d to 9s; tithe 7 pounds 4s, cess 15 pounds 1s; landlord Marquis of Londonderry.

Tinklers Ford: Protestants 11 males, 13 females; Roman Catholics 11 males, 14 females; population 49; 4 inhabited houses, 3 ruined or uninhabited houses, 1 outhouse, 8 buildings; size of farms 19 to 26 acres, rent 19s 3d to 1 pound 1s 7d; tithe 4 pounds 7s 7d, cess 4 pounds 12s; landlord Earl of Wicklow.

Tully: Protestants 9 males, 8 females; Roman Catholics 30 males, 30 females; population 77; 4 inhabited houses, 2 ruined or uninhabited houses, 8 outhouses, 14 buildings; 1 loom, 1 weaver; size of farms 4 to 12 acres, rent 5s 6d to 19s; tithe 6 pounds 5d, cess 7 pounds 15s 6d; landlord Revd John Leslie.

Tullybogley: Protestants 34 males, 30 females; Roman Catholics 10 males, 3 females; population 77; 8 inhabited houses, 1 ruined or uninhabited house, 11 outhouses, 20 buildings; 1 loom, 1 weaver; size of farms 25 to 42 acres, rent 14s 6d to 19s 2d; tithe 9 pounds, cess 15 pounds; landlord Captain Patterson.

Veagh: Protestants 24 males, 26 females; Roman Catholics 29 males, 36 females; population 115; 17 inhabited houses, 2 ruined or uninhabited houses, 6 outhouses, 25 buildings; 1 loom, 1 weaver; size of farms 1 and a half to 115 acres, rent 8s to 1 pound; tithe 17 pounds 2s 8d, cess 33 pounds 17s; landlord Marquis of Londonderry.

Woodhill: Protestants 6 males, 11 females; Roman Catholics 15 males, 17 females; population 49; 9 inhabited houses, 1 ruined or uninhabited house, 12 outhouses, 22 buildings; 2 looms, 2 weavers; size of farms 4 to 30 acres, rent 7s 4d to 19s 6d; tithe 7 pounds 8s 1d, cess 10 pounds 7s; landlord Revd John Leslie.

Total or average in the parish: Protestants 1,589 males, 1,593 females; Roman Catholics 1,172 males, 1,318 females; population 5,772; 744 inhabited houses, 105 ruined or uninhabited houses, 559 outhouses, 1,408 buildings; 159

looms, 158 weavers; tithe 641 pounds 12s 4d, cess 909 pounds 14s 4d.

Table of Schools

[Table contains the following headings: situation, number of pupils subdivided by sex and religion, remarks as to how supported].

Ballylawn: Protestants 15 males, 14 females; Roman Catholics 15 males, 10 females; this school is supported by the scholars. The teacher's name is Henry Murray, a Roman Catholic; value 18 pounds per annum.

Carricknamart: Protestants 17 males, 11 females; Roman Catholics 6 males, 3 females; this school is supported by the scholars. The teacher's name is Edward Laird, a Presbyterian, whose salary is about 10 pounds per annum with his board.

Dooish: Protestants 16 males, 9 females; this school is supported by the scholars. The teacher's name is Alexander Pilkerton, a Presbyterian; salary 9 pounds per annum.

Drumatoland: Protestants 5 males, 6 females; Roman Catholics 10 males, 8 females; this school is supported by the scholars. The teacher's name is James Carland, a Roman Catholic; salary 10 pounds per annum.

Galdonagh: Protestants 35 males, 23 females; Roman Catholics 10 males, 2 females; this school is under the direction of the Kildare Street Society. The teacher's name is James Porter, a Presbyterian, who receives 5 pounds per annum from the Marquis of Abercorn and 2 pounds per annum from the Revd Archdeacon Ussher, for which he is bound to teach as many children of poor people as make application gratis; and those who do not belong to that class pay for their children's tuition, which he values about 20 pounds, making his total emolument 27 pounds per annum. He also boards alternately with the scholars but for the last 2 years has not received any salary from the above society.

Labadish: Protestants 49 males, 26 females; Roman Catholics 8 males, 15 females; this school is taught by Thomas Tinnchame, a Protestant, who receives from an incorporated society residing in Dublin a house, fuel and 20 acres of land rent free, for which he is bound to teach 30 children gratis; and for all above that number he makes a charge which he values about 13 pounds per annum.

Manorcunningham: Protestants 31 females; Roman Catholics 4 females; this is a female school supported by a London society. The teacher's name is Miss Roseanna McKay, a Presbyterian, who receives from the society an emolument of 6 pounds per annum; also charges each female pupil from 1s to 3s per quarter of a year, according to their proficiency or ability. They are taught reading, writing, sewing and knitting.

Maybin: Protestants 3 males, 4 females; Roman Catholics 3 males; this school is supported by the scholars. The teacher's name is Francis Patterson, a Protestant; salary 6 pounds per annum. [Signed] I.I. Wilkinson, Lieutenant Royal Engineers, 18th January 1836.

Replies to Queries from North West Farming Society

NATURAL STATE

Situation and Extent

The parish of Raymoghy <Raymockey> is situated in the county of Donegal and in the barony and diocese of Raphoe. Its greatest length is 7 miles, in a line drawn from the southern extremity of the townland of Ruskey, where it joins the parish of Raphoe, to the northern boundary of Archdeacon Ussher's demesne of Sharon, where it meets the parish of All Saints. The greatest breadth, cutting the longitudinal line at right angles, is 3 miles from the townland of Maghremore West, where Connaghan river divides it from Leck, to the summit of Dooish hill east, where it [is] bounded by Taughboyne.

Archdeacon Ussher is the present incumbent, who has been continually resident in the parish since the year 1800.

Proprietors

2. The different landed proprietors are the Marquis of Londonderry, Earl of Wicklow, Marquis of Abercorn, Revd Mr Leslie, James Saunderson Esquire, [blank] Patterson Esquire, William Squire (a minor), the heirs of the late William Law Esquire, William Stewart of Hornhead, Esquire, Charles Colhoon (a minor), William Ball Esquire.

4. Not one of these proprietors nor an agent employed by any of them has been resident in the parish for many years except William Squire, a minor. There is no magistrate in the parish nor nearer to it than 5 miles.

Townlands

The townlands are Balleighan, Ballylawn, Ardnadishan, Teehirin, Veagh: these are the property of the Marquis of Londonderry. Dooish, Gentle Dooish, Bogtown of Dooish, Largey, Ballyboe, Castle Dooey, Sheskin, Drumatoland, Galdonagh Upper and Lower, and Lismoghrey belong to the Marquis of Abercorn. Mundooeys, Drumbarnet Upper and Lower, Forth, Castle Blagh, Killynorry, Moneymore, Miltown, Ballyboe, Earl of Wicklow's. Ruskey, Tully, Kincraigy, Labadish, Corkeys Upper and Lower, Carricknamarts, Drummoghill are the Revd Mr Leslie's.

Manorcunningham, Grakeys Upper and Lower, Maghremore, Dreanare, James Saunderson Esquire; [blank] Patterson Esquire has Lisclamerty and Tullybogley. William Squire has a part of Manorcunningham, Errity and Whitehill. Charles Colhoon has Drumcairn, Carrick and Ballyboe. William Stewart Esquire of Hornhead has the Munclink. The heirs of William Law have the Bays Upper, Lower and Middle. A small part of the townlands of Grakey, Ray and Galdanagh is glebe, the Revd Archdeacon Ussher's.

PRODUCTIVE ECONOMY

Farms and Herds

The size of farms varies from 6 to 60 acres, but there are many more from 20 to 30 than of any other number. All these are very ill enclosed; indeed, excepting a few they can hardly be said to be at all enclosed, for there is not one farm in the parish so well fenced as not to be easily found by the neighbouring cattle if suffered to run at large.

Very few farmers have their arable ground so well enclosed or separated from the pasture as not to require herdboys to watch their cows etc. These boys are paid from 12s to 20s for the 6 summer months. I suppose their food during that time worth 5 pounds. It is not a large average to say that a herd costs a farmer from May to November 5 pounds 10s. This sum, if expended in making fences, would in a very few years render herds altogether unnecessary.

Suggestions for Improvement

It is evident to everyone who examines the present state of the country that no effective improvement can be expected to take place until the terribly barbarous custom of what is called rundale is totally abolished, as also joint leases. An industrious active man bound in the same lease with a lazy, inactive or drunken co-partner, which is no uncommon case, is in as bad a situation as an energetic rower whose companion, though dead or dying, is still chained to the same oar with him.

My lords and gentlemen of the North West Farming Society, you have set out in such a manner as proves that you are really intent upon the improvement of the country. Begin then by encouraging the enclosing and fencing of the farms. Let the occupying [tenant] have the land, whatever it may be, entirely himself.

This is far from being the case at present in the parish: from the first week in November to the latter end of April the entire face of the country resembles a great common where cows, horses and sheep graze promiscuously. A man's cabbage garden is not secure from the depredations of his neighbour's cattle. It is no uncommon thing in winter to see a man drive his cows or sheep to a distance from his own farm and leave them in his neighbour's field, where he thinks the grass is better or the shelter greater.

I have dwelt on these particulars because I know what I have mentioned with respect to fences and enclosures in this parish to be generally the case throughout the county of Donegal. In the large mountainous districts, which are very valuable for rearing young cattle, no man can be said to have a distinct or separate right. The marches are just as well ascertained as the ideal line in the Mediterranean which divides the African part from the European. Without enclosures there can be no permanent or effectual improvement.

Rotation of Crops

Potatoes first, for which the ground is generally ploughed twice, they are then for the most part put down in beds and covered with the spade. Some few farmers sow them in drills with the plough. The latter mode produces more potatoes from the same quantity of ground and seed, but the cultivators all agree that the subsequent crops are never so good as when they are planted in beds.

The next crop after potatoes is generally barley, sometimes oats, then flax for the third, after which some sow oats, but this last crop is seldom such as to repay the farmer.

Such is the general routine of crops throughout this and the adjacent parishes. Indeed it is almost universal in the county of Donegal. The holders of small farms continue this practice for many years in succession, by which the land becomes quite exhausted. They are then forced to let it rest by leaving it for pasture in such poor state that it bears little or no grass until the second year.

The cultivators of larger farms generally turn their ground to pasture every fifth year, graze it for 4 and in the fifth plough it up. When being deeply hinted and well shovelled, it produces a good crop of oats and then potatoes, barley, flax, oats as before mentioned. The latter method is very profitable when compared with the former, but how much better would it be to lay the ground down when in good heart with clover or grass seed.

6. The quantity of pasturage in this parish is very small compared with the arable.

NATURAL FEATURES

Mountains

There are no mountains. The highest hill is Dooish, the western side of which is in Bay, is cultivated a good way up with improvable pasture to the top. The face of the country is most pleasing, varied by hills, dales and valleys. The hills are all capable of cultivation to the very summit.

Bogs and Woods

8. There is very little bog and that is very easy to be reclaimed; no timber worth mentioning found in the bogs.

There are no nurseries, plantations or woods except a few acres of the latter near the old mansion house of Mr Leslie, at a place called Kincraigy.

Some orchards of small extent have succeeded very well in proportion to the number of trees, bringing from 10 pounds to 35 pounds annually; the fruit, apples, pears, cherries and gooseberries.

10. All kinds of trees which would thrive in Ulster would grow very luxuriantly here, but few have been tried owing to the open unenclosed state of the country which I have already mentioned.

Rents

11. Good arable was formerly much sought for in this parish at 40s an acre. It would at present hardly bring 1 pound 2s.

12. There is very little turf bog. Tenants are not charged for any little that is.

Improvements in Tillage

13. Considerable improvements has been made in tillage and enclosures by a few individuals who are proper persons to correspond with the North West Society and to become members of the minor branches or local committees. Such are Mr A. Leslie, Ruskey; Messrs Thomas and William Colhoon, Labadish; John William Montgomery, Ray; James McIlhinny, Maghremore; Nathan Alexander, Balleighan; John Porter, Forth; and John Patterson, Tullybogley, post town Letterkenny.

The above-mentioned have made some very meritorious attempts at improvement by enclosing part of their grounds and sowing some clover and grass seed.

Fences

14. The description of fences they have generally made is quickset hedges; of the excellence of this it is unnecessary to say anything. If the field to be enclosed is stony I would recommend a stone wall for the double purpose of fencing the field and clearing the ground. The labour and expense of sinking the stones, which is often practised, would go a good way in building the walls.

Gooseberry cuttings grow quicker by far than whitethorns, make a most excellent thick hedge and may be trimmed to any shape. The common whin or furze is much cheaper than whitethorn and, if properly attended to, make a good fence.

I would strongly recommend the sowing of furze in the tops of fences in the mountainous districts. They will afford an excellent shelter and, in case of great scarcity of fodder in the beginning of spring, will afford a good supply of wholesome nourishing food for either cow or horse. I have known them carried 3 miles for that purpose. A man may cut and chop as much in a day as will feed their cows. This is no fanciful theory but a well-known fact.

Employment

15. Employment is very abundant in spring and autumn; during the winter months it is rather scarce, many hands unemployed. It is not easy to support any feasible plan for their employment. Much is to be done in the way of enclosing, improving and reclaiming the grounds. The farmers, I fear, have not the capital. Many of them are

Parish of Raymoghy

in arrears to their landlords which they can never hope to repay.

If an upright active man were, from avoidable circumstances, found in their situation, I would, with all that deference which the delicacy of the subject demands, beg leave to suggest that he might be forgiven the arrears in a certain proportion for every perch of sufficient fence he made around his farm. This would remove from the farmers dead weight and, I think, ultimately benefit the landlord by putting the ground into a better condition and giving the tenants a new stimulus to industry for the future, at the expense of a desperate debt.

Wages

16. Servants are paid during the spring and autumn from 10d to 15d per day and fed when there is a great hurry of business; but if you agree with a man for the whole year, you may have him for 6d a day and his food or 1s without food.

Crops and Drainage

17. Green crops are not cultivated nor are artificial grasses of any description sown except the individuals who I have mentioned at no.13.

19. Surface and underdraining are both used but to a very limited extent.

Manures

19. The manures in general are the produce of stable and cowhouse etc. Seaweed is a good deal used in the part which is convenient to Lough Swilly. Shells found in Lough Swilly and drawn up into the country from the distance of 3 miles, and are found to be excellent manure.

Clay is not burned. In some parts where there is a depth of turf or peat of a few inches and then clay they cut it into large sods and then burn them in heaps, the peat being sufficient to burn the clay, and the ashes make very fine manure but by no means equal to shells or lime.

The potato crop produced from the ashes of peat and clay burned together is equal to that produced from any other manure, but the subsequent crops are by no means so good.

Turf bog is much burned for potatoes.

Irrigation

The farmers are in the habit of watering their meadows but not judiciously. They have no idea of any regular system of irrigation, having never had the advantage of precept or example.

Dairies and Oxen

22. Mr Alexander of Balleighan has established a dairy. He is the only man in the parish who sows clover to any extent worth mentioning.

23. Oxen are not used for the purpose of husbandry. I have not during the course of 15 years seen more than 4 or 5 of them in draft.

Spade Tillage and Grain Crops

24. The spade in tillage is used only in planting and digging potatoes, hinting oats etc. There is very little ground prepared with the spade for any kind of grain.

25. Oats and barley are the only kinds of grain grown. An acre of barley, if a good crop for a number of years, averages 10 pounds to 12 pounds and oats 5 pounds to 7 pounds.

26. The measurement of land is computed by the English acre except in the estate of the Marquis of Abercorn.

Livestock

27. The farmers are in the habit of rearing the old native cows. There are, however, latterly in some parts crosses from Devonshire bulls which appear to do very well.

28. The small Irish sheep are still the most numerous, but the South Down and crosses with the South Down are increasing very fast. Cows, sheep and horses are kept on the pasture-grounds. The people in general are strongly impressed with the conviction that the old small native breeds are best adapted to the soil and climate.

30. Light horses from 7 to 20 guineas price are in general used for agricultural purposes. Such horses 12 years back would have sold for 13 and 35 guineas.

31. The average weight of swine generally reared is from 2 and a half cwt; very few of 4 cwt.

32. In the year 1817 the quantity of stock in this parish was diminished one-third or perhaps more. In the last 2 years it has increased very considerably and may be estimated at 1,375 head of black cattle, 459 horses, sheep about 700, pigs about 1,000. But if the present weather continues 8 days they will be reduced two-thirds.

33. The breed of horses was improving rapidly from the year 1800 until 1816, since which it has been visibly on the decline. Black cattle and sheep much improved by crosses with the Devonshire and South Down.

Natural Features and Natural History

Rivers

34. The only river in the parish is Ray <Rye> or Connaghan <Canahan> river, which rises in the small bog of Galdonagh and, after a winding course of about 3 miles, runs into the Swilly near the village of Manorcunningham. It is navigable for boats of 4 tons about 1 and a half miles from the Swilly, from which shells, an excellent manure, are carried up into the country. There are very few fish of any description in the rivers. They are annually destroyed by the flax water.

Mines and Minerals

35. No metallic mines have ever been discovered in this parish.

36. There was a slate quarry found some years since at the top of the hill just over Manorcunningham. It has never been worked to any extent, which is much to be lamented as it is most advantageously situated. From the quarry to the Swilly is a regular descent about 1 mile in length. At a place called the Black rock, sloops or brigs could put in at spring tides but boats of 5 or 6 tons could at all times; from this the slates could be taken at a very cheap rate to Ramelton [crossed out: Rathmelton], Rathmullan, Letterkenny, Fanad <Fanit>, Rosguill <Rosgul> etc. and all parts of the barony of Kilmacrenan.

37. Limestone of a fine blue is found in the townlands of Ray and Munclink, and good lime may be had at these places for 1s 2d per barrel.

39. No coal of any kind is found in this district. There is a tradition among the people that it was formerly found near to the slate quarry mentioned at no.36.

39. No mineral springs of any kind are yet known.

40. A bed of calcareous marl has been found in the townland of Mundooeys; it has not been used to any useful purpose.

Social Economy

Condition of the People

41. The situation of the great body of the people with respect to domestic comforts and conveniences is but very poor. Some of the best class of farmers live very comfortably but they are few indeed. The others are just struggling to make up their rents at the appointed day and at least two-thirds of the farmers find great difficulty in doing so.

The people in general are very well disposed to be industrious but they have no encouragement. There are no resident gentlemen to employ the labourers, to inspirit the farmers by his advice or more powerful example.

The general means of earning money is by farming, weaving, very little dealing carried on. Some few individuals who can collect together a trifling sum employ themselves in buying small quantities of flax and yarn, which they afterwards sell to the Derry merchants.

Houses and Fuel

43. The houses of the upper class of farmers are neat, clean and comfortable. Those of the middle sort are very indifferent. The cabins are cold, comfortless and wretched, owing in a great measure to the scarcity of fuel which in most parts is very high, the average price for a kish of good turf being from 2s 6d to 3s 4d.

Food

44. The general food of the farming class is meat of different kinds, fish, potatoes, oatbread, stirabout, potatoes for the first class of farmers. [Insert note: There is not one-fortieth of the meat used in this parish now that was 10 years back].

The middle class of farmers eat very little meat or fish; potatoes, oatbread, stirabout, butter, eggs, salt herrings in the season is their fare. The lower class eat very little butter or eggs. They sell the latter for the most part to procure tobacco etc.

45 and 46. The poor labourers are generally confined to potatoes and milk or a salt herring, sometimes stirabout and oaten bread in small quantities.

Education

47. There certainly is a very strong wish for education among all classes, but in general they are not able to pay proper masters. There is a school in the parish at Labadish where about 74 children are educated at the expense of the "Incorporated Society." The scholars were formerly boarded and clothed here but John Newport, Sir Robert Wilson, Mr Brougham and other excellent friends and supporters of the constitution, church and king have been successful in reducing the annual parliamentary grant. The society has reduced its establishment bay from a boarding to a day school.

There are 12 other schools in this parish, at which about 300 children are instructed in reading, writing and arithmetic. The average expense of each child is about 1 pound per annum.

Progress of Improvement

49. A very material change has taken place in the last 10 years in the peasantry. The children of the rising generation are certainly more attentive to public worship and more respectful to their superiors and more civilised in every respect.

Health

The general state of health is at present pretty good. The most prevalent diseases are fever, dysentery, rheumatism, ulcerous scurvy. Causes of the first: sudden change of temperature, weak and unwholesome food; of the third: humid state of the atmospheric; of the fourth: weak diet, moisture and want of cleanliness.

Friendly Societies

51. To relieve the poor from these calamities no societies of any kind have been instituted. The farmers are not able and there are no resident gentlemen.

Towns

52. The now ruinous village of Manorcunningham had once 2 fairs in the year but they have long been given up. There is no market town in the parish.

PRODUCTIVE ECONOMY

Improvements

53. The people as a yeomanry and peasantry are well informed, have a turn for improvement which might, to the great advantage of the community, be excited and called into activity by instruction, but more powerfully by example. Of these 2 most effective means of improvement, the inhabitants of the parish of Raymoghy are totally deprived. A few spirited and intelligent individuals, whose names and address are mentioned in no.23, by enclosing, sowing clover etc. [no further text].

Linen Manufacture

The linen manufacture in this parish is very much diminished. The quantity of flax grown has been nearly stationary for some years. The general mode of preparing land for a flax crop is by ploughing it early in the season, in the latter end of December. It is then suffered to stay until the latter end of April, when it is harrowed, then ploughed again and harrowed a second time, when the seed is sown and harrowed in. Some plough but once, but the former mode is proved by experience to be for the best.

The flax crop generally succeeds a crop of barley or oats. There is but little consumed in home manufacture. It is mostly taken to Derry market for exportation.

Preparation of Flax

55. The flax, previous to being broken or crushed, is generally dried over a moderate fire. At present it is not near so much dried as formerly. Indeed some farmers who keep it over years use no fire at all. They expose it to the sun in April and crush it under a stone drawn by horses. This is a vast improvement and is coming into general use. After this it is sent to be scutched in mills turned by water, when it is made to go into a quarter and a half hundred bundles for the market.

The flax consumed in home manufacture is generally spun into yarn from 3 to 5 hanks in the lb. At this, the spinner at present can earn on an average 2d per day. The price per spangle varies very much. I believe it has not been so low for the last 50 years as in the last summer (1821). The same species of yarn which has been sold in the markets of Donegal at 6s 5d and 4s 2d brought only 1s 4d, 1s 6d and 1s 8d. The yarn spun at home is generally sent to market. Very little linen cloth is manufactured.

Spinning of Flax

The lower orders, who are far the greater part, purchase the flax for spinning either from the neighbouring farmers who grow it, or at the nearest market town.

The spinners do not use the double wheel. It has never been introduced into the parish, nor has it succeeded in any of the neighbouring parishes in which attempts have been made to introduce it.

I mentioned before that very little linen cloth is manufactured here. If the manufacturer has a family able to spin, he has as much as he can spin at home. The rest he buys green at market and prepares it himself. The probable expense of preparing it is 3d per spangle.

There are no yarn greens in this vicinity, nor do I think it would be worthwhile to establish them in the present confined state of the weaving business here.

Quality of Webs

The linen manufactured here is generally of 2 kinds: wrappers, which are three-quarters of a yard wide, and what the weavers call 6 to 8 hundred; and finer linens from 12 hundred to 14 hundred, generally seven-eighths of a yard wide. Both go to Derry market; the present price: wrappers from 6d to 9d, broad linen from 1s 2d to 1s 8d per yard.

Flax Seed

Very little flax seed is saved in this parish, which is a circumstance much to be lamented. I know of nothing which should be so strongly recommended to the farmer of the north west of Ireland than to secure a sufficient quantity of seed from flax of their own growing. With all whom I have known try it, it has succeeded beyond their most sanguine hopes.

Since I began to write this article, I stopped to interrogate more minutely a farmer who had last year saved seed of 1 acre's produce. His flax he sold in the Derry markets and it brought him the average price which his neighbours who had not saved the seed got for theirs. The seed saved from an acre produced 8 pounds, from which may perhaps be deducted 10s for additional labour and that I am sure is enough. See what an immense profit on 1 acre: 7 pounds 10s. I saw him crushing this day as fine flax as ever grew, the produce of part of the above-mentioned seed.

If our people, after they know this, will persevere in purchasing foreign seed, they need no longer complain of that dreadful bane to Ireland, absenteeism, for they will knowingly and designedly derive from the country their best friends, guineas and sovereigns.

The best mode of saving flax seed is the following: the plant, when perfectly ripe, should be pulled and suffered to dry until it might be, with safety and without danger of heating, stacked up as hay, oats or barley. Let it then be thrashed off as oats, barley or any other grain, and the flax may then be steeped and treated in the usual manner. The seed will keep perfectly save[d] in any place where oats, barley or wheat may be stowed with security.

This is a better method than another which has been tried, namely stacking up the unthreshed flax till March or April. The seed will be equally good in the latter way but the flax loses something in quality. It is never so silky or fine in the reed as when prepared in the latter end of autumn. Besides, the farmer loses the interest on its price for 5 months.

Rippling flax or drawing it through an iron comb is still more unprofitable. The flax in this way is perfectly safe and secure but the seed is very liable to be injured.

In rippling, the fine extremities of the plant are not broken from, but generally drawn out of the bulb containing the seed; hence a small aperture is left in the under part of the bow, as the farmers call it (I don't wish to use learned botanical terms), into which, if the seed be dried in the open air, moisture more or less always enters and either blackens or rots the seed, according to the state of the weather. Some, to prevent this, dry the seed in corn kilns, but in this way it is so very difficult to adjust the proper degree of temperature that this is seldom or ever perfectly sound.

General Remarks on Flax

The parish of Raymoghy is the best flax district in Donegal. The farmers who have saved seed themselves or tried that raised by their neighbours think it preferable by much to the American, equal to the Riga. They never save the seed produced from American but from Riga or their own rearing. They mostly prefer the former.

Wool and Cotton

66. Very little wool is manufactured. Farmers who keep sheep generally make blanketing sufficient for their own families. There are no wool staplers or sorters. Any wool that is spun is on the small wheel. The females seldom or ever knit woollen stockings for sales. The markets are supplied from Boylagh, Rosses and Cloghaneely.

70. Some few farmers have shorn their sheep twice in the same years but they disapprove of it altogether and will never do so again.

71. No kind of cotton manufactory in this part of the country except now and then the knitting of a pair of stockings.

Kelp and Fisheries

73. No kelp of any description manufactured in the neighbourhood: that article is brought here from Rosses or Boylagh.

76. The Swilly washes this parish on the west till nearly the extent of the 3 miles. Salmon, cod, sole and mullet are taken here but not in such abundance as to be sent to market at any distance. They are generally consumed by those who take them or sold to the neighbouring farmers.

77. The herring fishery in the Swilly, once very extensive, is now hardly worth mentioning. Still, I think, it might be greatly improved and extended.

78. The time of fish making their appearance is very various and uncertain. Some years they come in great quantities and do not appear for many years afterwards. Hence it is that the people along this part of the coast are not always prepared for them, not knowing when to expect them. They should be encouraged to have their boats, nets etc. always ready, and then the quantity taken in a good year would more than compensate for the deficiency of the bad years.

81. The Swilly herrings have not of late years been taken to a greater distance than Londonderry. Formerly many Scotch vessels were employed in this fishery.

General Remarks: Improvements

The greater part of the above remarks are applicable to most parts of the county of Donegal. It is evident to every superficial observer how much this district suffers from late harvests. Might not this be in some measure remedied by sowing oats, our principal grain crop, in the latter end of autumn or beginning of winter? I know this cannot be done till the country be better enclosed than it is at present, nor can any other improvements whatever take place with any permanent effect.

I am induced to believe that winter oats would succeed very well from the following observations which I have made during the last 4 years. A farmer in this parish had his field of oats much shaken late in October. After drawing in the crop, he ploughed down the field and harrowed it. He had more than an average crop of good oats ripe early in the following August, solely from the grain shaken off before reaping.

Another farmer who was sowing a small field of wheat in November found himself deficient in seed. He sowed his ridges with blanter oats and had an abundant crop ripe early in August. Might we not hope that, if our fields were enclosed and drained and our grain sown at the above-mentioned periods, we might escape in a great measure the calamities arising from such wet and late harvest as the present?

The culture of the potato might be greatly improved. The quantity might be doubled on the same ground, and from less seed, by manuring better and moulding with more care.

A neighbour of mine had in his garden last year a single stalk which produced 18 lbs of potatoes. It occupied about a square yard. This would be a fair average crop for 2 yards in a good field of potatoes etc.

In the latter end of May last, after a potato house had been cleared out, I picked up a small bud from among the rubbish. It was not more than half or three-quarters of an inch in length. I planted it on the end of a carrot bed, where no seed had been sown. I took up 13 potatoes, the produce of that bud, early in September. 6 of them were large, 4 middle sized and 3 small. Might not a knowledge of this fact be of use in dear years, when many find it very hard to seed their ground?

A stranger riding through this country in summer or harvest might think that the growth of weeds was not only permitted but encouraged: thistles, docks, ragweeds, burs thriving in great luxuriance. Now it is certain that a crop of these impoverish a field very much; and if suffered to shed their seed, which is almost universally the case, they not only stock the adjacent grounds but disseminate their prolific seeds to the distance of many miles.

It would be profitable labour for a farmer to collect these weeds when green, even if he threw them into the next river. But the profit would be trebled did he convert them into manure, which is very practicable. I have known a poor man, who had not a pound of any animal manure, that in one season produced a rood of most excellent potatoes, raised entirely upon the manure he procured from weeds of every kind collected along the sides of the highway and adjacent fields.

That these hints may be of use is the sincere wish of J.E.

Parish of Taughboyne, County Donegal

Replies by Reverend Nathan Rogers to Queries of North West Farming Society

MEMOIR WRITING

General Remarks

It is a truth that agriculture is a science which requires the attention of the philosopher and too refined for the researches of the farmer, whose ideas are so limited by the usual labour of his forefathers without making himself acquainted with the different kinds of earths and cultivation proper for each. Experience only tells him that manure is good for potatoes and does not fail of producing a plentiful crop of weeds, but to plant early and dig deep (which is a great preventive of weeds) seems entirely a mystery to them; but in order to accomplish this piece of labour the farmer must provide himself with strong horses and some little capital.

The husbandman and merchant are both nearly alike in this, as the latter cannot embark in merchandize without capital or credit, so the farmer remains useless without means and labour.

Being favoured with one of the statistical queries of the north west district of Londonderry, I now offer the answers for this parish, which have been done in as accurate a manner as possible by personal experience. First, beginning with the answers to the statistical queries in a concise and comprehensive manner according with their respective numbers; secondly the names of all the farmers in the parish, the quantity of arable, pasture and bog or mountains, together with observations on the soil of each townland.

NATURAL STATE

Situation and Landlords

County of Donegal, diocese of Raphoe; Revd Edward Bowen, incumbent; 4 [sic] landowners, Lord Abercorn, Lord Wicklow, Revd Mr Cary, Revd Mr Knox, Mr Rankin and a small gort belonging to the Revd Edward Bowen, all non-resident except Mr Rankin.

Townlands

Altaskin Glebe, Ardaugh, Benson, Burnthaw, Ballylinin, Ballybow, Bready, Brockaugh, Clashagarvan, Creatland, Cavinaca, Castletown, Castlethird, Cavinshanagh Glebe, Carrickmore, Crohadoes Upper and Lower, Castle of Moneygelvin, Cross, Cuttamon Hill, Dundee, Drumdonaugh, Drummone, Drumfad, Drumcrow, Durnakally, Drummeen, Drummenan, Drumbeg, Drummucklough, Derrymore, Feddy Glass, Gills Tower, Hall, Hill Sead, Kinekally, Kilgort, Lettergul, Legnoha, Listonaugh, Lustikill, Maymore, Mahareelay, Monreagh, Momeen Upper and Lower, Whitehill, Moness, Rockfield, Rateen, Swilly, St Johnstown, Trentamucklaugh, Tullysape, Tully-own, Teroddy, Trensalaugh, Tonaugh, Trentaugh, Tibber and Woodland.

The arable in Lord Abercorn's estate are 3,865 acres, pasture 1,234 acres, mountain or bog 1,408. Lord Wicklow's estate in this parish is called Churchland, being in the see of Raphoe; contains 1,120 arable, 853 mountain or bog.

PRODUCTIVE ECONOMY

Farms

5. In general from 5, 10, 15, 20, 30, 40 to 100 acres. Very badly [fenced] with dry ditches. Mostly following the old method, with the common Irish plough and hinting. Potatoes, barley, oats and flax, lying lea and sowing grass seed and clover.

6. The arable ground left out in lea except where there is bog and mountain, by labour are in general capable of improvement.

NATURAL FEATURES

Hills and Bogs

7. Doe's hill, Brison hill and Mullaghsawey, the summit of each covered with heath and capable of improvement for pasture-lands, but not for crop in consequence of a mist resting on them.

8. [Bogs] Moneylea, Drumcrow, Swilly and Carrickmore; timber called bog fir at the depth of 8 to 9 feet.

Plantations and Trees

9. Feddy Glass, wood and woodland; Crohadoes, Whitehill, Moness, Trentaugh, Kinekally, Drummenan and Clashagarvan.

10. Ash, sycamore, Turkey sallow, mountain ash, alder and birch.

Parish of Taughboyne

PRODUCTIVE ECONOMY

Rents

11. Best 4 guineas per acre, middling 1 pound 14s 1d ha'penny, inferior 1 pound, moory pasture 10s.

12. [Charge for turf bog] On an average 1s per pound.

Agriculture and Fences

13. No improvements except the introduction of some Scotch ploughs, carts and cars.

14. [Fences] Mostly clay ditches, hawthorns and furze; stone ditches as they give no shelter to birds.

Employment and Wages

15. Employment abundant only in seed time and harvest: edging, ditching and draining.

16. [Wages] From 5d to 10d with victuals round the year.

Crops and Drainage

17. [Green crops] None except in culinary gardens.

18. [Artificial grasses] Grass seeds and white and red clover.

19. In general underdraining.

Manures

20. Lime, moss and dung mixed. Sods burned, which do well for 1 crop or for meadow but fail after that. Lime is preferable, lasting 2 or 3 years.

Irrigation

21. [Irrigation] They are but entirely ignorant of the right method, letting it run too long in one place, whereas it should be changed once every 10 days.

Farm Techniques

22. All substantial farmers have dairies which answer well, as they supply their houses with many conveniences.

23. [Oxen] None.

24. [Spade husbandry] It is not practised except in hinting and gardening.

Grain Crops

25. Barley, oats and some wheat. Barley on an average 1 guinea per barrel, oats from 7d to 10d a stone, potatoes from 20d to 2s per measure, meal from 13d to 16d per peck, butter from 7d to 8d per lb., beef from 3d to 6d per lb.

26. [Unit of measurement] By plantation and Cunningham measure.

Livestock

27. Cows of a middling size.

28. Cows, horses and sheep.

29. In general the small mountain sheep, except in the vicinity of Raphoe where they have got into the spirit of raising a superior breed from the dean's and bishop's. Both kinds are well calculated for soil and climate, but the small is considered the best mutton.

30. [Horses] A very imperfect breed for agricultural purposes, in consequence of the mixture of blood-horses with small horses.

31. [Swine] In general a good kind, in consequence of being supplied in Strabane market from the county Fermanagh.

Improvements in Stock

32. In general each farmer possesses on an average about half-stock. Since the conclusion of the last peace, the price of cattle fell considerably. The pressure of the times obliged the farmer to part with his stock, besides the driving of our young cattle into the Scotch and English markets, all of which lessens the stock in the country. Giving the farmer his land at a more reasonable rate would both give him spirit and power to raise a superior breed and quantity of cattle. He would then be able to rest his lands by sowing grass seed and clover.

33. The breed of horses and all kinds of cattle have rather degenerated than improved within these 20 years.

NATURAL FEATURES AND NATURAL HISTORY

Rivers

34. The River Foyle, commonly called Lough Foyle, is met by the RiversMourne and Finn a little above Lifford bridge. Those rivers have their source in the mountains of Barnesmore, all of which disembogue themselvesinto the harbour at Londonderry.

A small river called Swilly, separating the parish of Taughboyne from that of Lifford, falls into Lough Foyle at the turf bog of Carrickmore.

Another small river, separating the parish of Taughboyne from that of Ray[moghy], in its course supplies a number of flax and 1 corn mill, and empties itself into Lough Foyle at St Johnstown.

Lastly a small river rising from Port lough, separating Taughboyne from Killea and supplying the Carrigans mill, falls into Lough Foyle a little below that village. Foyle, Mourne and Finn produce salmon and trout.

Minerals and Quarries

35. Iron ore is to be found in Moneygelvin and Momeen, between 6 and 8 inches from the surface of the ground. It is also thinly dispersed about the parish but never has been investigated and worked.

36. 2 slate quarries, Trentaugh and Tibber, well situated for drawing to St Johnstown or Portstewart [sic] for exportation.

Limestone quarries in the following towns: Drummucklough, Ballylinin, Momeen, Ardaugh, Tonaugh and Crohadoes. The produce of the latter is drawn to Carrickmore ferryboat and exported to Derry for the use of Mr Walker's saltworks.

37. The limestone in this parish is all of a blue colour, of an ardent nature and medicinal. Thrown into a kiln and burned with peat the expense would be to the farmers about 6d per barrel.

38. Report says there is some coal at Binion but none has ever been found or worked.

39. Drummore an iron spa, 4 others: Lignatra, Tunsalaugh, Bready and Cloughfin. The latter is an excellent chalybeate, having cured a girl of a consumption which had baffled the skill of the physicians.

40. [Marl] None has ever been discovered in this parish.

SOCIAL ECONOMY

Condition of the People

41. The inhabitants are in general reduced in their circumstances, appear willing to be industrious, but altogether without the means, some by husbandry, others by manual labour and trade. They lay out [the fruits] of their labour to purchase the necessaries of life.

Houses and Food

42. In general farms and cottage houses are in bad repair, neither comfortable internally nor externally.

43. Turf is plenty and cheap.

44. [Farmers] Potatoes, buttermilk, stirabout and herrings.

45. [Manufacturing class] Potatoes and buttermilk.

46. [Labourers] Potatoes with salt.

Education

47. The Protestant class of the inhabitants appear extremely fond of education, for which purpose Sunday schools are dispersed throughout the parish. At the commencement Roman Catholics objected to Sunday schools but appear not so adverse to them now.

48. [Expenses] Reading 2s 1d, writing 3s and figures 5s per quarter. 8 schools in this parish, 5 of which are under the patronage of the Revd Mr Bowen.

49. There is a marked difference in the propriety of their manners and habits.

Health and Poor

50. [Health] Good in general but liable to scorbutic eruptions.

51. [Friendly societies] None.

Towns and Villages

52. In this parish there are 58 villages, none of any consequence except St Johnstown.

PRODUCTIVE ECONOMY

Improvements

53. They possess a turn for improvement, if encouragement was given to the linen trade, which is the staple commodity of the country.

54. [Practical farmers] John Alexander of Drummenan, Andrew Hamilton of Trentaugh, Hugh Stephenson, Lignatra, William McClean, Clashagarvan.

Linen Manufacture

55. [Linen trade] Rather increasing.

56. 12 flax mills work regularly every winter in the parish of Taughboyne.

57. [Flax] In general succeeds a crop of oats after lea ground, sometimes potato ground or barley leave.

58. In general it is manufactured by mills and little is worked by manual labour for home use, and fire is used in the preparation of it.

59. [Linen yarn] Fine yarn spun from 3 to 5 hanks out of the lb., coarse yarn from 1 hank to 1 and a half out of the lb. The spinner earns about 3d per day, allowing 1 hank a day, that is, at the rate of 1s per spangle.

60. [Price of yarn] From 20d to 2s both kinds per spangle and sometimes sold for exportation.

61. In general both farmers and cottagers sow their own flax.

62. [Double wheel] It has been introduced into a few families and is considered not to answer the purpose.

Yarn

63. The weaver purchases it himself in the green state from the spinner and prepares it for the loom, which preparation costs him about 6d per spangle.

64. [Yarn greens] There are none in this parish. The introduction of them would be of infinite use in promoting the linen manufacture.

65. [Quality of webs] Both fine and coarse; fine from 12 to 13 hundred, coarse from 7 to 8 hundred. The fine from 15d to 20d per yard, the coarse from 8d to 10d per yard and sold in Strabane and Derry markets.

Wool

66. There is none.

67. [Woollen manufactory] There are none.

68. [Knitting] It is generally spun on the small wheel for home consumption.

69. [Stockings] Families knit their own.

70. [Shearing of sheep] The year-old wool is considered, both in quantity and quality, superior to half-year-old wool.

Cotton

71. There is none except a little for home use in preparing a cloth called drugget.

72. [Cotton manufactory] There is none.

Kelp

73. [Kelp] None.

74. There are no materials in this parish for the manufacturing of kelp.

Fisheries

76. There is a salmon fishery on Lough Foyle.

77. 7 boats, burthen from 1 ton to 4.

78. Salmon and trout in general. As far as Port Hall, the fishermen always fish near the shore.

79. The men employed are 74 in number; their wages from 2s to 1d per day.

80. [Curing of fish] None salted but preserved with ice and sent to Liverpool. Lord Abercorn and Lord Erne claim the fishing above the islands to Lifford; rent it off at 60 guineas per year, supply Strabane.

81. They are capable of improvement by preserving the mother fish alive, by which means the fishery would double itself.

General Remarks on Economy

I conclude with a few observations. It appears that the farmers who are constantly turning up the bowels of the earth do not discover the utility of cultivation in autumn, as from that period during the winter the atmosphere discharges the valuable manures of oil and salts. If all blue clay bottoms were turned up and exposed to these enriching qualities, the farmer might expect the succeeding crop luxuriant.

Look behind a ditch where snow has lain for some time: you will find a greasy substance deposited which, if absorbed by the newly turned up earth, would modify and fertilize the most stubborn clay.

Another advantage attending early labour is that all weeds and stubble, being then turned down in their succulent and juicy state, would petrify and cause a fermentation which would enrich the ground considerably.

DIVISIONS

Townlands

Altaskin Glebe is situated at the Hill Heard [Head?] or suburbs of St Johnstown, subject to the deanery of Raphoe. There is another small property of Mr Rankin's held under the see of Raphoe. Blue clay bottom, 17 acres arable, total 64.

Ardaugh, in Lord Abercorn's estate, is situated on the south of Doe's hill and the farms all run up to the top of the hill. On a thin slaty bottom, limestone in these villages. No crop comes to perfection on the hill, in consequence of a mist resting on the top of it. On a south view it has the form of a haystack, flat north: arable 151, mountain 181 [acres].

Binion is a hill situated to the west and north of Crohadoes, in Lord Abercorn's estate. It overhangs that village, is steep and covered with whins on the east side, flat on the north. The summit is covered with heath and capable of improvement. It has a blue clay bottom: arable 30, pasture 30, mountain 40 [acres].

Burnthaw, in Lord Abercorn's estate, is situated on a round hill west of White Hill, has a red till with a blue clay bottom: arable 50, pasture 14 [acres].

Ballylinin, in Lord Abercorn's estate, is situated south west of Binion; is remarkable for nothing but limestone and has a blue clay bottom: arable 80, pasture 69, mountain 22 [acres].

Ballybow is also on Lord Abercorn's estate; is situated on an eminence which may be considered part of Binion and south of it; is steep and has a blue clay bottom with land rocks: arable 50, pasture 44, mountain 22 [acres].

Bready is in the churchland property of Lord Wicklow and situated a little above the church of Taughboyne; has a red till with blue clay bottom: arable 95, pasture 100, mountain 60 [acres].

Brockaugh is in Lord Abercorn's estate; has a blue clay bottom and a slaty red till in another: arable 85, pasture 8, mountain 25 [acres].

Clashagarvan is in Lord Abercorn's estate, situated north west of St Johnstown; has in it a corn and flax mill besides an orchard. The part next St Johnstown has a red till, that towards the mountain a blue slaty bottom and part of it rocky: arable 337, mountain 31 [acres].

Creatland, situated at the bases of Binion hill on the east side, has an orchard and towards the hill it has rather a slaty bottom: arable 31, mountain 34, pasture 25 [acres]; Lord Abercorn's estate.

Cavinaca, Lord Abercorn's estate, situated on the east side of Binion. It is intersected by the road which leads from St Johnstown to Raphoe. The land of the village runs up to the summit of the steepest side of Binion, where it is covered with furze and rocks. It has a blue clay bottom: arable 40, mountain 11 [acres].

Castletown, Lord Abercorn's estate, about 1 mile south of St Johnstown; has partly a blue clay and red bottom, mixed with slate. It has a flax mill in it: arable 236, mountain 6 [acres].

Castlethird, Lord Wicklow's estate, situated on an eminence south of the church of Taughboyne and has a blue clay bottom; it has a fort supposed to be Danish: arable 84, mountain 36 [acres].

Carinshanaugh is a glebe situated in the upper end of the parish of Taughboyne, surrounded almost by Lord Abercorn's estate. It is the boundary between Raphoe and Ray of [sic] this parish, and subject in rent to the rector of Lifford, though in the diocese of Raphoe. It is divided into 2 townlands, Carinshanaugh and Carrick-a-dawson. The former is excellent land, the latter is partly mountain and has a good turf bog in it besides limestone.

Castle of Moneygelvin in Lord Abercorn's estate is situated on the banks of Lough Foyle; has 4 turrets, appears in tolerable preservation and has a stone with the following inscription:

"The Honourable Elizabeth Hamilton, daughter of John, Lord Colepepper, and widow of Colonel James Hamilton, who lost his life in the service of his king and country, purchased this manor and annexed it to the opposite estate of the family, which paternal estate itself was improved by her prudent management to near the yearly income of the dower she received thereout. She hath also settled her son Mr Hamilton Esquire in an estate acquired in England of equal value in the purchase of this, and given every one of her numerous offspring descended from both branches some considerable mark of her parental care.

Her eldest, James, Earl of Abercorn and Viscount Strabane, hath caused this inscription to be placed here for the information of her posterity, from whom she hath merited their most grateful acknowledgements and to whom she hath set so valuable an example, anno 1704."

Another stone about 2 feet long and on one side has the following letters in alto: "ISEST ETATIS 24 161 1P." This inscription appears ancient, as some of the letters are almost effaced. The townland of Moneygelvin has a red sandy bottom.

Cross, in Lord Wicklow's estate, is situated about half a mile above the church of Taughboyne and about the same distance from Tibber; slate quarry, has a red blue clay bottom, also a flax mill.

Cuttamon Hill, Lord Abercorn's estate, is situated a little to the west of the castle of Moneygelvin, Lord Abercorn's estate. Has a red sandy bottom, towards the shore backwards a blue clay bottom. Iron ore is found here in abundance: arable 27, mountain 12 [acres].

Drumcrow, Lord Abercorn's estate, the land of which runs down to the River Swilly, is considered one of the best farms in the manor; pays 150 guineas rent, has a large turf bog in it: arable 50 [acres], pasture 20, bog 60.

Dundee, Lord Abercorn's estate, is situated in the vicinity of St Johnstown, on the Derry side of it; the land runs down to Lough Foyle. The farmers are inhabitants of St Johnstown who follow their respective trades, and as high as 4 guineas per acre [rent]. The land is of a superior quality, has a red till with a blue clay bottom.

Crohadoes Upper and Lower are situated on the south east side of Binion, at the base of the hill. The lands of the village are of a superior quality. They abound in orchards and limestone. There is also a good turf bog in it. In Lower Crohadoes is a spring well supposed to have its source in Binion, the current of which would almost turn a mill; commonly called the "boiling well."

Carrickmore, Lord Abercorn's estate, is situated near the banks of Lough Foyle. It is cut through the centre by the road leading to the ferryboat, at which place all goods or limestone can be exported to Derry or the opposite side. It has a red sandy bottom. There is also a turf bog, considered as large as the townland. Excellent brick is made here. The clay which lies under the bog is calculated for a pottery: arable 103, pasture 52, bog 12 [acres].

Drumdonaugh, Lord Abercorn's estate, situated on the south side of Doe's and at the base of the hill, has a blue clay bottom: arable 28, pasture 36 [acres].

Drummore, Lord Abercorn's estate, situated at the upper end of this parish and is the boundary between it and Raphoe. It abounds with flax mills and limestone, and has an iron spa. This village has a superior breed of sheep, in consequence of being near the deanery.

Drumfad, Lord Abercorn's estate, is also situated at the upper end of the parish, bordering that of Raphoe; has a Danish fort in it; heavy blue clay bottom.

Durnakally, Lord Wicklow's estate, situated north of St Johnstown, cut through the centre by the road leading to the church at Taughboyne; has a blue clay bottom: arable 166, pasture 41 [acres].

Drummenan, Lord Abercorn's estate, situated about 1 mile south of St Johnstown, intersected by the road leading from Raphoe and Strabane to Londonderry; has an orchard and a flax mill; blue clay bottom: arable 56, pasture 35, mountain 21 [acres].

Drummeen, Lord Abercorn's estate, situated on a rising ground a little west of Carrickmore, is intersected by the road leading to the ferryboats; has a sandy bottom: arable 36, pasture 30, bog 6 [acres].

Drumbeg, Lord Abercorn's estate, about one-half mile from Raphoe, on the road leading to that town, has 2 flax mills in it; a blue clay bottom.

Drummucklough, Lord Abercorn's estate, intersected by the road leading from Raphoe to St Johnstown; 2 picturesque grave knolls and limestone of the first quality, besides a large lime-kiln, built by the ancestors of the late Lord Abercorn for the use of his tenants: arable 51, pasture 57, bog 11 [acres].

Derrymore, Lord Wicklow's estate, situated between St Johnstown and the church of Taughboyne; has a blue clay bottom: arable 66, pasture 6 [acres].

Feddy Glass, Lord Abercorn's estate, on the banks of the small River Swilly; on the east side of this village is a wood containing 31 acres. It abounds with wood, wild pigeons and owls, has in it the following trees, oak, ash, birch and alder, besides a thick shrubbery; sandy and blue clay bottom: arable 33, pasture 84, mountain 8 [acres].

Gill's Tower, Lord Abercorn's estate, on the north east side of Binion, runs up to the summit of the hill and is intersected by the road leading from Lifford to St Johnstown: arable 20, pasture 12, mountain 6 [acres].

Hall, Lord Wicklow's estate, near and at east end of the church at Taughboyne; has a red till with a blue clay bottom: arable 86, bog 9 [acres].

Hill Head, part of which is in Lord Abercorn's estate and Mr Rankin's property, which latter is under the see and deanery of Raphoe; situated at the north west of St Johnstown on a rising ground; blue clay bottom: arable 12 [acres].

Kinekally, Lord Abercorn's estate, situated about 1 mile from St Johnstown, on the road leading to Letterkenny. It has in it flax mills, orchards and a nursery. The land abounds in whins and land rocks, which give part of it the name of the Craigs, and has a slaty bottom towards the mountain and the lowland red: arable 143, pasture 40, rocks 14 [acres].

Kilgort, Lord Wicklow's estate, situated about half a mile below Tibber slate quarry and south of the church of Taughboyne, has a blue clay bottom and an excellent turf bog in it: arable 50, bog 100 [acres].

Lettergul, Lord Abercorn's estate, situated on the south east side of Mullaghsawey hill, at the base of it; the lands of these villages are very steep and partly rocky. There is limestone here and an excellent turf bog. The young generation of these villages are making rapid progress in consequence of a Sunday school being established amongst them.

Lignatra, Lord Abercorn's estate, north of Binion hill and about 1 and a half miles south of St Johnstown, is remarkable for nothing but a spa well of iron ore; has a blue clay bottom: arable 145, pasture 61, bog 57 [acres].

Listonaugh, Lord Abercorn's estate, south of Binion, is intersected by the road leading from Raphoe to St Johnstown. The land is both productive and early; has a gravelly bottom and a turf bog: arable 24, pasture 24, bog 13 [acres].

Lustikill, Lord Wicklow's estate, situated a little north of the church of Taughboyne, on the road leading from St Johnstown to Newtown-cunningham. The land of this village runs in a moor up the side of Doe's hill; has a fort of Danish construction and a flax mill; a red and blue bottom with some land rocks: arable 170, b[og] 140 [acres].

Maymore, Lord Abercorn's estate, on the banks of Lough Foyle, 1 mile south of St Johnstown, has a commanding view of the surrounding country. Opposite to the village is a small island very productive of grass, on which the inhabitants graze their cattle at large. This village abounds in rocks and whins: arable 72, pasture 37, rocks 32 [acres].

Mahareelay, Lord Abercorn's estate, south of Trentaugh slate quarry, has a turf bog that supplies the inhabitants of St Johnstown and its vicinity; has a blue clay bottom: arable 32, bog 30 [acres].

Monreagh, Lord Wicklow's estate, on the east side of the church of Taughboyne and on the road leading to Carrigans <Carrickgen>. There is a Presbyterian meeting house and an orchard also. Sand pits calculated for making mortar; the land has gravel and blue clay bottom: arable 115, bog 51 [acres].

Momeen, Lord Abercorn's estate, at the base of Mullaghsawey and north of it, is intersected by the road leading from Raphoe to St Johnstown. It is divided into 2 villages, Upper and Lower, or new and old; has excellent spring water and limestone. The upper part of these villages abound in iron ore. In the lower part human bones and skulls have been found, supposed to be an ancient monastery or burying place. They have a blue clay and limestone bottom, with a small turf bog: arable 2,090, pasture 23, bog 26 [acres].

Moness (Lord Abercorn's estate), about 1 mile south of St Johnstown, has an orchard and blue clay bottom, a few rocks and whins: arable 56, pasture 5, bog 10 [acres].

Rockfield, held by the Revd Anthony Carey of Londonderry under the see of Raphoe. This land is surrounded by Lord Abercorn's estate and situated near St Johnstown. Cut through the centre by a road leading from Letterkenny to St Johnstown. This land is full of land rocks and a red till, with a blue clay bottom: arable 78 [acres].

Rateen is situated near the Crohadoes, a little below the road leading from Strabane and Raphoe; has a large lime-kiln built by the ancestors of the late Lord Abercorn for the use of the tenants. This village has plenty of limestone, which is exported to Derry for Mr Walker's saltworks, and has excellent spring water: arable 54, pasture 13, bog 1 [acres].

Swilly, Lord Abercorn's estate, so called from a small river that runs by it, is situated a little to the east of Crohadoes. There is a turf bog annexed to it which contains plenty of bog fir at the depth 7 or 8 feet. The village produces excellent crops in consequence of the ground being of a bituminous nature; might also be useful in pottery.

St Johnstown, situated on the banks of Lough Foyle, in Lord Abercorn's estate, being within the circumscribed limit of 6 miles from Londonderry has not the privilege of a weekly market. This is a serious disadvantage to the inhabitants and its vicinity, having a navigable river to the spot and being in the centre of a very fine and thickly inhabited country, being a town corporate and formerly having the power of sending a member to parliament. These advantages, together with 12 freeholds, might entitle it to the attention of the landed proprietors. All these freeholds contain 10 acres each, except the one called the proportion which has 18 acres.

As there is in this town but 1 fair in the year, I would suggest the improvement of one every quarter and a weekly market, and also a bleach green or any other manufactory, as there is command of water and a fine flax country all around. The freeholds lie all on the south side of St Johnstown.

Trentamucklaugh, Lord Abercorn's estate, a little to the south of Doe's hill, on a rising ground. The land of this village is blue clay bottom with the heads of slates. As the upper end of the townland terminates in the slate quarry of Trentaugh, a quarry of equal worth could be worked in this village. It is also conveniently situated for the purpose, having the road from St Johnstown to Letterkenny through the centre of it. There is a turf bog at the upper and lower end of this town.

Tullysape, Lord Abercorn's estate, situated at the upper end of this parish; bounded by the parish of Raphoe on the south and separated from the parish of Lifford on the east by the River Swilly which discharges itself into Lough Foyle. The lower part of the land towards the river is good, the upper inferior with a blue clay bottom; has in it a flax and corn mill: arable 32, pasture 26, bog 4 [acres].

Tullyown, Lord Abercorn's estate, south of St Johnstown, on the banks of Lough Foyle; this farm is in a romantic situation and well disposed for cultivation by fields regularly proportioned out, besides the farm and office houses are in good repair: arable 60, pasture 60, bog 6 [acres].

Teroddy, Lord Wicklow's estate, about half a mile north of the church of Taughboyne, has a red till with a blue bottom and a flax mill in it: arable 39, pasture or bog 40 [acres].

Trensalaugh, Lord Abercorn's estate, about 1 mile south of Trentaugh slate quarry, has a blue clay bottom; sycamore and ash trees thrive well in it, besides it has an iron mineral well in it.

Tonaugh, Lord Abercorn's estate, is the general name for a quarterland which comprehends Greenhill, Richfield and Cookstown. The latter has a small gort about 5 acres, the property of the rector. The 2 former are inundated by the overflowing of the river that takes its rise from the Port lough, which inundation takes place at the time of heavy rains, occasioning a flood on that part of the lands nearest the river. These villages have limestone, blue clay and hard gravel: arable 153 acres, bog 178, pasture 7 [acres].

Trentaugh, Lord Abercorn's estate, well known in consequence of having in it a blue slate quarry considered the best in the north of Ireland. The land has a red till, with a slate and blue bottom: arable 230, bog 60 [acres].

Tibber, Lord Wicklow's estate, west of the church of Taughboyne, has in it also a slate quarry but of a harder nature than that of Trentaugh. This quarry is not worked at present. The land in general has a red till but towards the quarry abounds with slates; has both a flax and corn mill: arable 194, bog 300 [acres].

Woodland, Lord Abercorn's estate, about 2 miles from Raphoe, has in it an orchard and wood of 7 acres containing the following trees: oak, ash, birch and alder, besides shrubs. Being scarcely a mile from Feddy Glass wood, it has the same description of game: arable 98, pasture 25, bog 38 [acres].

White Hill, Lord Abercorn's estate, situated on a rising ground about 1 mile from St Johnstown, has 3 orchards and the land is productive with a red till and blue clay bottom. It lies south of St Johnstown and Tullyown, on the left hand side of the road to Crohadoes: arable 132, pasture 18, bog 14 [acres].

Signed Nathan Rogers, curate of Taughboyne.

Parish of Templecarn, County Donegal

Memoir by Lieutenant W. Lancey, November 1835

NATURAL STATE

Name

This parish is said to derive its name from the old church having been built in the townland of Cairne, the vestiges of which, in an enclosed burial ground, are still to be seen.

Locality

It is situated in the county of Donegal, barony of Tyrhugh, diocese of Clogher and is surrounded on the north by the parish of Termonamongan <Tarmonamongan>; on the east and south by Templecarn and Drumkeeran <Druimkeiran> in Fermanagh and part of Lough Erne; on the west by Belleek and Drumhome.

This extensive district measures from south west to north east about 14 miles and 8 miles in breadth. It contains 38,244 acres, 6,857 of which are arable and cultivated pasture, 28,137 acres waste, bog or mountain, affording summer feeding for black cattle, and 3,250 acres of water, comprised in Lough Derg <Deirg> and 109 smaller lakes. The valuation to the county cess amounts to 179 pounds 18s 2d.

NATURAL FEATURES

Hills

The high grounds of Templecarn present no marked features worthy of very particular notice. The highest ground is at Blaberine or Cronyscairne, near the mearing of Termonamongan, and rises to a height 1,248 feet above the sea.

Crockeningo is the next in elevation, 1,189 feet, and is perhaps the most conspicuous mountain in this district. Its western descent falls in long slopes to Lough Derg but, except its elevation, it presents nothing to the observer but a high mass covered with bog, the strata occasionally showing themselves towards its summit.

The general position of the mossy lands is low, in long and gentle undulations, the eye embracing at one glance many thousand acres. Towards the south this tameness is broken by rising cultivated knolls which increase in number and fertility towards the neighbourhood of the village of Pettigo, where a thickly-peopled and well-cultivated district succeeds.

The average height of these hills above the sea is from 376 to 450 feet and the average level of the higher hills from 600 to 800, from which 400 feet may be deducted for the height of the plain on which they stand.

Lakes

The lakes amount to 110, of which Lough Derg is the most extensive. This fine sheet of water contains 42 islands, spreads itself over 2,140 acres and lies embosomed in wild hills and bog. Its depth is stated to be 120 feet. In some parts of it dangerous sunken rocks are met with. Its islands are low, rocky and usually covered with small shrubs. Their average height is 484 feet above the sea, the lough being 467 feet.

Saints Island contains 10 acres 1 rood 6 perches; the largest in the lough is Inisusk, 13 acres 2 roods 24 perches; Station Island, the place of penance, is 3 roods 26 perches and the islands decrease in extent to a few yards. All of them, except Station Island, are let for 5 pounds a year. No rent is demanded for it.

The loughs next in extent are those of Duanrack, 150 acres 2 roods 36 perches, Lough Mhriartigh, 112 acres 1 rood, Loch-a-bhiga, 90 acres, Lough Golagh, 84 acres 10 roods and Ruscrine, 56 acres 1 rood 7 perches. There are 6 between 40 and 50 acres, 5 between 30 and 40 and 3 between 20 and 30.

Note: 1 acre 22 perches of Lough Erne belong to this parish.

List of Loughs

Part 1: Duanrach or Lough Minaillum, 150 acres 2 roods 36 perches; Duanrach Lough Minagh, 40 acres; Lochaphise, 10 acres 1 rood 20 perches; Loch-at-the-gable, 1 acre 2 roods 28 perches; Duanrach Loch Beag, 9 acres; Loch-hole at the [?] Geaoel, 3 roods 29 perches; Lochnaagcunniog, 1 acre 3 roods 14 perches; The Blind Pool, 1 rood 4 perches; loch no.1, 3 roods 35 perches; loch no.2, 3 roods 2 perches; Lochvairderrig, 39 acres 3 roods 20 perches; Lochnanderne, 3 acres 3 roods 4 perches; loch no.9, 1 rood 25 perches;

Parish of Templecarn

loch no.8, 1 rood 19 perches; loch no.4, 1 acre 20 perches; loch no.3, 1 acre 10 perches; loch no.24, 1 acre 2 perches; loch no.5, 36 perches; loch no.6, 1 rood 7 perches; loch no.7, 23 perches; loch no.10, part in Drumhome, 2 roods 2 perches; loch no.11, part in Drumhome, 2 acres 3 roods 7 perches; Loch Golagh, 84 acres 10 perches; Lough Derg, including 58 acres 2 roods 14 perches, 2,199 acres 22 perches; Loch Beag, 4 acres 2 roods; Mur loch, 3 acres 2 roods 8 perches; Loch Binina, 7 acres 2 roods 14 perches; [?] Lochmonie, 4 acres 3 roods.

Part 2: Paddys loch, 1 acre 3 roods 39 perches; Acheson's loch, 2 acres 3 roods 27 perches; Loch Finghrian, 28 acres 2 roods 17 perches; Loughnaangeng, 37 acres 28 perches; Loughnabin, 7 acres 3 roods 20 perches; Lough Nachan, 3 acres 1 rood 8 perches; Lough Liffin, 2 acres 1 rood 2 perches; Lough Cearc, 4 acres 2 roods; Lochaghealbhan, part in Termonamongan, 3 acres 16 perches.

Part 3: Loch Iseapa, 12 acres 2 roods 28 perches, in Drumhome parish, [total] 23 acres 32 perches; Brin loch, 1 acre 3 roods 30 perches; Loch Tullighcross, 6 acres 16 perches; Lochnanbradanban, 6 acres 1 rood 4 perches; Rusaine loch, 40 acres 35 perches, in Fermanagh, [total] 56 acres 1 rood 7 perches; Loch Atheiarty, 111 acres 22 perches, in Fermanagh, [total] 112 acres 1 rood; Lochabhige 90 acres 12 perches; Lochnamnasmuirbh, 41 acres; Loch Cip, 10 acres 1 rood 32 perches; Loch Tulleghnabhascabhbeag, 2 acres 5 perches; Loch Aghuismore, 18 acres 2 roods 36 perches; Loch Dubhmor, 7 acres 1 rood; Loch Dubhbeag, 3 acres 20 perches; loch no.13, 1 rood 29 perches; Toobar loch, 2 acres 1 rood 28 perches; Loch Siabranach, 14 acres 2 roods 3 perches, in Drumhome parish, [total] 49 acres 3 roods 4 perches; Glasseasach loch, 1 acre 2 roods 24 perches, in Drumhome parish, [total] 46 acres 1 rood 8 perches; Lochaghuisbeag, 2 acres 2 perches; Lochalonigh, 39 acres 3 perches; Loch Allabuin, 1 acre 3 roods 9 perches; loch no.9, 28 perches, in Drumhome parish, [total] 1 rood 7 perches.

Loch Gorlachbeag, 3 acres 3 roods 8 perches, in Drumhome parish, [total] 8 acres 12 perches; Loch Aghuismor, 4 acres 2 roods 32 perches; Lochnasmatten, 13 acres; loch no.12, 1 rood 19 perches; Lochachadeagh, 3 acres 36 perches; Lochasmatten, 4 acres 2 roods 38 perches; Lochnagcollmor, 2 roods 22 perches; Lochachaillan, 1 rood 7 perches; Lochasaithire, 1 acre 7 roods; Lochalach, 1 acre 15 perches; loch no.10, 12 perches; loch no.11, 21 perches; Loch Sallagh, 4 acres, in Drumhome parish, [total] 8 acres 32 perches; Loch Geearach, 3 roods 7 perches; Lochnatragh, 4 acres 2 roods 18 perches; Loch Geragaonn, 1 acre 17 perches; Lochnatragh, 17 acres 3 roods 2 perches, in Drumhome parish, [total] 22 acres 10 perches.

Part 4: Lochmculbhan, 7 acres 3 roods 8 perches; Loch Currandale, 1 acre 3 perches; The Smultans, 3 acres 16 perches; The Smultans, 8 acres 20 perches; Lochunaibh, 9 acres 1 rood 8 perches; [?] Lochnananernagh, 2 acres 3 roods 38 perches; Lochanfarine, 3 roods 29 perches; Loch Fadda, 17 acres 2 roods; Black loch, 1 rood 27 perches; Lochnhamias, 2 roods 26 perches; Lochnasuofan, 10 acres 1 rood 32 perches; Loch Bormas, 36 acres 1 rood 33 perches; Loch Allan, 36 acres 2 roods 13 perches; loch no.1, 24 perches; Loch Sallagh, 4 acres 2 roods 36 perches; Lochaturribh, 1 acre 2 roods 34 perches; Loch Blanan, 7 acres 2 roods 32 perches; Drumgunna loch, 37 acres 3 roods 8 perches; Lochnamnameuibh, 45 acres 3 roods 8 perches; Lochamhadeadh, 8 acres 1 perch; Lochnagcunniog, 18 acres 1 perch; Lochamhadeadh, 15 acres 1 rood 19 perches, in Fermanagh, [total] 23 acres 1 rood 20 perches; Locharseghbeag, 4 acres 2 roods 3 perches; Lochchupam, 2 acres 1 rood; Loughcamambaluighibh, 2 acres 4 perches; Black loch, 6 acres 2 roods 16 perches; Loughaghnuisbeag, 4 acres 2 roods 3 perches; Loughaghnuismore, 18 acres 2 roods 36 perches.

Part 5: Black loch, 2 acres 3 roods 24 perches; Achafoi loch, 12 acres 31 perches; Achalach, 5 acres 2 roods 6 perches; Lochnambeadendearg, 5 acres 3 roods 13 perches; Loch Namnas, 2 acres 3 roods 24 perches; Lochnasinach, 2 roods 26 perches; Loch Allabuin, 2 acres 1 rood 3 perches; part of Lough Erne, 1 acre 22 perches.

Rivers

The river dividing the counties of Tyrone and Donegal on the north mearing of Templecarn receives the drainage of Lough Derg. It is about 40 feet wide and bounds about 5 miles of this parish, falling from west to east, and is from 400 to 600 feet above the sea.

Lough Derg, from whence flows at its north eastern corner a rapid stream, receives but few tributary waters; yet it is supposed sufficient in the mass to account for the whole overflow without supposing it to possess natural springs in itself. The lough and river mentioned above empty themselves into the Mourne and finally mingle with the ocean at Magilligan, whilst the waters of the southern part of this parish fall into Lough Erne and are discharged at Ballyshannon.

The county boundary of Fermanagh runs in the centre of a stream 40 feet wide flowing from north east to south west for 10 miles and turning the mill above the village, passes through Pettigo and falls into Lough Erne at Burnfoot. The mearing of Templecarn to the west of this is a stream flowing from the west for 5 miles and a half and emptying itself into the Erne. These rivers flow over gravel and rocks and are sufficiently powerful for mills and machinery.

The parish is well watered, possessing a considerable number of brooks and rivulets converging from north west and north east towards the south and finally falling into Lough Erne.

Bogs and Woods

There is a vast extent of bog in Templecarn in which fir and other timber are found. Nothing unusual was heard of in connection with these bogs except what has been stated, that cultivated knolls rise out of them.

There are very few existing traces of woodlands, if we except those deposited in bogs.

Coast and Climate

The coast of Lough Erne in this neighbourhood is low and a very small portion of it belongs to Templecarn.

The general climate of Tyrhugh is moist and damp.

NATURAL HISTORY

Zoology

Eagles build in the islands of Lough Derg, in places apparently very accessible to man. Foxes abound in Crockbrack and Crockeningo. Kites, curlews, partridges, hares, grouse and snipe are met with; badgers in Crockeningo, and otters, trouts, eels, pike etc. in Lough Derg.

Geology

This district is a primitive formation of quartz and gneiss with blue mountain limestone filled with organic remains on the margin of Lough Erne.

MODERN TOPOGRAPHY

Towns: Pettigo

Pettigo, situated on the county mearing of Donegal and Fermanagh: it is a neat village and has an excellent, clean little inn of superior description kept by Mrs Hamilton. The parish church in the village is much dilapidated and a new one is about to be built. It can contain 400 persons. A market house is also in progress. There are several good and substantial buildings in the town and Pettigo is fast rising into respectability.

The new road from Donegal to Enniskillen passes through the village. A mail coach, it is said, is to be run on this new line when completed, which will materially assist the people of Pettigo.

Public Buildings

The new Roman Catholic chapel lies at the west of the village. It was erected in [blank], cost [blank] and can hold [blank] persons. A new chapel is in progress in the townland of [blank] and a new church on a small scale for a schoolhouse and place of worship is also in progress.

The Presbyterian house stands in the adjacent parish of Drumkeeran and was erected in [blank] at a cost of [blank], and is calculated to contain [blank] persons.

The Methodist chapel in the village was built in [blank], cost [blank] and can hold [blank] persons.

Gentlemen's Seats

The only houses of respectability are Grouse Hall and the rector's. The former is now in bad repair, having been built 100 years ago by the grandfather of the present occupier. The Glebe House is a good and substantial building.

Mills

The mill is found in the townland of South Belalt. It is overshot, having a wheel of about 8 feet diameter. Any person may erect mills, but the exportation of corn has destroyed this particular branch of business.

Communications

The new road from Donegal now in progress appears to be well laid out. The old one is very bad in wet weather and for spring carriages scarcely passable at any season.

The road to Strabane is hard but hilly, and very little attention has of course been paid to the roads of the country, where few spring carriages are used.

Bridges

There is a new bridge at Pettigo, of substantial workmanship, over a rapid and turbulent stream in wet weather. The old bridge a little above it has a steep ascent, partaking of the rising ground east of the river, and the new erection is evidently of great advantage.

ANCIENT TOPOGRAPHY

Church

The ancient church in Cairne has only its burial ground to mark its site.

Magrath's Castle

The old ruin in Aghnahoo known by the name of Magrath's Castle belonged to the father of Magrath, first Protestant Bishop of Clogher. He defended his castle against Cromwell's troops who, after 3 days' firing, were in the act of raising the siege when a deserter from the castle, Hugh Monaghan, pointed out its weakest part in the right wing, to which the artillery were directed and a breach effected, upon which Magrath surrendered and suffered confiscation. His son recovered the property by conforming to the Protestant faith and, having received ordination, was preferred to the see of Clogher, where he died.

[Drawing of Magrath's Castle, main dimensions 60 feet 5 inches high, 33 feet wide, 38 feet high to the top of the battlements, 60 feet 5 inches high to the top chimney].

SOCIAL ECONOMY

Lough Derg Pilgrimage

The pilgrimage to Lough Derg is an ancient superstition still kept up with zeal, but not so vigorously as formerly. The old place of penance was on Saint's Island but now the Station Island; lies about 2,112 feet from the east coast of the lough. There is a rude ferry-house, the access to which is across a rough mountain a mile and a half from the nearest accessible point of road. A large boat capable of holding about 40 or 50 persons, called the *St Patrick*, conveys the pilgrims barefooted to

Station Island, Lough Derg

the island. The females do not uncover their heads. The men tie a handkerchief around their temples.

On their arrival at the shore, each produces a ticket with which they were presented on the payment of 6d ha'penny at the ferry-house. They proceed immediately to work. 3, 6 or 9 days are occupied in their devotions; usually only 3. During this period they eat but 1 meal, of oatcake, on the first and third days. The water of the lough boiled and turned into wine by the miraculous power of the priests afford them their only beverage. The second day is one of complete abstinence even from sleep.

6 circular paths of stone called the Beds about 15 feet in diameter afford the pilgrims the first penance, by traversing them all 3 times at 3 successive periods of the day, counting beads, saying prayers, aves etc.

The second day they are kept in prison in a large chapel without food, water or sleep for 24 hours, and any transgression of this rule entails eternal damnation on the offender. Priests or persons are engaged with long wands to keep the poor creatures, already exhausted perhaps by a long journey, from risk of slumbering, and it is reported that many have left the island in a state of distraction from having unadvisedly indulged.

The rest of the penance consists in perambulating the interior of the prison chapel 9 times. A second chapel is appropriated to confession, in which about 8 boxes for that purpose are arranged. The pilgrims state their sins, are forgiven them by the priests if they deserve it or, in other words, if they perform the station properly.

This superstition so directly opposed to the principles of the Christian religion commences annually from the 1st of June and lasts to 15th August, during which time about 15,000 persons, it is computed, visit the station. A prior and 6 or 7 priests paid by him for the occasion reside during this period on the island.

The buildings consists of a chapel called the prison, a confessional chapel, the prior's house, 4 or 5 lodging houses [crossed out: an old chapel not now used] and 1 or 2 outhouses. A boiler to make the water into wine which, however, possesses the taste and appearance of water after its supposed change, and an old broken cross dignified by the name of St Patrick's and a single tree complete the varieties of Station Island.

The expenses absolutely incurred consist of 6d ha'penny ferry money, which covers the inward and outward passage, 6d ha'penny to the prior and 3d for hot water, candles etc. To these sums the pilgrims may add what they please for masses, building funds etc., and respectable persons are said to give a pound and others as their conscience says or their resources dictate.

Ferryboat

Perhaps the 2 most striking things connected with the superstitions of Lough Derg are first the ferry is kept by a Protestant and he rents from the executive of the late Colonel Leslie at 65 pounds a year. The best way to see this place to advantage is first to row round it, as the prior stops everything directly a Protestant lands on its shores. A boat can be hired in Ballymacavenny.

When you leave the station a bell is rung and, on looking round, you perceive the hundreds in its confined space hard at work at the beds, prison etc. There were about 300 persons on the island on the 7th June 1835, but the weather was bad and the season had only commenced.

Sometimes the number towards the close of the patton [pattern] amounts to 1,000. The boatmen averaged the pilgrims of 1834 at 300 a day, making 22,800 for the season. Men and women came from all parts of Ireland to the station, some even from America and the Continent, but it is said the whole affair is not so respectable in the class of pilgrims or in number as formerly.

Stone at the chapel door Station Island, Lough Derg, county Donegal. A. Dogherty was prior in 1763. [Drawing of arms engraved on stone tablet 2 feet 3 inches high by 1 foot 9 inches wide, showing a cross and deer, with inscription: "Acresty [sacristy?] ye house was built Fr Anthony Dogherty for ye use of ye conven[t] of Donegal, his age 68 ye 8th September AD 1763"].

This cross is in the centre of one of the beds and retains traces of characters now not legible [drawing, 2 feet high, 2 feet long].

St Patrick's Cross [drawing, 3 feet 9 inches high, 4 inches thick].

Station Island in Lough Derg [tracing showing main buildings, with a key].

A very good sketch of Station Island in Lough Derg, 1835.

ANCIENT TOPOGRAPHY

Forts

Forts, usually called Danish, are found in the townlands of Barnas, Drumceiribe, Gortnessey and Drumahare. The centre of the latter is a standing stone and the townland has also a holy well.

Modern Topography

General Appearance and Scenery

The general appearance of Templecarn as an agricultural district is wild and unpromising, except in the immediate vicinity of Pettigo and Lough Erne, the shores of which, being low and lying on limestone, are cultivated; neither is there any striking scenery unconnected with Lough Erne.

Lough Derg is a large sheet of water surrounded by black bogs relieved only by a few detached cabins and patches of cultivation and its groups of islands. There are no less than 110 loughs in the parish. They present no picturesque features but rather blend to the general gloom of its mountain districts.

Social Economy

Early Improvements

The people have settled themselves on the shore of Lough Erne following the general law observable in every parish where cultivation is usually commenced on the sea-coast, the shores of lakes or the banks of rivers. The beds of mountain limestone and the accessible nature of the country is perhaps a better reason than the above for the settlement of this part.

No obstructions to the general improvement of the country have been heard of; run and dale and other similar ancient customs are becoming obsolete.

Local Government

There are no magistrates residing in the parish. Enniskillen and Ballyshannon are the nearest places where troops are quartered. A small detachment of constabulary is stationed in Pettigo.

Illicit distillation is kept up but the crimes of the district are confined to those usually settled at petty sessions.

Dispensaries

An establishment of this nature is in the village, supported by subscription and a grant from the grand jury.

Schools and Poor

There are 4 schools, 2 under the management of the Hibernian Society, the parish school and 1 supported by the scholars. Mrs Leslie gives 3 pounds a year each to the 3 first, which averages 50 scholars at each school. Added to these there are [blank] hedge schools under no society.

Poor: no provision for them except the collections at the public places of worship.

Religion

Templecarn contains 794 families, 1,987 males, 2,185 females, 1,728 Established Church, 2,568 Roman Catholics, 97 Presbyterians, 4,393 total. From the above it will be seen that an unusual number of Protestants, compared with the rest of the population, reside in Templecarn. The neglected state of the Established religion has caused Methodism to prevail in this district.

Habits of the People

The style of cottage is the same as that generally met with in the north of Ireland. Potatoes, milk, meal and occasionally fish and meat afford sustenance to the people. The average number in a family is 5 and a half. There is nothing new to be remarked under this head. A general want of cleanliness and comfort prevails, but there are various degrees of it; and what in one district would be considered clean, in another is looked upon as unclean, but anything in the cabins like real neatness has not been observed.

Productive Economy

Spinning

Spinning and general dealing in flax and yarn are common; weaving has fallen into much decay, in consequence of the decrease of the linen trade. Good millstones are worked at Lathaircranny (see Memoir of Killymard).

Rural: Proprietors

The chief proprietors are the representatives of the late Colonel Leslie, who hold 45 townlands out of 50, 2 belong to the Revd Mr Dixon, 2 to Mr Aitcheson and the glebe to the clergyman.

The size of the holdings varies in different parts of the parish according if it be arable or mountain. The townland of Tibhetiobar is occupied by 2 tenants as a grazing farm at 14 pounds a year. All the islands in Lough Derg and the eel rivers are let for 5 pounds. Crockbrack is held by 2 tenants at 10 pounds and the arable lands vary in price, according to their relative value, from 10s to 25s an acre. Colonel Leslie's property is bishop's land and is held at the usual term of 21 years. Mrs Leslie bears a high character for kindness to her "tenants."

Farms

There are no farms cultivated by the landlords as examples for the people; lands are not let in conacre. The farmers appear to labour more for subsistence than for the realization of capital. Their fields are tolerably well laid out near Pettigo but generally they are of all sizes and shapes, fenced with stone walls. The farm buildings are erected by the tenants, assisted occasionally by the landlords in a trifling way but afterwards kept in repair by the occupiers.

Agricultural Methods

Lime and compost are the only manures. The kilns belong to the tenants and are usually of small dimensions and of a temporary description. Carts and cars are in common use. The better kinds of agricultural implements are scarce. Rotation in crops is a matter not thought of, except potatoes, oats and potatoes, till the land is destroyed. This of course is not so much the case near the village, where a better style of farming is practised and wheat, flax and clover are grown.

Produce and Markets

The produce is taken either to Castlederg, Donegal or Ballyshannon markets, all of which are at extremely inconvenient distances. This will, however, shortly be amended by making Pettigo a weekly market as soon as the market house is erected.

Grazing and Livestock

There are some large townlands in the northern part of the parish occupied as grazing farms. Artificial grasses for this purpose are not sown, nor is irrigation practised for the improvement of the herbage to any extent. In the townland of Crockbrack 40 head of cattle at 3s are generally put on it during the season. Towards the south west and the vicinity of the road to Donegal grazing has been spoiled by enclosing the best spots for tillage.

There are good slopes for corn and cultivation on the hills falling into Lough Derg on its southern shores, and these of course in process of time by the opening of roads will be turned into arable districts.

The usual mixed breeds of cattle, pigs and horses prevail in Templecarn.

Uses made of Bogs

The bogs are grazed and used as fuel; no efforts have been made to drain them except those carried on by the tenants on a small scale.

Planting

There is very little, if any, planting of modern date in this large district, except a few trees here and there around the cottages. At Grouse Hall, a place of 100 years standing, the timber has attained a fine growth and much land in that vicinity might be advantageously laid down with trees. This branch of profit so highly useful and ornamental has hitherto been neglected.

Fishing

There are good trout in Lough Derg which are sometimes taken by anglers Salmon towards the autumn ascend the Pettigo river from Lough Erne. The loughs generally have trout.

The legend of St Patrick having "banished" the salmon from Lough Derg is religiously believed by the people, who state the saint was tripped up by a large one when wading to Saint's Island, the original station. The absence of salmon from Lough Derg is not difficult to be accounted for: the shores are studded with low rocks in almost every part and very little gravel is met with for the fish to spawn in.

The Rivers Derg and Mourne on its north have fords and shoals which, being congenial to the nature of the fish, are preferred to the deep and rocky shores of Lough Derg, and the salmon, arriving at the junction of the streams which drain the 2 loughs, are said to continue their ascent by the Mourne.

Large pike are found also in Lough Derg and report states that Lough Mourne about 16 years ago contained good trout which were destroyed by a shoal of these fish which found their way to it by following the course of the 2 rivers. An eel-weir is on the river draining Lough Derg.

General Remarks on Economy

There is yet much land in the parish capable of being turned to agricultural purposes. The new road from Donegal to Pettigo will doubtless facilitate this and a new road from Castlederg <Castledeirg> to join the unfinished one between Lough Derg and Crockeningo, said to be about to be made by Sir R. Ferguson, will add much to the convenience of the inhabitants, open a better egress for the produce in that quarter and bring a vast number of waste acres under the spade and plough.

The highest point yet cultivated is 705 feet above the sea, in the townland of Cullion. The general level of the highlands averages 600 feet, those of the neighbourhood of Pettigo varying from 300 to 400 feet. The general fall of the country is to the south, to the shores of Lough Erne, and is protected on the north by highlands.

Lime could easily be got for manure. Sheepwalks would not answer in this district, it being too wet. Planting might be advantageous[ly] laid down and fuel and water power are abundant.

Lough Erne is at hand, were it made navigable to Ballyshannon, and the roads could easily be made good for any description of carriage. [Signed] William Lancey, Lieutenant Royal Engineers, 25th November 1835.

ANCIENT TOPOGRAPHY

St Deavog's Chair

[Insert note by Lieutenant Larcom: Will you add this to the Memoir of Templecarn, [by] W. Lancey, Lieutenant Royal Engineers, 7th December 1835].

St Deavog's Chair, situated on a height in the townland of Seabogue and in view of Saint's and Station Islands [drawing with dimensions and annotations].

Replies to Queries on Termon Magrath District from North West Farming Society

MEMOIR WRITING

Composition of Memoir

The author of the following brief sketch, on first receiving a copy of the statistical queries, was for a considerable time in doubt whether to forward any answer to the inquiries proposed. The barren subject on which he was invited to communicate his knowledge and observations presented an appalling obstacle to a successful execution of such a project.

Meagre and dry to the last degree must appear the description of a region where the hand of nature, severely parsimonious, has been very niggardly aided by the ingenuity of art or the tasteful design of scientific industry. Beautiful indeed and picturesque in many places the scenery must appear to the eye of the poet, but when considered in an agricultural, commercial or manufacturing point of view, it presents a spectacle little fitted to captivate the fancy of the theoretical or invite the labours of the practical improver.

And this discouragement, great in itself, was rendered still more powerful by considering the vantage ground on which others would stand, to whose lot would fall the description of more favoured districts. There the abundant profits of a well-directed cultivation, the happy results from varied combinations of art accomplished in extensive manufactories, the rich tide of wealth flowing in from commercial pursuits and the numerous mines everywhere underfoot, pregnant with precious ores, all concur in affording rich materials to the narrator and in attracting and affixing the attention of the interested reader.

Such are the motives which operated to deter the writer of the present article from venturing to exhibit his pitiful stock of wares in a mart where they must encounter a comparison so unfavourable. Still, however, the request of the society so earnestly urged, and the hope that the diffused knowledge of the wants and hardship of this district may lead to their amelioration or removal, have prevailed on the author to contribute his mite to forward the views of the society, so honourable to themselves and so likely to prove beneficial to the community at large.

NATURAL STATE

Name and Locality

Name of the district, situation, extent and divisions: the parish of Templecarn is situated partly in the county of Donegal and partly in the county Fermanagh. That portion included in the former county (to which the present report is confined) is denominated Termon Magrath, so called, it should seem, from the first Protestant Bishop of Clogher, who in the reign of Queen Elizabeth resided at the castle, the shell of which is still marked by his name.

The district is situated in the barony of Tyrhugh and diocese of Clogher; the present incumbent is the Revd Robert Staples Jacob.

Proprietors

The only landed proprietor is the Bishop of Clogher, under whom Colonel Charles Powell Leslie holds the entire of this district. This gentleman is non-resident, scarcely indeed ever visiting his property.

Townlands

Names of townlands as taken from the vestry book: Ardnaglass 21 acres arable, Aughafy 44 acres arable, Aughalough 72 acres arable, Aughaloo 95 acres arable, Ballymacavenny 57 acres arable, Banis 37 acres arable, Bualt 141 acres arable, Billory 7 acres arable, Bircog 16 and a half acres arable, Boeshall 27 acres arable, Carrickrory 75 acres arable, Meenanellison half an acre arable, Oughtkenley 5 acres arable, Pettigoe 66 acres arable, Carne 204 acres arable, Corley 26 acres arable, Carntressy 119 acres arable, Croagh 64 acres arable, Croaghbrack 6 acres arable, Cashlinny 66 acres arable, Crilly 45 acres arable, Cullion 190 acres arable, Drumawark 162 acres arable, Drumcrin 42 acres arable, Drumgim 102 acres arable, Rushen 11 acres arable, Tamlaght 86 acres arable, Tullylack 105 acres arable, Drumherriff 35 acres arable, Drumnescue 55 acres arable, Fencashel 67 acres arable, Glasskeeragh 77 acres arable, Gortnessy 123 acres arable, Grousehall 388 acres arable, Kimmitt 128 acres arable, Lettercran 117 acres arable, Margy 44 acres arable, Mulnagode 58 acres arable, Minchifrie 4 acres arable, Sessaghkilty 116 acres arable, Tievemore 35 acres arable, Taver 50 acres arable, Tullycarne 158 acres arable.

Extent of Parish

By the late census, the number of arable acres (as marked in the list of townlands) amounts to 3,397 acres; on the same authority the number of horses is fixed at 595 and that of the inhabitants at 3,195.

It is impossible to ascertain the number of acres of mountain and bog, as in the vicinity of Lough Derg, Rushen, Glasskeeragh and some other places the eye is fatigued traversing the boundless extent of heathy ground, unmixed with arable or meadow. When the extent of the district is considered, being upwards of 10 miles in length and on an average nearly 4 in breadth, the quantity is surely not exaggerated when taken at nearly 20,000 acres.

PRODUCTIVE ECONOMY

Nature of Farms

Section 2: nature of the farms, fences, crops, grounds etc. There are no farms in this tract on an extensive scale. The size is very different, varying from 30 to 40 acres down to 3 or 4; the general average is about 8 acres. These farms are in general but indifferently fenced. According to the different nature of the soil, they are enclosed either with earthen ditches or in rocky grounds with stone fences. Quickset hedges are very rare.

The general, or indeed the universal, mode of cultivation is carried on in the following rotation of crops: first year potatoes, second barley or oats, third year flax.

Improvements in Agriculture

Of improvement as the cultivation is at present managed, there is not great degree of capability. A considerable amelioration might indeed be looked for were the growing of green crops, artificial grasses etc. once introduced; but as this, at least to any great extent, is, from causes hereafter to be explained, not to be expected, any valuable improvement seems to be removed to an indefinite distance.

To pasture-grounds too, the same observations may be extended. They are in general not of a good description: those particularly situated on the northern side of the hills are worse than indifferent, nor is any considerable improvement contemplated as likely.

NATURAL FEATURES

Mountains and Hills

Of mountain and hills there is a great number. The whole face of the country indeed consists of hills separated by narrow valleys. These hills are usually denominated from the townlands in which they are situated. The most considerable are Crocknacunny, Mindilpier, Croaghbrack and Rusheen.

Overrun as they are with heath, they are pasturable to a certain degree, being covered in summer with considerable herds of black cattle. Cultivation had during the last war crept up their sides to a good height but, through the low prices of agricultural products and the bad prospect of remuneration, has since reverted again to the vales.

Bogs

Though the number of bogs in this district is considerable, yet few of them reach to any great extent. Those at present used have been but lately entered upon and consequently contain a great quantity of fir and oak. These trees are to be met with at no great distance from the surface, generally at 8 or 10 feet depth.

Woods

Of woods, nurseries or plantations, this tract is at present completely destitute, though there is every appearance of it having been formerly well supplied with timber. To iron works formerly carried on in the neighbourhood, the present bare appearance of the country is chiefly to be ascribed. There are few orchards and these very diminutive indeed.

Parish of Templecarn

From the few samples that are to be met with, it is to be presumed that trees would thrive tolerably well. Oak, ash, poplars seem to suit the climate best, as also all the different species of fir, Scotch and larch particularly.

Productive Economy

Value of Land

The value of land in this quarter is as variable as can well be imagined, the degrees between best and inferior of arable and pasture-grounds being almost infinite, though the acreable rents bear no such proportion to the variety of degrees. The following table will show the highest acreable rent of the several descriptions: arable, green pasture and meadow grounds, best 2 pounds 10s, middling 1 pound 5s, inferior 15s. The rent of moory pasture is not calculably by the acre, as such description of land is let by the lump and there is no great diversity in its quality.

Of turf bog, the value is not easily to be ascertained as no rent is paid for it by the tenants, who are accommodated with it in proportion to the farms they hold. However, as nearly as can be guessed, the value of it should seem to be about 20s per acre.

Improvements in Husbandry

There have been no improvements as to tillage, enclosures, descriptions of fences, implements of husbandry recently made, unless in the adoption of 2-wheeled carts, a few of which are here and there to be met with but which have by no means come into general use.

The fences mostly in use have been adverted [to] above. They indeed are of a most sorry description. Quickset hedges would undoubtedly be the most eligible in general, both for defence and shelter, but in the rocky grounds here frequently to be met with stone ditches are the most easily made, indeed the only ones possible to be constructed.

Employment and Wages

Section 3. Servants and labourers find pretty general employment here during the year, though from the prevalent modes of cultivation, averse to change and not found [fond] of making experiments, the contrary might be respected. Indeed in cheap times labourers are with difficulty procured, especially in harvest. The introduction of manufactures might give employment to persons at present not much regarded, such as young boys and girls, whom in other places we see gain very considerable wages; but agriculture as at present practised seems fully adequate to give general employment to all others.

The wages of servants and the prices of labour by the day or piece vary considerably at different times and are always exactly regulated by the plenty or scarcity of the preceding harvest. At present menservants can get from 3 pounds to 5 pounds yearly, female servants 2 guineas per annum. Daily wages are 1s per day.

Green Crops and Drainage

Section 4. There are no green crops sown of any description except clover and that very rarely, nor are artificial grasses much used. The little that is to be found is the perennial rye grass. Draining too, though much wanted in many places (as may easily from the nature of the country be supposed), is but very imperfectly executed. Surface draining and underdraining are both partially carried on.

Manures

The manures most in use are lime, dung, bog, clay and compost of bog, clay and lime. The soil in barren grounds and such only is generally burnt for potatoes. This indeed is the process used for bringing in bad ground and is never made use of in soil naturally good or improved by labour. The crop of potatoes thus raised is tolerably good but the aftercrops are very deficient.

Irrigation

The irrigation of meadows has very lately been introduced and, notwithstanding its perceptible advantages, is not carried on to the extent that it deserves or that might be expected. And yet from the local situation of such grounds, generally inclined plains on the slopes of hills, or low grounds lying at the bottom of adjacent heights from which constant rills of spring or rain-water might be derived, the process could be carried on with great facility.

Dairies

Few dairies have been established in this district, and those few very insignificant. Every little farmer indeed has as many cows as he can afford to buy, and has grass to feed, for the sale of butter is at present found to be the best article to ensure the payment of rent.

This butter is sent to a distant market and the buttermilk either used to fatten swine or sent to the village of Pettigo, where a few artificers and a constant garrison of soldiers kept there for the suppression of illicit distillation encourage its importation.

Oxen and Spade Husbandry

Oxen have never as yet (as far as the author has learned) been employed in husbandry; and as for spade tillage, whenever it occurs, it is the effect of necessity arising either from the want of horses or the wetness of the land, where no other mode of tillage could be used.

Grain Crops

The grains here sown are all the different kinds of oats and barley. The ground is generally found inadequate to the growing of wheat, which is therefore never attempted. Prices of late years have fluctuated greatly: good oats may be bought at present for 10d a stone and barley for 11d, potatoes may be had at 2d a stone.

The measurement of land is computed by the Irish acre.

Livestock: Breeds of Cattle

Section 5. The black cattle, horses, sheep and swine usually reared by the farmers are of the old Irish breed and of an indifferent kind. Some exceptions to this are to be met with in the horses and swine. A few Manx horses have been introduced and, from their hardy nature, have been found to answer well; and some swine of the Dutch breed have found their way into this district.

As the attention of the natives is at present chiefly turned to the butter business, which is found to answer best for the payment of rents, which cattle form the predominant share of stock occupying pasture-grounds. The following table will shew the probable quantity of each description of stock in this division of the parish.

Best draft and saddle horses 12, valued at 10 pounds, total value 120 pounds; inferior draft and saddle horses 40, valued at 5 pounds, total value 200 pounds; milch cows 200, valued at 4 pounds, total value 800 pounds; sheep 350, valued at 10s each, total value 175 pounds; mules 5, valued at 30s, total value 7 pounds 10s; asses 30, valued at 8s, total value 12 pounds; hogs 350, valued at 6s, total value 105 pounds; total 1,419 pounds 10s.

Improvements in Stock

No improvement has been made in the different breeds of stock within the last 20 years, nor are any likely at present to take place; though it cannot be denied but there is ample scope for such improvement in all its several kinds. In the case of sheep particularly, which are of a description very inferior both in point of wool and of flesh, the present breed ought to be extirpated or at least amended by the introduction of a new breed of rams.

NATURAL FEATURES

Rivers and Lakes

Section 6. There are 3 small rivers which, after watering or bounding this district, fall into Lough Erne: the Pettigo river, the Omna and the Letter river.

The Pettigo river rises about 5 miles north of Pettigo and runs in a southerly direction about a mile north of the village. It receives the tributary waters of the Omna, which rises in the mountains near Lough Derg and runs in a south easterly direction. After this junction the united stream passes through Pettigo and falls into Lough Erne about a mile south of that place.

The Letter river rises in the mountains north west of Pettigo and, running but a short distance in a south easterly direction, falls into Lough Erne about a mile south west of Pettigo.

The lakes in this quarter are numerous. Besides Lough Erne, a small part of the shore of which borders on this district, and Lough Derg, of far-extended notoriety which is enclosed in the heart of it, there are many others of smaller extent, all of which produce great quantities of excellent fish.

SOCIAL ECONOMY

Lough Derg Pilgrimage

The annual pilgrimage to this lake constitutes one of the great curiosities and a not inconsiderable branch of the traffic of this district. It has been averaged some years back at 11,000 or 12,000 persons. This present year the numbers, it is computed, will exceed 15,000.

The Saint's Island formerly was the seat of this austere but gainful superstition, where a cave denominated Patrick's Purgatory, and supposed to lead to the confines of Hell and which had been much abused to sinister purposes, was in the time of the Commonwealth closed up by order of the lords justices.

This island being, however, accessible in dry weather from the mainland has been deserted and the scene of penance removed to another called thence the Station Island, of much less extent but greater difficulty of access. There are 2 large chapels lately erected on it, besides other buildings for the accommodation of the prior and confessors and for the use of the pilgrims.

The ferry is let and brings in 260 pounds annually to Colonel Leslie.

Natural History

Mines and Minerals

No metallic mines have as yet been discovered in this neighbourhood, though the numerous chalybeate and sulphurous springs everywhere oozing out might scorn to give indications of the existence of such. Quarries of limestone, freestone, whinstone are found in great quantities, as also a species of dark-coloured rough marble of which chimneypieces might be constructed. There are quarries also from which millstones are cut out. Of these articles, there is at present no convenient exportation.

The limestone found in this tract is of a light, sky-blue colour producing excellent lime. From the abundance and consequent cheapness of turf with which it is universally burnt, the price of lime is very low, not exceeding 10d a barrel, and the expense might be rendered still lighter if perpetual kilns, at present unknown here, were gradually adopted.

Of coal, no mines have hitherto been discovered, though a considerable vein has lately been found at no great distance in the neighbouring parish of Drumkeeran. With what success the mineral spring, both chalybeate and sulphurous, might be attended if used for medicinal purposes is problematical, as they are seldom or ever made use of in that way. Of marl, no traces whatever are visible.

Social Economy

Condition of the People

Section 7. As to the general situation of the natives and their domestic comforts, the writer of this article regrets that he is unable to give a more pleasing report. Notwithstanding the general disposition to industry, the means of earning money are scanty and limited in the extreme; and scarcely have the poor inhabitants a choice in the mode of expending it. After the demands on them for rent, tythes and taxes have been discharged, very little remains for the supply of food and apparel; and this little, it may be easily conceived, admits as little of the profession of prodigality as of the provident disposal of it for future contingencies in savings banks.

Houses

Yet with all these disadvantages, a stranger might be led to form a more favourable idea of their domestic comforts, from the neatness of dress displayed at their several places of worship or at fairs and other public places. Their cottages too, for under this denomination the generality of houses here to be met with are to be included, though sometimes very poor in their external appearance and seeming to totter to their fall, if destitute of other comforts possess at least that of cleanliness.

Another internal comfort they universally enjoy is the abundance of turf, of which a backload may be procured at present for the small sum of 2d ha'penny.

Food

The farming, manufacturing and labouring classes of inhabitants are not usually discriminated by any difference in point of diet, as masters, labourers and servants generally partake at the same table of the same frugal fare. The usual food of all these classes consists of potatoes, oaten meal, butter and milk. Of animal food, they seldom taste except on festival occasions.

Education

The wish for education is very prevalent in all these classes, though from their poverty and the necessity of providing for the more immediate demands of their situation in life they cannot gratify the desire to any extensive degree. The recent establishment, however, of hibernian schools in this and the adjacent districts is calculated to obviate the first of these obstacles, as that of Sunday schools, an institution too of modern date, promises to relieve the pressure of the latter.

The observation shortly before made that the poverty of the country militates against the extent of education might lead to the supposition that the expenses attending it are high, whereas on the contrary they cannot be imagined more reasonable. The charges usually made are as follows: tuition in reading 2s 6d, in writing 3s 11d and in arithmetic 5s 5d per quarter. Of these private schools, there are 4 in this district, besides a school established by Hibernian Society alluded to above.

The author, from his short residence of 12 years in this parish, during which the state of education has continued much the same, is not well qualified to decide concerning whether the state of the peasantry has been ameliorated to any observable degree, in consequence of the more general diffusion of education. Still, however, by comparing the manners and habits of the rising generation who have enjoyed the advantages with those of their immediate predecessors less favoured in this respect, the difference undoubtedly will authorize the assertion that the superiority lies wholly on the side of the former.

Health

This tract of country is healthy in an uncommon degree, so that a physician or even an apothecary would find it impossible to support himself by his practice. The prevalent diseases are fevers and pleurisies, which probably have their origin in the blood being heated excessively by labour without using due precautions to guard against the effects.

Friendly Societies

The state of civilisation, as may be well conjectured, admits not of the establishment of friendly societies for bettering the condition of the poor. In fact no such societies are to be met with.

The only town or rather village in this parish is that of Pettigo.

PRODUCTIVE ECONOMY

Improvements

The natives of this district are wonderfully bigoted to the routine of labour and habits transmitted to them from their forefathers, nor is their attention directed to the effects of improved modes, as exemplified in the conduct of more wealthy or more scientific neighbours. No doubts, however, are to be entertained but that they would follow wherever the good effects of such imitation would be held up to their view.

The writer of this sketch would be extremely happy were it in his power to give in the names and address of any proprietors that would be likely to add to the stock of information desired by the North West of Ireland Society; but [that] there are intelligent farmers here in their own way cannot be denied; but that any important results would follow from a correspondence with them is a matter of very doubtful complexion.

Linen

Section 8. Linen manufacture has never been carried on to any great extent in this neighbourhood. From the total want of millworks and bleach greens, it never reaches farther than the operations of weavers. At present it seems pretty much at a stand, neither increasing nor yet, under all the present disadvantages attending the manufacture, appearing to diminish.

Preparation of Flax

The land is prepared for the inception of flax seed merely by ploughing and harrowing; the flax crop usually succeeding that of barley, sometimes that of oats. The flax thus raised is chiefly employed in home manufacture, little of it being sold for exportation. The natives have not as yet got into the secret of saving the seed without injuring the flax; of course little seed is saved.

The flax is prepared for manufacture partly by scutch mills and partly by manual labour, and in the preparing of it fire is universally used.

Yarn

The grist which yarns are spun to in this neighbourhood are as follows: tow yarns are usually spun to a hank in the lb.; flax yarns are from 2 to 4 hanks in the lb. The prices of spinning are lamentably low at present, by no means affording to the labourer the means of subsistence.

The good effects indeed of habitual industry are in nothing more apparent than this fact: that the labours of the wheel are still continued under the discouraging circumstances of unrewarded exertions; for, if the prices of flax are considered and compared to the out-proceeds of yarn, it will, I am sure, be found on the computation that the spinner has little or nothing for his labour.

The prices of yarn by the spangle are 2s for coarse and 1s 8d for fine. This yarn is partly employed in home manufacture, partly sold for exportation. The spinners usually grow their own flax. The double wheel for spinning with both hands is unknown.

Preparation of Yarn

The weaver purchases yarn in the same state in which it is seen in the market and afterwards prepares it for the loom himself by an imperfect process of bleaching. The ashes used for this purpose will cost 2s 6d; the yarn is afterwards to be spooled and warped. The former operation costs 1s 6d, the latter 1s 1d.

There are no linen greens in this vicinity; by the establishment of such greens, the manufacture would undoubtedly be much facilitated and improved.

Quality of Webs

The description of linens manufactured in this quarter is that denominated the Coleraine web, consisting of upwards of 50 yards and varying from 11 hundred to 13 hundred. The present prices of such linen is from 11d to 1s 1d per yard. The market of Strabane is that where the linen is sent to be disposed of.

Wool

The woollen manufacture in this district is inconsiderable: I might say a nonentity. A few people manufacture woollen cloths for their own apparel, and these are coarse and, though strong, not well-looking. This manufacture was, I understand, formerly more extensive, but since the establishing of shops in the neighbouring towns, where handsome woollen cloths are to be purchased, is almost entirely done away.

There are no woollen staplers or sorters here at present and the little wool here made use of is spun universally on the small wheel.

A few females are occasionally employed in knitting woollen stockings, but the sale of such commodities is very limited and uncertain; inconstant employment is to be found by such manufacture.

Farmers generally, I might say universally, shear their sheep twice in the year, first in May and afterwards about the first of November. More wool, it is said, is thus saved nor is the practice with any inconveniences.

Cotton, Kelp and Fisheries

There is no cotton manufacture here of any description nor any kelp as the country is inland.

And for the same reason no fisheries have been established. There are indeed great quantities of fish caught both in the lakes and rivers of this district, such as pike, trout, eel, perch, bream etc. These, when the quantity exceeds immediate consumption, are salted and dried, and go a great way in supporting a number of poor people.

But no markets are hence supplied nor indeed is the fish thus caught often disposed of by sale.

They are rather applied to answer the wants of the original captors; nor could any constant supply of fish be expected from this source, for as waterkeepers are established on all the rivers for the preservation of the salmon, who prevent fishing a great part of the year, an interruption would be thus put to any commercial speculation of this kind.

General Remarks on Economy

It will be seen from a cursory view of the preceding sketch that the district the subject of the above report is wretchedly behind in the 3 great sources of natural prosperity: agriculture, manufacture and commerce.

It may be worthwhile to consider to what causes this slowness of progress in the march of improvement is to be ascribed. And these causes it will not require much sagacity to determine: to the non-residence of landlords or (to speak more properly) the total absence of gentry; the want of roads, canals and other means of communication, and the distance of regular markets, where to dispose of the superabundant produce of industry; to these causes especially, the whole or the greater part of the evil is to be attributed.

It may at first sight seem that the only mischief arising from the non-residence of gentry is the drain of rents thereby occasioned; but this, though the great[est], is not the only complaint. The streams of wealth flowing in from different quarters of an estate into the reservoir of the landlord, to be thence again returned in plentiful and opportune supplies for the improvement of his tenantry, is the happy effect necessarily resulting from the residence of a gentleman on his own property.

The contrary practice cannot be too much duplicated, as cutting the very sinews of industry and destroying in its germ the principle of improvement; but there are other evils, though less apparent yet perhaps of greater malignity, to which this practice gives rise. Among these, one of the most prominent is the want of that spur to industry which the example of the upper ranks is so well calculated to impart.

It has been often justly remarked that example is far more effectual than precept: we imitate when we will not be taught. A gentleman residing on his own estate has it greatly in his power to forward by his own practice the general improvement of all around. He can set before the eyes of the surrounding farmers improved methods of cultivation, useful changes in agricultural instruments of labour etc.; and when the utility of any novel practice is apparent, his neighbours will not be slow to follow in the track.

It cannot be expected that the poor farmer will readily adopt the novelties in these points without the powerful influence of such a example. It is much more likely that he will continue [in the manner] to which he has been accustomed.

His finances are too contracted to hazard contingent experiments. He knows that should such experiments fail, inevitable ruin will stare him in the face. Should the report of the happy effects of the late innovation reach his ears, he disbelieves the rumour. If the testimony be too strong to admit of doubt, he fears lest some unknown circumstance, the difference of soil, the variety of climate, or some untoward accident, should mar the undertaking; but when success invariably attending such innovations is proposed to his view, he cannot but attend to them, he cannot but wish to share in the profits arising from those new discoveries.

Obstructions to Improvement

Another very material obstacle to the improvement of this district is to be found in the want of roads, canals and other means of communication. Shut up on the north west by a chain of craggy mountains, and on the south by Lough Erne, it seems almost wholly excluded from human society. For here that element intended for facilitating the commerce of nations serves only, through want of sufficient nautical vehicles, to bar almost entirely all intercourse.

The only road too, and that very badly kept up, is that which leads from Strabane to Pettigo which, after passing through this village and proceeding about a mile, parts into 2 branches, one of which leads in a south westerly direction to Ballyshannon, the other in a more westerly route to Donegal.

The late Captain Aiken attempted by a new line of road to open the communication between Pettigo and Stranorlar, but from the very inadequate presentments granted by the Donegal grand jury it was never carried farther than about 2 and a half miles and is now, it is feared, abandoned forever since his death.

This district, being bishop's property, is from its tenure unrepresented on the grand jury and consequently the wants and hardships of its inhabitants is scarcely attended to.

Inland Navigation

A few years ago an engineer employed by the Commissioners of Inland Navigation surveyed the grounds in this district situate between Strabane and Lough Erne in order to judge of the practicability of carrying on the canal in that direction. He also surveyed a small easterly line for the same purpose. It was, it is said, clearly ascertained that in consequence of the few locks requisite to be constructed and the abundant supply of water to be derived from the Derg river and other streams contiguous to Lough Derg, the cheapness of expense was decidedly in favour of this district.

At the same time it was hinted that the poverty of the district, affording but scanty supplies of articles for internal commerce, would prove an insuperable obstacle to the furtherance of such a project: were the work intended to be carried on by private subscription, the views of the subscribers looking forward to immediate remuneration should undoubtedly be attended to. But if the undertaking be one designed to be carried into execution by a national grant, might not a question be started whether the advantage, though remote, of improving and rendering valuable in the scale of cultivation a tract now comparatively neglected, should not preponderate against forwarding the interests of a district already far advanced towards the ne plus ultra of cultivation?

Remoteness from Markets

A third obstacle to the improvement of this district is its remoteness from markets whence its superabundant produce might be disposed of. The nearest market towns of any consequence are those of Strabane, Enniskillen and Ballyshannon. Strabane is 20 miles distant from Pettigo, Enniskillen 16, Ballyshannon 12.

The market of Strabane is that to which the linen here manufactured is sent for sale; and generally speaking the poor weaver sets out with a solitary web on his back (for his means will not admit of a more extensive trade) for this distant market. He must be part of at least a day [crossed out: 2 days] on the road; the second he spends in Strabane, either in selling his linen or waiting for payment; and the greater part of a third is taken up in his journey home. It may easily be imagined what a drawback this must be upon industry when considered both in point of expense and waste of time.

A linen market, it is thought, might easily be established in the town of Pettigo which, from its distance from the competition of other markets and the quantities of linen manufactured in the neighbourhood, would probably succeed. But this requires at its first establishment considerable funds for the giving of premiums and the encouragement of buyers; and a non-resident landlord, though the most likely to profit by such a speculation, is the last to look up to for assistance to such a project.

Such are the causes to which the wants and hardships of this district may fairly be laid; and when they are materially considered it will not, methinks, appear surprising that the state of its population should be sent as it is.

The above sketch, hasty and indigested as it must appear, speaks more than volumes to the hearts of the intelligent and humane; and should the perusal of its few pages contribute in the remotest degree to the removal of the distresses of the natives and the improvement of their means of industry, the writer would consider himself amply rewarded.

Parish of Tullaghobegley, County Donegal
Brief Memoir, 1834

SOCIAL ECONOMY

Schools

The underneath sheweth the number of schools in the parish of Tullaghobegley, together with the number of scholars, both males and females, Protestants and Catholics, attending at each school at the time that I visited them, about the beginning of last October. And also the names of the schoolmasters and the amount of their salaries and how paid etc. [Table contains the following headings: name of townland, name of schoolmaster, number of scholars subdivided by religion and sex].

Killult, schoolmaster Jack Smullin; 24 scholars: Protestants 10 males, 6 females; Catholics 5 males, 3 females.

Bedlam, schoolmaster Mr Byrns; 10 scholars: Catholics 6 males, 4 females.

Maherarorty, schoolmaster John Gallagher; 11 scholars: Protestants 2 males; Catholics 8 males, 1 female.

Ardsbeag [insert alternative: Ardsbeg], schoolmaster William Olphert, 3 scholars, all Catholics and males.

Dunlooye [insert alternative: Dunluhy], schoolmaster James McFaddin, 14 scholars, all Catholics, 10 males, 4 females.

[Total] 62: Protestants 12 males, 6 females; Catholics 32 males, 12 females.

NB 4 of the above teachers, namely James McFaddin, William Olphert, John Gallagher and Mr Byrns, have no fixed salary or means of subsistence, only 2d per week from each scholar, which petty sum is paid by the parents of those children that are sent to school under the instruction of these most sublime luminaries of literature. But Jack Smullin, whose name is first on the list, has a salary of 12 pounds a year, exclusive of 2 or 3 pounds sterling that is laid out in supplying his scholars in books and paper, which salary of 12 pounds Smullin gets of Bishop Robison's [Colonel Robertson's] donation. He also gets about 2 acres of land and a free house.

Tradition: Thoar McBride

The following tradition is concerning Thoar McBride. Thoar is the name of a small village in the mountains of Tullaghobegley parish and in the triangle ZY and Blue hill. The village Thoar above mentioned has got its name from a large pyramidical stone which is placed on the summit of a circular, small green hill.

The word thoar is an Irish term signifying "a bush," "a tower" or "a pyramid;" and the reason of it being called Thoar McBride is in consequence of a man of the name of McBride having brought a young woman up to the top of the stone, on the pretence of showing her the natural curiosities of all the rugged and barren appearance of the mountains contiguous in view; but instead of so doing, he ravished her on the top of said stone, as the narrowness and dangers of the place admitted of no defence or assistance on the part of the young woman. From thenceforth said stone is called Thoar McBride and the village is called after the same name.

Tradition: Fairies

NB 'Tis to be observed that the above village Thoar has some singular curiosities both natural and supernatural, as it has of modern date, or those few years back, become the most splendid theatre of the fairy tribe as they infrequently made their appearance in various parts of the said townland to a man by the name of Cauhall Sharkey, whose residence is in the neighbourhood of Thoar.

Said Sharkey is a man of sincerity and truth, of morality, piety and Catholicity. He is also a man of an undaunted courage and mostly sees those supernatural beings in the daytime. The last interview he had with them was in or about 16 months ago. They appeared to him in the human and ordinary size.

He tells that he knows or is acquainted with several of them, i.e. such of them as he knew in this life or before they died, although they appear very pale and discoloured and in a mutinizing and fighting appearance. He tells that they have their regular chieftains and officers, and sometimes the Connaught party offers violence and abuse to him but always relieved by the Ulster division. Nor would he always escape their violence with safety, were it not for the interference of a young man by the name of O'Neil from Connaught, who was killed in battle fought in the parish of Conwal near Letterkenny, in a place called Castle Wholme, which was anciently called in Irish Brissue-na-scaribheshoilsea.

And that was the time that the townland of Drimmenaugh got its name, which is a townland between Letterkenny and Rathshedog. The reason of it being so called: after the above battle was fought, a great number was found dead on each side, to such a degree that their military horses were without a single person to own them. They grazed about at pleasure until the saddles fell off, either rotten or by other movements, at which time many of them, were found on the above-named place. Drim signifies "a back" and eagh signifies "a steed." When the word drim is applied when speaking of land, it shows that it is a rising ground with a descent on each side and so Drimmenaugh appear in like form.

But to return to my former subject concerning those spirits that frequently appear to Mr Sharkey, I have to observe that there is another man, a resident of the town or village of Thoar, by the name of Daniel Gallagher, whom I have heard telling that he was coming home after night with 2 cwt of meal in a sack on his back, he met with a crowd of the above species. They played the violin very melodiously and travelled slowly along with him.

They all appeared to be in men's dress with the exception of 1 woman. They asked him to dance to their music. He consented as he dare not refuse, and danced with the woman. They lifted the sack on him again, the woman always desiring him to not fear. They played their music and left him safe at his own house, and went off without any harm.

Several other of such similar circumstances have happened in Rosses, which may be recorded if this meets your honour's approbation.

[Countersigned] W.E. Delves Broughton, Lieutenant Royal Engineers, 1st January 1835.

Parish of Urney, County Donegal

Statistical Report by Lieutenant I.I. Wilkinson, March 1836

NATURAL STATE

Name: Urney

Urney "the nurse of health," which is supposed to be the English meaning of the word, is pronounced as it is written. The proportion of the inhabitants who lives to 70 and 80 years age is greater than in many of the neighbouring parishes.

Locality

The parish of Urney is situate partly in the county of Tyrone and barony of Strabane and partly in the county of Donegal, barony of Raphoe. The Donegal portion occupies the south east extremity of the barony of Raphoe.

Urney is bounded by the parishes of Camus juxta Mourne, Ardstraw and Skirts of Urney and Ardstraw in the county of Tyrone, Donaghmore and Clonleigh in the county of Donegal. It belongs to the diocese of Derry.

The greatest length from north east to south west is about 8 and a half miles, the greatest breadth from south east to north west about 5 and three-quarter miles; mean length 6 and a half miles, mean breadth 3 and a half miles.

The Tyrone portion includes [blank] townlands, containing 9,185 acres 8 perches of land and 99 acres 1 rood 25 perches of water. The Donegal portion includes 36 townlands, containing 5,172 acres 1 rood 30 perches of land and 32 acres 2 roods 6 perches of water. The whole parish therefore contains land 14,357 acres 1 rood 38 perches, water 131 acres, 3 roods 31 perches, 14,489 acres 1 rood 29 perches.

NATURAL FEATURES

Hills

The hills are not generally distinguished by name from the townland in which they are situated. The principal are Fearn hill in the Donegal portion, which rises to the height of 753 feet above the sea; and in the Tyrone part Whiskey hill, 667 feet, Urney hill, 473 feet and Carricklee, 235 feet above the sea.

Rivers and Floods

The 2 principal rivers are the Mourne and Finn, the former separating the parish of Urney from that of Camus on the east and the north, the latter in its course dividing the parishes of Donaghmore and Clonleigh from the parish of Urney on the west and north, and also separating some portions of the parish that are situated in the county of Donegal from others in the county of Tyrone. It is not, however, the chief boundary or division. Many townlands in the parish that are situated in the county Donegal lie to the south of those that are situated in the county of Tyrone.

These 2 rivers, though running for some miles of their course within a few miles of each other, are as dissimilar in character as it can be well conceived. The Mourne, for the entire of its course through the parish of Urney, is shoaly and rocky, very picturesque, but totally useless in point of navigation. There is not sufficient depth for the smallest row-boat to come up to Strabane, which is not more than three-quarters of a mile from its junction with the Finn.

This latter river, on the contrary, is deep and sluggish, running through a valley of the richest soil and navigable in its whole course through the parish for boats of a certain construction carrying from 60 to 80 tons. Were it not that there are 3 fords, one near Urney House, another at Clady <Claudy> and a third at Magheracallaghan, vessels of any tonnage might ply safely between Lifford and Castlefinn, a distance of 7 miles.

A company, consisting of landed proprietors chiefly, was formed for the improvement of the navigation of the Finn, and a steamboat was built so constructed as to draw but a very few inches of water, for the purpose of towing vessels to and from Derry; but the reaches of the Finn were found too short and numerous and the steamboat was given up.

One enterprising member of the company, who has property in the neighbourhood of Castlefinn, has built vessels that seem to answer for the navigation of this river very well. In contrary winds and calm they are obliged to be tracked by men. It would be very expensive to form a towpath, particularly on account of the floods which rise very suddenly after heavy rains. When these happen at new moon and full, the spring tides cause the river to rise more than 12 feet and the whole valley of the Finn becomes one sheet of water.

The deposit left by the subsiding of these floods is of the most fertilizing kind and the meadows and pasture are consequently very luxuriant, but the value of them to the tenant is much diminished in consequence of the hay crop, when growing or cut, being liable to the flood. A small outlay of capital by the proprietors along the river, in throwing up an embankment sufficiently high to keep out the summer floods, would much increase the value of these meadows and the comforts of the tenants.

The floods in the Mourne rise very rapidly, but from the precipitous nature of its channel the deposit left by it is rather hurtful than beneficial. It sometimes so happens, from the falling of rain in the Tyrone mountains, that a high flood will rise in the Mourne while the Finn remains at its ordinary height. In this case the waters of the Mourne run for some miles up the Finn and cause the townlands to be overflowed.

The town of Strabane suffers much from the spring and autumn floods. They have been known to rise so high in the houses built in the lower grounds as 5 and 6 feet. When the flood rises in the night, the distress to the inhabitants is greatly augmented.

Both these rivers abound in salmon but the fish of the Finn are very easily distinguished from those of the Mourne, which are of a darker colour and are thickly covered with bright red spots.

The parish is well supplied with water from rivulets and springs. No mineral springs have been discovered.

Bogs

The bogs are generally small and are quickly being cut out; most of the turf burnt in the parish is cut in the mountains. There is in almost every bog an indication of the presence of bog iron.

Very little timber occurs in these bogs.

Climate and Crops

The climate, though humid, is not unhealthy. The quantity of rain that falls between the months of September and March is very considerable. For some years past there has been very little frost or snow, and the severity of the winter has been perceptibly extending itself into the spring of the year while the months of December and January have been unusually mild.

The severe storms generally set in from the north west and are usually accompanied by heavy showers of rain or sleet. It has been remarked during the last 3 winters that much vivid lightning and occasional heavy peals of thunder have been concomitant on these storms.

The summer seasons have been of late years very favourable to the agriculturalist, so dry that the turf has been uniformly well saved, and yet the rain has fallen so seasonably in the month of July that the potatoes have been very abundant. A warm summer is quite essential to the hill farmer: in cold damp summers his crop does not ripen.

In this place it may not be amiss to allude to a disease that for the last 4 or 5 years has shewn itself to an alarming extent in the seed of the potato and which is attributed, among various other causes, to the mildness of the winters occasioning vegetation among the crop soon after it had been dug and pitted in the fields.

It was first observed about 4 years back in this district of Ireland that, in several instances, the seed when set did not germinate but mouldered away with something of a dry rot. At first this was very partial but for the 2 succeeding years it was so general as to excite alarm that the staple esculent of the country was about to desert it. Last year, however, the evil was very apparently declining, the number of missed crops being very few.

There have been premiums offered for the discovery of a remedy for this disease in the potato seed by the Dublin Society but hitherto no specific has been obtained. The farmers have been recommended not to dig their crop till fully ripe and to be very particular in pitting them dry.

Modern Topography

Public Buildings: Church

The church is a plain building without a tower, little more than a century old, calculated to hold about 300 persons. It is found insufficient for an increasing congregation. The rectory, called Urney House, is a very handsome commodious house situated between the mail coach road to Derry from Sligo and the River Finn, over which it looks into the county Donegal. The former residence of the clergyman was accidentally burnt down about 40 years since.

The present Bishop of Ossory, Dr Robert Fowler, was at that time rector of Urney and it is owing to his taste and liberality that the parish of Urney enjoys one of the best clerical residences in this province. The present rectory house was built by him at his own private cost and it must have been very considerable.

Presbyterian Meeting House

There is a Presbyterian meeting house and Roman Catholic chapel, both plain modern buildings.

The former is situated on the crossroad from Clady to Newtownstewart. It is stated to have been built upwards of a century and will contain about 600 persons.

Catholic Chapel

The Roman Catholic chapel is situated in the townland of Dunnyloop and was originally built in 1735. It was rebuilt in 1824 at an expense of 370 pounds by the congregation and will contain about 800 persons. The parish priest, the Revd Mr O'Donnell, has 2 curates. The Roman Catholic parish includes the parish of Skirts of Urney and Ardstraw.

Seceding Meeting House

There is a Seceders' meeting house in the townland of Upper Alt, built in the year 1834 by the congregation at an expense of about 176 pounds. It will hold about 300 persons. The Revd Samuel Stewart officiates. He receives the sum of 30 pounds annually from the Home Mission Society and about 25 pounds per annum from his hearers.

PRODUCTIVE ECONOMY

Fairs

There were 4 fairs in the year at Clady, an inconsiderable village situated on the Finn river. 2 of these fairs have been transferred to Strabane, the others are held on the 16th May and 16th November. They are commonly called "rabble fairs" and are merely for the accommodation of the neighbourhood in changing servants. No cattle are brought to them, but coarse stockings and socks manufactured in the country are sold and little else with the exception of whiskey.

The fairs in fact seem to benefit no portion of the community but the keepers of public houses and, as being a source of quarrels and disorderly conduct on the part of those who frequent them, it is desirable that they should be altogether abolished.

MODERN TOPOGRAPHY

Gentlemen's Seats

Urney Park, the seat of the late Sir James Galbraith Bart and at which his widow Lady Galbraith is constantly resident, is a handsome modern house with portico situated in an extensive demesne looking over the plantations which divide it from the mail coach road to Sligo and over the grounds of Urney House to the River Finn, the picturesque hill of Crohan on the opposite side of the river forming a pleasing background and termination to the prospect in the north west.

In the grounds here, which were much improved by plantations and enclosures in the lifetime of the late proprietors, is one of the most perfect and well-placed Danish forts that I have yet seen. It commands the country on all sides and is not, as is most generally the case, commanded by any adjacent height. There has been no discovery of any entrance into it.

Gallony, John Smith Esquire, and Finn Cottage, belonging to Conolly Gage Esquire, situated on the banks of the Finn river near Castlefinn.

The landed proprietors of the parish are chiefly non-resident or have their country residences in other parts of the country, such as Lord Abercorn who has a large property in this parish while his country seat is at Baronscourt in the parish of Ardstraw, the Revd Peter Maxwell residing at Birdstown in the county of Donegal.

Manufactories and Mills

Weaving is general in the winter months when the people are not employed in husbandry. The females in the cabins were formerly much employed in spinning, but since the flax spinning mills have been introduced there is so little to be obtained by the wheel that it is fast falling into disuse.

There is at this moment a most extensive flax spinning mill being erected by a Belfast company, who have recently obtained by lease from Lord Abercorn the most advantageous site on the River Mourne. Much benefit is likely to be derived to the poor of this neighbourhood from this establishment, in the increased means of employment it will offer, and the flax grower will find a ready and convenient market for his produce at his door, which he is now obliged to carry to Derry for sale.

The price of flax has been greatly increased since the spinning [of] it by machinery has been introduced and the result already is manifest in the improved circumstances of the farming class. The females find occupation now in preparing the flax for the scutching mills, of which there are several in the parish. These, however, appear of but an indifferent construction and are already found quite inadequate to prepare the increasing supply of flax for the market.

Parish of Urney

There are no breaking mills in this side of the north which are so common in Antrim and Down and by which the process of making flax ready for market is much expedited. There are a few oatenmeal mills in the parish, generally on the same site with the flax mills and turned by the same stream.

The Sion mill was built in 1828 by the Marquis of Abercorn and intended for a flour mill. It is now let as a flax mill with 100 acres of land to Lions Herdsman [Lyons Herdman] and Co., at a rent of 200 pounds per annum. 100 females are employed at the mill at from 1s to 6d per day, 40 hacklers at from 1s to 2s per day and about 12 boys at 4d per day.

The machinery cost about 5,000 pounds, is of 20 horsepower and will spin 1 and a half tons of flax per diem. The diameter of the wheel is 18 feet, breadth 5 feet and fall of water 10 feet.

The tenants of Conolly Gage Esquire are bound to the corn mill and kiln in Magheracallaghan, which is held forever by Mr McCurdy, with a farm of 20 acres, at a chief rent of 56 pounds per annum. He charges the 30th grain, the diameter of the wheel is 12 feet, the fall of water 26 feet.

The same stream is conveyed from the corn mill to a flax mill, where the charge for cleaning flax is 5s per cwt. The diameter of the wheel is 10 feet and the fall of water 6 feet; both wheels are middle-shot.

Communications

The mail coach roads from Londonderry to Dublin and to Sligo pass through this parish, the former parallel to the Mourne and close to its bank, the latter parallel to the Finn and in view of it.

There are numerous crossroads which are kept in repair by the grand jury presentment. Many of them are not in the best order, owing to the absence of the landlords from their properties and the want of influential persons to forward the necessary presentments on them at road sessions and assizes.

Bridges

Clady bridge, a structure of 9 water arches and 5 land ones to increase the passage of the water in time of floods, crosses the Finn on the road from Strabane to Sligo, at about 4 miles from the former place; the date of erection unknown but it is stated that the bridge was broken in the year 1688 to stop the advance of King James' army.

The bridge was built and repaired at the expense of the county by grand jury presentments and in 1832 the company for improving the navigation of the river rebuilt 3 arches with a greater height and span, to admit the passage of the steamboat.

SOCIAL ECONOMY

Early Improvements

There has been a considerable improvement in the mode of agriculture in this part of the country, chiefly owing to the encouragement given by the North West Farming Society for several years in the shape of premiums for best plowing, crop and stock. The drill husbandry is very general in the lower portion of the parish, but where in the hills the ground is being reclaimed the spade is used exclusively. There is a large portion of reclaimable land in the hilly district of the parish on which are limestone and fuel.

Conolly Gage Esquire gives his tenantry great encouragement to reclaim land by allowing them so much per perch for fencing, and limestone and turf to burn it with. Were the same policy generally adopted, I am persuaded many of the farming class who now emigrate to America would remain at home and find their native hills a more lucrative, as well as agreeable, field for their industry.

The ground is certainly reclaimable at a very small proportional expense and when the risk and cost of removal is taken into account, there can be no question between such a location at home and a settlement in the western forests.

Obstructions to Improvement

The chief obstacle to improvements appears to be the absence of the fostering and enlightening presence of the landed proprietors on their several estates, which are too generally exclusively under the management of agents or rather receivers, who have no sympathies with the people and seem to have but one object in view, viz. the levy of the rent whatever that may be. This would seem but a small portion of the duties of an agent, but it is all that too many of them conceive they are called upon to do, and they make little or no enquiry into the circumstances of the tenantry over whom they are placed.

The consequence is that lands have been divided and subdivided till the same portion of ground that formerly was considered only sufficient to keep up one or two respectable farmers is now occupied by several struggling families who would be considered paupers rather than farmers in any other country.

The former elective franchise, when a 40s freeholder was considered the qualification for a voter, was an additional means of increasing the number of petty landholders, and while the linen trade flourished, the evil of overpopulation was not felt as the loom paid the rent, which it is now entirely left for the land to do.

The low price of grain is much against the agriculturalist, where a farm is of sufficient magnitude and good quality of ground. The improved price of flax latterly has told much in the farmers' favour.

Local Government

This parish, though of so great extent and so populous, has not a magistrate residing in it nor is there a single policeman within its bounds. The habits of the people are industrious and peaceable. The cases that arise in it requiring the intervention of the law are very few compared with the neighbouring parishes, and the magistrates presiding at the neighbouring petty sessions of Strabane have fewer offences brought before them from this than any other portion of their district.

Those who are competent to decide on the point with whom I have conversed attribute much of the peace of the parish to the absence of party feeling. All religious denominations are on a friendly footing and it is remarkable, as I am informed, that in the case of an Urney man being attacked in a distant fair or market, the men of the same parish, without respect to sect or political opinion, will one and all come to the assistance of their neighbour.

Dispensaries

There is a dispensary at Strabane which takes Urney parish under its care. Many subscribers live in this parish and the poor are reasonably well-off for medical assistance.

The principal diseases among the people arise from bad food or damp houses and are rheumatism, dyspepsia and typhus fever. The latter has not been so prevalent since the introduction of the Asiatic cholera, while the increase of stomach complaints is very evident. The scrofula is common among even the lowest class of the peasantry and the itch is so ordinary a complaint that is not considered in the light of a disorder by the people. The younger portion of each family, in numerous instances among the lower orders, have this very filthy and infectious complaint. It is attributed to the general use of oatenmeal as food.

Poor

The destitute poor, by which term I mean to describe such persons as from age or infirmity are unequal to labour, have no settled provision; their condition is about the most wretched that can be well conceived. They are generally the remnant of some farming families who either by misfortune or, what is oftener the case, by improvidence and profligacy have been compelled to give up the lands which was formerly their support.

They maintain themselves chiefly by begging and collect from the farmers of the country (many of whom are hardly in a better condition than themselves) potatoes and meal. They reside in wretched hovels which are usually granted them by the present occupier of the farm which formerly belonged to themselves or families. For some of these miserable huts they will pay so much as 1 pound per annum, but how they are enabled to make up such a sum it is hard to imagine.

Benevolence

There is a sum of 25 pounds per annum, the interest of a legacy left for the benefit of the poor of this parish by a Mr Sproule, annually at the disposal of the clergyman of the Established Church, for their use; to this he has been able to procure subscriptions from a few of the absentee landlords amounting to 22 pounds annually. Many of the most wealthy proprietors in the parish give nothing, nor can I discover any trace of their contributing either directly or indirectly to the support of the destitute poor on their estates.

With the monies arising from the above very limited sources, the rector has this year been enabled to relieve with clothing and money about 170 individuals. It were much to be desired that some means could be devised to ensure support to the aged and infirm when they are no longer able to maintain themselves.

Charitable Report

Copy of printed report, parish of Urney. First annual report of the distribution of clothing and cash from the Sproule and other charitable monies in the parish of Urney for the year ending December 31st 1835.

80 blankets, 40 yards printed long cloth, 60 yards grey calico, 20 yards of cloth for coating 2 yards wide, 35 yards grey clothing 2 yards wide, 30 yards of corduroy, 40 yards of flannel, 2 quilts, thread and buttons.

By the distribution of the above articles, with cash to 14 individuals in sickness or extreme distress, upwards of 150 of the destitute and deserving poor of the parish have been relieved at an expense to our funds of about 40 pounds, leaving a balance in the treasurer's hands, when the subscriptions shall have been received, amounting to about 6 pounds 5s, as the annexed account will show.

In making this our first report, we beg to offer our thanks to those landlords who have so kindly contributed to our fund and at the same time to express our deep regret that in future years we shall be obliged to limit our distribution to the poor on those estates alone, the proprietors of which contribute to our funds.

We have this year broken through the rule of our society which limits the objects of our charity to the poor on the properties of subscribers. The hope that the liberality of those landlords who have hitherto been solicited but in vain to subscribe to our funds will enable us at our next annual distribution to include the many very wretched objects on their lands among the persons to be relieved. Robert Hume, rector, R. Porter and John Crowe, churchwardens, Jeremiah Gill, William Inch Senior, John Patton, James Hamilton.

NB It having been supposed that the children at the Urney female schools were clothed out of the charitable monies of the parish, we beg to state that about 40 of them received cloaks or frocks as a reward for their diligence and good conduct from the patroness of the schools, without the aid of 1s from our funds.

The dinner also which was given on Monday last to the scholars of both the male and female schools of Urney, and at which were present 95 children besides their teachers, was from private sources.

Accounts for the year 1835: interest of Sproule fund 25 pounds per annum; Lieutenant-Colonel Barnard 10 pounds per annum; Conolly Gage Esquire 4 pounds per annum; Miss Jones Agnew 3 pounds per annum; Daniel Wauchob Esquire 1 pound per annum; John Chambers Esquire 1 pound per annum; Revd Robert Hume 5 pounds per annum; [total] 49 pounds.

Expenditure on purchasing blankets etc. 40 pounds; cash to 14 individuals in sickness and distress 2 pounds 15s; balance in favour of charity 6 pounds 5s; total 49 pounds.

Names of those landlords not resident on their properties within this parish who have been applied to but without effect in aid of our fund for clothing and supporting the poor: Most Noble the Marquis of Abercorn, William Law Bestall Esquire, Revd P. Maxwell, Revd Charles Irving, Donaghmore, John Fenton Esquire, Dublin.

Religion

As is the case generally in this division of the country, the religion of the community is divided into Episcopalian, Protestants or members of the Established Church, Presbyterians and Roman Catholics. The members of each, according to a very accurate census lately made by the Commissioners of Education Enquiry, are as follows: members of the Established Church 1,136, Roman Catholics 4,060, Presbyterians 1,670, total 6,866; and from enquiry made in 1835, vide table, it appears that in the Donegal portion of the parish there were 366 families which, on an average of 5 to each, would give a population of 1,830 persons for that part.

Habits of the People

The people are industrious, and if there were employment in proportion to the willingness of the peasantry to work, much benefit would result to the community at large. The character of the lower order here is peaceable and orderly, and I am informed there is no party work on one side or the other.

In the winter months weaving and spinning forms the chief occupation of the cottagers and in the other seasons they are busied in agriculture.

Their chief food is the potato and salt herrings with milk where a cow is kept, and oatenmeal. Though the weekday clothing of the lower orders is often of the worst appearance, still on Sundays and market days they are most comfortably clad with the exception of the destitute poor. In their cabins they are dirty to a degree. Many stow their potatoes under their beds and the manure heap is generally at the threshold of the door.

PRODUCTIVE ECONOMY

General Economy

Besides the produce of the land, which is generally wheat, oats, potatoes, hay and flax, there is a considerable quantity of linen wove in the parish which is carried to the neighbouring markets of Strabane and Newtownstewart. Much butter is also made in this district which meets a ready sale at Strabane.

Several industrious poor women obtain a livelihood by gathering eggs through the country and selling them to the dealers, who take them to Derry for exportation. Pigs are fed by even the poorest cottiers and usually share the house with him, claiming right to do so as contributing to pay the rent for him.

Proprietors

The Bishop of Derry, Marquis of Abercorn, heirs of Sir James Galbraith Bart, Conolly Gage Esquire, Revd Peter Maxwell, Lieutenant-Colonel Bernard, Miss Jones Agnew and several landlords, deriving from 100 to 500 [pounds] per annum. None of the above are resident within the parish except the widow of the late Sir James Galbraith; consequently there is a great drainage of rents constantly being carried off to be spent elsewhere. This is not so great an evil as the absence of the protection and fostering care of the natural guardian of the tenantry, many of whom do not see their landlord for several years.

Rents

On the whole, the rents may be considered as moderate. Tenants holding from year to year a few acres with a house will be able to procure often so much as 100 [pounds?] for their goodwill of a farm that they have not an hour's lease of. The average of the best lands, I should say, is 30s per acre, while the next class is about 1 pound per acre. The mountain farms are let in the lump.

The cottier tenants, that is the persons who work for the farmer, are generally much oppressed. I have known several farms of considerable extent, a few acres of which have been set off with some miserable huts to a few cottiers whose rents have enabled the immediate tenant of the head landlord to sit rent free.

Many of these poor people pay their rents in labour which is lower than the general rates of the country, but they are so bound to their landlords that they are obliged to submit to their terms, however unfair they may be. I attribute all this wrong to the inefficiency or inactivity of the agents on the properties where it occurs, and might readily be prevented by a little more surveillance on their parts.

Husbandry

Crops and grazing and planting: in the low grounds the drill husbandry is very generally followed with rotation of crops, viz. 2 crops of corn out of the lea ground, then potatoes with manure, afterwards lay down with wheat, flax or oats. In the upper portion of the parish the spade is necessarily used from the nature of the ground and oats and potatoes seem to be the alternate crop sown.

The tenantry in the high grounds grow no hay and feed their cattle in winter usually on oaten straw, which is shorn very close to the ground, and much grass is consequently in the butts of the sheaves.

Except along the banks of the Finn little is done in the way of grazing, and even here there is a great interruption to the graziers' proceedings by means of the floods that often cover their fields so long as a week at a time.

The cattle of this part of the country are of a very middling description. Any of a superior class are purchased up the country, chiefly in the fairs of Sligo and Fermanagh.

Draining is not carried on to the extent it might be with great benefit to the tenantry, where labour is so cheap. As usual there is little or no planting in this parish, though much of the ground could not be put to any more profitable use.

River Fisheries

The proprietors on the banks of the Finn and Mourne have the right of fishing with nets for salmon. They are not, however, taken in sufficient quantities in either river to dignify them with the name of fisheries.

SOCIAL ECONOMY

Advowson

The living of Urney is a rectory entire in the gift of the Lord Bishop of Derry. The tithes are valued under the Tithe Composition Act at 700 pounds per annum, liable to a deduction of 15 pounds per cent to the landlords under Lord Stanley's act and to a considerable percentage to the Ecclesiastical Commissioners.

The present rector, the Revd Robert Hume, is constantly resident and employs 2 curates, the senior at a salary of 100 pounds per annum. The patronage of the perpetual cure of the Skirts of Urney is in the rector of Urney for the time being, this district having been separated from the parish of Urney about 30 years ago.

The glebe is set to a respectable tenantry at 200 pounds per annum.

ANCIENT TOPOGRAPHY

Antiquities: Stones

In the townland of Upper Alt, close to the east side of the road from Castlefinn to Castlederg and

Parish of Urney

about 3 miles from the former place, are some remarkable stones bearing the appearance of antiquity and called the Giant's Grave. The stones are 5 in number, 3 standing and 2 fallen. The largest standing stone is 5 feet high and seems sunk about 1 foot in the ground. The 2 fallen are each 6 feet in length about 4 broad and 2 thick.

Danish Forts

There are several of the circular enclosures called Danish forts. The most perfect and best placed is in Urney Park. A passage has been discovered in one situated in the townland of Scot-town, the sides built with large stones and covered with single flags. Nothing remarkable was found in it.

Another fort in the townland of Drimdoit is still well defined on its western side.

Mansion

There is an old mansion about 10 perches to the south of Clady village which by some people is called the Castle but more generally the Grave. It was built in 1764 by a Mr Maxwell, but the property is said to have been presented to him by the Hamiltons.

SOCIAL ECONOMY

Table of Townlands

Statistical table of the parish of Urney, as taken from census and enquiry made in the year 1835. [Table contains the following headings: name of townland, number of houses and families, name of landlord].

Alt Lower, 8 inhabited buildings, 10 dwelling houses and families, 7 outhouses, 2 in ruins, 17 total buildings, landlord Mr Lecky.

Alt Upper, 32 inhabited buildings, 40 dwelling houses and families, 29 outhouses, 3 in ruins, 64 total buildings, landlord Revd Mr Irving.

Ballylast, 9 inhabited buildings, 10 dwelling houses and families, 3 outhouses, 2 in ruins, 14 total buildings, landlord Lady Galbraith.

Calhame, 8 inhabited buildings, 13 dwelling houses and families, 8 outhouses, 3 in ruins, 19 total buildings, landlord Revd Mr Irving.

Cavanaweery, 4 inhabited buildings, 4 dwelling houses and families, 1 uninhabited house, 4 outhouses, 1 in ruins, 10 total buildings, landlord Conolly Gage Esquire.

Cloughfin, 10 inhabited buildings, 10 dwelling houses and families, 6 outhouses, 1 in ruins, 17 total buildings, landlord Lady Galbraith.

Cormakelly, 18 inhabited buildings, 22 dwelling houses and families, 7 outhouses, 5 in ruins, 30 total buildings, landlord Conolly Gage Esquire.

Coolyslinn, 12 inhabited buildings, 13 dwelling houses and families, 12 outhouses, 1 in ruins, 25 total buildings, landlord Conolly Gage Esquire.

Drimdoit, 22 inhabited buildings, 29 dwelling houses and families, 11 outhouses, 3 in ruins, 36 total buildings, landlord Conolly Gage Esquire.

Drimnaha, 7 inhabited buildings, 9 dwelling houses and families, 3 outhouses, 2 in ruins, 12 total buildings, landlord Conolly Gage Esquire.

Drimbane, 8 inhabited buildings, 17 dwelling houses and families, 3 outhouses, 1 in ruins, 12 total buildings, landlord Conolly Gage Esquire.

Dunnyloop, 4 inhabited buildings, 4 dwelling houses and families, 3 outhouses, 7 total buildings, landlord Conolly Gage Esquire.

Dresnagh, 7 inhabited buildings, 7 dwelling houses and families, 6 outhouses, 13 total buildings, landlord Conolly Gage Esquire.

Fearn, 31 inhabited houses, 35 dwelling houses and families, 2 uninhabited houses, 21 outhouses, 54 total buildings, landlord Conolly Gage Esquire.

Foyfin, 12 inhabited buildings, 15 dwelling houses and families, 8 outhouses, 3 in ruins, 23 total buildings, landlord Conolly Gage Esquire.

Gortnagrace, 35 inhabited buildings, 40 dwelling houses and families, 13 outhouses, 2 in ruins, 50 total buildings, landlord Mr Browne.

Gortkelly, 8 inhabited buildings, 10 dwelling houses and families, 2 outhouses, 10 total buildings, landlord Conolly Gage Esquire.

Graffy, 9 inhabited buildings, 13 dwelling houses and families, 6 outhouses, 15 total buildings, landlord Conolly Gage Esquire.

Halftown, 7 inhabited buildings, 14 dwelling houses and families, 6 outhouses, 2 in ruins, 15 total buildings, landlord Conolly Gage Esquire.

Kellysmeadow, landlord Conolly Gage Esquire.

Magheracallaghan, 4 inhabited buildings, 4 dwelling houses and families, 7 outhouses, 11 total buildings, landlord Mr McCurdy.

Millfarm, 4 inhabited buildings, 6 dwelling houses and families, 3 outhouses, 7 total buildings, landlord Mr McCurdy.

Mullanbwee, 7 inhabited buildings, 8 dwelling houses and families, 2 outhouses, 1 in ruins, 10 total buildings, landlord Dr Finton.

Rogan's Park, 1 inhabited building, 1 dwelling

house and family, 2 outhouses, 3 total buildings, landlord Conolly Gage Esquire.

Skelpy, 19 inhabited buildings, 19 dwelling houses and families, 12 outhouses, 2 in ruins, 33 total buildings, landlord Conolly Gage Esquire.

Tullyard, 9 inhabited buildings, 13 dwelling houses and families, 5 outhouses, 14 total buildings, landlord Conolly Gage Esquire.

Totals: 295 inhabited buildings, 366 dwelling houses and families, 3 uninhabited houses, 189 outhouses, 34 in ruins, 521 total buildings.

Schools

[Table contains the following headings: situation, number of pupils subdivided by religion and sex, remarks as to how supported].

Urney Glebe, Protestants 20 males, 30 females, Presbyterians 10 males, 20 females, Roman Catholics 5 males, 10 females, total 95; this school is supported by the rector and Mrs Hume, by a subscription of 3 pounds per annum from Lady Galbraith and by the children's payments. The master's name is John Crowe, the mistress Jane Gwynne.

Upper Alt, Protestants 2 males, 1 female, Presbyterians 9 males, 9 females, Roman Catholics 16 males, 8 females, total 45; the master of this school has nothing to depend on but the children's payments, which amount to about 13 pounds 10s per annum. His name is Francis McDivett, a Roman Catholic. The scholars are taught reading, writing and arithmetic, and are charged the sum of 1s 6d each quarter.

Upper Alt, Protestants 32 males, 10 females, Presbyterians 6 males, 7 females, Roman Catholics 1 male, 1 female, total 57. This school was supported by Kildare Place Society but, owing to the government grant being withdrawn, the master only receives an acre of land from the society and is supported by the children's payments, amounting to about 6 pounds per annum, and a donation of 2 pounds per annum from the rector. The scholars learn reading, writing and arithmetic, and are charged 1s 1d each per quarter. The master's name is William Katerson, a Protestant. Divine service is performed in this schoolhouse on Sunday afternoons.

Drimdoit, Protestants 8 males, Presbyterians 1 male, 6 females, Roman Catholics 8 males, 11 females, total 34. The master of this school is John Elliott, a Presbyterian. He has nothing to depend on but the children's payments, which amount to about 10 pounds 4s per annum. The scholars learn reading, writing and arithmetic, and are charged the sum of 1s 6d each per quarter.

Tullywhisker, Protestants 8 males, 9 females, Presbyterians 39 males, 45 females, Roman Catholics 7 males, 5 females, total 113. This schoolhouse was built in the year 1822 by subscription, the Marquis of Abercorn giving the ground and timber. The master's name is Andrew Smiley, a Protestant. He receives the sum of 10 pounds per annum from the marquis and about 5 pounds per annum from the children, those who are able to pay being charged 1d per week. The school is taught under the system of the Kildare Street Society.

Sion, Protestants 7 males, 1 female, Presbyterians 59 males, 15 females, Roman Catholics 37 males, 9 females, total 128; this school is supported by payments from the scholars. The teacher's name is M. Wade, a Protestant.

[Signed] I.I. Wilkinson, Lieutenant Royal Engineers, 3rd March 1836.

Miscellaneous Papers, County Donegal

Statistical Report of the North East District of the Barony of Raphoe

SOCIAL ECONOMY

Early Improvements

[Copy of] Statistical report of the north east district of the barony of Raphoe in the county of Donegal, comprehending the parishes of All Saints, Taughboyne, Killea, Clonleigh and Raymoghy, 1821.

Sketch of history: the greater part of the inhabitants of these parishes, in common with those of most of the neighbouring districts, are the descendants of emigrants from north Britain who settled here in the reign of James I about the year 1611; and even at present, after a lapse of more than 2 centuries, the language, customs and manners of the people themselves bear indubitable marks of Scottish origin.

They are chiefly of the Presbyterian persuasion and, though their discipline seems now to be rather on the decline, they were formerly exemplary in the observance of religious duties. According to their own account, their clergy enjoyed the church-land and tithes of their respective parishes from their first establishment in Ulster till they were deprived of them in the time of the Commonwealth for refusing obedience to the usurper.

Agriculture and linen manufacture are the principal employments, occupations which have doubtless in many instances descended from sire to son since time immemorial.

NATURAL FEATURES

Climate

No theory whatever appears to be better confirmed by fact or experience than that which accounts for the wetness of the climate of Ireland. The vapours of that part of the immense Atlantic which lies between our extreme parallels are collected by the general prevalence of westerly winds and condensed and deposited on meeting the range of mountains by which our shores are for the most part surrounded. Hence all continued rains and most squalls proceed from that quarter. A north east wind is commonly dry, a south wind more rarely but a continued west wind scarcely ever.

Vide origin, progress and present state of the fund called regium donum prefixed to Dr Black's *Substance of 2 speeches* etc. Dublin 1832.

Soil

A number of well-conducted experiments in different parts of the country are wanting to furnish a complete analysis of the subject, in the absence of which perhaps little more can be done than to give a general idea of the predominant loams and substrata which characterise the soil in different circumstances.

The face of the country for the most part presents the appearance of a vast number of little hills or uplands entirely capable of cultivation, the surface of the southern declivities of which is chiefly composed of a warm, friable brown loam varying in depth from 6 inches to 2 feet, with a subsoil of gravel or red clay and well adapted to the common purpose of vegetation.

In northern aspects a cold, heavy, adhesive, external substratum of a lead colour prevails from 6 to 18 inches in depth on a wet bottom of blue clay mixed with soft slaty stones, to the unproductive quality of which draining and liming are found to be powerful correctives. It may, however, be remarked that lime is of itself an adhesive substance and, though it may warm and fertilize such lands to a certain degree, it is to be doubted whether it increases their viability.

A method lately introduced of applying bare sand to fields of this description has been practised for some time on the shores in the neighbourhood of Newtowncunningham and is found to be amazingly efficacious. The writer has seldom observed a field of this cold quality in a southern exposure except when something negative, a marsh or ill-defined stream immediately above, had been for ages suffered to contaminate the lower lands.

Drains of a sufficient depth, either open or covered according to the nature or value of the waste, would doubtless in few years, with proper cultivation, render the description of loam on lands fronting the south general without a single exception. With a single exception with respect to situation these observations apply to the middle region.

Near the verges of mountains or bogs the above soils in their respective aspects are found to mix gradually with peat, a surface which obtains in the extremes of elevation or depression.

Natural State and Modern Topography

Situation and Boundaries

This district comprehends the north eastern part or half of the barony of Raphoe in the county of Donegal, its eastern boundary lying a little more than 2 miles west of Londonderry and the western limit about 8 miles from the same place. It contains 253 townlands. According to the late returns, the number of acres is 31,235, of houses 4,148 and the population 22,285.

The peculiar fertility of the soil has contributed much to increase the number of inhabitants, which is very considerable with respect to the geographical extent, it being no more than 12 miles by 7 at the utmost computation. It is subdivided into 5 parishes which are as follows.

All Saints, the most northerly of the district, is bounded on the north by the parish of Templemore in the barony of Inishowen, on the east by Killea, on the south by Taughboyne, on the south west by Raymoghy and on the west by Lough Swilly; the greatest length being from Killea bridge on the eastern side to the shore at Ballybegly upwards of 4 miles and a half and the greatest breadth about 2 miles and three-quarters.

There are in this parish 34 townlands containing 5,669 acres, of which 5,281 are arable, 276 mountain and about 112 bog, exclusive of the principal tracts of that description. The number of houses is 634 and of inhabitants 3,682, about 236 of whom are farmers. The highest acreable unit of land 30s for the best land, 20s for middling and about 15s per acre for an inferior description.

The measurement of land is computed by the Scotch or Cunningham measure of 6 and a quarter yards to the perch all over the district, with the exception of Marquis of Abercorn's estate where the plantation or Irish acre prevails.

Newtowncunningham

Newtowncunningham is the only principal town. It has 4 fairs yearly but no market, and it contains 169 inhabitants who subsist chiefly by agriculture and dealing on a very limited scale. It may be proper to remark that the ancient custom of holding courts baron for the manor of Castlecunningham, though long discontinued, has been lately revived in this town.

Ecclesiastical Administration

All Saints was formerly a part of the parish of Taughboyne but in consequence of a misunderstanding between the inhabitants respecting the parish cess, an act was obtained about the year 1772 to enable each part to hold its own vestries, support its own church and perform other separate functions.

During the operation of the late disastrous Townland Fine Bill, the affinity of these parishes was a continual source of ludicrous embarrassment to excise men. Both constitute one distinct living, the same as before their separation. The present rector is the Revd Edward Bowen, a gentleman deservedly beloved.

Boundaries of Taughboyne

Taughboyne, the central parish of the district, is bounded on the north by All Saints, on the north east by Killea, on the east by the River Foyle, on the south by Clonleigh, on the west by the parish of Raphoe and on the north west by that of Raymoghy. The greater length may be [reckoned] from Teroddy north north east to Tullysape south south west upwards of 6 miles and the greatest breadth from Dunmore on the west to Carrickmore on the east about 3 miles and a half.

This parish contains 66 townlands, in which there are 8,667 acres, 7,890 of which are arable, 413 moor or mountain and 364 bog and the same restriction as before. The houses are ascertained to be 1,186 and the inhabitants 6,283. About 373 are farmers and the highest rent is about 2 guineas an acre for the best land, 30s for a second quality and 1 pound per acre for bad land. In the neighbourhood of St Johnstown some of the fields are set so high as 4 guineas and the lowest is said to be 3 per acre.

The general complaint of high rents seems in no part of the district to be better founded than in the latter place as, were it not for the earnings of trade and other similar means, the holders of such lands must soon sink into a state of insolvency.

St Johnstown

St Johnstown is the principal town of this parish. It had formerly a provost and 12 burgesses, and was represented a borough in the Irish House of Commons. Since the Union, by which it was divested of these privileges, its importance has rapidly declined, notwithstanding the natural advantages of its situation, its central position between Londonderry and Strabane and the commercial facilities of which the Foyle is susceptible.

This town contains at present 334 inhabitants, chiefly supposed [supported] by small trades, dealing and agriculture. There is a burying place with a river (probably the remains of a monastery) in this neighbourhood but of its origin no account could be obtained.

Somewhat more than a mile further up the riverside the old castle of Moneygelvin is still seen in tolerable repair. There had been a portico with a winding staircase in front but it has long since been removed. The arched gateway of the courtyard is still standing.

This edifice, which is now converted into a farmhouse, was an ancient residence of the noble family of Hamilton, as appears by an inscription on a marble slab found amongst the rubbish.

It is a curious fact that the glebe land of Carnshennagh in this parish has immemorially belonged to the successive incumbents of Clonleigh.

Boundaries of Killea

Killea, the smallest of these parishes, has Inishowen on the north, the liberties of Derry on the east, the River Foyle on the south, Taughboyne on the south west and All Saints on the west. The greatest length is from the barony mearing on the summit of the Holywell hill north, to Carrigans south about 3 miles, but the breadth is nowhere more than 1.

In this parish there are 13 townlands, 188 houses and 987 inhabitants. The total number of acres is 1,265, of which 1,234 are arable, 31 of mountain, but with the exception of a small common in the neighbourhood of Newtownhamilton, there is no bog of any importance. The rent in this parish in general (does not exceed) 1 guinea per acre for the best, 15s for second sort and for worst about 5s.

Towns in Killea

Carrigans and Newtownhamilton are the principal towns, the former containing 49 houses and 246 inhabitants, the latter 19 houses and 99 of a population. In these, as in other similar towns of the districts, the manner of living is the same as already described. The farmers of this parish, who are but 65 in number, complain much of their rate of tithe. The incumbent for the time being is the Revd Samuel Law of Ashgrove in the vicinity of Carrigans.

Boundaries of Clonleigh

Clonleigh, the southernmost parish of this district, is bounded on the north by the parish of Taughboyne, on the east and south east by the River Foyle, on the south by the River Finn and part of Donaghmore, and on the western side by the parish of Raphoe. The length from the mouth of Sooly at Porthall to the River Finn at Cloughfin, nearly 6 miles, is the farthest computation of this dimension and its greatest breadth somewhat more than 3 miles.

The townlands or subdenominations into which this parish is divided are about 90, Croaghan chapel having no land attached to it and but 1 house and 7 inhabitants. The aggregate of acres is 7,211, the arable 6,892, the mountain land 211 and the quantity of bog 108 acres, subject to the aforesaid limitation. The houses of this parish are 1,136 and the population 6,002. With respect to rent, the lands are set here much the same as in All Saints.

Towns in Clonleigh

Lifford is the principal town not only of this parish but of the county of Donegal. The courts of assize and general sessions of the peace are held here. It contains, according to the late census, 139 families and 914 inhabitants.

There is another town called Ballindrait in this parish, which contains 50 houses and 210 inhabitants. It has 4 fairs annually which consist in sales of cattle, yarn etc. The proximity of Strabane to the above towns is a great obstacle to their improvement and one which no remedy can remove.

Ecclesiastical Administration

This parish belongs to the diocese of Derry. Its last rector was the late Revd Averell Daniel, a gentleman who lived to an advanced age, much esteemed. The lands of Clonleigh were originally granted by James I to Richard Hansard, on the conditions of endowing a classic and English school and furnishing 30 Protestant families with 3 acres of land, a house, garden and commonage to each respectively. The ruins of the old parish church of Clonleigh are still seen in an old burying place at Edenmore.

Boundaries of Raymoghy

Raymoghy or, as it is commonly called, Ray is bounded on the north and north east by All Saints, on the east by Taughboyne, on the south by the parish of Raphoe, on the south west by Leck and on the west by Lough Swilly. The length may be reckoned from Ardee to the southernmost part of

Mondooey 5 miles and a half and the breadth from Taughboyne mearing or Dooish to the shore at Draina little more than 3 miles.

It contains 50 townlands and in these there are 1,004 houses and 5,331 inhabitants. The number of farmers is about 397 and the quantity of land 8,423 acres; the arable is estimated at 7,694, the mountain 529 and the bog at 186 acres. The highest rent in this parish is 1 pound 10s per acre. There is middling land let in some places at a guinea and bad land at 15s per acre.

The principal town is Manorcunningham, which contains 60 houses and 227 inhabitants; there are fairs held here.

The rector of this parish, the Revd John Ussher, archdeacon, a gentleman venerated by all classes of his acquaintance and who needs only be heard of to be esteemed.

At the graveyard of Balleaghan in this parish there is the remains of a religious edifice.

PRODUCTIVE ECONOMY

Proprietors

The principal landed proprietors of the north districts are as follows. Non-resident: Marquis of Londonderry; Marquis of Abercorn (a minor); Earl of Wicklow; Earl of Erne; Bishop of Raphoe; Bishop of Derry; the Revd Charles Leslie; the Revd Thomas C. Cowan; James Law Esquire; Harvey Ferguson Esquire; [insert addition: James Sinclair Esquire, Holywell; the proprietors of Argory quarterland; Thomas Patterson Esquire; the proprietors of Plaister].

Resident: Robert Beatson Esquire; William McClintock Esquire, Dunmore; Robert Maxwell Esquire, barrister-at-law; John Chambers Esquire, Lifford; Tasker Keys Esquire, Mullenagung; Miss Keys, Cavanacor; William Patterson Esquire, Mason Lodge, besides several others who hold inconsiderable property in perpetuity in the different parishes yet pay a chief rent to one or other of the above.

Improvers

The phrase "intelligent persons" would doubtless, with few exceptions, be more generally descriptive of this class than that adopted for the sake of method. The following are, however, some of the principal. In the parish of All Saints: Mr James Fulton, Gortenlearm; Mr Alexander Thompson, Moyle; Mr [?] Mallow Hood, Moyle; Mr Henry McCay, Newtowncunningham; Mr John McCay, Newtowncunningham; Mr Samuel Fisher, Drumbwee; Mr William Park, Ballybegley; Mr William Gallagher, Rusky.

Taughboyne: Mr Hamilton Patterson, Churchtown; Mr Oliver Whyte, Clasygowan; Mr David Whyte, Clasygowan; Mr William Latta, Braidy; Mr Henry Wark, Teroday; Mr Hugh Stevenson, Legnathraw; Mr William Smyth, Carrickmore; the Revd Matthew Rodgers, Taughboyne; the Revd Matthew Heron, Haugh.

Killea: Mr William McCrab, Altaghaderry; Mr John Osborne, Maghaderry; Mr George Crockett, Drumnasheer; Mr Thomas Culbert, Killea bridge; Mr James Baird, Carrigans.

Clonleigh: John Chambers Esquire, Lifford; the Revd John Graham, Lifford; Mr Thomas Keys, Clonfad; Mr James Stevenson, Churchminister; Mr Andrew McCrea, Tobwee; Mr Archibald McCrea, Argory; Mr Samuel Blackburn, Mullaghaevny; Mr John McCrea, Mullaghaevny.

In the parish of Raymoghy: Mr William Boal, Forth; Mr Samuel Cunningham, Forth; Mr Thomas Colhoun, Mr William Colhoun, Labadish; Mr John Marshall, Moneymore; Mr Nathaniel Alexander, Balleaghan.

NATURAL FEATURES

Mountains and Hills

Perhaps no part of the country of any considerable bounds can with propriety be termed champaign; nevertheless this district viewed as a whole is one of the least mountainous of Donegal. Dooish, which occupies a part of the parishes of Taughboyne and Ray respectively, is the most important hill with respect to elevation and extent. It has long been famous for its slate quarries, of which that of Glentown, the property of Mr James Alexander, is the only one worked at present, that of Tubber in the land held by Mrs Elizabeth Marshall having been closed on the 18th of August last.

The reason assigned by the proprietor for its failure was that the vein or the practicable part of the quarry being exhausted, it became doubtful whether the present markets would indemnify her in clearing another. It had been worked unremittingly for nearly 50 years.

Mr Alexander's quarry employs at present about 30 men but formerly the number was upwards of 90. The wages of each labourer, according to their several employments of raising, splitting and forming, is from 10d to 1s per day. There is but little demand at present for the produce of this quarry, owing to the low state of improvement. Formerly the markets were Omagh, Sligo, Galway, Great Britain and sometimes America, besides supplying Derry, Buncrana and the neighbouring farmers. The situation is somewhat more than 2 miles from conveyance by water.

This hill is chequered pretty much with rude attempts at cultivation. It has 3 principal summits which repel the efforts of agriculture, generally speaking, from a quarter to a half a mile.

On the north easterly side, at Braidy and Lustical, a stratum of iron ore projects to a great distance on the declivity and presents an appalling sight to the eye of industry. Some abortive trials have been made to break up those parts by Mr Porter and his neighbours the proprietors, but the scanty crops have forced them to relinquish the idea.

It may perhaps be allowable in this place to remark that the above townlands of Taughboyne and that of Drumbarnet in the parish of Ray furnish the chief depositions of iron ore in the district. Nevertheless, as no regular vein has been discovered but only an assemblage of detached pieces, it remains doubtful on either place whether a real mine exists.

Other Hills

The only remaining hills which lie entirely within the boundary under consideration and claim particular attention are Binion in the parish of Taughboyne and Croghan in that of Clonleigh. They are both in many places cultivated nearly to their respective summits. Binion on the eastern side is so extremely steep that there is no probability of the advance of agriculture in that direction. The precincts of these bleak elevations afford an asylum to a large proportion of the poorer class of cottagers.

These subsist almost entirely by an indifferent crop of potatoes raised by paring and burning annual patches of the vast tracts of heath which surround their little dwellings. The occupiers of mountain farms find their account in holding out to the industrious poor man the inducement of a hut and privilege of cutting rough heads or heath parings for his fire at a reasonable rent, as their quantity of arable increases progressively in proportion to his exertions in raising potatoes.

The pasture of these regions is of the worst quality, consisting for the most part [of] heath and rushes, yet during summer young stock, nay even milk cows, have in many places no other foods.

Bogs

It is highly probable that the different tracts of the peculiar kind of surface known by this appellation and which, for the most part, occupy our valleys were originally swept in a state of fluidity from the summits of mountains into the hollow parts where they settled in, in manner of sediment, after the deluge had subsided.

The following considerations seem to strengthen this hypothesis. In the first instance, there is a striking affinity in the qualities of that stratum in both situations, the colour and general properties being exactly the same; secondly, it is observable that whereas the declivities of the mountains approximate to a level, the soil more or less partakes of the nature of peat again.

Bog peat is more ductile and free from stones or gravel than that of the mountains, which has never been decomposed, and it appears to have been deposited in layers according to the specific gravity of each respectively. Hence fuel procured at or near the bottom is the most hard and brittle when dry, and affords the best fire. The soft whitish peat of the surface appears in many respects to be nothing more than the concreted remains of mosses and other vegetable substances, in which consideration the usual name for such places was perhaps founded.

The principal bogs of the district are those of Ballyhasky, Letrim, Argory <Argony> and Creeve in All Saints, Newtownhamilton bog in Killea, Sooly partly in the respective parishes of Taughboyne and Clonleigh. In the latter parish there are besides Clonleigh bog and the old bog of Lifford. The largest tract of this kind in the parish of Rye (with the exception of particular property) is one of about 10 acres in the townland of Mondowey.

Fir and oak trees and blocks of both kinds are found in most of these bogs but chiefly in those of Ballyhasky, Argory and Sooly. They are various in their degrees of depth, some lying at or near the surface and others perhaps 9 feet below. It is very remarkable that rocks are principally found near the verges and firs for the most part in the interior parts.

These bogs are for the most part occupied by the tenantry of the respective estates to which they belong, nor is any rent paid for the privilege with the exception of a trifle for the purpose of draining and other occasional expenses. The tenantry of Castlecunningham estate, however, having no bog in their own lands, are obliged to purchase a supply in the contiguous estate of Castle Forward at the rate of from 6 to 12 pounds an acre, according to the quality.

Springs

In Ballyhasky bog (commonly termed the Flow moss), in the immediate vicinity of Castle Forward demesne, the best mineral spring of the district is to be seen. By the taste, which is highly acidulous, it appears to be a very strong natural chalybeate water, though no other symptoms of iron have appeared around this interesting fountain. The late Earl of Wicklow entertained a favourable opinion of its medicinal properties.

There are, besides the above, innumerable springs of this kind in the different parishes. The most considerable in point of strength, as far as these observations have extended, are those of Lustical in the farm of Dr Porter, of Brady in that of Mr Latta and another at Drumbarnet in Rye; no use whatever is made of these waters.

River Finn

Although this district is watered by innumerable native streams, yet no river of any considerable size rises within its boundaries. There are, however, 3 which, as they either wash or intersect it, deserve to be noticed under this head. These are Finn, Burndale and Sooly.

Finn, the largest of the number, rises from Lough Finn in the confines of Boylagh and, after an irregular course in a south easterly direction, winds between Stranorlar and Ballybofey. It runs thence east to Clady, where it becomes a boundary of the district, and afterwards north east to its junction with the River Mourne above Lifford.

The offspring [of] this union is the noble river of Foyle where, with many other commercial advantages, there is a considerable fishery of salmon and trout. There are at present 11 boats of different sizes, with from 2 to 6 oars each and carrying upon the whole 105 persons, chiefly employed in taking the fish. A yawl with 4 men conveys the fish when taken to an ice-house on the other side of the river erected for the purpose of preserving them. During the season 2 men are here engaged in icing, as it is termed. In all 111 persons [are employed].

The principal market is Liverpool, to which place the produce of this fishery is regularly conveyed in smacks. Glasgow and other parts of Scotland are also occasional purchasers.

The range of the boats is from Lifford downwards, and all over the river several depredations are made on the fish in the winter season by mischievous persons, to prevent which a number of waterkeepers are then employed. Mr James Baird of Carrigans is the present manager of this concern. The Foyle is also said to abound with eel of great size.

Burndale River

Burndale rises from the mountains westward of Aghygalt and, after an irregular course of nearly 20 miles, falls into the Foyle at Islandmore nearly east south east of its source. This river, like the Finn, abounds with fish of the same description. In wet seasons frequent floods make great havoc in the valley through which it passes. The public road at Rossgeer bridge has been frequently rendered impassable excepting to people on horseback, and the hazard even to these often imminent.

This road has lately been embanked here at a great expense, being now 30 feet wide and considerably higher than the usual floods.

Sooly Burn

Sooly burn rises in the parish of Raphoe, runs nearly half its course eastward to Mullinaveigh, to where it becomes the mearing of the parishes of Taughboyne and Clonleigh, and, continuing so after an irregular course (upon the whole east north east) of about 3 miles, falls into the Foyle between Porthall and Carrickmore.

Lakes

The only lake of any size in this part of the barony is Portlough in the parish of All Saints, which gives its name to an adjoining townland. It is upwards of half a mile in length and near the middle up what more than a quarter broad. For several years eels were the only species of fish found here, but latterly it is said perch has made its appearance.

A canal intersecting this lake in a longitudinal direction, and connecting the waters of the Foyle and Swilly, would in the writer's opinion give increased importance to all the towns of the western coast of the country and also be the means of extending the inland market of the fisheries.

A legend in the tradition of the neighbourhood ascribes the origins of this beautiful lake to enchantment.

Shores and Ferries

The only shores are those of Foyle and Swilly. These waters have each a very irregular outline. The former is navigable for small craft to Strabane, the latter to Letterkenny. The shore of Swilly is remarkable for affording an inexhaustible store of seaweed and glar to the adjacent farms as manures, and furnishing a multitude of poor families with a nutritious and ample supply of shellfish, chiefly oysters, mussels and cockles.

Ferries: these are Dunnelong on Foyle and Fort Stewart on Swilly.

Woods and Plantations

The soil is in general well adapted to the production of the common species of forest trees. Nevertheless upon the whole, there is a great deficiency in planting ash, sycamore, beech, elm. Fir and elder are the kinds mostly seen but rather in detached clumps promiscuously ranged around farmhouses than in the form of woods or plantations.

The chief of these in All Saints are at Castleforward and Bogay, the former the beautiful paternal seat of the Right Honourable the Earl of Wicklow and the latter the much improved residence of the Revd Edward Bowen, who has lately planted and otherwise improved very extensively.

The judicious and tasteful arrangement of Robert Beatson Esquire has in this way much embellished the townlands of Gortinleave and Ballyboe. There is also a plantation at Plaister, the property of Thomas Patterson Esquire, but apparently in a state of decay.

In the parish of Taughboyne, excepting the small woods of Phiddyglass and woodland consisting chiefly of stunted oak, ash and elder trees, there is little planting deserving of notice.

Killea has its principal scenes of these kind in the vicinity of Carrigans, whence the seats of Dunmore and Prospect have an agreeable appearance.

Killandarrogh wood, the property of Lord Erne, and a belt at Argory, that of James Sinclair, are the principal plantations of Clonleigh. These, with Kincraiggy, a wood or rather shrubbery of about 14 acres, and Sharon, the beautiful retreat of the amiable Dr Ussher, furnish a general idea of the district in this respect.

PRODUCTIVE ECONOMY

Orchards

To give an account of these particularly would far exceed the limits of this sketch and be little else than the history of every farmer's garden in the district. The size of the plots of ground occupied in this manner varies from 20 perches to 3 or 4 acres.

The principal orchards are those of Moyle, Newtowncunningham, Portlough, Clashygowan, Cretland, Craghadooes, Moneygelvin, Clonfad and in the neighbourhood of Ballindrait. The nipping frosts of last spring have diminished the average of fruit.

Agriculture

The practice of resting the land (as it is called) for 3 years at least between each series of crops has been general amongst the cultivators of this country since the earliest times. Its advocates seem chiefly to rest its utility on the idea that ground by too frequent tillage, like the human frame, as it were, after a long course of intemperate exertion, becomes lax and debilitated and consequently unfit to perform its assigned functions with uniform vigour.

Indeed, it is observable even in the richest lands of the district that, when cropped several seasons in succession, the growth of weeds increases progressively with each ploughing but, be they never so foul, a rest of 3 years banishes gradually every excrescence and clothes them in their pure and primitive verdure.

The drilling system it must be confessed, though scarcely known here, has a decided superiority over the common broadcast method of depositing seed, as it affords every facility towards the eradication of weeds of all kinds.

Draining

The most approved method is that of the underdrain or (as it is here denominated) the French drain. Much labours in this way has been done in Rye, All Saints and elsewhere, yet by far the greater part remains to be effected. Surface draining, excepting of meadow, is seldom or never practised.

Agricultural Methods

Picking and turning: this is a mode of agriculture preparation for cold, shallow soils, of late invention and surprising effect. Mr William Boal of Forth, by whom it was first brought into operation and notice, as an assiduous and enterprising improver claims without doubt the highest encomiums. During the distressing season of

1817, this true philanthropist tried an experiment on a part of his farm where the hard blue subsoil lay half exposed to view under a broken moory surface.

In order to afford employment to poor neighbours whose families must otherwise have starved, trenches were made 18 inches deep and of a convenient breadth, the whole length of the field. These immediately communicated, that is, no partition of the subsoil intervened, the clearing of the last still replenishing the former until the whole was overturned.

The stones raised during the process (some of which probably a ton weight) liberally covered the surface. These were of course appropriated to the construction of fences and filling of French drains; and the land cleared in this manner, manured and cropped the following year equalled his best fields in produce.

The success of this first essay induced him to carry the plan into effect on every perch of this quality in his possession and the same success uniformly crowned his exertion. He has in this manner reclaimed 9 acres. The operation was at first performed with a pick but latterly the followers of Mr Boal's plan turn the land more speedily with a crow.

Mr Robert McLeland and Mr Samuel Cunningham of the same place were the first to follow Mr Boal's method, which was at first looked on by the neighbours as a paroxysm of insanity. The first of those persons has turned 4 acres, the other 5 after this manner.

Well were it for their landlords and well for themselves did the high fliers of the day but endeavour to resemble this true farmer in plain good sense, industry and simplicity of manners. The bare turning of the above land cost Mr Boal no less than 18d a perch. The whole expense per acre of turning, draining and fencing is estimated at 22 pounds; upon the whole for 9 acres, 198 pounds.

Fences

The parishes of All Saints and Killea are doubtless best secured in this respect, yet even these are extremely deficient. With the exception of gentlemen's seats and the enclosures of a very few farmers, the greater part of the district bears the resemblance of a vast common. Perhaps 7 years of unremitting industry are requisite to bring it to the state of which it is susceptible. The few enclosures are chiefly fenced with quicksets, a species of hedge highly suitable.

Irrigation

This very necessary and useful operation, notwithstanding an abundance of water, is greatly neglected. Meadows, it is true, are tolerably supplied but arable lands extremely seldom.

Manures

These are 1 animal ordure, 2 mire, 3 earth, 4 lime, 5 ashes, 6 sand, 7 glar. The most general compost of the district is that of the first two, though lime is lately resorted to (especially on cold lands) as an excellent auxiliary.

It is proper to observe that mire is a species of peat which has been often stirred by tillage or otherwise, or exposed to frequent extremes of drought and inundation, which in time degenerates into the black friable mud so called and is of essential service to the cultivator. It is drawn during the summer months in great quantities and, after being broken with a spade or shovel sufficiently fine, is deposited in ditches and other receptacles for the purpose of fermentation.

Lime abounds [in] all the district with the exception of Killea. The principal places for lime are Montglass, Creghadoos, Cavin and Montolink. The quality is in general good but that of Creghadoos is preferred.

Limestone of the purest slate blue is said to be the best, but the colour of lime for building in a great measure depends on the quality of the fuel. For this purpose peat, having white ashes, are much in request. No coal is used in preparing it [insert footnote: none has been discovered]. The expense of from 10d to 13d per barrel will purchase lime of the best quality.

The earth of old fences, mounds, verges etc. makes, with dung, mire and lime, an excellent compost. It is often used separately on shallow grounds with good effect.

Ashes are chiefly procured from paring and burning of moors, fens or other old swards, whether the surface be composed of peat or earth, and most commonly served as a manure to the spot producing them.

The use of sand as a manure has been already described. Glar is the rich deposit of the sea and produces the most luxuriant crops of itself without other mixture. These 2 last are entirely local.

Implements of Husbandry

Implements are the old Irish or wooden plough, the iron plough introduced a few years ago, the Scotch plough; the common harrow, a few brake harrows; the old wheel-cart growing scarce, the cart car very common, large cart in use where there are good horses, the old sliding car or slipe nearly done away excepting on steep rugged lands; the spade and shovel, these are most common. The iron plough, cart car and the brake harrow are late improvements.

Ploughing

This operation commences in general about Christmas and continues on large farms till the month of April. Crops: 1 potatoes, 2 barley, 3 oats, 4 flax, 5 oats and afterwards rest; on good lands perhaps 6 flax, 7 oats, then as before.

Potatoes

This crop is usually planted on ridges. After ploughing and manuring, the seed is sometimes introduced with a spade previous to the throwing up of the trenches, but often laid on the ridge and then covered. Both methods are in use but the former is chiefly practised. The first mode is usually termed kibbing. In this crop the spade and shovel are always used.

Barley and Oats

Barley: many have discontinued this crop on account of the restrictions on illicit distillation. It is usually sown in April.

Oats: this crop is put down in March. The occupiers of mountain farms often lose their whole labour by sowing at a late period. They seldom take pains to drain their lands, and delay their sowing until the warm weather sets in. The consequence is that before the seed germinates, it is literally burned up with the heat which acts with intensity on light soils.

Mr John Alexander of Drumennan, an experimental farmer whom the writer has before omitted to mention, sowed for 2 successive seasons lands of the above description in the month of February, leaving at each time a ridge which was afterwards sown in April. In both trials the early sown oats were luxuriant; in the others, land, seed and husbandry the same, not half a crop.

Flax

In this crop the land is ploughed and harrowed, the first time in January or February and the second at the time of sowing, which is from the middle of April to that of May. The wetness of the climate and the injuries sustained by the flax and saving the seed are material obstacles to the advancement of this desirable process.

Flax, when dried from the steeping place, is usually crushed with a brake, which is a crooked wooden mallet, for the purpose of facilitating the operation of cleansing or scutching, but the flax must be sufficiently dried before either process can take place with proper effect. For this purpose it is placed, about 20 lbs weight each time, and weighs on a small kiln whilst a strong fire from below prepares it speedily for the brake.

There are in the parish of All Saints 18 flax mills; in that of Taughboyne 19; in Killea 6; in the parish of Clonleigh only 2; and in that of Ray 16 or more. Owing to the low state of the home manufacture, by far the greater part of the flax produced in this district is sent to foreign markets. The present prices are from 2 pounds to 3 pounds per cwt.

Wages

The farmers usually hire their servants by the half-year. The terms of such contracts are the 12th of May and of November. Wages are at present from 2 pounds 5s 6d to 3 pounds for the above period. Day labourers during harvest have from 8d to 10d per day besides food; at other times only the last sum without any sustenance. Reaping by the piece is from 6s to 7s 6d an acre; ditching from 10d to 2s 2d by the perch, according to the dimensions of the work; and draining from 6d to 1s, subject to the same restrictions.

Markets

The low state of the agricultural resources producing an immediate and uniform demand on the fruits of labour for sundry emergencies is a principal cause of cheap markets. The following are the present prices of some necessaries of life: oatmeal 1s 3d per peck, potatoes 7s per load of 3 measures or 24 stones, beef 4d per lb., butter 9d per lb.; oats and barley sell the former 9d, the latter 1s per stone.

Improvements: Green Crops

The cultivation of these is yet in a state of infancy or rather of bare existence, a circumstance which the state of fences will readily explain. Patches of clover from 1 rood to 2 acres raised merely as a supply for milk cows appear thinly dispersed over the district.

Mr Nathaniel Alexander of Balleaghan is the most extensive grower of clover, raising from 4 to 5 acres annually; other cultivators of this crop are Mr James Fulton of Gortenleave, Mr John Osborne, Altaughaderry, Mr John Key, Cavin, and a few besides.

Turnips are seldom or never cultivated by the mere farmer. Mr Hamilton Patterson of Churchtown is almost the only person in this way; his crop this year is very good.

Artificial grasses are nearly as rare as clover. The kinds are rye grass, white grass and, on some swampy spots, fiorin.

Livestock

These are in general bred from *cast racers*, which is a radical error in their raising of cattle for agriculture. Every useful consideration is sacrificed to the hope of obtaining a fine shape, and the consequence is that the offspring often inherits no other characteristic of the size than his imbecility. Mr Middleton's estimate of 1 horse to every 15 acres of arable land might, in the absence of certainty, be assumed as data for the district.

The breed of black cattle and every other in these parishes is promiscuous. The best of the native stock are of an old English descent, but of whose first introduction the writer, at this distance of time, could obtain no satisfactory account. The descriptions kept on farms are for the most part milk cows, the young cattle being usually sent to pasture in spring to the mountains of Inishowen and elsewhere.

Dairy Cattle

The practice of selling milk and butter and sending occasional supplies to the principal towns gives the stock of almost every farmer more or less the appearance of a dairy. A cart, car or other vehicle brings the produce to market, by which a description of persons termed *buttermilk drivers* obtains a livelihood, as the farmers attach a certain degree of infamy to its personal conveyance! Strictly speaking, however, there are few established dairies. Mr Gallagher of Tubberlawn in the parish of Killea is perhaps the only one in the district. The number of cows belonging to this concern are usually from 12 to 15. A few males of the Ayrshire breed have been recently introduced and are highly approved of by the best judges.

Robert Beatson Esquire is famous as a breeder of cattle. The Devonshire are seen on the lands of Gortygrana, the property of Robert Maxwell Esquire. These are the chief improvements in black cattle.

With respect to the use of oxen in husbandry, the practice is hardly known in these parishes. The proportion of black cattle to that of horses are nearly as 4 to 1.

Sheep

Since farmers have become too refined to wear their own manufacture, the garb of better days, sheep have in a great measure, except on mountainous lands, been eradicated. The few remaining are chiefly the small mountain sheep. In the present destitute state of the country, they are perhaps best adapted, if not to the soil, at least to their scanty accommodations. Their meat is the most delicious but their wool is not of the best quality.

Mr William Latta of Bready, with a laudable zeal for ancient economy, has had a web of flannel, one of blanketing and one of wearing apparel for some time annually manufactured from his flock.

No South Down, Leicester etc. are seen with the common farmers. The average quota of sheep perhaps does not exceed 3 to each farmer, a number little more than sufficient for providing them in stockings.

Swine

Swine are common all over the district but little is known in this quarter relative to the different breeds of this animal. Mr Hugh Collins of Lisclamerty has the best boar in his possession for size and every requisite doubtless in the barony. Swine may be one for each of two-thirds of the houses.

General Remarks

It should have been remarked that some few farmers whose pastures or other means afford them proper facilities occasionally raise the beef cow for their own table. The best pastures for this purpose are those which produce abundant herbage, well sheltered and convenient to good water. The pressure of the times, however, will not allow the farmers in general to lay down good lands for the length of time necessary to produce this effect.

Suggestions for Improvement

1st. As experimental farming is the only rational path whereby agriculture can possibly arrive at the perfection at present contemplated, it would be well to stimulate a spirit of enquiry among the intelligent landholders of every district and to induce them at stated times to report to the North West Society, or any contiguous branch of society, the result of their researches exerted on all subjects connected with this invaluable art.

2nd. It might likewise be advisable, so soon as proper materials could be procured, having due respect to local situation, to publish a farmer's calendar adapted to the soil and climate of the north of Ireland, by authority of the same enlightened body. Such a work would be of incalculable utility and would remain to latest time an undoubted record of their patriotism and philanthropy.

Linen Manufacture

In the latter part of the last century and commencement of this, the linen manufacture had acquired an importance in this district which forms a striking contrast when compared with its present state. It has been lately remarked to the writer by a gentleman whilst discoursing on this subject that 20 years ago there was scarcely a common weaver who had not temporarily 10 pounds to lend, whereas an equal sum would, at this day, purchase at this day almost any individual of that class of society out of a habitation.

It was usual at that time for the farming heads of families to put their younger sons into this employment, many of whom were enabled, by proper economy and application, in a few years to purchase farms, but this practice has been long discontinued. There is a perceptible balance, it is true, on the side of weaving at this moment from that some time ago, but as it arises rather from a comparison of the respective prices of cloth than yarn than from any increased demand for the former, it becomes a matter of domestic competition, upon the whole no favourable symptom.

Domestic Labour

The female inmates of the labouring class can seldom afford to pay 12s or 13s, the rent set by the farmer on half a rood of flax ground, besides 5s or perhaps more for seed. Hence the greater part of poor spinners are obliged to purchase the raw material from the farmers at the highest rate. Often when their little stock is exhausted and they are no longer able to buy flax, the last resource presents itself, that of spinning by the spangle to farmers' wives for different purposes, at the rate of a hank per day, work for a good spinner.

The spangle of course occupies 4 days which, at the common rate of 1s per spangle, amounts to but 3d for each day! To purchase the flax is preferable by a ha'penny on each hank, at the present prices of single hanks, as, it is necessary to remark, the rate of these is always lower than that of large quantities, *bunches*.

Yarn

The common grist for fine yarn is called {spangle} yarn, that is 4 hanks to 1 lb. The prices are 2s 6d for 3, 4, 5 or 6 hank yarn and for tow or coarse yarn from 1 hank to 20 cuts (twelfth of a hank) to a lb., 2s 4d per spangle.

The late-invented double wheel has made but slow progress, as a material objection appears against its introduction in the inferior quality of the yarn, to make which good on the common wheel both hands are necessary. This is the general opinion on the subject; no double wheels are used in this district.

Weavers are generally supplied with yarn in the public markets, though they sometimes purchase it from spinners of the neighbourhood.

Preparation of Yarn

No bleached yarn is purchased for manufacturing into cloth. The buyer always prepares it himself and in a manner, it is presumed, less injurious to the texture than that of public greens. The common setts of linen manufactured in the north east district are 12 hundred and 13 hundred, and the prices are 1s 4d to 1s 9d per yard, according to the quality of the manufacture.

Markets for Cloth

Londonderry is the principal market for the cloths of All Saints, Taughboyne and Killea. It also receives a considerable part of those woven in Clonleigh and Ray. For the residue of the former, the market is Strabane; for those of the latter, Letterkenny. These remarks of general convenience, however, often yield to the hope of obtaining a high price.

Social Economy

Domestic Economy

Unavoidable dispatch (October 8th) obliges the writer to observe on this and the following article as briefly as possible.

Farming class: the greater part of the habitations of these appear in a state of decay. The window tax, obliging the farmer to keep a number of these lights below the operation of the statute, gives to farmhouses a dismal and ruinous appearance; and when they consist of 2-storeys, as most late erections do, so much the worst. A common error is that cow-houses, stables etc. are often either immediately in front of the dwelling house or on the same range.

The food of this class differs less at present from that of the others than formerly. Oatcake, porridge, potatoes, milk, butter, beef, bacon and tea are their common subsistence.

Manufacturing and Labouring Classes

The high rents paid by these for their little tenements are yet undiminished from times of the greatest prosperity. If farmers wish for reduction themselves, they ought of course to set the example. The writer himself pays for a cow's grass, half an acre and half a rood of land, and a hovel without a window and almost without a door, the annual sum of 7 pounds.

2 guineas or upwards for a cow grass have debarred nearly four-fifths of the cottages from keeping any. A goat must now be substituted: this useful and economical animal will produce from 1 pint to 4 or 5 quarts of milk daily.

The beginning of summer and the time of harvest are the periods of greatest employment. During the winter and other intervals the labourer collects manure for raising potatoes, the chief support of his little family.

These classes live at present in the same manner, chiefly on potatoes, porridge, milk etc.

Education

Country people at present seem more desirous of learning to live than of living to learn. The expenses of education are reading 2s 6d, writing 3s 4d, English grammar and arithmetic 4s 2d per quarter; from 12 to 24 poor children in each parish of the diocese of Raphoe are taught gratis.

In All Saints there are 7 schools; in Taughboyne 11 or more; in Killea 1; in Clonleigh upwards of 9; and in Raymoghy 10. Much yet remains to be done. The Lancasterian system would produce in some time amazing effects.

There are no established societies.

Conclusion

The writer's warmest acknowledgements are due to the Revd Edward Bowen; Andrew Ferguson Esquire; the Revd Ewing, All Saints; John Chambers Esquire, Lifford; and many others. End of the report (copy).

Appendix to Statistical Report, 1821

SOCIAL ECONOMY

All Saints: Census of Townlands

Appendix no.1, All Saints according to the census of 1821 by Mr John Aikan.

Ardee, 300 acres arable, total 300 acres; 16 houses, 111 inhabitants.

Ballybegley, 268 acres arable, 268 total acres; 18 houses, 125 inhabitants.

Ballyboe, 80 acres arable, 80 total acres; 3 houses, 21 inhabitants.

Ballyhasky, 216 acres arable, 27 acres bog, 243 total acres; 44 houses, 257 inhabitants.

Bogay, 80 acres arable, 21 acres mountain, 9 acres bog, 110 total acres; 6 houses, 26 inhabitants.

Callhame, 86 acres arable, 86 total acres; 15 houses, 75 inhabitants.

Castle Forward, 75 acres arable, 75 total acres; 6 houses, 25 inhabitants.

Castrews, 200 acres arable, 59 acres mountain, 259 total acres; 24 houses, 153 inhabitants.

Cloon, 195 acres arable, 195 total acres; 12 houses, 68 inhabitants.

Colehill, 131 acres arable, 131 total acres; 18 houses, 105 inhabitants.

Corncammon, 206 acres arable, 206 total acres; 20 houses, 114 inhabitants.

Creeve, 152 acres arable, 152 total acres; 19 houses, 84 inhabitants.

Drumbarnett, 104 acres arable, 50 acres mountain, 154 total acres; 17 houses, 86 inhabitants.

Drumbwee, 240 acres arable, 240 total acres; 16 houses, 74 inhabitants.

Drumlougher, 66 acres arable, 66 total acres; 12 houses, 96 inhabitants.

Drumay, 188 acres arable, 188 total acres; 25 houses, 154 inhabitants.

Garshuey, 107 acres arable, 107 total acres; 29 houses, 159 inhabitants.

Gortenleave, 128 acres arable, 44 acres mountain, 28 acres bog, 200 total acres; 21 houses, 83 inhabitants.

Gortree, 215 acres arable, 215 total acres; 23 houses, 136 inhabitants.

Keshends, 99 acres arable, 99 total acres; 17 houses, 96 inhabitants.

Killdrum, 412 acres arable, 412 total acres; 36 houses, 230 inhabitants.

Letrim, 137 acres arable, 137 total acres; 6 houses, 31 inhabitants.

Moneygreggan, 140 acres arable, 140 total acres; 7 houses, 53 inhabitants.

Monfad, 135 acres arable, 135 total acres; 20 houses, 120 inhabitants.

Montglass, 102 acres arable, 48 acres bog, 150 total acres; 29 houses, 162 inhabitants.

Moyle, 130 acres arable, 130 total acres; 10 houses, 75 inhabitants.

Murlough, 48 acres arable, 48 total acres; 5 houses, 34 inhabitants.

Newtown Cunningham, 201 acres arable, 201 total acres; 25 houses, 169 inhabitants.

Plaister, 96 acres arable, 96 total acres; 16 houses, 99 inhabitants.

Portlough, 189 acres arable, 69 acres mountain, 258 total acres; 21 houses, 134 inhabitants.

Roughan, 169 acres arable, 169 total acres; 8 houses, 51 inhabitants.

Rusky, 251 arable, 251 total acres; 48 houses, 238 inhabitants.

Tinnyhatbuck, 52 acres arable, 52 total acres; 18 houses, 107 inhabitants.

Tullyannan, 83 acres arable, 33 acres mountain, 116 total acres; 24 houses, 131 inhabitants.

Total: 5,281 acres arable, 276 acres mountain, 112 acres bog, 5,669 total acres; 634 houses, 3,682 inhabitants.

Taughboyne: Census of Townlands

No.2, Taughboyne according to the census of 1821 by Mr David Stevenson.

Ardagh Irish, 60 acres arable, 40 acres mountain, 100 total acres; 19 houses, 95 inhabitants.

Ardagh Scotch, 328 acres arable, 328 total acres; 19 houses, 112 inhabitants.

Balliboe, 92 acres arable, 92 total acres; 9 houses, 56 inhabitants.

Ballycushion, 66 acres arable, 66 total acres; 10 houses, 43 inhabitants.

Ballylennon, 168 acres arable, 12 acres bog, 108 total acres; 22 houses, 117 inhabitants.

Binnion, 94 acres arable, 94 total acres; 8 houses, 45 inhabitants.

Brady, 55 acres arable, 90 acres mountain, 148 total acres; 16 houses, 94 inhabitants.

Brockagh, 134 acres arable, 134 total acres; 16 houses, 78 inhabitants.

Burnthaw, 43 acres arable, 43 total acres; 7 houses, 38 inhabitants.

Carnshennagh, 349 acres arable, 9 acres mountain, 358 total acres; 49 houses, 258 inhabitants.

Carrickmore, 157 acres arable, 4 acres bog, 161 total acres; 28 houses, 172 inhabitants.

Castlethird, 95 acres arable, 95 total acres; 23 houses, 123 inhabitants.

Castletown, 232 acres arable, 232 total acres; 32 houses, 184 inhabitants.

Cavanacaw, 49 acres arable, 49 total acres; 15 houses, 65 inhabitants.

Churchtown, 20 acres arable, 20 total acres; 9 houses, 51 inhabitants.

Clashigowan, 310 acres arable, 310 total acres; 41 houses, 224 inhabitants.

Cloghfin, 197 acres arable, 8 acres bog, 205 total acres; 27 houses, 156 inhabitants.

Corporation Land, 50 acres arable, 50 total acres; 19 houses, 89 inhabitants.

Cragadooes Lower, 120 acres arable, 48 acres bog, 160 total acres; 45 houses, 203 inhabitants.

Cragadooes Upper, 93 acres arable, 56 acres mountain, 149 total acres; 23 houses, 124 inhabitants.

Cretland, 58 acres arable, 35 acres mountain, 93 total acres; 9 houses, 46 inhabitants.

Cross, 125 acres arable, 125 total acres; 20 houses, 108 inhabitants.

Cuttimonhill, 30 acres arable, 12 acres bog, 42 total acres; 7 houses, 41 inhabitants.

Derrymore, 103 acres arable, 103 total acres; 6 houses, 31 inhabitants.

Drumbeg, 70 acres arable, 70 total acres; 7 houses, 29 inhabitants.

Drumcrow, 100 acres arable, 44 acres bog, 144 total acres; 10 houses, 51 inhabitants.

Drumdoonagh, 62 acres arable, 62 total acres; 10 houses, 56 inhabitants.

Drumeen, 34 acres arable, 34 total acres; 12 houses, 58 inhabitants.

Drumfad, 184 acres arable, 184 total acres; 7 houses, 40 inhabitants.

Drumennan, 140 acres arable, 38 acres mountain, 178 total acres; 13 houses, 74 inhabitants.

Drumucklagh, 44 acres arable, 44 total acres; 16 houses, 86 inhabitants.

Drumore, 233 acres arable, 233 total acres; 24 houses, 131 inhabitants.

Dundee, 55 acres arable, 55 total acres; 10 houses, 55 inhabitants.

Durnacally, 189 acres arable, 189 total acres; 12 houses, 59 inhabitants.

Glentown, 37 acres arable, 25 acres mountain, 62 total acres; 11 houses, 71 inhabitants.

Gilliestown, 18 acres arable, 6 acres mountain, 24 total acres; 7 houses, 41 inhabitants.

Haugh, 70 acres arable, 70 total acres; 4 houses, 25 inhabitants.

Killgort, 80 acres arable, 80 total acres; 12 houses, 65 inhabitants.

Kinnycally, 161 acres arable, 161 total acres; 24 houses, 142 inhabitants.

Legnathraw, 240 acres arable, 240 total acres; 25 houses, 156 inhabitants.

Lettergull, 211 acres arable, 211 total acres; 56 houses, 237 inhabitants.

Listannagh, 61 acres arable, 61 total acres; 2 houses, 18 inhabitants.

Listicall, 300 acres arable, 84 acres mountain, 384 total acres; 32 houses, 171 inhabitants.

Magheracloy, 60 acres arable, 60 total acres; 3 houses, 21 inhabitants.

Maymore, 61 acres arable, 61 total acres; 5 houses, 33 inhabitants.

Moymeen, 310 acres arable, 310 total acres; 41 houses, 251 inhabitants.

Moness, 74 acres arable, 74 total acres; 6 houses, 41 inhabitants.

Mongavelin, 99 acres arable, 99 total acres; 15 houses, 68 inhabitants.

Monreagh, 181 acres arable, 181 total acres; 28 houses, 124 inhabitants.

Nethertown, 75 acres arable, 75 total acres; 10 houses, 48 inhabitants.

Pheddyglass, 189 acres arable, 189 total acres; 41 houses, 111 inhabitants.

Rateen, 39 acres arable, 39 total acres; 13 houses, 63 inhabitants.

Rockfield, 48 acres arable, 48 total acres; 6 houses, 32 inhabitants.

St Johnstown, 69 houses, 334 inhabitants.

St Johnstown Glebe, 74 acres arable, 74 total acres; 7 houses, 40 inhabitants.

Swilly, 44 acres arable, 31 acres bog, 75 total acres; 12 houses, 75 inhabitants.

Teroddy, 65 acres arable, 40 acres bog, 105 total acres; 9 houses, 62 inhabitants.

Tonagh, 174 acres arable, 161 acres bog, 335 total acres; 21 houses, 117 inhabitants.

Trensallagh, 167 acres arable, 167 total acres; 19 houses, 110 inhabitants.

Trentagh, 168 acres arable, 168 total acres; 14 houses, 100 inhabitants.

Trentaghmucklagh, 118 acres arable, 30 acres bog, 148 total acres; 24 houses, 136 inhabitants.

Tubber, 165 acres arable, 165 total acres; 19 houses, 99 inhabitants.

Tullyown, 100 acres arable, 100 total acres; 7 houses, 39 inhabitants.

Tullyrap, 100 acres arable, 100 total acres; 14 houses, 73 inhabitants.

Whitehill, 151 acres arable, 12 acres bog, 163 total acres; 12 houses, 81 inhabitants.

Woodland, 111 acres arable, 111 total acres; 17 houses, 107 inhabitants.

Total: 7,890 acres arable, 413 acres mountain, 364 acres bog, 8,667 total acres; 1,186 houses, 6,283 inhabitants.

Killea: Census of Townlands

No.3, Killea according to the census of 1821 by Mr John Aikin.

Altaughaderry, 393 acres arable, 31 acres mountain, 424 total acres; population: 94 under 18 years, 82 between 18 and 45, 36 above 45, 36 houses, 212 inhabitants.

Ardnamoghal, 55 acres arable, 55 total acres; population: 27 under 18 years, 21 between 18 and 43, 11 above 45, 13 houses, 59 inhabitants.

Ash Grove, 26 acres arable, total 26 acres; population: 1 under 18 years, 52 between 18 and 40, 1 above 45, 1 house, 4 inhabitants.

Carrigans, 55 acres arable, 55 total acres; population: 104 under 18 years, 78 between 18 and 45, 64 above 45, 49 houses, 246 inhabitants.

Drumnasheer, 60 acres arable, 60 total acres; population: 4 under 18 years, 5 between 18 and 45, 1 above 45, 1 house, 10 inhabitants.

Dunmore, 283 acres arable, total 283 acres; population: 59 under 18 years, 34 between 18 and 45, 35 above 45, 25 houses, 128 inhabitants.

Glassmullen, population: 9 under 18 years, 21 between 18 and 45, 9 above 45, 10 houses, 39 inhabitants.

Imlick, 128 acres arable, 128 total acres; population: 26 under 18 years, 25 between 18 and 45, 11 above 45, 11 houses, 62 inhabitants.

Lagnaduff, 20 acres arable, 20 total acres; population: 18 under 18 years, 9 between 18 and 45, 4 above 45, 5 houses, 31 inhabitants.

Magerabwee, 15 acres arable, 15 total acres; population: 6 under 18 years, 3 between 18 and 45, 2 above 45, 1 house, 11 inhabitants.

Newtownhamilton, 16 acres arable, 16 total acres; population: 46 under 18 years, 30 between 18 and 45, 23 above 45, 19 houses, 99 inhabitants.

Tubberslawn, 131 acres arable, 131 total acres; population: 18 under 18 years, 12 between 18 and 45, 6 above 45, 7 houses, 36 inhabitants.

Whitehouse, 52 acres arable, 52 total acres; population: 22 under 18 years, 15 between 18 and 45, 13 above 45, 10 houses, 50 inhabitants.

Total: 1,234 acres arable, 31 acres mountain, 1,265 total acres; population: 434 under 18 years, 337 between 18 and 45, 216 above 45, 188 houses, 987 inhabitants.

Clonleigh: Census of Townlands

No.4, Clonleigh according to the census 1821 by Mr J. Mellon.

Aghawee, 60 acres arable, 60 total acres; 4 houses, 25 inhabitants.

Ardnaglass, 149 acres arable, 5 acres mountain, 154 total acres; 18 houses, 99 inhabitants.

Ardnasool, 50 acres arable, 50 total acres; 4 houses, 20 inhabitants.

Back Hill, 10 acres arable, 10 total acres; 2 houses, 8 inhabitants.

Ballinabrine, 96 acres arable, 2 acres mountain, 98 total acres; 16 houses, 88 inhabitants.

Ballindreat, 131 acres arable, 131 total acres; 50 houses, 210 inhabitants.

Ballyboggan Churchtown, 124 acres arable, 124 total acres; 21 houses, 104 inhabitants.

Ballyboggan Milltown, 73 acres arable, 73 total acres; 17 houses, 81 inhabitants.

Ballyminister, 90 acres arable, 90 total acres; 4 houses, 24 inhabitants.

Birdstown, 68 acres arable, 68 total acres; 14 houses, 61 inhabitants.

(+) Blackrock, 74 acres arable, 74 total acres.

(+) Boyagh, 120 acres arable, 4 acres bog, 124 total acres.

(+) Braid, 137 acres arable, 28 acres mountain, 165 total acres.

Callhame, 50 acres arable, 50 total acres; 7 houses, 33 inhabitants.

Carrickannaslate, 26 acres arable, 4 acres mountain, 30 total acres; 5 houses, 31 inhabitants.

Calms, 60 acres arable, 60 total acres; 6 houses, 27 inhabitants.

(+) Cavan, 112 acres arable, 112 total acres.

Cavanacor, 65 acres arable, 65 total acres; 6 houses, 28 inhabitants.

Clamperlane, 14 acres arable, 14 total acres; 6 houses, 30 inhabitants.

Cloghfin, 99 acres arable, 99 total acres; 19 houses, 84 inhabitants.

(+) Cloncash, 57 acres arable, 57 total acres.

(+) Clonfad, 211 acres arable, 5 acres bog, 216 total acres.

(+) Coolatee, 84 acres arable, 84 total acres.

Corcan Island, 47 acres arable, 47 total acres; 2 houses, 11 inhabitants.

Croghan Chapel, 1 house, 7 inhabitants.

Croghan Crawford's, 40 acres arable, 40 total acres; 3 houses, 20 inhabitants.

Croghan New Rowin, 13 acres arable, 4 acres mountain, 17 total acres; 4 houses, 22 inhabitants.

Cunninghamstown, 72 acres arable, 72 total acres; 9 houses, 38 inhabitants.

Cunnyberry, 29 acres arable, 29 total acres; 8 houses, 40 inhabitants.

Doorish, 35 acres arable, 35 acres mountain, 70 total acres; 3 houses, 18 inhabitants.

Drumbwee, 95 acres arable, 95 total acres; 15 houses, 88 inhabitants.

(+) Drumina, 36 acres arable, 36 total acres.

(+) Drumleene, 144 acres arable, 144 total acres.

Drumnahaw, 42 acres arable, 42 total acres; 3 houses, 24 inhabitants.

(+) Drumore, 71 acres arable, 6 acres bog, 77 total acres.

(+) Edenmore, 105 acres arable, 11 acres mountain, 116 total acres.

(+) Glebe, 19 acres arable, 19 total acres.

Glensmoyle, 105 acres arable, 41 acres mountain, 146 total acres; 10 houses, 58 inhabitants.

(+) Gort, 5 acres arable, 5 total acres.

(+) Gortgranna, 110 acres arable, 110 total acres.

Gortin, 61 acres arable, 61 total acres; 4 houses, 19 inhabitants.

Gortinbeg, 38 acres arable, 38 total acres; 4 houses, 24 inhabitants.

Gortinmore, 126 acres arable, 126 total acres; 22 houses, 116 inhabitants.

Gortinreagh, 62 acres arable, 2 acres bog, 64 total acres; 10 houses, 54 inhabitants.

Gortnagole, 78 acres arable, 78 total acres; 8 houses, 36 inhabitants.

Gortnavilly, 38 acres arable, 38 total acres; 7 houses, 18 inhabitants.

Guystown, 84 acres arable, 84 total acres; 7 houses, 40 inhabitants.

Hall, 85 acres arable, 85 total acres; 10 houses, 54 inhabitants.

Hermitage, 40 acres arable, 40 total acres; 3 houses, 12 inhabitants.

Hollands, 42 acres arable, 42 total acres; 12 houses, 69 inhabitants.

Inshany Lower, 50 acres arable, 50 total acres; 3 houses, 7 inhabitants.

Inshany Upper, 36 acres arable, 10 acres mountain, 46 total acres; 2 houses, 11 inhabitants.

Islandmore, 114 acres arable, 114 total acres; 3 houses, 16 inhabitants.

Keelogs, 81 acres arable, 81 total acres; 7 houses, 37 inhabitants.

Kirkminister Lower, 122 acres arable, 122 total acres; 16 houses, 95 inhabitants.

Kirkminister Upper, 117 acres arable, 117 total acres; 15 houses, 82 inhabitants.

Leggandarrough, 30 acres arable, 10 acres mountain, 40 total acres; 2 houses, 13 inhabitants.

Legnaniel, 19 acres arable, 19 total acres; 3 houses, 14 inhabitants.

Lifford, 235 acres arable, 235 total acres; 139 houses, 914 inhabitants.

Lifford, suburbs of, 108 acres arable, 26 acres mountain, 134 total acres; 22 houses, 100 inhabitants.

Lisky, 96 acres arable, 96 total acres; 5 houses, 36 inhabitants.

Lurganshenny, 86 acres arable, 86 total acres; 5 houses, 28 inhabitants.

(+) Mass Hill, 96 acres arable, 96 total acres.

Millsessaugh, 20 acres arable, 20 total acres; 47 houses, 107 inhabitants.

Monen, 76 acres arable, 4 acres bog, 80 total acres; 10 houses, 33 inhabitants.

Mossbeg, 96 acres arable, 56 acres bog, 152 total acres; 7 houses, 34 inhabitants.

Mossmore, 64 acres arable, 64 total acres; 2 houses, 13 inhabitants.

Mullaghawney, 118 acres arable, 118 total acres; 12 houses, 75 inhabitants.

Mullen, 8 houses, 51 inhabitants.

Mullenagung, 112 acres arable, 20 acres bog, 132 total acres; 28 houses, 157 inhabitants.

Mullenaveigh, 78 acres arable, 78 total acres; 37 houses, 166 inhabitants.

Murlogh, 131 acres arable, 131 total acres; 28 houses, 155 inhabitants.

Nassau Hall, 36 acres arable, 36 total acres; 4 houses, 24 inhabitants.

New Bridge, 27 acres arable, 27 total acres; 3 houses, 14 inhabitants.

(+) New Row, 65 acres arable, 2 acres bog, 67 total acres.

Portanure, 40 acres arable, 4 acres mountain, 44 total acres; 5 houses, 32 inhabitants.

(+) Porthall, 231 acres arable, 231 total acres.

Roghan, 28 acres arable, 28 total acres; 5 houses, 25 inhabitants.

(+) Rossgeer, 193 acres arable, 2 acres bog, 195 total acres.

Shannon, 249 acres arable, 249 total acres; 17 houses, 104 inhabitants.

Shearcloon, 82 acres arable, 7 acres bog, 89 total acres; 14 houses, 77 inhabitants.

(+) Sixty Acres, 46 acres arable, 46 total acres.

Spring Grove, 45 acres arable, 20 acres mountain, 65 total acres; 1 house, 10 inhabitants.

Spring Hill, 34 acres arable, 5 acres mountain, 39 total acres; 4 houses, 20 inhabitants.

Tamnawood, 14 acres arable, 14 total acres; 14 houses, 68 inhabitants.

Terkeerey, 70 acres arable, 70 total acres; 2 houses, 14 inhabitants.

Tobwee, 45 acres arable, 45 total acres; 7 houses, 50 inhabitants.

Tubbernabrock, 87 acres arable, 87 total acres; 5 houses, 36 inhabitants.

Tubberoneill, 145 acres arable, 6 acres mountain, 131 total acres; 22 houses, 117 inhabitants.

Wood Island, 20 acres arable, 20 total acres; 1 house, 5 inhabitants.

Marked thus (+) 19 townlands, [subtotal] 280 houses, 1,509 inhabitants; [insert note: thus marked were taken, for want of time, in the aggregate].

Total: 6,892 acres arable, 211 acres mountain, 108 acres bog, 7,211 total acres; 1,136 houses, 6,002 inhabitants.

Raymoghy: Census of Townlands

No.5, Raymoghy according to the census of 1821 by Mr J. Stevenson.

Ardnadittion?, 62 acres arable, 21 acres bog, 83 total acres; 15 houses, 68 inhabitants.

Balleaghan, 132 acres arable, 132 total acres; 20 houses, 117 inhabitants.

Balliboe, 56 acres arable, 56 total acres; 9 houses, 40 inhabitants.

Ballylawn, 200 acres arable, 200 total acres; 20 houses, 116 inhabitants.

Ballylevin, 148 acres arable, 148 total acres; 9 houses, 60 inhabitants.

Broadlee, 24 acres arable, 24 total acres; 9 houses, 34 inhabitants.

Carrickballydowey, 90 acres arable, 90 total acres; 16 houses, 73 inhabitants.

Carricknamart, 187 acres arable, 38 acres mountain, 10 acres bog, 235 total acres; 34 houses, 192 inhabitants.

Castleblaugh, 219 acres arable, 20 acres bog, 239 total acres; 15 houses, 78 inhabitants.

Corky, 162 acres arable, 162 total acres; 31 houses, 162 inhabitants.

Doorish Balliboe, 84 acres arable, 19 houses, 109 inhabitants; Doorish Bogtown, 92 acres arable, 5 houses, 27 inhabitants; Doorish Castle, 225 acres arable, 39 houses, 213 inhabitants; Doorish Gentle, 142 acres arable, 16 houses, 93 inhabitants; Doorish Larggy, 36 acres arable, 4 houses, 23 inhabitants; [subtotal] 201 acres mountain, 10 acres bog, 790 total acres.

Drain, 99 acres arable, 99 total acres; 14 houses, 51 inhabitants.

Drumatoland, 186 acres arable, 44 acres bog, 230 total acres; 33 houses, 124 inhabitants.

Drumbarnet, 269 acres arable, 269 total acres; 34 houses, 177 inhabitants.

Drumcairn, 332 acres arable, 332 total acres; 27 houses, 118 inhabitants.

Drumoghal, 133 acres arable, 12 acres bog, 145 total acres; 26 houses, 109 inhabitants.

Erritty, 168 acres arable, 168 total acres; 13 houses, 64 inhabitants.

Forth, 307 acres arable, 307 total acres; 12 houses, 75 inhabitants.

Galdannagh, 295 acres arable, 295 total acres; 34 houses, 190 inhabitants.

Galdannagh Glebe, 228 acres arable, 228 total acres; 26 houses, 142 inhabitants.

Grawky, 206 acres arable, 206 total acres; 21 houses, 112 inhabitants.

Hunger's Mother, 100 acres arable, 50 acres bog, 150 total acres; 16 houses, 73 inhabitants.

Killyverry, 224 acres arable, 224 total acres; 23 houses, 132 inhabitants.

Kincraiggy, 125 acres arable, a wood, 139 total acres, 23 houses, 125 inhabitants.

Labadish, 244 acres arable, 244 total acres; 25 houses, 130 inhabitants.

Lisclamerty, 145 acres arable, 116 mountain, 261 total acres; 21 houses, 113 inhabitants.

Lismoghery, 80 acres arable, 101 acres mountain, 181 total acres; 21 houses, 92 inhabitants.

Magherabeg, 125 acres arable, 125 total acres; 13 houses, 55 inhabitants.

Magheramore, 67 acres arable, 67 total acres; 7 houses, 50 inhabitants.

Mailin, 50 acres arable, 50 total acres; 2 houses, 12 inhabitants.

Manor Cunningham, 70 acres arable, 70 total acres; 50 houses, 227 inhabitants.

Monclink, 94 acres arable, 22 acres mountain, 10 acres bog, 126 total acres; 23 houses, 117 inhabitants.

Mondowey, 376 acres arable, 10 acres mountain, 386 total acres; 46 houses, 243 inhabitants.

Moneyhaughley, 127 acres arable, 127 total acres; 18 houses, 105 inhabitants.

Moneymore, 300 acres arable, 300 total acres; 39 houses, 345 inhabitants.

Ruskey, 217 acres arable, 3 acres mountain, 9 acres bog, 230 total acres; 45 houses, 186 inhabitants.

Ray, 257 acres arable, 26 acres mountain, 283 total acres; 34 houses, 203 inhabitants.

Raylands, 264 acres arable, 6 acres mountain, 270 total acres; 18 houses, 114 inhabitants.

Sharon, 79 acres arable, 79 total acres; 5 houses, 33 inhabitants.

Sheskan, 47 acres arable, 5 acres mountain, 52 total acres; 7 houses, 39 inhabitants.

Terheeron, 68 acres arable, 68 total acres; 2 houses, 12 inhabitants.

Tully, 26 acres arable, 26 total acres; 13 houses, 56 inhabitants.

Tullybogley, 129 acres arable, 129 total acres; 11 houses, 72 inhabitants.

Veagh, 262 acres arable, 262 total acres; 20 houses, 130 inhabitants.

White Hill, 29 acres arable, 29 total acres; 8 houses, 41 inhabitants.

Wood Hill, 107 acres arable, 107 total acres; 13 houses, 59 inhabitants.

Total: 7,694 acres arable, 529 acres mountain, 186 acres bog, 8,423 total acres; 1,004 houses, 5,331 inhabitants.

NATURAL FEATURES

Weather Journal in 1821

[Table contains the following headings: date, direction of wind, observations].

No.6, register of weather for August 1821. 1st: south westerly wind, variable to north westerly, bright, a slight shower a.m.; 2nd: south westerly, brisk, rain at intervals; 3rd: easterly, mostly calm, fair and sultry; 4th: south easterly, variable to southerly, rain, a hazy day; 5th: south westerly, rain; 6th: south westerly, brisk, rain; 7th: south westerly, variable to westerly, brisk, rain, heavy showers in the forenoon; 8th: south westerly, brisk, rain afternoon, very wet; 9th: south westerly, a high wind, rain; 10th: westerly, rain; 11th: south westerly, rain; 12th: south westerly, rain trifling; 13th: south westerly, rain; 14th: westerly, fair; 15th: southerly, variable to south westerly, rain, dark and hazy; 16th: south westerly, fair; 17th: south westerly, rain, ominously dark; 18th: south westerly, fair and sultry; 19th: south westerly, fair; 20th: south westerly, variable to easterly, fair; 21st: easterly, fair; 22nd: south easterly, very slight towards night, fair, a warm cloudy day; 23rd: north easterly, variable to south westerly, fair, a very warm day; 24th: easterly, fair, very warm; 25th: easterly, fair, very warm, evening cloudy; 26th: north easterly, fair, moderately warm; 27th: easterly, rain, somewhat cold; 28th: easterly, a sharp cold wind, rain throughout; 29th: easterly, rain, very wet; 30th: easterly, fair; 31st: easterly, fair.

No.7, register of weather for September 1821. 1st: southerly wind, variable to westerly and northerly, fair, very warm; 2nd: south westerly, rain; 3rd: easterly, fair excepting a slight shower; 4th: south easterly, high wind, rain, cold; 5th: south easterly, variable, rain; 6th: southerly, fair; 7th: south westerly, rain; 8th: south westerly, rain and thunder; 9th: south westerly, rain; 10th: south westerly, rain and hail; 11th: southerly, rain, a very wet evening; 12th: south westerly, rain; 13th: south westerly, rain, extremely wet; 14th: south westerly, rain; 15th: south westerly, rain; 16th:

south westerly, rain; 17th: south westerly, rain, morning very wet; 18th: westerly, rain; 19th: westerly, rain slight; 20th: north westerly, fair excepting a slight shower; 21st: easterly, fair; 22nd: northerly, fair; 23rd: south westerly, rain, a wet day; 24th: south westerly, rain trifling; 25th: south westerly, fair excepting a slight shower; 26th: south westerly, rain; 27th: south westerly, fair; 28th: westerly, variable to south westerly, rain, very wet; 29th: south westerly, high wind overnight, rain, very wet; 30th: south westerly, variable to southerly and south easterly, fair excepting a slight shower.

www.ingramcontent.com/pod-product-compliance
Lightning Source LLC
Chambersburg PA
CBHW082337300426
44109CB00045B/2403